110
120
Yellow Sea
CHINA
Nanking
Shanghai
Hankow
R. Yangtse-kiang
Ningpo
JAPAN
Foochow
Kilung
Amoy
Formosa St.
Formosa
Tropic of Cancer
Swatow
Canton
Takao
Tongking
Hongkong
Macao
Hanoi
Haiphong
Gulf of Tongking
Hainan
Vinh
SOUTH CHINA SEA
LUZON
Hue
Manila
ANNAM
Philippine Is.
Mindoro St.
Nha-trang
Saigon
Palawan
Sulu Sea
C. Cambodia
Mindanao
Labuan
Sulu Is.
SARAWAK
Celebes Sea
Nantuna Is
Malacca
Singapore
Kuching
Molucca Str.
BORNEO
Carimata Str.
Simpang
Macassar Str.
CELEBES
Sula Is.
Molucca Sea
Java Sea
New Guinea
Macassar
Batavia
Madura I.
Flores Sea
Sunda St.
110
120
130

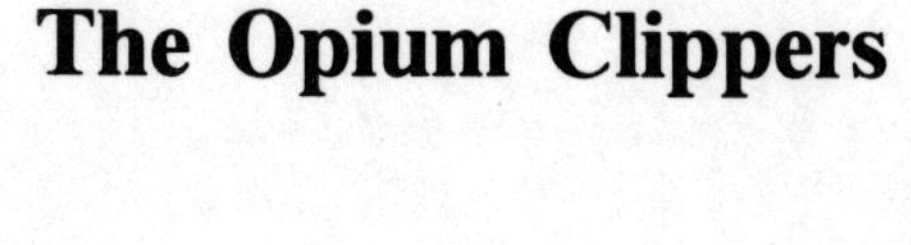

The Opium Clippers

BY THE SAME AUTHOR

The China Clippers
The Colonial Clippers
The Blackwall Frigates
The Log of the "Cutty Sark"
The Western Ocean Packets
The Last of the Windjammers, Vol. I
The Last of the Windjammers, Vol. II
The Down Easters
The Nitrate Clippers
The Arctic Whalers
The Coolie Ships and Oil Sailers
Bully Hayes — South Sea Pirate

THE AUTHOR

[*Frontispiece*

THE
OPIUM CLIPPERS

BY

BASIL LUBBOCK

WITH ILLUSTRATIONS AND PLANS

GLASGOW
BROWN, SON & FERGUSON, LTD., NAUTICAL PUBLISHERS
4-10 DARNLEY STREET

New Edition - 1933
Reprinted - 1976
Reprinted - 1992

ISBN 0 85174 241 6

Printed and made in Great Britain

Dedicated to
The Old China Coaster

PREFACE

NO man lives at the present day who actually saw an opium clipper at sea and the memory of them has almost faded away, yet these beautiful little ships are not worthy of oblivion, for were they not the first trading craft with clipper lines? Did they not produce an incomparable race of seamen and were they not also the chief means by which China and Japan were opened up to the outside world?

It has taken close on 25 years collecting the material for this book, and my thanks are due to numbers of old hands on the China Coast, notably the descendants of the Dents, Mathesons, Forbes and Pybus brothers, of many of the captains and of more than one naval officer.

The illustrations have been specially hard to find, for even the famous MacPherson Collection only possesses a few prints of opium clippers. The beautiful little drawings by A. G. Dallas, a partner in Jardine Matheson's which were lent me by the late Major-General A. G. Dallas, were a find indeed.

The opium trade was so inextricably mixed up with the first Chinese war that I have felt compelled to give a slight sketch of the operations, such operations as have never been features of any war, before or since.

I have tried also to show some of the glamour and romance of the life on the Coast when captains had to present a dauntless front to the typhoon and the pirate, and pit theirs wits in business against the wily Celestial, the shrewd Parsee and the artful Malay.

BASIL LUBBOCK.

CONTENTS

CHAPTER IV.—A BOOMING TRADE.

CHAPTER V.—THE OPIUM WAR.

ILLUSTRATIONS

PLANS

THE OPIUM CLIPPERS

THE OPIUM CLIPPERS

CHAPTER I.

INTRODUCTION.

Ye bloods of the present day,
To you I have nothing to say,
Except ye are able;
To splice a chain cable,
And get a sheer hulk under way.

The Romance of the Opium Trade.

N these modern days when the Seven Seas are slowly growing desert of ships, and sea life has become nought but sordid monotony made up of weary bridge pacing, dull office work and a never ending multitude of petty worries, the word "clipper" sets one longing for the brave old days.

When ships are run to time like trains and buses with very little to fear from the elements or the enemy, to read of a rakish schooner thrashing to windward in the teeth of the monsoon, of a taut-rigged brig battling it out in a howling typhoon or of a tall skysailyard barque fighting for dear life against a circling swarm of piratical prahus or lorchas, is to admit with a sigh that the glorious profession of seafaring has lost a good deal of its romance.

Certainly there was no lack of romance on the China coast a hundred years ago.

What more could a merchant adventurer ask for than a trade whose profits were often five hundred or even a thousand fold, albeit the risks were of equal magnitude?

What more exciting employment could be found for a sailor than that of running contraband on an uncharted and hostile coast amidst pirate junks and great winds!

When fortunes were made out of a six months' voyage, it is not surprising that the salaries of officers were regal, that the little clippers were fitted out with the best of everything and carried crews twice and three times as large as those of ships double their tonnage.

What more thrilling task for a shipmaster than that of outwitting wily mandarins, out-manoeuvring Imperial war junks and out-sailing every merchantman, aye, and man-of-war that he encountered in his racing passages between India and the Canton river!

What greater delight for a watch officer than that of handling a beautiful schooner in narrow waters or backing and filling a smart brig up the twists and turns of a Chinese river, with the knowledge that one small mistake in pilotage meant far worse than a mere stranding!

Small wonder that seamanship was at a premium in the opium clippers or that gun laying was a necessary qualification in their officers and petty officers.

Their hands, too, had to know their manuals both for big guns and small arms; besides being able to refit a clipper at sea from truck to keel, cutlass drill was as regular a part of a clipper's routine as it was that of a man-of-war.

The service, if well paid, was a hard, dangerous one, with not only pirates, typhoons and hostile mandarins to encounter, but deadly fevers, unknown plagues, and, in the event of capture, unimaginable horrors of cruelty to endure.

Yet who would exchange such a life—a man's life—for the slavery of the modern machine? Who would not jump out of his soft bed and sling his hammock aboard an opium clipper, could we but put the clock back? And who of us would not prefer the hardships and hard knocks of that forbidden trade to the soul-destroying emptiness of our present day workless conditions?

The Dangers of the China Coast.

Under this heading should also be included the Indian Ocean and the Java Sea, for the opium trade extended from Bombay to Korea, from Calcutta to Japan and from Moulmein to Manila.

The dangers of these seas were real enough. The percentage of casualties in the trade was always a high one. Quite a quarter of the clippers disappeared leaving no trace, and it is probable that fully a third fell victims to the pirate and the typhoon.

Rust and decay were seldom the lot of the opium clipper.

The dangers of the navigation have been vividly touched on by Joseph Conrad. "The China Seas," he wrote, "North and South, are narrow seas. They are seas full of everyday eloquent facts, such as islands, sandbanks, reefs, swift and changeable currents—tangled facts that nevertheless speak to a seaman in clear and definite language."

Though the lordly East Indiamen were the first visitors to these seas, they only voyaged in the fair monsoon and therefore had little need to diverge from the straight-ruled track up and down the middle, taking care to keep well clear of such well-known obstacles as the Paracel and Pratas Reefs and that archipelago of coral rocks and shoals lying to the West of the Palawan Passage, which even in modern charts is still marked "Dangerous Ground."

But the prime object of the opium clippers was to get the Indian drug to the Chinese market twice or even three times a year, and that in the face of an adverse monsoon.

Working up from Singapore against the N.E. monsoon, it was a steady slog to windward with never a let-up. Clever pilotage was very necessary. The strong foul current, often as much as 600 or 700 miles in a month's passage, had to be cheated by risky work along an uncharted coast. And when the monsoon fell light, the land and sea breezes had to be wooed along the Cochin China and Borneo Coasts, the captains standing boldly into shoaling water until there were only inches under their keels.

In later days, when the surveyors of Her Majesty's Navy came on the scene, such splendid Hydrographers as Kellett, Collinson, Belcher, Bate and Yule always acknowledged their great indebtedness to the officers of the opium clippers. Let me give two quotations from technical papers, written by naval officers in the *Nautical Magazine*. The first comes from Commander Blake of H.M.S. *Larne*, describing his passage down the China Sea in 1839.

"I gathered the foregoing information from comparing the

abstract of reckonings with an opium vessel, whose captain had had much experience and which arrived at Singapore from Macao the same day as ourselves, although she had left ten days after us."

Then in an article by Captain Mundy, of H.M.S. *Iris*, on how to beat North against the monsoon, I find the following:

"I have also been assisted by information which from time to time I have received from the masters of the clippers, whose opinions I consider valuable from their long experience."

The names of the opium clippers and their captains are studded all over the charts of the Java and China Seas, marking shoals and reefs which they discovered and reported.

Taking a random glance at an old track chart one's eye is at once caught by such significant names as "Johnson's Reef"; "Rob Roy's Shoal"; "Pearl Island"; "Ardaseer Breakers"; "Louisa Reef"; "Swallow Rocks"; "Wallace Bank"; "Owen's Shoal"; etc., etc.

Typhoons and Pirates.

The chief dangers of these uncharted, unlighted waters were not due to reefs and currents, but rather to the fury of the typhoon wind and the boldness of the wild pilong or pirate.

During the hot summer months on the coast the "great wind" had always to be watched for. Known as the cyclone in the Indian Ocean and Bay of Bengal; in the China Sea it was equally dreaded under the local term of "typhoon." Yet "typhoon" is not really the correct term for the hurricane or circular storm. The Chinese called the worst form of wind known on this earth the "Teet-Kiey," which means "iron whirlwind." This word, however, was never added to the English language, that of "typhoon" taking its place.

In this history of the opium clippers, typhoons occupy an important place. How the tiny, tall-masted, long-sparred ships of the opium fleet ever survived these cataclysms of Nature was truly astounding and speaks volumes for the skilful seamanship of their captains. Many, as we shall see, disappeared—never to be heard of again. Occasionally, however, in that uncanny way in which murder will come to light, it was proved that the typhoon was not the cause of some missing vessel but the pirate.

The whole of the Southern Coast of China swarmed with pirates.

Piracy was considered to be in the blood of the Cantonese, and *bona fide* fishermen, given the opportunity, left their nets to combine in spoiling some helpless trader becalmed amongst the islands. The Cantonese were always a lawless, fighting race, who looked with contempt upon the Northerners. It is interesting to read that, in the Taeping Rebellion, Cantonese were brought North by the Imperialists to fight against the terrible Taepings and given twice the pay of the ordinary Imperial troops. And, when in the Second Chinese War, Canton was captured by the British, the Emperor, on the news being brought to him, is said to have remarked: "I wish them joy of their task. If they can govern the Cantonese and keep them quiet, it is more than I could ever do."

In later days when Hongkong had become one of the great ports of the world, the pirates actually had their agents in the town, and the pilong junks had the audacity to venture within the confines of the port and even follow their prey from the very anchorage. A case of this description was that of the English brig *North Star*, which was captured and her crew murdered when she was in full sight of the signal station at Victoria Peak.

The Case of the "North Star."

The *North Star* sailed from Hongkong one morning at the beginning of the 'sixties. She was bound for Japan in ballast. Her personnel consisted of 17 souls including two passengers, who brought with them treasure to the tune of 12,000 dollars in specie. The wind being very light, the brig made slow progress and about sunset was still within 7 miles of the anchorage, lying almost becalmed. A junk had left Hongkong a few minutes behind the brig and had followed close in her wake all day.

And now as the sun sank significant events began to take place. First of all, the Chinese pilot of the *North Star* calmly dropped into his sampan and was yoloed across to the junk.

Next the Chinese steward came on deck with the captain's revolver in his hands and blandly asked if he might clean it. The unsuspecting master of the brig discharged each barrel—it was apparently of the early pepper-pot variety of pistol—and handed it back to the steward.

Meanwhile the junk in a light air, which barely gave the brig steerage way, was edging down upon the latter. Too late it was suddenly realised that she was alive with men, who had previously remained hidden. These now manned their long sweeps and pulled straight for the *North Star.*

The latter's armament only consisted of four muskets in a rack in the cabin. The captain, at last realising his danger, yelled to the crew to arm themselves and rushed to seize a musket. He was followed on deck by the second mate and two passengers, each armed with a musket, but these were soon found to be useless for the rascally steward—who had already put the captain's pistol out of action—had filed the nipples.

Just as the after-guard reached the deck of the brig the pirate junk crashed alongside, and as the two vessels ground together a shower of stink-pots fell aboard the *North Star*, killing the man at the wheel and burning two of the crew severely.

Forward the mate snatched up a hand spike, the carpenter laid hold of his axe, and the rest of the crew armed themselves with sheath knives and belaying pins. It was evident that all hands were ready to put up a desperate resistance. The after-guard sighted their muskets into the brown of a hoard of boarders, but when they pulled the triggers the caps snapped without effect. Before they could even club their useless weapons, the captain, second mate and one of the passengers were cut down or speared whilst the other passenger jumped overboard.

The mate and the carpenter at their end of the brig, with the watch on deck, were soon overwhelmed by numbers. The mate, after cracking a few skulls with his handspike, received a slash with a sword across the face, which blinded him.

The carpenter sank his axe in the brain of one pilong, but was at once cut down by another. And so the slaughter went on. One after the other the hands on deck were struck down until only two men and a boy remained. These three were the last to obey the captain's cry of "All hands on deck!"

The first sight to dismay them as they put their heads above the hatchway was that of one of their shipmates lying in his blood under the folds of the fore trysail, the halliards of which had been let go by the pirates so that they could use the halliard belaying pins to make the junk fast alongside. At the same moment a horrid shrieking came from aft where the last of the crew to keep on their legs were fast being hacked to pieces.

The terrified three, being screened from observation by the foresail, went hand over hand up the forestay and so into the fore-top where they lay flat in such a way that they were hidden from the pirates.

The latter wasted no time; quickly plundering the *North Star* of everything valuable, including the specie, they went off under their sweeps.

It was not until the pirate junk was well away that the three survivors descended to the deck. They found their shipmates literally cut in bits with such effect that only the mate and three foremast hands were still breathing.

After doing what little they could for the dying men, the brig was headed back for the anchorage under a light air. But at midnight it fell calm again, so two of them jumped into the dinghy and pulled for the nearest ship. This was the *Emeu.* As she had no surgeon they rowed off to H.M.S. *Imperieuse.* Their story speedily set the bosun's pipes wailing, and in less than no time an armed cutter with a surgeon in the stern sheets raced away in the direction of the dark loom of the brig. But the condition of the four who still breathed was beyond the doctor's skill, and in the end only one man survived besides the three who had lagged behind in the fo'c'sle—this was the passenger who had jumped overboard. At first the pirates who saw him jump had lunged at him with their long bamboo spears, but having grimmer work on hand aboard the brig soon paid no further attention to him.

The passenger was not hit by any of the spears thrown at him, but found them convenient as a support; and whilst the pirates were occupied with their killing and looting, he remained hidden under the counter, the bamboo spear shafts and rudder chains serving to support him. Yet being a fine swimmer, he did not wait long, but set off to swim for the shore, 7 to 8 miles away, without being noticed. After a swim of nine hours he actually reached the land and was taken back to Hongkong by some fishermen.

Murder Will Out.

The pirates who captured the *North Star* within sight of Hongkong anchorage got clean away with their booty.

About two years later the pilongs were not so lucky. This time the merchant vessel, a brig named *Fanny*, was barely outside Green Island before a fast lorcha, when passing in a light wind, suddenly put her helm over and sheered alongside. But this time a British gunboat—there were something like sixteen or twenty of these little vessels on the East India Station in the late 'fifties and early 'sixties—hove in sight and interrupted the usual proceedings.

The pilongs managed to slip away but left the brig in a condition that could not but attract attention, with her braces cast off the pins and her yards swinging to and fro as she kept coming up and falling off.

This time amongst the dead and dying aboard the *Fanny* the captain was discovered to be worth attention, and he was rushed off straight away to the hospital ship *Melville*. He was placed in a cot on the starboard side close to a porthole, which gave a view of the gangway ladder. To his amazement he had barely been dressed and made comfortable before the very same lorcha, which had attacked him, came ranging up alongside the hospital ship and he was able to see two or three wounded men, including the captain of the pilongs, carried up the ladder. Luckily he had all his wits about him in spite of his wounds, and he immediately reported that these wounded Chinamen were his assailants.

A signal was quickly hoisted and in a very short time an armed launch from the flagship had captured the lorcha. There was a quick trial and the captain and five of his crew were condemned to death.

In both these cases the pirates probably obtained their information in the alleys round West Point and such haunts of iniquity as Endicott Lane.

The Pilongs and the Opium Clippers.

Of all the ships sailing the China Sea, the most attractive prey for the pirate was undoubtedly the opium clipper, for she was

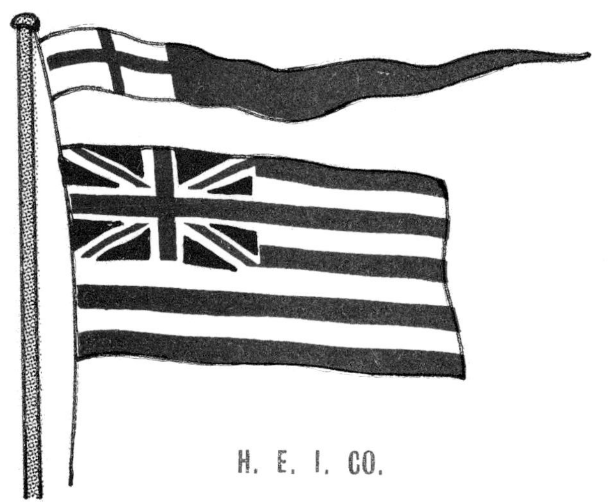

H. E. I. CO.

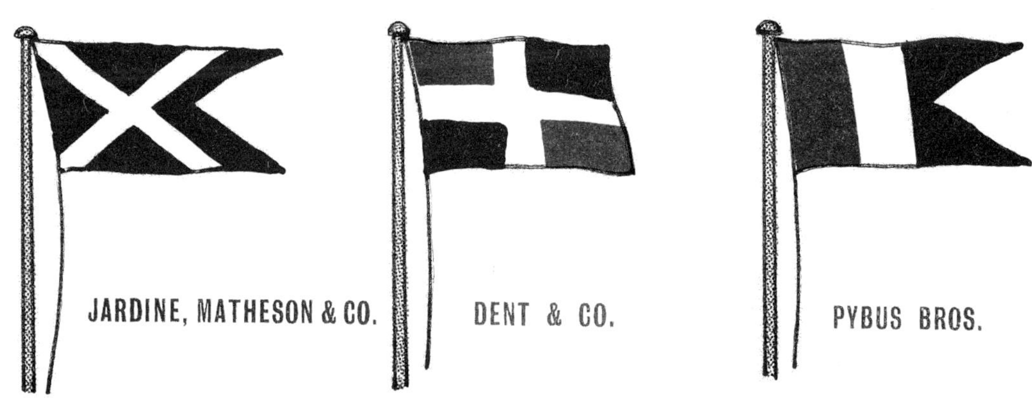

JARDINE, MATHESON & CO.

DENT & CO.

PYBUS BROS.

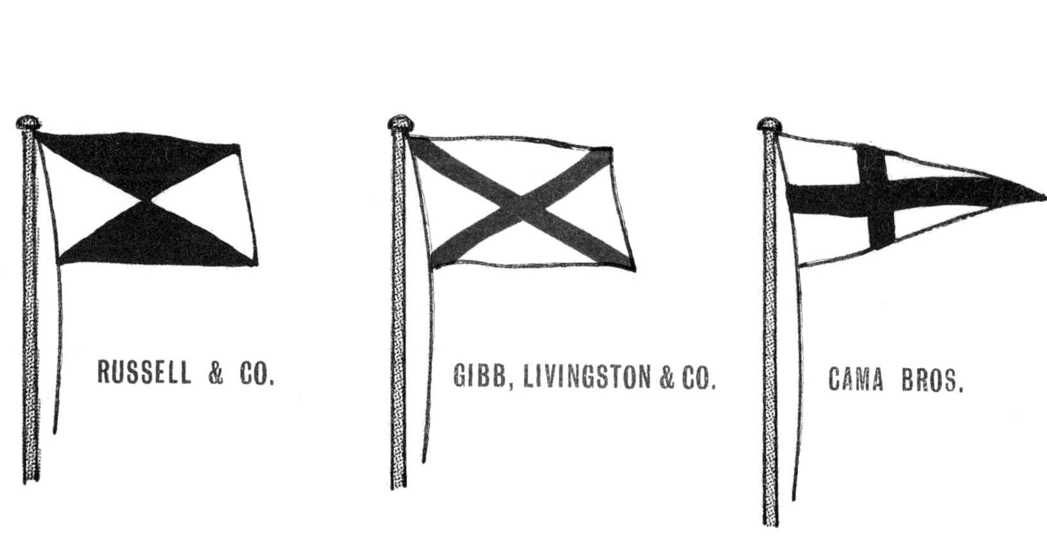

RUSSELL & CO.

GIBB, LIVINGSTON & CO.

CAMA BROS.

either full up with opium or else specie. Unfortunately for the high sea robber she was invariably well armed and well manned. Until the late 'forties, though there were many fights, none of the clippers was captured by the pilongs so far as is known though other ships continually suffered.

But about that date two very successful pirate chiefs, Shap'-ngtzai and Chuiapoo, each with a large fleet, began to play havoc with the shipping, and no less than seven noted clippers, which were posted missing in 1848-49, were considered to be their victims.

Sometimes ships were traced by some bit of their gear being discovered in Hongkong itself. This happened in the case of a ship, which had a name like "Cumana;" a skipper, on the prowl one day in Endicott Lane, came upon a nice chronometer, which was marked down at such a give-away price that he bought it there and then.

As it had run down, he took it round to Falconer, the Hongkong optician, to be overhauled. To his astonishment Falconer at once recognised the chronometer and declared that he had had it in his shop only a few weeks back and that it had belonged to the *Cumana*. Under such suspicious circumstances a search was made by the police and other gear of the unfortunate ship discovered in the purlieus of Hongkong which confirmed the optician's statement. It appeared that the *Cumana* had been cut off when lying anchored for the night just outside the Ly-ee-moon Pass. She was loaded with cinnamon wood, which made a big blaze when the pilongs set fire to her. This was noticed but thought to be nothing more important than a junk in flames, so nothing was done.

On the Pratas and the Paracels.

Many of the ships which such super-pirates as Chuiapoo and Shap'ngtzai had captured were at first supposed to have been wrecked on the Pratas or the Paracels. These two obstructions, the first a mere sandspit surrounded by a ring of coral, and the second a perfect maze of nigger-heads, mushrooms and coral islets, extending over 120 miles of longitude and 80 of latitude, are the two chief graveyards of the China Seas.

In the days before the Western Pacific was surveyed, there were reckless skippers of racing ships, such as the opium and tea clippers, who dared to steer a course right through the middle of the Paracels and actually came through without touching.

Sandy Nicholson, for instance, of the tea clipper *Argonaut*, on a calm clear moonlight night with a hand lead going in the chains, conned his ship from the foreyard and brought her safely through. Others were not so successful. The opium brig *Antonio Pereira*, when racing the *Sylph* to the Canton market in 1838, is supposed to have tried a tack through the Paracel Reefs. Some time afterwards a ship reported two masts showing cross-trees out on the edge of the North Reef and that was all that was ever heard of the *Antonio Pereira*, though both the gun brig *Algerine* and the sloop *Larne* went in search of her.

Chinese wreckers made a very fair living out of both the Pratas and the Paracels.

The "Childers" Leaps the Reef.

Only one ship ever bumped on the Pratas and came off—and that was Her Majesty's gun brig *Childers* which topped the barrier reef on the crest of a typhoon wave on October 10, 1848.

She was running from the stormfiend like a tired hare before a pack of noisy beagles. Her mainmast had gone by the board. Her guns, shot and much other gear had been sacrificed to Davy Jones. Her worn-out crew hung desperately to life lines which had been stretched fore and aft. Her commander and officers vainly tried to pierce the driving sheets of spray with bloodshot, salt-rimmed eyes. A weird screech from the lookouts forward was unheard in the wild hooting of the elements, but its cause was soon apparent to all hands. Stretching for two points on either bow, there suddenly appeared a snow-white ridge, for all the world like the view of the Himalayas from the Simla hills. It was the mountainous surf breaking on the horseshoe-shaped coral reef, which bounded the Pratas on the North.

The *Childers* was that same lively brig whose keel Harry Keppel caught a glimpse of in a Mediterranean squall. She was travelling then but she was actually flying before the typhoon, flinging half her length out of the water at each plunge and recovery. As she leaped nearer and nearer the line of surf a deep booming began to be distinguished, making a thunder-like base to the shrill screaming of the typhoon.

There was nought to be done—no possible way of avoiding the jagged rocks—no time to round her to, even if this had been possible without a capsize.

"Steady your helm!" was all Commander Pitman said, or rather bellowed into the ear of the helmsman.

"Steady it is, sir," returned the quartermaster, directing the helmsmen with a hand on the spokes.

"Keep her dead before it!" went on his commander.

"Aye, aye, sir," growled the old sea-cunny at the con, his chew high under his cheek bone and his jaws working. He was not the man to get rattled.

A second later and the brig rose on a gigantic sea, up, up, up, throwing the spray on either bow as high as her foreyard, as she cleft the great breaker in twain.

"Hang on all!" roared the commander through his speaking trumpet.

There was little need of such a caution. All hands had lashed themselves with the running gear to life line, fiferail or belaying pin.

The next moment the *Childers* was right on top of the reef. There was a dull, grinding crash—the old quartermaster and his two helmsmen were sent sprawling as the wheel kicked violently. The wheel spun: three pairs of hands grabbed it and held on, but to their astonishment it was like a feather for lightness—the rudder had been torn from the sternpost !

For perhaps a split second the *Childers* hung poised, shaking from stem to stern, her decks hidden in a cloud of thick spray—then she leaped forward again. The gallant sloop had jumped the reef. Suddenly she lay quiet, then began to twist and turn in a maelstrom of swirling soapsuds under the lee of the reef. Though the nigger-heads literally bristled all round her, she had landed after her giddy leap in a clear patch of deep water with a white sand bottom under her.

Such an escape from almost certain destruction is scarcely believable, and one would not dare to put it into a book of fiction, but the *Childers*' adventure may be found in calm official language in the Admiralty records. The anchor was let go and the hard tried vessel lay at peace with the hurricane still screeching overhead.

For fifteen days she was compelled to remain at anchor in the Pratas lagoon whilst her people sought to find a way out by sounding. All her boats had gone except for a tiny dinghy. By this means a channel sufficiently deep to float the sloop was eventually found and the lame duck was piloted to sea after perhaps the most marvellous escape that ever happened in the China Seas.

A Chinese Wreckers' Paradise.

Other vessels were not so lucky. Only a year or two later the steam sloop *Renard*, which had gone to the Pratas to rescue a shipwrecked crew, was caught in her turn by the treacherous reefs and became a total loss.

More than one opium clipper came to her end on the Pratas—notably the *Carthage* and probably the *Coquette*, if the pirates did not get her. The reason for so many wrecks on this tiny reef is chiefly owing to the very strong currents—the set from West to East often being as much as 60 miles in the 24 hours.

The shoal water to the Southward extends for a distance of 2½ miles from the island itself but light draft junks and lorchas can sail right in to about 400 yards off the white coral beach. Here used to come the wreckers, mostly fishermen but on occasions pirates on holiday. These rarely failed to find good pickings amongst the pile of wreckage which littered the strand above high-water mark.

The beach of white coral sand surrounded a little hump of land, which was mostly covered with a coarse grass and low scrubby weather-beaten shrubs like giant cabbages. A few living and many dead trees stood or leaned about the highest part of the Pratas, which was nowhere more than 30 feet. This stunted growth was overrun with luxuriant convolvuli. Here, in a bower of gay flowers, the wreckers built a joss-house, which they decorated with figureheads, stern emblems, wreaths of carved gingerbread work, ornamental teak stanchions and balusters, brass-bound rails, cabin mirrors, birds-eye maple panelling and even plate and pewter from many a ship's pantry and saloon.

Besides the hardy sunburnt Chinese fishermen and wreckers there was little life on the Pratas beyond a warren of shipwrecked rats, a few domestic pig run wild, a flight of plover, a few dotterell and sandpipers and the usual colony of foolish gannets. Yet what stories these rats and birds could have told about the gaunt ribs and fragments of planking which lay half sunk in the sand, about the broken spars and bits of keel—aye, and about the opium and specie chests, gaping open and empty.

No doubt the wreckers could have solved the mystery of many a fine ship's disappearance could they have read the names on the gilded trail-boards with which they fed their fires.

The Opium Fleet.

The opium fleet, which throughout the short 25 years of its existence did not exceed 100 ships all told, was divided up into three classes known as the clippers, the coasters and the receiving ships.

The clippers were vessels specially built to beat to windward against the monsoons. They carried the drug from Bombay and Calcutta to the Canton River and Hongkong *via* Singapore; making the return passage with specie and occasionally a few choice Chinese wares. In the early days the clippers delivered their outward cargoes to the receiving ships lying off Macao or at the Lintin and Cap-sing-moon Anchorages: but after the opium war Hongkong became their usual discharge port.

The coasters—so called because they delivered the precious balls and cakes of opium to every coast town and fishing village, with which they were able to open communication, from the Gulf of Tongking along the whole length of the China Coast as far North as Korea—were mostly smart little brigs and schooners, the smaller vessels of the fleet being selected for this duty, as it was easier for a light draft vessel to find her way amid the sandbanks of an unsurveyed river mouth, through rock strewn passages or over bars of barrier coral.

There was one exception, however, to the general small size of the coasters, and that was Jardine Matheson's famous full-rigged flagship *Falcon* of 351 tons. She carried the drug to ports which were far outside the treaty areas, her most important duty being the discovery and opening up of new markets. She was an impressive looking vessel with the row of broadside guns poking out through her white strake and her long-toms amidships and on fo'c'sle-head so that pirates and Imperialists, wreckers and marauding fishermen, all hesitated before attacking her, though they thought little of trying to cut off a small schooner.

The third class—the receiving ships—were usually teak-built country ships or Indiamen with roomy hulls, specially strong ground tackle, large arms chests, and bright polished broadside guns, for they had to be ready to fight off surprise attacks by day or night, their cargoes being an overpowering temptation to Chinamen of every degree; they also had to ride out typhoons in anchorages where there was often little room to drag.

Besides a fighting crew, they also had a large staff of schroffs for the difficult matter of weighing and checking the chests of opium and the cases of shoe or Sycee silver.

A receiving ship that dragged ashore or fell a victim to surprise attack was considered a heaven-sent gift in the Celestial's kingdom.

The Country Wallahs.

In the very early days of the opium trade when John Company's word was law for all Englishmen East of Suez, the drug was carried to China by the Indian country craft. These were everlasting but quaintly shaped vessels built of Malabar teak in the shipyards of Bombay and the Hooghly, whose rounded lines were very little fitted for beating to windward. Thus it happened that until the advent of the clippers, opium, like the other commodities of the China trade, had to put up with one season a year. The country wallahs ran up the China Sea before the S.W. monsoon and returned with the North-east

These country craft, or wallahs as they were called by the British officers who invariably commanded and often owned them, formed in their day a by no means unimportant section of the traders in Eastern waters.

To Canton they brought raw cotton as well as opium from India, and rice, pepper and tin from the Malay States. Their business was always known as "The Country Trade" and their masters were called "Country Captains."

There was even a favourite cuddy dish called "Country Captain" in the far-off days of the Napoleonic wars—something made up of rice and raisins, hot chillis, jungle fowl and Bombay duck.

Here is a note on the country wallahs, written by a country captain in 1836:—"Into this snug bight we used to bring our country ships under convoy to and from China, particularly the Bombay ships, for which craft I have a sort of affection—they were kept so clean, were so well ordered and navigated—heavy, ugly teak vessels, very true, of from 500 to 800 tons; but their condition on board was admirable with their sea-cunnies, tindals and Lascars—obedient and good sailors in those days. The only Europeans on board were the captain and his three mates. All the duty was carried on in the Hindoostanee language—'Moors,' a tongue, by the way, almost rivalling the musical softness of the Malay and so easy to acquire that most of us lads picked up a smattering of both."

The late Captain Shewan, of the tea clipper *Norman Court*, also has borne witness to the way in which the country ships were looked after:—"The ships were kept in beautiful order, more like a man-of-war than a merchantman: the decks holystoned white; copper sheathing polished and oiled; yards all a-taunt-o; and the furled sails rolled up in snow-white sail covers."

Many of the early country wallahs were known as grabs owing to the peculiar form of their bows, which projected, as Commander Coates, their historian, relates, like that of a Mediterranean galley. This grab bow was decked over flush with the maindeck, but bulk-headed off to form quarters for the crew. It must have been an exceedingly damp and uncomfortable spot when the heavy old craft was pitching into a head sea.

The Indian ship designer considered imitation the sincerest form of flattery, and in both lines and rig he was an iron-bound conservative, thus even as late as the 'fifties there were almost exact replicas of caravels, carracks and galleons to be seen wave-crushing, as it was called, in the Bay of Bengal, the Arabian Sea and the Gulf of Siam.

These old timers were fitted with a high narrow roundhouse,

on top of the cuddy, whose heavily leaded windows looked out of sumptuously carved and gilded quarter galleries.

In a short, high-bulwarked waist, guns on elaborately carved hardwood carriages poked their muzzles out of ports, with gilded wreaths encircling them with other fancy wood carving. The guns themselves were beautifully chased with trunnions, handles and tompions representing some very strange birds, beasts and fishes of which tiger's and dolphin's heads, snake's jaws and eagle's talons were the most common.

The chase, too, and the reinforces of the cannons were often damascened with anchors and coats-of-arms like the culverins of a royal Stuart ship.

Aloft these ancient country craft were equally interesting to the nautical eye with their yellow narrow-cut canvas and coir standing rigging, their fibre chafing gear and grass mattings, their bamboo stunsail booms and big clumsy tops.

No wonder their British officers took a pride in keeping such museum pieces in the shape of ships in spick and span order! Numbers of these country wallahs were centenarians. One of the oldest was the *Pestonjee Bomadgee.* How old she was when picked up abandoned in the Red Sea about 1750 history does not relate; but with pointed prow, low waist and narrow poop, her tapering yards and lateen-rigged gaffs she was still a familiar sight in the Indian Ocean when the nineteenth century was half over. She was finally lost in a Madras cyclone about 1879.

Then there was the *Sulimany,* built in Bombay in 1779, and the *Cornwallis,* built at Surat in 1790; both of these lived to a great age, the former being burnt in 1842. The little *Java,* which is still doing duty as a Gibraltar coal hulk, gives one an idea of an early nineteenth century country wallah, though she was a crack Indiaman in her day.

When the clippers ousted the country craft from the opium trade several of these veterans ended their days as receiving ships or "floating godowns" in Chinese waters.

Clipper Types.

The greater number of the opium clippers were built at the

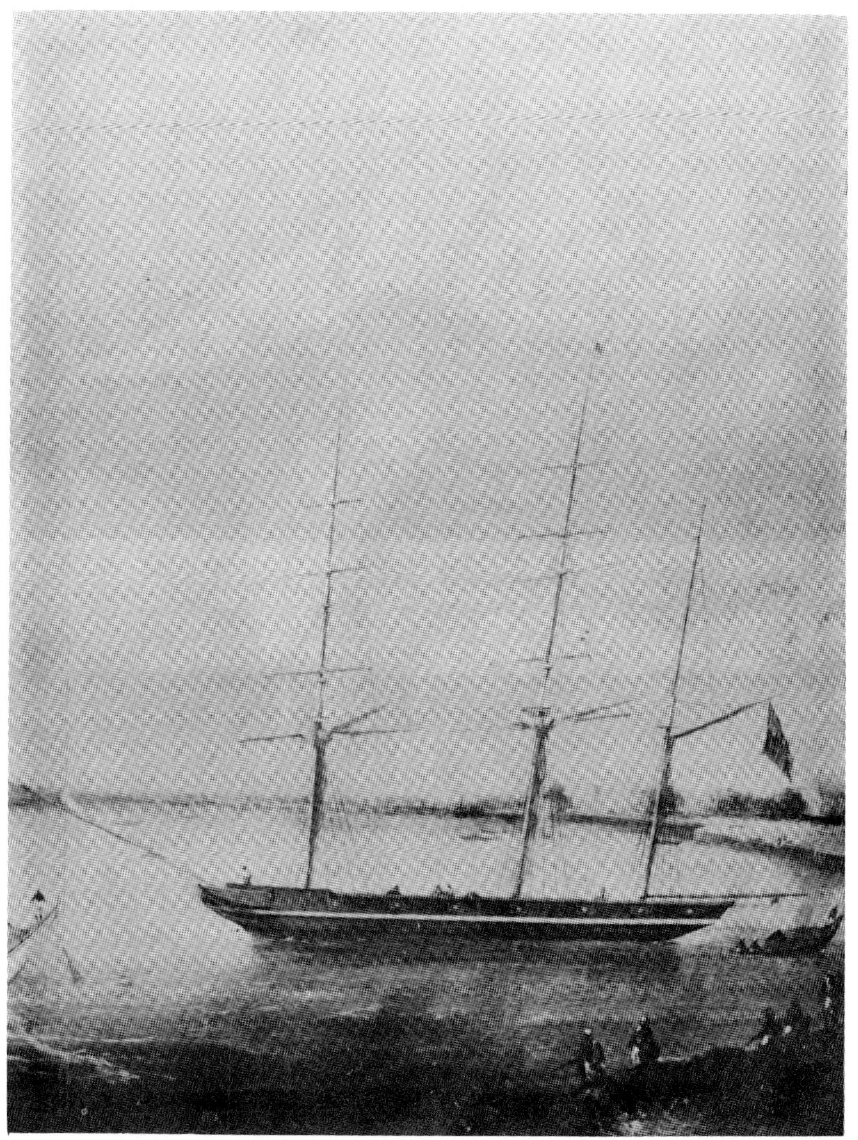

"RED ROVER" OFF FORT WILLIAM

National Maritime Museum, Greenwich [*See page* 16

DOCTOR WILLIAM JARDINE
National Maritime Museum, Greenwich

JAMES MATHESON AS A YOUNG MAN
National Maritime Museum, Greenwich [*See page* 32

various yards on the banks of the Hooghly. The shape and lines of these Calcutta built clippers followed two rather different types.

The first type copied the plans of the *Red Rover*, which were the exact replica of those of a very famous American privateer. The second Calcutta type followed the lines of the *Sylph*, which was specially designed for the trade by Sir Robert Seppings, the Surveyor of the Navy.

There was one other opium clipper which probably influenced the Hooghly shipyards, and that was the schooner, *Syed Khan*, an ex-slaver of an undoubted Baltimore model.

Three very well-known clippers came out of the Bombay Dockyard, and they were all considered very smart sailors indeed.

The first of these was the brig, *Lady Grant*, which astonished local shipping people owing to the unusual sharpness of her lines and tallness of her rig. It was predicted that she would never live through her first typhoon, and it is probable that she was somewhat overhatted.

Some half dozen clippers were built at Moulmein. The first of these was the *Sir Edward Ryan*, a sturdy barque of the *Sylph* pattern. The others were schooners, built on the lines of the little *Time*, considered the smartest fruit schooner in the Mediterranean and afterwards a very successful opium clipper.

Four very famous yachts, belonging to the Royal Yacht squadron, ended their days in the opium fleet. These were the two *Falcons*, belonging to Lord Yarborough, Rajah Brooke's old schooner *Royalist*, and the *Anonyma*, a very lofty brig.

The *Syed Khan* was not the only ex-slaver; there were several others, such as the brig *Ann* and the schooners *Black Joke*, *Kelpie* and *Nymph*.

There were also other old fruiters in the fleet, the schooner *Hellas*, for instance.

Some of the opium clippers came from the famous Thames shipyards, as the brig *Antonio Pereira*, the ship *Mor*, and the schooner *Sidney*; but Jardine Matheson's brig *Lanrick* was the only one that was built on the Mersey.

Hall of Aberdeen supplied the trade with several of his clipper schooners, headed by the *Torrington*, whilst White of Cowes sent several of his yacht-like schooners to Chinese waters for the coasting trade. Only three opium clippers were actually built on the spot; these were the schooners *Harriet* at Macao and *Celestial* and *Undine* at Hongkong.

Turning to the American built clippers, the schooners *Anglona* and *Mazeppa* were of the New York pilot boat type; and so was the *Spec*, once tender to Commodore Wilkes' expedition, under the name of *Flying Fish*.

There were some half dozen Boston built clippers in the trade—all of them noteworthy vessels.

Lastly, there were one or two ex men-of-war, such as the *Jamesina* ex *Curlew*, and the *Pelorus*.

The above slight survey of the fleet will give some idea of the great variety of types. Unfortunately there are no plans or lines to be had, and in many cases it has not even been found possible to give the dimensions.

The whole trade was wrapped in secrecy; the movements of the ships were not always reported in the local papers; few, even of the later clippers, were registered at Lloyd's; and the nautical historian, however clever a researcher he may be, will find very little information about them either in the British Museum or elsewhere.

It is only in private hands that any records remain; and these records, scattered letters and sheets from old logs, have only been preserved in most cases by sheer luck, and stumbled upon in the most haphazard manner.

The Personnel.

Most of the early masters in the opium trade were either ex-naval officers or officers who had been brought up in the Honourable East India Company.

When world peace after long years of war came in 1816 scores of naval officers preferred active work in the Mercantile Marine to idleness on half pay; and when the Company's monopoly came to an end, their officers mostly went into the country trade or joined the opium clippers. But so lucrative did this contraband trade prove to be and so high was the pay received by those engaged in it that in a very short time there was quite a competition amongst British seamen to get into the service.

Here is what an officer wrote about it, who served in the late 'thirties and 'forties:

"The officers were for the most part the younger sons of good families at home, who had to use every effort and wait long to fill a vacant appointment, which was very difficult to obtain as applicants had to undergo the severest tests of fitness, both mental and physical. Some acquaintance with nautical astronomy and the physical sciences, with a taste for Eastern languages, and a tongue and turn for Eastern colloquials; approved physique; steadiness and courage; reliability of temper; with the higher moral gifts of coolness and patience under trial and provocation—all these were essentials.

"And it may be remembered that among the officers were many sons of clergymen, who, after a period of active service afloat, would retire to succeed ultimately to their fathers' livings or to practise at the bar, not a few finding their way into Parliament."

The opium clippers carried very large crews for two reasons: firstly, they were racing ships; and secondly, they always had to be ready to fight against odds in the shape of Malay, Dyak or Chinese pirates.

Of the larger vessels, *Sylph's* complement was 70 all told, *Falcon* and *Cowasjee Family* also carried 70; the *Rob Roy*, a barque of 380 tons, had a complement of 80 men; and the brig *Anonyma* in 1842 had 74 men. Of the smaller vessels, the schooner *Hellas* seems to have had the largest crew with 45 hands; *Time* only had 22 and *Syed Khan* 25; the American built *Ariel* running up the East coast only had 8 hands at one time, but this was quite exceptional, for schooners of her size usually had from 20 to 30 hands.

The early clippers followed the example of the country craft in carrying Lascars, Malays and Manila men in their fo'c'sles.

Their sea-cunnies (a good old sea term, which seems to have dropped out of the language) were generally Portuguese from Macao or the Malabar coast or else Manila men. They were responsible petty officers, being in charge of the steering, the lead, and even of the broadside guns in some ships.

For men born in the tropics the winter passage up the China

Sea in the N.W. monsoon was a very hard service. The ships had fo'c'sles of the most niggardly dimensions owing to their sharp forward lines, so that whenever it was possible the hands preferred to live on deck. But this was a damp business in a clipper carrying sail in a dead beat to windward with her decks a smother of sprays. Under such conditions there was no comfort and very little rest, and for this reason not only Lascars but European seamen fought shy of the opium craft in spite of the extra pay and no stint in anything.

Here is what an American foremast hand who shipped on an opium clipper at Calcutta has to say on the subject:

"With her low black hull, tall rakish masts and square yards she was a regular beauty, just such a vessel as it does an old tar's heart good to set eyes on—though, for the matter of comfort, keep me out of them, for what with their scrubbing and scouring in port and their carrying on sail at sea to make a good passage and half drowning the crew, there's very little peace aboard them. We went aboard to take a look at the beauty and before we left her had shipped for the voyage. After taking a cruise around Calcutta for a couple of days, we went on board, bag and hammock (for no chests were allowed in the forecastle). Our pay was to be 80 rupees per month with half a month's advance."

This was written in the middle 'forties, when the clippers were striving to get British or American seamen into their fo'c'sles. Though the Oriental was a faithful, reliable seaman, quick and skilful at his work, he was not at his best when battling with a typhoon or a pirate; and whenever he had the chance the skipper of an opium vessel was only too glad to ship deserters from the British and United States Navies, a few of whom were generally to be found lying hidden in the low sailor haunts of Bombay or Calcutta, Hongkong or Shanghai.

Crimps were just as much a necessity in those early days in the East as they were in later days in the West. At Bombay and Calcutta these dealers in human flesh were called "ghaut serangs" and they were every bit as heartless and callous as the Caseys and Muldoons of later years; and what is more, they took a six months' advance out of the wretched Lascar.

As a rule, only about two-thirds of a crew shipped in Bombay or Calcutta in the 'thirties had ever been to sea before; the rest were hill coolies, bullock drivers, and other landsmen, who had either been caught in the crimp's net by false promises, or owed him money or what was rather more rare were young Indian boys with an inborn taste for the sea.

There was an instance of a ship arriving at Whampoa, amongst whose crew was a syce aged 70 years, who was making his first voyage to sea.

The financial concerns of the native crews were entirely arranged by the ship's serang or boatswain; and he distributed their pay to each member just as he thought fit. His mates, the two tindals, headed the watches, and the European officers of the ship issued all commands to them. It was the duty of the ghaut serang, in return for the six months' advance, to provide each Lascar with a sea chest, an outfit of clothes and also provisions for the voyage.

The first only lumbered up the deck—there was no room for it in the tiny forecastle—and it speedily became firewood or found its way overboard. The clothes were the usual cast-off rags supplied by crimps, and the food, generally some dried fish and curry stuff, only lasted a week or ten days, after which the Lascars had to subsist on a straight diet of rice and ghee, provided by the ship.

In the honest, tubby country wallahs, which only voyaged with the favourable monsoons, "calashie" crews of Indians or Malays were comfortable enough, for they had fair winds, fine weather and quick passages and it was no hardship to live on deck even in their scanty cotton rags—but it was a very different matter aboard the clippers. So much did these racing ships come to be dreaded by Lascar seamen that "shanghaiing" often became necessary. Indeed it is possible that the term originated with the opium clippers.

Most of the clippers which came out from England did their best to hang on to their European crews by dint of raising the pay and other attractions. But merchant jack was not always willing to risk his skin in such a dangerous trade. When the schooner *Time* arrived in China her crew became thoroughly scared by the yarns they heard about shipwrecked and captured crews being tortured by the mandarins or else the pirates; and when the schooner left Canton waters for a trip up the coast, they signed a round robin demanding to be taken back to Macao.

Captain Pybus acted in the decisive manner customary with the masters of the clippers. Arming himself and his two officers he seized the ringleaders and put them in irons. He then ran back to Hongkong, where he turned his cowardly crew ashore and shipped a crowd of Malays.

Captain Wallace of the *Sylph* had rather the same trouble in 1833. He discharged 5 refractory seamen, consisting of 3 Englishmen, 1 American and 1 Bermudan, at Macao. According to the East India Company's regulations their return to England had to be provided; this not being possible, the Select Committee would only renew the *Sylph's* licence on condition that Captain Wallace reshipped these men.

No sooner had they been reshipped than it was discovered that they had planned with one, Henry Steele, the mate of a New Zealand ship, to seize the Company's cutter *Louisa*, with the intention of capturing and running off with one of the receiving ships lying off Lintin. The date arranged for this piratical attempt was the day following that on which they had been reshipped—thus their scheme fell to the ground. The mate, Steele, was arrested and sent to England for trial and Captain Wallace had to put up with five prospective pirates in his forecastle.

The Crew of the "Falcon."

If we can believe one of her officers, the *Falcon*, Jardine Matheson's flagship in the 'forties, must have had one of the smartest all round crews in Eastern waters.

Here is what he writes about them:

"Our spars from deck to truck were, or had been, modelled by rough and ready artists, in the persons of our carpenter and his mates, who had sometimes more than they could do to supply our frequent losses. Famous among us as he was—and as he deserved to be—our carpenter yielded to the superior art of our sailmaker. Much as they did to enhance each other's merits, the sailmaker bore the palm. No Academician ever draped a classic figure with more consummate taste and art than that with which our sailmaker draped the *Falcon* . . . . I cannot honestly proceed further without a word in praise of another deserving petty officer, the boatswain, who, with a couple of mates and four quartermasters, had come out from England in the *Falcon.* The boatswain had been a foreman rigger in one of the great commercial docks at home, where his daily practice for many years had familiarised him with every description of craft of every possible rig, and with fittings and refittings to suit almost any taste. He was a master of his craft, and was as intelligent as he was expert.

"His leading peculiarity was his faculty of teaching and communicating to others not only the mode but the philosophy and the spirit and beauty of his own gifts, so that the three years that we had spent together in the *Falcon* had made us all riggers.

"All able seamen, by mere use of the term, profess to be competent to 'hand, reef and steer and heave the lead'; but there wasn't a seaman on board the *Falcon,* who couldn't—besides these requisites—turn in a dead-eye, gammon a bowsprit, fish a broken spar, rig a purchase of any given power, knot, point, splice, parcel and serve, spinning his own yarn or lines, of such length and dimensions as could be adapted to the power of our winch and rope-walk.

"With such a crew the state of our rigging, stays, backstays, standing and running gear and fittings may be accepted as most perfect and complete.

"As an instance of the capacity of the *Falcon's* crew, I may state that we have stretched, cut and fitted a set of coir lower rigging on our own decks at sea; and at sea we have placed it over the naked lower mastheads and set it up, one mast at a time, completing the whole work in three days.

"And at sea we have constructed a raft of spare spars and transferred to it our guns, stores and much of our ballast. And to the raft so loaded, we have hove down the ship and repaired and cleaned the copper from keel to bends in two days.

"Our crew was a large one, I admit, sufficient in number to make three strong watches, either of which could reef the three topsails together. . . . If I am asked why such feats should have been performed at all, or even attempted, I may say that the *Falcon* was always at sea; that her cruising grounds were over a long extent of coast that, in those days, swarmed with pirates; that it afforded no place of shelter where strangers could safely enter; that the whole coast was *terra incognita*, except to the lawless, rapacious natives and to the few like ourselves who had spent many years in its navigation in all weathers."

The Poppy Plague.

Though we are not concerned in this book with the ethics of the opium trade, but only with its one bright spot—its beautiful clippers and their hardy crews—it is necessary to understand not only how the trade was carried on but its effect upon the Chinese nation.

The contraband traffic in the "Black Smoke" roused a veritable ferment in England. The Anglican Church denounced the hideous trade in strongly worded tracts, eloquent sermons and prosy digests; the Nonconformist conscience thundered abuse and prophesied damnation; yet the opium smugglers continued to make fortunes in a business in which the power of money stifled all other considerations.

It is not altogether easy to get at the truth about the opium traffic. The British Government, like all democratic Governments, appointed Commissions of Inquiry and published Blue-books of many pages but continued to temporise until one day it found that it had a war upon its hands.

Old China hands declared that it was the drain of silver from China in order to pay for the drug which caused the opposition of the Emperor and his advisers. They also maintained that the Chinese were so addicted to opium smoking that they were quite unable to do without it, and if imports were stopped it would have to be cultivated more extensively in China. The opium poppy was grown in China in some places, but the drug resulting from it was not nearly so good as the Indian opium.

The chief argument of the opium smuggler was that opium when smoked in the Chinese fashion was no more harmful—indeed very much less—than beer and spirits to the Briton or arsenic to the Circassian. The health of the lower class Chinese certainly seemed to confirm this. They were invariably active, muscular, hard-working, cheerful, frugal and intelligent in those days before Western civilization had invaded their country. They could live on less and work harder and longer than possibly any other nation on this earth. They were supremely enduring, extraordinarily healthy and were quite ignorant of all the petty yet troublesome ailments from which the people of Europe suffered. In cultivation, in manufacture, in all kinds of handicraft and art they were not only exceedingly industrious and painstaking, but skilful to a degree that has seldom been equalled.

These qualities, the opium traders contended, could not last if opium smoking was really so harmful. The truth, however, was that the poorer class of Chinaman could only afford to buy opium in a very diluted form, which dilution rendered it practically harmless.

It is certain that Commissioner Lin was sincere in his strong opposition, though one is not so sure if his Emperor was, for it was rumoured that most of his Court used the drug.

Lin published some very long diatribes against the opium trade, but his argument is well summed up in his own words:

"Though not using opium oneself, to venture, nevertheless, on the manufacture and sale of it, is to seek one's own advantage by other men's injury; and such acts are utterly abhorrent to the nature of men, and are utterly opposed to the ways of heaven."

The Effect of the Black Smoke.

Dr. MacPherson, of the Madras Army, who came to China in the Indian Expeditionary Force during the first Chinese war, has given such a detailed and vivid account of the effect of opium smoking that I have been tempted to quote the following from it:

"When introduced into the system through the lungs its effects are far more immediate and exhilarating as well as more transient than when taken internally. The pulse vibrates, it becomes fuller and firmer; the face glows, the eyes sparkle, the temperature of the skin is elevated and it becomes suffused with a blush: the organs of sense are exquisitively sensitive, perspiration flows profusely, respiration becomes quicker, the action of the heart is increased, the nervous energy is exalted, and a glow of warmth and sensations similar to those which often attend highly pleasurable and agreeable feelings overspread the body. Every organised tissue shares the impression and the whole system becomes preternaturally excited and assumes the characteristic of disease.

"The perceptions become more vivid, the imagination more prolific with ideas and these of a more brilliant and exalted nature. Fancy is awakened and creates new and bright associations. The pleasurable scenes of former life are again recalled, events and circumstances long effaced from recollection, facts long forgotten, present themselves to the mind. The future is full of delightful anticipations, whilst the most difficult schemes seem already accomplished and crowned with success.

"Under its operation every task seems easy and every labour light. The spirits are renovated and melancholy dissipated, the most delightful sensations and the happiest inspirations are present, when it is only partaken to a limited extent, and to those not long accustomed to its use.

"If persevered in, pleasing feelings vanish, all control of the will, all functions of sensation and volition as well as reason are suspended. Vertigo, coma, irregular muscular contractions and sometimes temporary delirium supervene."

After this terrible piece of word painting he declares that "opium smoking is almost universal amongst rich and poor throughout China."

The Opium Den.

The opium den, very often an underground lair, was something like an old wooden ship's forecastle with its surrounding bunks or couches and its close foul air. At the head of each wooden couch stood the smoker's lamp. The pipe was a reed about an inch in diameter with an aperture in the bowl for the admission of opium no bigger than a pin's head. A ghoulish attendant waited upon the smokers, to fill and light the pipes. A single pipe only sufficed for one or two whiffs, the black smoke being taken into the lungs as from the hookah in India.

The occupants of an opium den were far from being a pleasant sight. The idiot smile and death-like stupor of the opium smoker after a few pipes strike the onlooker with a horror, more sickening than the worst bestiality of the drunkard. The state of bliss, which the smoker seeks, is corpse-like in its outward appearance so that as the night hours pass the opium den gradually assumed the aspect of a dead-house. The noisy gambling parlour, which usually adjoined it, only served to attract the tyro, the habitué of the den, half distracted by his cravings through the day, rushed straight to his couch, pallid and haggard, his face a skull, his body a skeleton.

The Curse of the Drug.

It was commonly believed in the East that the effects of opium extended far beyond the ruin and degradation of those who used it.

Men, even of education, declared that those who bought and sold it, those who carried it, in fact all those who handled it and lived by its means, were brought under its evil bane, so that sooner or later the curse of the drug fastened itself upon them in some way or other.

Even the captains and officers of the opium clippers themselves were not considered exempt from the blighting influence of the "black mud." As for the merchants who engaged in it, though they amassed enormous wealth, bad luck haunted them and their ends were often tragic in the extreme.

I find this belief confirmed in that interesting little book, *The Old Country Trade of India*, by Commander W. H. Coates. I will quote his words:

"Curiously enough the opium trade brought no luck. A prominent Parsee gentleman, member of a family distinguished in Indian shipping history, while indulging in reminiscences, told me of the ill luck which had persistently dogged those who had made their fortunes in opium. He instanced several, including his own family. I reminded him of a baronet, recently deceased, who left behind him not far from two millions sterling, much of which was derived from this nefarious traffic.

"The Parsee rejoined that the baronet in question was formerly in command of one of the clippers belonging to the Banaji family and, though it was true he had made a fortune, he was a physical wreck, which no doubt greatly clouded his latter days."

One could easily bring examples of opium dealers whose days of retirement were not exactly happy or even healthy.

But there have been many Britishers who have paid a price for their years of exile in the East without being in any way connected with the opium trade.

Yet equally true is it that you cannot touch pitch without being defiled, and in some mysterious way the terrible drug certainly did leave its mark upon those who derived the most worldly profit from it.

The Opium Sales.

The opium grown in India, which the clippers loaded in Bombay and Calcutta, was produced in several localities and was thus of different grades. The best of these was Malwa, the poppy of which was cultivated by the native chiefs and rajahs. It fetched on an average from 400 to 450 rupees a chest at Bombay, where a duty of 125 rupees had to be paid. A chest of Malwa weighed about a picul or 100 catties (133⅓ lbs.) The freight during the thirties ranged between 25 and 32 rupees the case, but in most cases the merchants who traded in the drug owned their own clippers. Malwa opium was made up in balls, which in size were compared to 32-pounder shot. Each of these was packed in dried leaves.

The Patna and Benares opium, the cultivation of which was entirely in the hands of the East India Company, was never considered equal to Malwa and it only fetched about 300 rupees a chest of about 120 catties. This was made up in small cakes.

The East India Company tried its best to corner opium; besides growing the Patna and Benares, it bought up all the Malwa in the early days at a fixed price. Perhaps it would be more correct to say that the great John Company did not succeed in buying up all the opium grown in the native States, for some of it was smuggled down to the coast by secret native channels and shipped from the Portuguese ports of Daman and Goa in country craft. This was known as Daman opium and was handled almost entirely by Portuguese merchants.

At the opium sales at Bombay and Calcutta there was a great deal of heavy gambling in the price. Many a Jew and many a

Gentile burnt his fingers badly over this speculation in opium. Many a well-known Indian or Parsee house went down in the fray. A few lucky ones made fortunes, especially when the price rushed up during the opium war. Opium sold on the China coast at between 700 and 800 dollars, over £150; but on the outbreak of war it went to 1200 dollars a case or nearly £260.

When the East India monopoly was given up, the Bengal merchants endeavoured to cut out those of Bombay by increasing their supply, but the Parsees of Bombay were not to be out-manoeuvred. They at once sent their agents to Calcutta to bid the price up; thus the cost of the drug was raised to a fictitious level, and in this game of diamond cut diamond it is impossible to say who had the best of it.

The war ruined many an opium dealer, but it was not nearly so fatal as the financial crisis of 1849 when the Union Bank failed, involving all the biggest houses in tremendous losses.

Besides Indian opium a small amount of the drug, just two or three ship-loads, was brought to China from Smyrna, and was known as Turkey opium.

This Turkey opium was due to the enterprise of some American captains. The first of these was a Captain Dobell of the Philadelphia brig *Sylph.* He arrived at Macao on July 22, 1811, with a cargo of opium from Smyrna; and his speculation was so successful that other ships were soon loading the drug at Smyrna. One of these, the *President Adams* of Boston, with 170,000 dollars in specie and a quantity of Turkish opium on board, came to grief on St. John's Island to the Westward of Macao on October 6, 1813. This was unfortunate, for the war with Great Britain was already checking the American effort to run Turkish opium into China. The news of the outbreak of hostilities between Britain and America was not known in Canton until February 5, 1813, when the *Ann* of Baltimore arrived in the Pearl River with a copy of the declaration of war. After the war the Smyrna trade continued in the hands of the Americans.

Full statistics of the opium trade up to the end of 1833, giving the number of chests imported into Canton each year, are given in Morse's *Chronicles of the East India Company.*

CHAPTER II.

IN THE DAYS OF "JOHN COMPANY."

"Which I wish to remark,—
And my language is plain,—
That for ways that are dark
And for tricks that are vain,
The heathen Chinee is peculiar
Which same I would rise to explain."

The Chronology of the Opium Trade up to 1820.

PERHAPS a short chronology of the opium trade in the early days will be the best way of leading up to the stirring times of the clippers.

1700.—The Portuguese began importing about 200 chests a year into Macao from India.

1729.—First Chinese edict against opium.

1745.—The Emperor Yung Ching ordered all foreign trade to be confined to Whampoa, the port of Canton.

1753.—An import duty of 3 taels (equivalent to 20 shillings) per picul placed upon opium.

1760.—Total import of opium equalled 1000 chests.

1769.—The East India Company countenanced the trade, but as the drug was contraband in China the Court of Directors considered it beneath the dignity of the Company to smuggle and would not allow their Indiamen to carry opium.

1773.—First opium imported into China by ships under the British flag. These were Indian country craft.

1781.—Warren Hastings, as Governor of Bengal, sent a cargo of opium to China.

1785.—Export of silver, to pay for opium, forbidden by the Emperor of China.

1799.—A formal edict sent out making opium contraband throughout China.

1800.—All sale of opium forbidden; nevertheless both the use of opium and its import into China increased.

1809.—Further edict forbidding import of opium.

1811.—American brig *Sylph* arrived in the Canton River with first cargo of Turkish opium loaded at Smyrna.

1815.—Chinese dealers in opium arrested at Macao. American schooner *Lydia* searched for the drug.

1816.—The season's fleet at the Whampoa Anchorage numbered 87 foreign merchantmen under a senior captain of the Hon. East India Company as commodore. This fleet included 28 British East Indiamen (flagship *Earl of Balcarras*) and 39 country ships. This was the year of Lord Amherst's embassy.

On July 14 the American brig *Macedonian* arrived in the Canton River, having made the round trip to New York and back in 290 days.

1817.—The Indiaman *Vansittart* arrived with a cargo of Turkish opium.

1015 chests were imported into Macao by the Portuguese ships *Principe Regente, Angelica, Belisario* and *Ramha dos Anjos.*

This year the prices at the Company's sales in Calcutta were soaring.

1819.—An opium mart opened at Bombay. The British brig *Mentor* was stated to be acting as an opium "godown" at Whampoa, and was thus the first opium "receiving ship."

1820.—The anchorage off Lintin became a rendezvous for outside shipping, especially for opium smugglers.

Opium Traders at Canton and Macao in 1821.

By this date the opium smuggling in the Pearl River had assumed a magnitude and importance which even the most careful secrecy, camouflage and "palm oil" could not hide. Each season more Europeans and Parsees, with no connection whatever with the authorised factories, were appearing at Canton and Macao.

Most of these independent European merchants cloaked their business under the flag of some insignificant nationality, for whom they acted as consul. For instance the three Magniacs represented the unimportant state of Prussia, C. Magniac being Consul, H. Magniac, vice-Consul, and D. Magniac, secretary. These three brothers formed the free-trading firm of Magniac & Co., the predecessors of Jardine, Matheson & Co.

Thomas Dent, the founder of the famous firm of Dent & Co., was at this date Sardinian Consul. The first members of Thomas Dent & Co. were Thomas and his brother Lancelot Dent and Charles Blight, an American; the latter, however, was out of the partnership by 1827.

Of the other Consulates in Canton, Sir Andrew Ljungstadt, though he did not leave China, handed over the Swedish Consulate to an Englishman named Robert Berry.

In the same way James Matheson became Danish Consul. The story of how Matheson came to China is worth telling, as showing how fortune plays tricks with a man. As a young man he was taken into his uncle's counting house in Calcutta (Mackintosh & Co.). One day his uncle gave him a letter to deliver to one of his captains who was about to sail for China. Young James Matheson put the letter in his pocket and forgot all about it. At this his irate uncle declared that he was no use to him and had better go back to England. Matheson took his uncle at his word and went off to engage a passage. Luckily for him, the first Indiaman commander to whom he applied for a passage was, like most East India skippers, a very shrewd business man, and he strongly advised young Matheson to make his way to Canton instead of England.

Matheson took his advice and in less than 20 years had made his fortune. He is described by his contemporaries as a man "of great suavity of manner and the personification of benevolence."

Doctor William Jardine, the senior partner in Jardine, Matheson & Co., settled in Canton in 1819. Born at Broadholm in the parish of Lochmaben, on February 24, 1784, this shrewd Scottish physician made his first essay in trade when a surgeon aboard one of John Company's East Indiamen, when he availed himself of the privilege

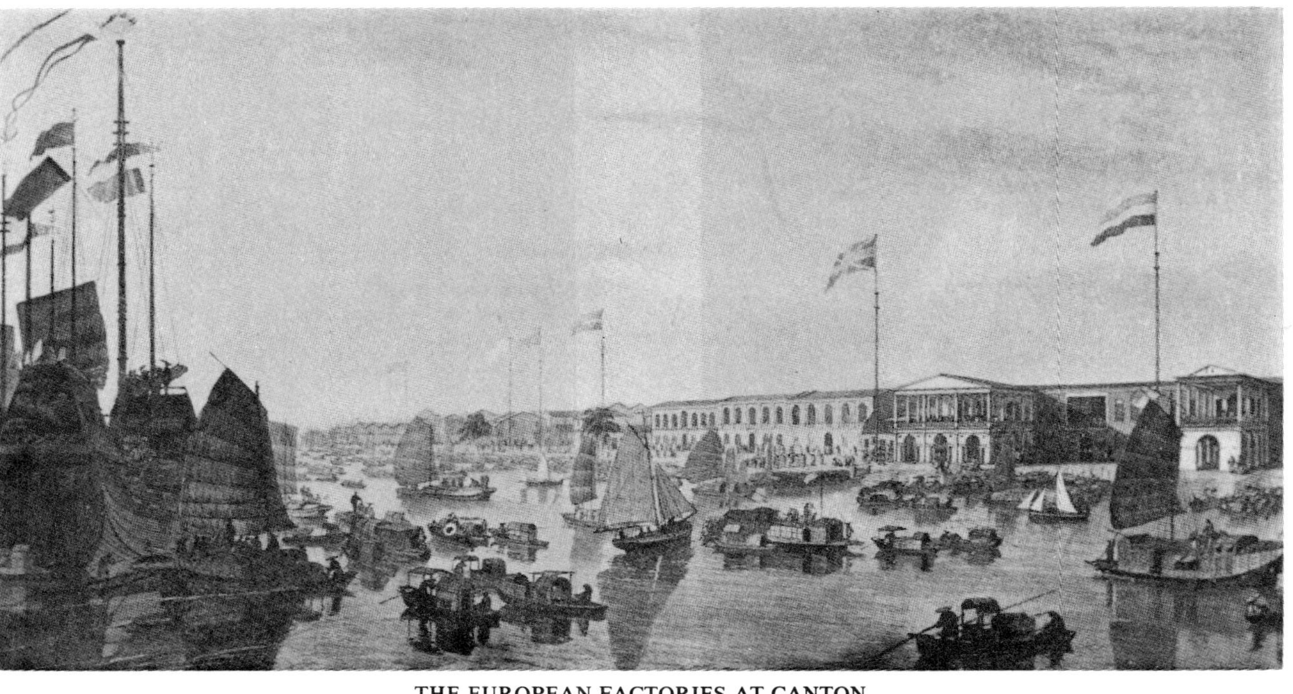

THE EUROPEAN FACTORIES AT CANTON

National Maritime Museum, Greenwich

[*See page* 38

"HOUQUA", HEAD OF THE CO-HONG
Lent by Mr. Allan Forbes

SAMUEL RUSSELL
Lent by Mr. Allan Forbes

[See page 44

of so much cargo space, so generously allowed by the Company to its officers.

From the first his business ventures were very profitable, but he always gave the credit for this to his friend and agent in India, the great Parsee merchant and philanthropist, Jamsetjee Jeejeebhoy.

On arrival in China Dr. Jardine never cloaked his business under a Consul's flag, but in a very short time he joined the three Magniacs in partnership. These Magniacs, by the way, were of Swiss descent if of English nationality. William Jardine was a man of untiring energy, a worker who showed little mercy to himself or to his employees, in a climate where easy-going methods and slack ways were the general rule.

Keenly intelligent, he was quite ruthless in business and pursued the opium trade with all his might and without any moral scruples. It is not surprising to find such a man described as "steady and ardent as a friend, equally steady and implacable as a foe." Yet he was most generous and hospitable and many a young man owed his first rise in life to Doctor William Jardine.

The chief American firm in Canton at this date was that of Samuel Russell & Co., founded on December 26, 1818. It was known amongst the Chinese as "Kee-Chang-Hong," and at first was only an agency conducted by the two partners, Samuel Russell and Philip Ammidon.

The following description of Samuel Russell I have taken from *The Fan Kwae at Canton*, an interesting little booklet written by W. C. Hunter, a member of his staff.

"Mr. Russell was a native of Middletown, Connecticut, a person of singularly gentle and benevolent disposition. There was about him a suavity and charm of manner which under no circumstances ever deserted him. Throughout a long life he enlisted the esteem and respect of all who knew him. Of his considerate forbearance under great provocation I can vouch from personal experience."

The Parsees were represented at Canton in 1821 by Mirwanjee Monockjee and Johangee Framjee. The first member of the great, firm of Rustomjee & Co. to visit China was Dadabhoy Rustomjee in 1827. He was a nephew of Johangee Framjee and son of the great Parsee shipowner, Rustomjee Cowasjee Banajee.

The Parsees were closely allied in business with the British firms in the early days, especially in the ownership of the clippers. Often many sixty-fourths were held by Jardine, Matheson & Co. in ships which were nominally under the ownership of the Banajees or the Camas and *vice versa.*

By the year 1831, in addition to the East India Company's officers and clerks, there were 26 British merchants, 21 American and 26 Parsee.

These free-traders were by no means welcome as far as the lordly John Company was concerned; indeed, every season the Select Committee in China—as the chief executive officers of the Company were called—issued a notification ordering all British subjects, who were not specially authorised (as foreign Consuls) to leave China, but none of these adventurous traders paid any attention to it.

As the opium trade was contraband, those who engaged in it cared little for the regulations of the Honourable Company. Their dealings were with the mandarins and Hong merchants. Sometimes a new Chinese official tried a little "squeeze pigeon" on these unauthorised traders, but their profits were so great and their methods of business so underground, that they could well afford to buy up the higher ranks of the mandarins and treat zealous or interfering Custom-house officers with contempt.

They must have been men of great strength of character, these opium smugglers of the early days, for the Chinese were notoriously difficult to handle and it was far from smooth sailing even for the mighty John Company itself.

The Foreign Devils.

Before the opium war all foreigners were contemptuously styled "barbarians" or "Fan kwae," "foreign devils" by the Chinese.

The British were always alluded to as the "red-haired devils." The Americans were called "Hwa-ke" or "flowery-flag devils"; and the Portuguese "Se-yang kwae" or "devils of the Western Ocean," though those who were born in Macao were known as "Oman kwae" or "Macao devils."

The Danes went by the name of "yellow flag devils" and the

Parsees "white headed devils" because they shaved their heads. The Dutch were always "Ho-lan kwae" or "Holland devils" and the French "Fat-lan-sy."

Of all the foreigners in Canton; the only ones whom the Chinese οι πολλοι really respected were the officials of the great John Company—that is to say, previous to 1840. As soon as the Celestial Empire had felt the weight of the British right arm its mandarins and its merchants, its townsmen and countrymen and even its priests and pirates only dared to address Britishers as "most honourable gentlemen."

The term honourable which up to that date had been reserved entirely for the great East India Company, henceforth was addressed with much kow-towing to any drunken foremast hand or beachcomber.

The Honourable East India Company.

Over a hundred years of honest and successful trading had given the East India Company a prestige which perhaps has never been equalled in the world of commerce since the days of the Phoenicians. At the end of the seventeenth century when the old and the new East India Companies were amalgamated under the title of the United East India Company, a trade mark was adopted in the shape of a heart, divided diagonally into four partitions, one for each letter of their title, thus:—

So great did the Company's reputation for honest dealing become, that no case or bale stamped with that trade mark was ever opened or inspected by the Chinese, whether Customs officials or merchants. The stamped heart was considered sufficient guarantee that the contents of the case were exactly what they were declared to be, and not only that, but "well up to sample" as the expression goes.

The Select Committee, who managed the affairs of the Company at Canton, always took infinite pains to carry on their business and all intercourse with the Chinese in the dignified and ceremonious fashion which was customary between educated people in China. They never acted hastily. They never acted pettily. Their attitude was ever one of solemn dignity and unvarying justice and honesty; and in this way the great Company impressed the Chinese in a way which no other nationals succeeded in doing.

Amongst the Chinese the Company was called "Kung-se," meaning "United Affairs," but with their fellow traders they were always known as "The Honourable John Company" and referred to in Canton as "The Factory."

The East India Company had a lordly way of carrying on business; they despised niggling and parsimony and no firm of employers have ever been more generous to their employees.

Besides the officers of their ships having space allowed them for private ventures, every man on their staff at the Factory was allowed a share of the profits, fixed by a sliding scale, which amounted to as much as six shillings per £100 in the case of the president; this was in addition to a salary which ran to well over four figures.

The staff of the Factory at Canton consisted of a president, treasurer, superintendent of exports and superintendent of imports—these four men made up the Select Committee as a rule.

Next came three supercargoes; the first carried out the duties of sub-treasurer and compradore; the second that of accountant and the third that of secretary. There were usually about ten writers, as clerks were named out East. The senior of these was assistant secretary; then came the superintendent of the office, the collator of records, and the deputy superintendents of imports and exports. It was the sole duty of three writers to copy out the records. These men were paid salaries of from £400 to £600 per annum besides a percentage on the sales of the cargoes in London. One of the most highly paid members of the staff was the tea inspector, who besides commission received a salary of £2000 a year, a princely stipend in those days. The surgeon attached to the Factory received £1300 and his assistant £1000 per annum. The translator and interpreter, who, in the last days of the Factory, was the celebrated Doctor Robert Morrison, received £1000 a year and the chaplain £800. Of the lesser members of the Factory staff, the steward, who was also clerk in the chapel, received 1100 dollars and the butler 800 dollars. Of Chinese servants there were a great number, headed by the schroffs.

Dining at the Factory.

The East India Company set the fashion of entertaining in the Far East in a style which was truly princely and ever since their day the hospitality of the Britisher East of Suez has ever been proverbial.

To be asked to dine at the Factory was always considered to be a great honour by any newcomer to Canton. The guest, after being let in through the great outer gate, found a broad paved walk in front of him, which led up to a wide flight of stone steps. On one side of this walk stood the chapel, upon the spire of which a large chiming clock set the time for everyone within the European area of Canton.

At the top of the flight of steps was a verandah, across which the guest stepped up to the door of the Factory library, which served as a reception room. In the last days of the Company's regime the librarian was Doctor Pierson, who took a pride in his well-filled shelves; the billiard room, to the right of the library was, however, a more popular room with the young writers.

Each guest was received by the president of the Factory with a good deal of old-world courtesy and ceremony, and when all the diners were assembled generally to the number of about 30—the tall folding doors into the dining-room were thrown open and dinner was announced by the dignified English butler of the Factory.

The dining-room was of the dimensions of a banquetting hall. The long table of polished mahogany in the centre was lit by a row of superb cut-glass chandeliers hanging from the ceiling. In these the best spermacetti candles provided a perfect blaze of light. And as if these were not enough there were also magnificent silver candelabra upon the table itself, which served to set off the valuable plate and choice glass and china of the dinner service.

Behind the president hung a life-size portrait of King George IV. in royal robes and wearing his crown. This was the portrait which Lord Amherst had taken to Pekin to present to the Emperor, only to have the gift spurned in the most contemptuous manner. At the other end of the room hung a full length portrait of the unlucky Ambassador himself. As in India and Malaya, so in China, when asked to dine, one always brought one's own servant to wait at table and look after one's own special wants. These Factory khitmutgars were all Chinese, dressed in caps and long robes.

As hosts and guests advanced into the dining room, a veritable phalanx of spotless Chinamen formed up in a line at the further end—and no sooner were the diners seated than each Chinaman slipped silently to his place behind his master's chair.

Then followed the long old-fashioned English dinner, washed down with sherry, madeira, champagne, claret and port.

Dining was a very important function in those days. The president took wine with each guest down to the humblest writer, and no man left the Company's table on steady feet. Yet decorum was never absent from these functions, and the dignity of the Factory was always worthily upheld.

The Canton Factories.

There were thirteen foreign factories or merchant houses standing in a line facing the river opposite the island of Honain at Canton.

These reading from East to West were the Creek Factory, Dutch Factory, East Indian Company's New Factory, Chow-chow Factory, East India Company's Old Factory, Swedish Factory, Imperial Factory, Paou-Shan Factory, American Factory, Chunqua Factory, French Factory, Spanish Factory and Danish Factory.

Between the factories and the Pearl River measuring about 250 yards in length and 50 yards in depth was the Square.

This Square was usually filled with a gaping loitering crowd of Chinamen, through whose curious ranks the Fan Kwae had to jostle their way.

Lines of booths faced the paved pathway; some of these were red, and contained side shows, something like Punch and Judy; from others, sellers of fruit, sweetmeats, and the quaint eatables beloved of the Celestial bawled out their wares. Then there were barbers plying their trade in the open air, wizened old crones with needle and thread, tinkers, cobblers and vendors of dogs, cats and chickens. Amongst all this rabble dignified Chinese merchants, often carrying tame birds perched on sticks, promenaded to and fro.

At the Eastern end was the Creek, which though dry at low water, or at least a muddy, smelly ditch, was always thronged with sampans, which never left it. On the far side of this ditch stood the great hongs or warehouses of Kingqua, Mowqua and Houqua.

At the other end of the line of Factory buildings Pwanting-qua Street led to the city from the river. Running parallel to it were Old China Street, New China Street and the notorious Hog Lane.

Old China Street, running between the Chunqua and the American Factory, was closed at either end by a heavy gate, the one guarded by an aged watchman, the other sanctified by an ancient stone altar. This street, with a span of 12 feet, was perhaps the widest street in Canton. It was blocked in its turn by ragged fortune tellers, more than one of them Buddhist, and Taon priests. Each of these had his circle of idlers. Then there were quacks selling patent medicines and narrow-faced money-changers.

At the North end of Old China Street stood the Consoo House or public hall of the Hong merchants, where all matters of dispute were discussed with the Fan Kwae, where children were vaccinated and criminals tried.

Against the American Factory was a guard-house occupied by some half-dozen Chinese soldiers whose only accoutrements were rattans, raw-hide whips, lanterns and conch-shells, which last they blew during the night to let all robbers know that they were on guard.

Hog Lane, known by the Chinese as Green Pea Street, led down to the ferry. This was the sailor-town of Canton, where Jack bought tobacco, samshoo or straw hats from "Old Jammy Apoo," "Old Good Tom" or "Jemmy Young Tom."

In front of each factory or Hong stood its flagstaff, flying its national flag.

On the river bank, at either end of the Square as well as about the centre, stood three chop or Custom-houses, branches of the Hoppo's or chief Custom officers' department. Just East of the main chop house was the well-known Jack Ass Point.

The factories did not belong to the different nationalities but to the Hong merchants, from whom they were rented.

Each factory contained on its ground floor the rooms of the compradores, schroffs, personal servants and coolies. Here also was the counting house as well as large godowns or store rooms. As there were no banks in Canton in the old days each factory stored its bullion, silver and gold, in a specially built strong room of granite with iron doors. All money transactions took place on a paved space in front of this treasury; and here stood indispensable scales and weights, for everything went by weight in China.

On the first floor, surrounded by a broad verandah and reached by a broad flight of stone steps, were the sitting and dining rooms of the European staff, whilst on the floor above were their bedrooms.

The compound of the new East India Factory was enclosed by a high wall, within which there was a garden. The Company also had its own landing stage, alongside of which in the twenties a smart little white-painted schooner was often to be found. This was the *Lavinia*, used for conveying the Company's staff and guests up and down the river.

The head of each factory was called the "taipan," but some of the factories such as the Danish and Imperial (Austrian) were only used to house their representatives, no trade being carried on with China. The French, after an interval of 30 years, only started trade with China again in 1832, the tricolour being hoisted on December 13 of that year.

The Creek Factory was occupied by Magniac & Co. and their successors, Jardine & Matheson. In the private room of Doctor William Jardine there was no chair to be seen, for that energetic man objected to his time being wasted in business hours by idlers and those who dropped in merely to have a quiet gossip.

Small wonder that he amassed a fortune running into six figures in twenty years.

The Co-hong.

In 1720 the Emperor of China first gave licences to certain Chinese merchants, allowing them to trade with the "foreign devils" on condition that they went security for their good behaviour and their proper payment of Custom dues.

These Chinese merchants were presently formed into a corporate body called the Co-hong, and thus the merchants themselves came to be known as the Hong merchants.

The Hong merchants built the factories on the banks of the Pearl River, opposite the great city of Canton and facing South. The site was 10 miles from the Whampoa Anchorage, 40 miles from the Bogue Forts, 60 miles from Lintin and 80 miles from Macao. It was the only piece of ground where a foreigner was safe from molestation in the days before the first Chinese war and this fact was entirely due to the good offices of the Hong merchants. They were not only held responsible for every foreigner in Canton but for every ship at Whampoa, the port of Canton.

It was through them that the Hoppo or mandarin of the Customs received all payments of duty. Each young blood, each newly arrived writer, was immediately put under the protection of one of these dignified merchants, thus they were accustomed to be called "our horse god-fathers."

The position of a Hong merchant was undoubtedly very profitable, though their losses were occasionally large and the "squeezes" almost without end, their purses being emptied for every kind of public requirement from contributions towards famine relief, to those for the repair of flood damage or for the erection of municipal buildings. From one end of the immense Empire to the other calls came in upon the Hong merchants.

Hunter in his *Fan Kwae at Canton* declares that a licence paid to Pekin by a Hong merchant often amounted to 200,000 taels or £55,000 sterling. He also gives the following instance of a typical squeeze:

"Well, Houqua, has got news today?"

"Hav got too muchee bad news; Hwang Ho hav spilum too muchee."

That sounded ominously.

"Man-ta-le (pigeon English for mandarin) hav come see you?"

"He no come see my, he sendee come one piece 'chop'. He come to-mollo. He wantchee my two-lac dollar." It was the old complaint, a squeeze, and this time a formidable one.

"You pay he how mutchee?"

"My pay he fitty, sikky tousant so."

"But spose he no contentee?"

"S'pose he, No. 1, no contentee, my pay he one lac."

In 1841 the burden of ransoming Canton from the troops of Sir Hugh Gough fell chiefly upon the Hong merchants, Houqua giving 1,100,000 dollars, Pwankeiqua 260,000, and the rest of the Co-hong 640,000 dollars.

This was not the only time that Houqua paid out a million. On another occasion the Viceroy compelled the Co-hong to pay up the debts of Hingtai, Mouqua and Kingqua. The sum required was made up as follows:—

Houqua	1,000,000 dollars	Footoi	90,000 dollars
Pwankeiqua	130,000 ,,	Samqua	50,000 ,,
Pwan Hoyqua	70,000 ,,	Saoqua	50,000 ,,

As the business of a merchant was very much looked down upon in China, the great Hong merchants purchased mandarins' rank in order to maintain their dignity.

Mandarin, by the way, is a pigeon English word, derived from the Portuguese mandar, to order. Mandarins were people having authority; in other words, they were Government officials of some sort or other, the grade being denoted by the colour of the button worn in a mandarin's cap. The grade purchased by Hong merchants was as a rule that of the blue button.

The Chinese have always been noted for their honesty in business, however slim and adroit they might be in driving a bargain or negotiating a "squeeze." They were set a fine example by the East India Company, which they strove their hardest to follow.

When a Hong merchant went security for a ship, the captain and supercargo of that ship came to him in all their troubles, financial and otherwise, and many a young East India officer owed his fortune to a Hong merchant.

Ship	Tons	Security in Taels 1832	Security Merchant
Lord Lowther	1447	3992	Mowqua
Thomas Coutts	1393	4021	"
Canning	1308	3990	Puankhequa
Earl of Balcarras	1370	4087	"
Duchess of Athol	1349	3992	Goqua
Reliance	1518	4137	"
Abercrombie Robinson	1391	3992	"
Edinburgh	1444	3961	Kingqua
Sir David Scott	1358	3954	"
London	1324	3964	"
Berwickshire	1461	4008	Fatqua
Dunira	1375	4035	"
Macqueen	1415	4014	Chungwo
William Fairlie	1399	4035	"
Orwell	1426	4023	Hengtae
Charles Grant	1297	3783	"
Asia	1046	3552	Shuntae
Windsor	1577	4030	"
George the Fourth	1366	4011	Yunwo
Marquis of Camden	1500	3957	"
Barossa (for Quebec)	730	3242	Mowqua
Broxbornebury (for Quebec)	751	3265	Puankhequa
Moffat (for Halifax)	821	3265	Fatqua
		1933	
Marquis of Huntly	1348	3994	Houqua
Duke of Sussex	1336	4071	Mowqua
Herefordshire	1354	3942	"
Buckinghamshire	1369	3983	"
Scaleby Castle	1242	3831	Puankhequa
Inglis	1321	4026	"
Waterloo	1325	4068	Kingqua
Kellie Castle	1332	4158	"
Farquharson	1406	4030	Fatqua
Vansittart	1311	3906	"
Warren Hastings	1068	3623	Hengtae
Thames	1425	4009	Chungwo
Lowther Castle	1507	4141	"
Lady Melville	1350	3995	Shuntae
Castle Huntly	1353	3954	"
Bombay	1279	3771	Yunwo
Rose	1024	3574	"
Minerva	989	3692	Goqua
Thomas Grenville	886	3358	"
Prince Regent	992	3550	Hengtae
Larkins	700	3036	Toughun
William Money	750	3349	Fatqua
Moira	550	2973	Kingqua

The foregoing list of the last two years of the great John Company's monopoly gives some idea of the extent of the Company's business with the Hong merchants.

This list is interesting for two reasons: Firstly, it gives a hint of the magnificent fleet sailing under the Company's red and white striped ensign just before the ships were dispersed far and wide by the non-renewal of the Company's charter. Secondly, it names all the Hong merchants. These were limited to 13. The affix "qua," by the way, was not part of the name, but a term of respect, meaning literally "controller," but usually translated into the equivalent of our "mister."

Howqua or Houqua.

It will be noticed that Houqua, the greatest Hong merchant of them all, was only responsible for one ship, the *Marquis of Huntly*.

He had asked to be excused from securing any ships in 1832 on the plea that he was retiring from business, but the true facts seem to be that he was devoting himself almost entirely to outside business, chiefly American and Indian.

Houqua was by far the greatest character amongst the Hong merchants as well as being the richest. In 1834, he estimated his fortune at about 6,000,000 sterling; thus he must certainly have been one of the richest men in the world at that date.

Like many another millionaire, he lived very simply and with no great ostentation, but his generosity was notorious, especially amongst any foreigners who got into trouble or difficulty.

One of the senior American merchants in Canton owed Houqua close on 100,000 dollars. In the Hongs it was known that this man had long been desirous of retiring, but could not leave China whilst his unpaid promissory notes remained in Houqua's treasury.

One day Houqua said to him:—"You and I are No. I olo flen: you belong honest man, only no got chance."

With this he tore up the promissory notes and tossed the pieces into the waste paper basket.

"Just now hav settee counter, alle finishee; you go, you please." He went on in the quaint pigeon English, meaning that their accounts were now settled and he could go home when he liked.

In appearance Houqua was a thin, wizened, frail, ascetic looking man with calm bearing and thoughtful eyes.

Most of the other Hong merchants were bon-vivants of jovial disposition, who loved a good table and a hearty laugh; but Houqua lived in the greatest simplicity. In business he was methodical and precise, and renowned for his rigid honesty. On November 16, 1826, he gained the consent of the Hoppo to his retirement from active business, and henceforth his Hong was under the management of his fourth son, Wu Show-chang; but Houqua still remained a directing figure in the background.

Like most of the Hong merchants he owned large tea estates, the famous chops of Congo, from the Woo-E (Bohea) country, being grown on land which had been owned by his family for generations.

When the East India Company retired from China, Houqua transferred his business to the agents of Baring Bros., the American Russell & Co.

Born in the same year as Wellington and Napoleon, this remarkable Chinaman was the last chief of the Co-hong. He died at Honam on September 4, 1843.

The Outside Merchants.

Though the thirteen members of the Co-hong, headed by Houqua, went security for every foreign ship that wished to trade with China, it must not be supposed that they were the only Chinese who had dealings with foreigners in the early days.

There were a number of "outside" Chinese merchants as they were called, men like the members of the Co-hong, of great wealth. great integrity and great intelligence. Of such were Washing, Cumwa, Linchong, Wo-Yun, Yeeshing, Keeb-chong and many other "outside" merchants.

In those early days a Chinese business man, though slim and, to use an old American expression "cute" enough in his bargaining, prided himself on his honesty, you could rely on his promises and his word was his bond

To illustrate the lengths to which this honesty was carried, here is a story told of Yeeshing at the time of the great fire in 1822.

It is given by Mr. Hunter in his most interesting little book of reminiscences, *The Fan Kwae at Canton.*

Mr. John P. Cushing, of the American house of Perkins & Co., had entrusted Yeeshing with 5000 pieces of crape, worth about $50,000, for the purpose of being dyed.

Let me give the story in Mr. Hunter's words. "A day or two after the fire Yeeshing entered Mr. Cushing's office, exclaiming: 'Hae-yah! Hae-yah!'

"'Well, Yeeshing,' enquired Mr. Cushing, 'how fashion?'"

To which he replied: "My have loosum my house, my shop—alla finishy, too muchee trub."

Mr. Cushing began to express his sympathy with the conviction that he too was involved in the loss—there was no insurance—nothing of the kind existing at Canton—when Yeeshing continued:

"My alla finishy, only when my take out you crape (to save it) hav loosum 84 piecee, how can my, no, too muchee trub?"

He had saved Mr. Cushing's crapes, but had lost his own dwelling and its contents, with an important quantity of his own goods in doing so.

The Chinaman, an ancestor worshipper, is very proud of a long lineage and keeps his genealogical tree with great care.

Keet-Chong, for instance, whose family had resided on their own estate on French Island for more than 800 years, once showed his ancestral tree to Mr. Hunter. It went back to the Sung Dynasty (967-1281 A.D.)

Chinese Names and Mottoes.

It was perhaps owing to this reverence for the family name that it was never used in business.

For instance, Houqua's real name was E-Woo or Woo-E; Mowqua's was Kwonglee; Pwantingqua's was Tung Foo; Manhop's Folung; Washing's Moo and so on.

The signs in Chinese characters on pillars outside shops never gave the names of the proprietors but some such fantastic inscription as "The Record of Perpetual Harmony," "Current Gains," "Perfect Concord," and even "Tan-E," the "solitary idea."

Then within the shop, above the all important weighing machine at the foot of the stairs, over the inner door, on narrow sheets of red paper were many characteristic mottoes and sayings.

Above the outer door you might read "May the five happinesses enter the abode," or "May wealth flow in abundantly"; or the more mundane—"For idle persons there is no admittance," and "Rich customers are perpetually welcome."

Over the scales a common prayer was "From a single cash may 10,000 be derived."

Some of these inscriptions were very amusing; over a water-butt you might read "The bucket of superlative peace," and above a sandalwood chest "The box of great tranquillity."

Even sampans and junks were not without their beautifully written adage on bow or stern. One of the most common was "Good wind, good water!"

A bow maxim meaning "May we have a successful voyage" in literal translation read "The dragon's head produces horns of gold."

Another poetic wish was "May the moon's rays shine upon and enliven the waters."

The Linguists.

But I must get back to Canton. There are so many fascinating aspects of Chinese life and manners that one is tempted to digress.

The Chinamen who had most to do with the ships themselves were not the Hong merchants but the linguists.

The linguist's chief duty was to accompany the foreign seaman and prevent him from getting into trouble owing to his ignorance of the language and the customs of the country. He was, in fact, the buffer between the sailor and the native. He was ready to undertake any duty night or day—all details of business or pleasure were entrusted to the linguist attached to the ship. He obtained permits either for pleasure trips or for cargo shipments and accompanied the trippers or the goods. He dealt with the Hoppo and the Customs and his duties were no sinecure.

The best known of the linguists was a calm, suave, tactful man named Tau, but always known as "Old Tom."

Alert and active, both physically and mentally, his self-possession was only equalled by his skill in composing differences which seemed almost irreconcilable.

Then there was Tung—known as "Young Tom" though no relation whatever to Old Tom.

These two and Alantsae were the leading linguists in the 'twenties and 'thirties.

Compradores and Schroffs.

There was one other class of Chinaman who was closely connected with the foreign trade, and this was the clerk class, known as schroffs, and headed by the compradore or chief clerk.

The compradore was not only head of the office, cashier and custodian of the treasury, but the confidential secretary of the Taipan, who attended not only to his public business, but his private, not even excepting the catering for his table.

Though the compradore of each foreign merchant house was secured by a Hong merchant, the case of a compradore betraying his trust, embezzling or taking even the smallest advantage of his most responsible position was practically unknown.

Yet his pay was small, often not more than 300 to 500 dollars per annum, but, according to "ole custom," his cumshas were very profitable and he was not likely to die a poor man.

The pursers and supercargoes of the ships were dependant greatly on the compradore and his schroffs. Even a small coaster carried her two schroffs. Their chief duty was to test the silver, whether it happened to be in coined dollars or lumps shaped like a Chinese lady's shoe, which were called "Sycee silver."

The schroff, in passing a dollar as good, stamped it with his own particular sign, and if it afterwards proved to be base metal he had to refund the amount. When ashore he usually carried a small pair of scales attached to a belt at his waist.

The Canton River and its Craft.

Canton was not only a city of houses, but a city of boats. Not even the Pool of London was more crowded with various types of shipping than the Choo or Pearl River opposite the factories in

WHAMPOA ANCHORAGE, H.E.I.C. "WATERLOO"

National Maritime Museum, Greenwich

[*See page* 48

OPIUM SHIPS AT LINTIN IN 1824

National Maritime Museum, Greenwich

[*See page* 52

the days of the Honourable John Company and the opium clippers. Not only were there all kinds of queer river craft, but great coasting junks all the way from Manila, Borneo, Java and Singapore came right up to the city and disputed place with tiers of salt junks from the South-West Coast.

Then there were whole streets of shop and store boats, selling every kind of article from food to flowers, from toys to trousers. There were barbers' boats, fortune-tellers' boats, theatrical boats and palatial house-boats belonging to wealthy Chinamen. There were boats like farmyards with families of ducks swimming alongside and boats of singing birds. In and out amongst this busy throng plied the sampans and tanka boats and large ferryboats.

From well below Dutch Folly Fort to the landing place at Jackass Point there was no room to row and oars had to be replaced by paddles in the captains' gigs and ships' galleys which came up from the big ship anchorage in Whampoa Reach.

Whampoa had been the harbour of Canton ever since the year 1745, when, by order of the Emperor Yung Ching, foreign vessels were not permitted further up the Canton River than the Wang-Po or Yellow Anchorage.

The Prophecy about the Grey-eyed People.

The reason for the Emperor's hostility to foreigners can be traced back to a mysterious letter dated January 10, 1618, which was sent to the East India Company from someone at Bantam—probably a cunning Dutchman who feared British competition, yet there was undoubtedly a substratum of truth in it. The letter stated:

"It was revealed by oracle unto the Emperor that his country should be subdued by a grey-eyed people, and we do thereby forbid all Christians his country."

Some years later when the second English venture into Chinese waters reached the Canton River, the Portuguese at Macao accounted for the strange fear the Chinese had for the new barbarians by the fact that the latter had blue eyes.

Whampoa.

During the season in the days of sail the anchorage in Whampoa Reach was a sight of fair ships. For instance, in 1816 there were 87 ships lying at anchor, including 28 East Indiamen and 39 Indian country ships. This vast fleet was regulated and kept in order by the senior officer amongst the Honourable Company's Indiamen, who acted as commodore, fired a gun morning and evening and was responsible to the Hoppo for the good behaviour of the foreign seamen.

He issued a daily rosta, each ship having to provide a boat in turn, as a packet boat to Canton city.

The "Vansittart's" Band.

These lordly Indiamen even had ship's bands. But European music was not appreciated by the Chinese. On one occasion the *Vansittart's* musicians were sent up to play in the Square in front of the factories. Mr. Hunter of Russell & Co. gives an amusing account of the incident in *Fan Kwae.*

"The bandsmen wore a uniform of red coats. We were all looking on and listening when a Chinaman exclaimed:

" 'What for he makee so muchee noisee?'

" 'Noise!' said one of the barbarians. 'May Fo run away with you—that no belong noise, belong music. You no likee?'

" 'Hae-yah! My how can likee, all make mixee—my China music No. 1; he too muchee fools!'

"Soon afterwards the crowd became so numerous and so noisy that to avoid further complications the band was withdrawn inside the Company's Factory and the Square cleared, and not very quietly as the Chinamen's bareheads resounded with the thwacks which were laid on them, but it took place with great celerity.

"That was the first and only time a foreign band of music was heard to play in the Square."

Opposite the anchorage at Whampoa were three islands, Dane's Island, French's Island and Wang-po Island. The latter in the early nineteenth century supported a town of over 1000 inhabitants, mostly the families of those Chinese who were connected with the foreign shipping, such as compradores, stevedores, shipwrights, caulkers, blacksmiths, etc. French's Island and Dane's Island, which had once been used by those nationalities, only contained ruined buildings and half-buried tombstones.

In the very early days, there were opium receiving ships lying at Whampoa—the first of these—then called an opium "godown"—was the brig *Mentor* in 1819.

Stealing Copper Sheathing.

One of the troubles of the Canton River like that of the Thames at the same date was the river thieves. Although guard-boats rowed round the anchorage at night, it was quite common at one time for ships to find they had lost several sheets of copper sheathing. The thieves would float down stream with only their faces above water, hidden under a bit of flotsam, such as a piece of matting or old basket. Arrived alongside a ship they would anchor themselves to her cable by means of a length of coir rope, and then under the very eyes of her watchman prise the plates of copper off under water.

The late Captain Shewan of the tea clipper *Norman Court* related an amusing example of this clever robbing of copper sheathing. In the early 'fifties the *Mirage* (Captain Roberts) and the *Blackburn* (Captain Douglas) were lying abreast of each other in Whampoa Reach, half laden with tea. A severe gale arose which heeled the two ships over and brought their port bilges out of water. The *Blackburn* lay to windward on the flood, and Captain Douglas, observing that the bilge of *Mirage* lacked several sheets of copper, attracted Captain Roberts' attention to the state of his ship's bottom with sundry comical wavings and pointings.

If he was amused, his brother skipper was far from being so, for it not only meant serious risk of worm but certain loss of speed.

However, Roberts had his laugh when the tide turned—for then the *Blackburn's* bilge shewed even more missing sheets than the *Mirage's* had done.

The Lintin Anchorage.

By 1824 the country ships had ceased to bring the opium as far as Whampoa; indeed, the notorious *Merope* had for the past three years acted as an opium godown without the confines of the port, lying under the shelter of Lintin during the winter months when the N.E. monsoon was blowing and in the Cap-sing-moon Anchorage off Macao Island during the heat of the summer.

The Hoppo protested vehemently against the iniquity of the country ships keeping outside the limits of his jurisdiction. In vain he sent a mandate to the Co-hong ordering the ships away from Lintin. The Hong merchants had no influence over the independent captains of the country craft.

On March 28, 1824, the *Valetta* and *Jane* arrived with opium from Calcutta and brought up off Lintin Island; they were followed by the *Eugenia* on May 1 and the brig *Jamesina* (ex H.M.S. *Curlew*, 18-gun sloop) in September. It was during this year that Huggins painted the opium ships lying off the island.

Behind the brig *Jamesina* will be noticed a fore-and-aft schooner. This was either the Company's yacht *Lavinia* or the Baltimore-built *Dhaulle*, belonging to Jardine & Matheson.

The Hoppo enquired of the pilots why they did not bring the ships on to Whampoa. The pilots replied of each ship in the same tenor—that the captain was villainous and wicked and refused to say why he anchored off Lintin or to produce his list of men, guns and goods, and that he swore that he "should consult his own convenience in his future movements."

Besides the five ships named, the *Samarang*, 505 tons (Captain Glover), was known to be an English opium ship, as were the country craft *Nearchus* and *Janet Hutton*; and the brigs *Venus* (English), *Cadet* (American) and *Quirogo* (Spanish) all had the drug on board.

On January 30, 1826, the Select Committee wrote to the Bengal Government per the brig *Venus*, as follows:

"The brig *Venus* will sail in a few days from Lintin, at which island many of the vessels engaged in the country trade now remain during their stay in China without coming further up the river.

"Every facility is there afforded to the opium traffic and smuggling transactions to a considerable extent in other articles are all carried on. A vessel frequently remains there until a cargo of opium is delivered and a lading of rice has been obtained, which according to the fiscal regulations lately established in this country give an exemption from port charges. . . . . The fees formerly paid to the officers of the Government, for their connivance, have been very materially diminished, the opium trade has nearly entirely forsaken Macao and a security has been given to it at Lintin, which it has never previously possessed."

The Committee also recorded the following minute:—"The consumption of opium in China continues progressively increasing and from the facilities which are afforded to the traffic by the ships which now remain throughout the year at Lintin, the interruptions to which it was formerly exposed have in great measure ceased to exist."

In the days before the clippers, that is to say, previous to 1830, the new season's opium only arrived during the S.W. monsoon, but the institution of floating "godowns," later called "receiving ships," at Lintin made it possible for the trade to be carried on at all seasons.

The Business of Dealing in Opium.

The actual buying and selling of the opium in Chinese waters was carried on by brokers. The Hong merchants had nothing to do with this illegal trade—at any rate openly—witness the following letter:—

The Hong Merchants to the Select Committee of the Honourable East India Company.

Gentlemen,—

We approach to state that opium is a commodity which the laws have heretofore prohibited most strictly, and we have before respectfully received commands to order all the respective ships that they must not bring it.

It has occurred not a second nor a third time only.

Last year Captain Hogg's ship (the *Eugenia*), Captain Robson's (*Hooghley*), Captain Parkyns' (*Merope*) and Captain Coupland's (American ship *Emily*) all brought opium into the port; and these, when it was discovered, were in obedience to the Imperial will, sent away and not allowed to trade; and it was decided that afterwards, if any opium were smuggled into the port, the implicated ship was to be treated in the same manner.

We will trouble the Chief and Committee (of the H.E.I.C.) to send a letter to the Company and to India and to the Marts, informing everyone that opium must not be smuggled into Canton, for if, reverently, orders be received to search and discovery ensue, the ship will be rejected and not allowed to trade; and if this year any ship, not knowing the prohibition, should bring opium, we beg you to inform her that she must not on any account enter the Port, but set sail immediately, for if she do enter and we find it out, we positively cannot become security, but must assuredly and immediately report it to the Great Offices of Government that the affair may be prosecuted according to law. This is an affair which concerns our persons, families and lives, and we are compelled to proceed in the straight road of management.

We hope you will excuse us and with Compts. we remain,

2nd Moon 12th day. GENTLEMEN
March 6th 1822. (Signed by the Hong Merchants.)

It must not be supposed that the Hong merchants were actively in opposition to the trade. They only took action when compelled to for their own safety; and the above letter was no doubt due to the "mandate prohibiting the opium trade," issued by the Imperial Government on November 17, 1821.

The opium lying afloat at Lintin was sold by the opium brokers at Canton for cash only; and orders to deliver the opium were sent down to the captains of the receiving ships by what the English called "smug boats," or the Chinese with their quaint nomenclature "scrambling dragons" or "fast crabs."

The captains of the receiving ships were paid five dollars per chest cumsha (literally "gold sand") and two dollars for demurrage, if the order was not presented within seven days. These payments had to be made when the opium was delivered to the agents in the smug boats.

The opium was taken from the chests of the receiving ship and packed in Chinese matting bags, and at the same time each mat was marked with the weight of its contents and the private sign of the new owner.

It took but a few hours unpacking, weighing and repacking, though as many as 100 chests, worth 150,000 to 200,000 dollars, were often delivered at a time. The Canton agent at first received as much as 5 per cent. commission on these sales, but it was later reduced to 3.

The receiving ships were well prepared to defend themselves and usually had boarding nettings triced up at night. Their crews at first were generally Lascars, Malays and Manila men, officered by Europeans, but with Chinese schroffs, carpenters, boats' crews, cooks and body servants.

Smug Boats, Fast Crabs or Scrambling Dragons.

The smug boats or scrambling dragons differed from the common chop boats in being small imitations of the imperial war dragons or mandarin boats. The latter, besides having more rowers, were painted black and red, whereas the hulls of the smug boats were always kept bright-varnished.

The smug boats had, as a rule, from sixty to seventy oarsmen, sitting like galley slaves on low benches, ranged along the deck on either side. There is no finer boatman in the world than the Canton Chinaman, who besides being most enduring and incredibly active was a very skilled waterman and uncannily intelligent. The smugglers' boats, however, did not entirely depend on their oars, but had large "mat and rattan" fore and main sails. Besides being of great length, the smug boats were beamy, and broadened out in the stern sheets so as to provide living quarters for the brokers' agents. They were, of course, well armed with a cannon of sorts in the bow, swivels along each rail, and a motley armament of spears, swords, creeses and flintlock muskets.

These weapons were ostensibly for use against pirates, who swarmed outside the Bocca, but there was many an occasion when a scrambling dragon came off best in a running fight with an imperial dragon.

Macao.

The Portuguese colony on the island of Macao has the distinction of being the oldest European settlement in the East. Just before Lintin became popular as an anchorage it was at the height of its prosperity, being an old world walled city with grim forts frowning from its heights, and solidly built churches and houses bounding its plazas and streets, including a convent and a senate house. Here came the jaded Europeans from Canton as soon as the tea season was over and the ships despatched to their destinations.

Crowned by the Monte Fort and circling round its bay, Macao has been called the Naples of the Orient. The broad esplanade of the Praya Grande with its well built row of houses, facing out across the outer harbour, had a fine view over the water towards the

"Nine Islands" in the North, and Lintin and Lantao to the North-eastward.

The inner harbour, too shallow to accommodate large ships, was bounded by the island of Lappa, once built over with Portuguese villas and beautifully laid out with gardens, but abandoned to decay through the difficulty of combating raiding pirates.

In spite of its beautiful situation and its fine climate—it rejoices in ever refreshing sea breezes—Macao, the "land of sweet sadness," has gradually lost its position as a world port. Two reasons may be assigned to its gradual decay—its shallow ever silting harbour and the rise of the free port of Hongkong only a few hours away to the Eastward.

Macao is now little more than a large fishing village as regards its trade, and junks with dark red or pearly grey blue hulls, yellow mat sails and barked nets, hung up to dry, occupy the anchorage where majestic East Indiamen, rakish opium clippers and yacht-like tea ships used to lie. Macao has become the Monte Carlo of the East, a gambling city of fan-tan houses, whose Government lives on the sale of lottery tickets.

The Praya Grande is now occupied by wealthy retired Chinese merchants; beneath the banyan trees that fringe the mile and a half of low sea wall one no more sees the "Omunkwae" and other foreign devils dozing in the shade, but a band plays in the Plaza, below the railed-in grotto and garden of Camoens, where black-eyed Portuguese signoritas flirt their fans at young garrison officers. Macao, even in its most busy and prosperous days, was a sleepy, easy-going port, which only woke up for a while on the arrival of the Factory of John Company at the end of the N.E. monsoon. Then indeed the influx of young English and Americans caused a flutter amongst the Dago dovecots; picnics were promoted; sailing matches took place; and daring cavaliers stormed the barred windows of the old Praya Grande mansions.

The Migration of the Factory.

The actual migration from Canton was conducted with some ceremony. It is so well described by W. C. Hunter in the *Fan Kwae at Canton* that I do not think I can do better than quote his words.

"The departure from Canton of the Factory was annually quite a circumstance. From 15 to 20 chop boats were drawn up at the Company's landing, of which some were converted into sleeping apartments, for which their high decks and capacious holds, which were floored off, afforded ample space. On either side were large windows, with curtains and movable shutters, for protection against rain. Others were appropriated to several milch cows and their keepers, for supplies for the journey, as well as books and papers of value.

"The members of the Factory, rarely fewer than 20 to 25, occupied the others with their personal servants; and what with compradore's men, cooks and coolies, the entire number was not less than 250 to 300 persons including the boat's crews.

"On the arrival of the linguist with the Government permit, the fleet set sail amidst the beating of gongs, burning of fire-crackers and small squares of red paper, as a propitiation to the gods presiding over rivers and streams. The boats always took the Macao Passage, as it was called, which is a broad stream branching off the Pearl River, about a half-mile westward of the Factories and running due South: consequently they passed the Factories, affording altogether a fine sight. The distance to Macao, taking the curves of the river, is about 120 miles and the journey averages three or four days."

Hunter, though an American, was invited to make the return trip to Canton in October, 1831, by the then Chief of the Company, Marjoribanks. Again I cannot resist quoting his letter, as it gives such an admirable sketch of the ways and customs of that date.

On board the *Golden Galley*, Macao to Canton.
October 4, 1831.

It was the intention of the Factory to embark on the 1st, but the departure was postponed to the 2nd.

A circular was then sent to the members, requesting them to be on board their respective boats, by half-past ten the next morning, at which time they were to get under way. Accordingly my chum (John Robert Morrison) and I joined our chop boat, anchored in the inner harbour with 13 others, which composed the fleet.

Presently a signal was made by the boat of Mr. Davis, Chief of the Select Committee, hoisting its mainsail, and in a few minutes we were sailing in line through the harbour. We numbered, including invited guests, 38 foreigners. Three of the boats (which in foreign measurement would be of, say, 120 tons) were full of Factory coolies, cows and provisions, the latter in addition to each one having a supply on board sufficient for three days. Our "chop" is large and comfortable; we have a cabin, by means of partitions, 14 feet by 10 and 7 feet high, and forward of it is another for our servants, the cook, and stores. Two couches, one on either side, serve for beds, added to which are tables, toilette arrangements and everything complete, with cleanliness the most perfect.

We breakfast and dine as regularly and in as good style as on shore. Some boats have four gentlemen and others five, as arranged among themselves.

They are chartered by the Factory twice a year, and each one receives one hundred Spanish dollars for the trip up and down. Provisions and furniture—in fact all things needful—are also supplied by the Company. We have not with us all the members, some remaining a while longer at Macao; but amongst those now on their way to Canton are Dr. Colledge and Padre Vachell, as well as that other important personage, the Steward Canning. The Company's compradore also accompanies the fleet, with three or four fast boats under his control for carrying messages, making visits, or distributing fresh milk. So you see everything is as cosy as possible.

The crews, numbering about 15 men to each boat, manage them with surprising dexterity. These Chinese boat people are perhaps unequalled by any others in the world. They are not only active and intelligent, but good-natured and obliging, and seem anxious to get on as quickly as possible.

Now that I have given you a sketch of our accommodation, I will go on with our passage from the inner harbour. While passing through it, volleys of fire-crackers were let off, and gongs were beaten by way of "chin-chining Joss" for a safe and pleasant passage. A little later dinner was served, and a No. 1 dinner it was. Crab soup to begin with, an ample dessert, Hodgson's pale ale, superb La Rose and sherry, with custard-apples, plantains and other fruits.

We turned in at 11, but slept little, as the wind was dead ahead after entering the "Broadway," so I was up early and on deck. The fleet was hard at it, tack and tack to windward. We found ourselves in the middle of it, those to windward about 3 miles off, and those to leeward about the same distance.

At 8 o'clock we passed the Mo-tow or "Knife-grinding" Fort, which was once a stronghold of the celebrated pirate Apotsae, who pillaged all the country round about. Near to it were lying two of His Celestial Majesty's men-of-war junks.

The day's supply of fresh milk was brought on board and at 8 breakfast, which was attended with difficulty, from the heeling over of the boat.

We entered the Heang-Shan ("Fragrant Hill") River, but at 11·30 were obliged to anchor within 5 miles of the city, as it had begun to blow a violent gale, the rain coming down in torrents.

On the morning of the 5th, cloudy and rainy, but the wind abating somewhat and the tide being favourable, we hove up and at 8·30 passed Heang-Shan.

We expected to anchor to receive the customary visit of the mandarin, but he may not have felt inclined to turn out in such weather. It happened that the compradore, who had gone up in a fast boat the evening before, procured from him his seal to the

Company's chop, which allowed us to go on without anchoring; but through all this fuss and his absence we lost the milk for our after-dinner tea!

On the morning of the 6th the compradore was again alongside, and made it "all right" with us by threatening to come again with mutton for dinner; and considering what we have "undergone" since leaving Macao it will be very acceptable.

The scenery on both sides of the river is celebrated for its beauty and we enjoyed it much. The banks are lined with orange and lemon trees, peaches and lyzee.

On the summit of a high hill stands a seven storey pagoda. If you ask a Chinaman its object or use, he replies that it is "Joss pigeon" and you are as wise as you were before. In reality, the Chinese believe that these buildings bring prosperity on the region and ward off evil influences.

The river is crowded with boats crossing from one bank to the other, filled with all sorts of country produce or passengers, who stare their very eyes out in looking at us. Further on we pass another fort with a curious name, the "Old Duck," and on the riverside opposite is another called "Greatly Excellent."

In the afternoon a fine strong breeze sprang up, and we made rapid progress, passing still another fortification called the "Mouth of the Great Gate." We were compelled to dine on a superb roasted capon with et ceteras as usual. We just touched at "Che-nae" for the official formality, and soon after the Western Fort was passed, when we saw the innumerable lights and lanterns of the provincial city; and at 8 p.m. glad enough we were to find ourselves once more in "Old Canton."

Modern Piracy in the Canton Delta.

Very different was this leisurely and luxurious chop boat voyaging to the present day method of travelling between Macao and Canton.

Nowadays Canton, Macao and Hongkong are connected by means of swift twin-screw river steamers, carrying armed guards and steel grills, as a protection against pirates. In many ways and many parts of the world life is less safe than it was a hundred years ago.

Only a few years ago the river steamer *Sui Au* on her way back to Hongkong with returning gamblers from Macao was captured by pirates.

The story is worth telling for comparison with the days of John Company. She left Macao with 60 cabin and 300 steerage passengers at 5 o'clock one Sunday evening. At about 5·45 the Indian guard in the steerage was suddenly held up without any warning by eight passengers flourishing revolvers. One of these shot him in the leg. Immediately there was a wild stampede—

somehow the gate through the grill was opened—probably by confederates, and passengers and pirates poured into the intermediate quarters. Several of the pirates rushed the companionways and succeeded in gaining the upper deck. Amongst these were three women, one of whom, travelling in the first class, played a leading hand with a levelled pistol in each fist.

The two Indian guards who attempted to stem the rush of pirates up the stairs on to the saloon deck were shot down and thrown overboard, the remaining four guards on that deck being captured and disarmed. When the affray began the captain had been sitting on the maindeck. He was on his feet in an instant and made for the bridge, but before he could take two steps he was shot down from behind and then bashed on the head with the butt of a gun.

The bridge, however, was not captured without a hard fight. Here two of the pirates were killed as well as one of the women pirates, whilst two more Indian guards, two European and one Chinese passenger were wounded.

In a very few minutes the pirates were in full control of the ship, the first class passengers were locked in their cabins, the ship turned off her course into the open sea, and throughout the night a systematic looting by the pirates took place.

At daybreak the pilongs calmly transferred themselves with plunder estimated at 50,000 dollars to a fleet of waiting junks.

The native passenger boats between Hongkong and Canton are accustomed to travel in convoy, but even then they have been plundered by the notorious pirate chief of the Shekki district, named Lam Choy.

Even the soldiers in the Government gunboats play the pirate in these chaotic days, when their pay has been long overdue.

Up the Coast.

Except for the Canton waters the coast of China was almost unknown to Europeans in the days of John Company. And the first vessels to venture into these uncharted seas were Indian country wallahs with opium on board.

One of the first of these daring country craft was the notorious

Merope, commanded by Captain Parkyns, which attempted to open trade up the coast in 1821, under the direction of James Matheson. In 1823 the enterprising Matheson went 400 miles along the coast as far as Chinchew in the country ship *Eugenia*, but failed to make a profit though he managed to open up a small trade. Then in 1824 he sent the *Merope* to the Eastward, and she did a considerable business with Taho, a few miles from Namoa; but was nearly wrecked on an unknown rock on March 4.

The mandarins, however, came down on the opium traders and burnt their houses, and this for a time stopped any more trading around Namoa.

Then in January, 1827, the American brig *Nile*, commanded by Robert Bennet Forbes, went up the coast with George Beale, Thomas Dent and a quantity of opium on board. This was probably the first trip made up the coast by an American vessel. Forbes went as far as Amoy but no merchants dared to come off to the stranger, and after waiting about for several days Captain Forbes, in accordance with the orders from his owner, Mr. Cushing, sailed back to Lintin, much against the wishes of Beale, who was confident that only patience was needed to start a trade.

Robert Bennet Forbes was a young captain, barely 23 years of age, the employee of his uncles, the brothers J. & T. H. Perkins. We shall hear a great deal more of him later on, for he was head partner of Russell & Co. for several years and directly responsible for practically all the American clippers in the opium trade.

On April 8 the Baltimore clipper schooner, *Dhaulle*, which either belonged to or was chartered by James Matheson, arrived at Macao, after having followed on the heels of the *Nile*, and she seemed to have been able to tempt the people of Amoy a bit more than the *Nile* had done, and made a slight profit on her trip.

It was not until 1831 that a receiving ship was actually stationed on the East Coast. She was the *Colonel Young*, and on her first arrival under Captain Innes she was reported to have disposed of 330,000 dollars worth of the drug.

She was owned by Jardine, Matheson & Co., and the first coaster in the trade was the little *Fairy* which ran up and down the coast between the *Colonel Young* and Lintin Island.

CHAPTER III.

THE FIRST OF THE CLIPPERS (1830-1831).

Where lies the land to which the ship would go?
Far, far ahead, is all her seamen know.
Where lies the land she travels from? Away
Far, far behind, is all that they can say.

Captain William Clifton.

CAPTAIN WILLIAM CLIFTON might well be called the father of the opium clippers, for it was entirely due to his enterprise, his far-sightedness and his professional knowledge of naval architecture that the beautiful little *Red Rover*, the first of the opium clippers and one of the longest lived and most successful, was launched into the Hooghly River by the Howrah Dock Company.

Like many another merchant sailor during the period of peace following the Napoleonic war, Captain Clifton was an ex-naval officer.

Born in 1795, he entered the Royal Navy in 1809 as a midshipman in the *Warrior*, 74 guns.

To the captain of the *Warrior*, Viscount Torrington, Clifton owed not only his sea education but his chance to make a success in the Mercantile Marine when peace spelt unemployment and half pay in the British Navy.

Lord Torrington was one of those naval officers who proved a friend through thick and thin to all who had once served under him; and when such a man has rank and power he is a patron, to use the old eighteenth century term, such as any seaman would thank his stars for. It made no difference to him whether his protege was a soured old first lieutenant, a boisterous master's mate, a skylarking midshipman or even a loplolly boy with a tarry jacket, his influence and his purse were at the disposal of every old shipmate.

Lord Torrington was promoted to flag rank in June, 1814, and Captain J. T. Rodd was appointed to the command of the *Warrior*. In January, 1815, the *Warrior* sailed for the West Indies, with Admiral J. Erskine Douglas, the new commander-in-chief at Jamaica, on board.

Now here is a curious fact—even as late as 1815 it was not usual for British men-of-war to be supplied with chronometers except when on convoying duty. Young Clifton's first four years of service had been spent in the East, and it was whilst the *Warrior* was on convoy duty with East Indiamen that he gained a good knowledge of her chronometer. Now Admiral Douglas was the possessor of a chronometer of his own. The *Warrior* was convoying a large fleet of West Indiamen, and in undertaking to look after the Admiral's chronometer as well as the ship's, Clifton gained the friendship of the Admiral, who transferred him to the *Shark*, his stationary flagship at Jamaica, as soon as they arrived out; and, very shortly afterwards, a vacancy occurring in the crack brig-sloop *Royalist*, of 18 guns, promoted him to a lieutenancy in that vessel. Clifton's new captain, Commander Houston Stewart, also proved a good friend until one of those sudden reverses in fortune occurred which seemed at first to be the shattering of his career but in the end turned out to be the reverse.

It happened that one day when at anchor at Port Royal, Clifton was in command of the deck, the other executive officers being ashore.

The doctor and a Mr. Grant asked for a boat to go ashore. The young lieutenant refused, with the explanation that it was just noon, the ship's company's dinner hour, added to which the heat was excessive. Two days later, without anything further having passed, an order came on board to discharge Clifton into the *Sabine*, a 16-gun brig, commanded by Alexander Campbell. But here again he fell on his feet, for Captain Campbell took to him as much as Viscount Torrington, Admiral Douglas and Commander Houston Stewart had done.

Campbell, too, was one of the smartest officers in the Navy—and his brig was in a high state of efficiency. Let me quote from Clifton's private memoir:—"When the *Sabine* came to anchor in Port Royal all eyes both on shore and on board used to admire the cloud of canvas which disappeared at our commander's quiet word of 'Shorten sail and let go the anchor.'"

The *Sabine* arrived in England to pay off late in 1816, and Clifton relates that the first words of the pilot as he stepped over the gangway were "It's peace with all the world!"

The young naval officer found that this was not altogether a blessing in his service. His first task on arrival home was to pass an unusally stiff lieutenant's examination. This was due to the astuteness of Wilson Croker, the very unpopular secretary of the Admiralty, who strove by setting these exceedingly difficult passing papers to keep down the number of commissioned officers and so to curtail the Navy estimates and lessen the congestion which succeeded the war. However there was no keeping down young Clifton and he passed that dreaded examination with flying colours. He immediately received an Admiralty order to proceed to the Jamaica Station.

"This," he wrote, "after what had occurred I had no great heart for: also I began to look the position of a lieutenant in the Navy at £120 a year for life in the face. I thought I might do something better.

"I had no family friends and hardly one in the world of any power but my old commander, Lord Torrington. I went down to his lordship's seat in Kent to talk the affair over. Of course he was angry and much against my leaving the Service; but he yielded when I pointed out to him that the Honourable East India Company's service was open to me. He then gave me letters to a very rich and powerful East India house, the firm of Alexander & Co. They appointed me third mate of their ship, the *Royal George*, but when I got on board, to my grief I found their uniform was more expensive than the Navy, and their mess expenses twice that of His Majesty's ships."

In this dilemma Clifton found himself obliged to write to Lord Torrington, thanking him most gratefully but stating that

JAMES MATHESON

National Maritime Museum, Greenwich

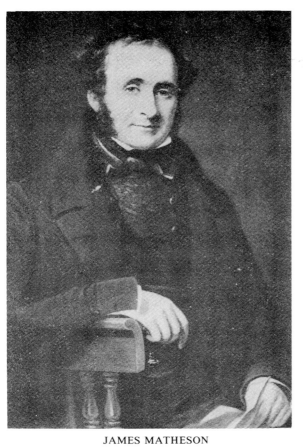

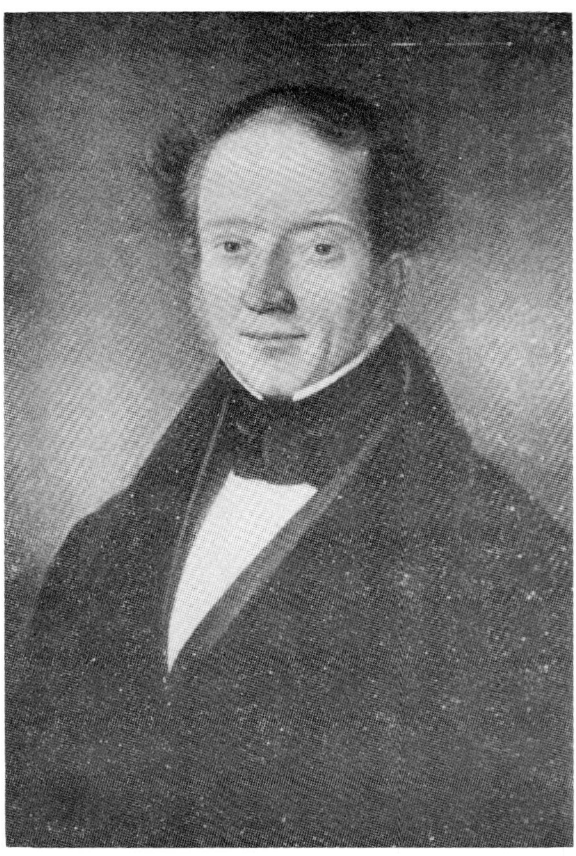

CAPTAIN CLIFTON

National Maritime Museum, Greenwich [*See page* 62

"RED ROVER" SAILING OUT OF PENANG ROADSTEAD

From a Painting lent by Miss A. M. Clifton [*See page* 72

under the circumstances he would have to return his appointment to Messrs. Alexander & Co.

And here we see what sort of a friend Lord Torrington was to all those who had served under him.

"Two days later," Clifton's memoir goes on, "a man came on board with a letter from his lordship enclosing a cheque for £200, and then he said: 'I am his lordship's tailor and have his orders to fit you out for the voyage.'"

The *Royal George* was one of the smaller Indiamen, a vessel of 486 tons, not to be confused with the *Royal George*, of 1333 tons, which was burnt at Whampoa on December 24, 1825.

Nine years later, in 1825, Clifton retired from the command of the *Royal George* with £15,000 to his credit with Alexander & Co. Those were the days when shipmasters could make a fortune in a few voyages.

Clifton's First Attempts to Conquer the N.E. Monsoon.

Captain Clifton gave up the lucrative command of the little Indiaman for a special purpose.

In a memoir of the old East India captain, which appeared in the *Western Daily Mercury* of September 24, 1875, appears the following: "He volunteered to find out the North West Passage to China, and lost three ships in the undertaking, one of them being only a pleasure yacht of 70 tons, belonging to Sir Thomas Turton."

This was not the only pleasure yacht to find herself in Eastern Seas. In the year 1824, Lord Yarborough sold his little brig, *Falcon*, of 175 tons, and celebrated his succession to the title and his election to the commodoreship of the Royal Yacht Squadron by building the second *Falcon*, the famous full-rigged ship of 351 tons, which 14 years later became an opium clipper under Jardine Matheson's flag.

In 1825 the first *Falcon* sailed for Calcutta. On July 25, 1825, Captain Clifton was granted a free mariner's covenant by the East India Company and it is possible that he acted as agent for the Company and brought the *Falcon* out. He recognised that the bluff-bowed tubby Indiamen and country craft though fast enough off the wind were not close-winded enough to conquer the N.E.

monsoon, which prevailed in the China Sea throughout the winter months.

The *Falcon*, though much faster to windward than the Indiamen and country craft, was also overpowered by the monsoon.

In May, 1826, Captain Clifton married Anna Vrignon, daughter of François Vrignon, the well-known Calcutta shipbuilder; it is fairly safe to conclude that his interest in ship designing was the direct cause of his friendship with the Vrignons.

It was probably in the following year that the little Baltimore built schooner *Dhaulle* distinguished herself by succeeding in reaching Macao in the teeth of the monsoon. I have been quite unable to find any reliable details of this first conquest of the N.E. monsoon. The *Dhaulle* was employed by the Magniacs and it hardly seems likely that Captain Clifton had anything to do with this performance. In the same year, 1827, Vrignon laid down the brig *Louisa* of just under 200 tons for his son-in-law.

The Unlucky "Louisa."

The *Louisa* was launched on April 1, 1828. The difficulty of getting her afloat was by no means a good omen for her future. The local reporter gave the following details: "She was christened at abour ¼ before 3 p.m., but hung fast several times, and was not finally launched until 5 minutes to 4; and it was then in a great measure owing to the assistance rendered by several professional gentlemen present that she was got off. Captain Clifton more particularly distinguished himself by his extraordinary exertions and was justly complimented at the tiffin which followed, as having saved the vessel. The launch was not accomplished until after 23 starts, which may give an idea of the laborious exertions required to effect it."

The Calcutta Tug-boat "Forbes."

On January 29, 1829, a specially-built tow-boat named the *Forbes* was launched from the New Howrah Dockyard, Kidderpore. Her owners, Mackintosh & Co., proposed to use her in a novel way—she was to tow a sailing ship out to China against the monsoon, the sailing ship providing the coal from her own hold. Such an expensive proposition could only have been entertained in the opium trade, nevertheless it was actually brought to pass.

The *Forbes* was built of teak with two 60 h.p. engines by Boulton & Watt and a copper boiler. Her engines had a stroke of 4 ft. and made from 22 to 24 revolutions per minute at full speed. Her light draft with coal for two or three days and in her best trim was 10 ft. With 11 days fuel and all stores on board she drew another foot. She registered 302 tons.

Her first attempt to tow a loaded opium trader was disastrous.

The "Louisa" lost on the Mizen Sand.

At 7 a.m. on Sunday, July 26, 1829, the *Forbes* left Calcutta with the *Louisa* in tow. The latter's cargo consisted of 260 chests of opium besides saltpetre, etc. By 7·30 p.m. Kedgeree was astern and the *Forbes* was well on her way to Saugor Roads: but at 8·15 the steamer struck heavily on the Mizen Sand, and before the hawsers could be either slipped or cut the *Louisa* ran up behind the *Forbes* and not only got foul of the latter but got hard and fast on the sand. The brig was holed by her own anchor, as the counter of the *Forbes* carried away her cathead and allowed the anchor to drop under foot. Then as the *Louisa* drove over it, it was supposed to have twisted off her forefoot. In ten minutes the water was up to the 'tween deck beams of the *Louisa,* but at low water there was scarcely 4 ft. under her.

The *Forbes* sent her boat off to the Indiamen lying at Saugor for help; and a little before 3 a.m. a boat from the Indiaman *Duke of York,* in charge of her fifth officer, Mr. Stewart, arrived to the rescue.

At this time the flood tide was just making, and the Hooghly was not only breaking all round but over the *Louisa.* To get alongside safely required real good watermanship, but after being nearly stove several times young Stewart succeeded in putting most of his boat's crew aboard the brig. They turned manfully to the pumps, but by daylight it was recognised that all their efforts were useless. The tide was fast covering the brig, she was rail under forward and threatened to capsize at any moment. In this case Captain Clifton decided to leave his vessel. His stern boat had been knocked to pieces by the *Forbes*, and his long-boat, which had been launched during the night, lay to a grapnel quite indifferent to the commands of her captain. There was also a native boat within hail but she also kept clear, thus all hands were compelled to get into the *Duke of York's* boat, which they could only do by dropping off the bowsprit and jibboom.

Just about this time, 8 a.m., the *Forbes*, which had been bumping heavily all night, managed to get off by means of her own steam, and a quarter of an hour later the brig's crew were put aboard her. From this moment until Wednesday evening the *Forbes*, which in spite of the weight of her machinery had not strained in the least, stood by to receive the valuable cargo of the *Louisa*, which the boats of the Indiamen at Saugor were busy salving.

Captain Clifton behaved splendidly, sacrificing all hopes of saving the brig, which wholly belonged to him and was uninsured, in order to make sure of the cargo. When asked to allow the decks to be scuttled and thus do away with his last chance of getting his vessel off, he instantly replied: "The cargo is infinitely more valuable; let the brig go."

The weather turned bad on the Wednesday, and Clifton nearly lost his life by lingering too long aboard, having to cross a tremendous surf to get clear.

At this time only 50 chests had been saved; though the officers of the Indiamen worked without thought of self or of danger night and day, the hands unfortunately got at the liquor and gave themselves up to plundering the brig; in this way her captain lost everything he had aboard.

By high water on the Wednesday morning the sea was breaking nearly as high as the brig's tops. It had blown hard and rained heavily all night, and there seemed little hope of saving any more opium; the evening before the brig's long-boat had been swamped with four chests in her, and when at low tide another attempt was made, the boats had to leave the wreck in a hurry. With the wind blowing a gale the tide made a clean breach over the unfortunate *Louisa*, and it was lucky that none of the Indiamen's boats was swamped. With the brig sunk deep in the sand and the weather behaving its worst, the *Forbes* weighed and ran down to Saugor.

During the night one of the *Louisa's* masts went and when the *Forbes* reached her at daylight she looked like breaking up. Whilst crossing over from Kedgeree to Mud Point, the tug-boat picked up a man floating on a piece of wood, who proved to be one of the crew of the swamped long-boat.

The *Forbes*, with the passengers and crew of the *Louisa* aboard, got back to Calcutta at 10 p.m. on the Thursday.

The "Jamesina."

It was the custom in the days of our wooden walls for the Admiralty to sell ships by auction, either at home or abroad; but they made this proviso, that these ships must be bought by a British subject, and nothing above a sloop in rating should be repaired or fitted out again.

It was in this way that H.M. brig *Curlew* of 18 guns (382 tons) became Matheson's barque, *Jamesina*, as far back as 1823.

The *Curlew* belonged to a class of 18-gun brig-sloop, which was considered without compare in Nelson's day, and did more work, year in and year out, than any other rate in the British Navy. Extremely fast, with good fighting powers and being at the same time magnificent sea boats, these brigs must not be confused with the little 10-gun brigs—they were the eyes of a fleet, the destroyers of their day.

They were designed by that excellent shipwright, Sir William Rule; the *Cruiser*, the pioneer ship of the class, being built at Ipswich and launched in April, 1797.

At the end of the Napoleonic wars there were over 80 of these crack brig-sloops in commission, and when in their old age they were put up for sale they were eagerly snapped up.

At first her old rig was kept on the *Jamesina* but towards the end of the 'twenties she was refitted as a barque.

The Barque Rig.

Curiously enough, in the original design of the *Cruiser* allowance was made for this change from a two-piecey bamboo to a three-piecey bamboo.

In the late 'twenties and 'thirties the barque rig was a great favourite with seamen. At that time the fastest ship in the British Navy was the *Columbine,* first of the Symondites, which was commissioned as an 18-gun barque in December, 1826.

> Of all the ships that e'er were built
> To sail the ocean's brine, sir,
> Throughout the fleet not one can beat
> Our saucy *Columbine,* sir.

In the French Navy also, as far back as 1801, a wonderful corvette, barque rigged, was built on lines from the board of Mons. Ozanne. Forty years later she was still considered to have been the fastest vessel in the French service and they had tried to build after her in vain.

In 1829, the *Jamesina* was one of 10 ships consigned to Magniac & Co., but she was the only one engaged solely in the opium trade, and her commander applied for exemption from giving the usual bond for vessels bound to China, because he did not intend to enter the port of Canton "nor can the Hon'ble Company's Supra Cargoes take any cognizance of me or my ship, being expressly prohibited by the orders of the Honourable Court of Directors from acknowledging in anyway the existence of the opium trade."

In the year 1829, 7006 chests of Bengal opium were received on board the receiving ships at Lintin, 137 chests landed at Macao; 6542 chests of Malwa were put aboard the receiving ships, 233 chests were lost in the wreck of the *Louisa* and 315 chests were landed at Macao. Besides this 700 chests of Turkey opium were brought to Lintin in American bottoms. This year the Company's Indiamen were ordered to avoid all communication with the opium squadron which either anchored at the Nor'-west end of Lintin or in Macao Roads; so the Indiamen were allotted an anchorage to the East of Lintin between the Island of Toon Koo and Castle Peak, or else in the Cap-sing-moon Passage.

The result of allowing the opium ships to monopolise the best anchorages was that the first class Indiaman *Bridgewater* got ashore in a typhoon on August 8. She had only arrived from Calcutta that very day; at nightfall with the wind increasing in squalls from the N.E. to East, she housed her topmasts and upper yards, but with both bowers and sheet anchor out began to drag.

Finally her masts were cut away, but still she dragged until brought up by the tail end of Lintin. She was got off, but had to be taken up to Whampoa for repairs.

The "Red Rover," First of the Clippers.

Undeterred by the financial loss incurred by the wreck of the *Louisa*, Captain Clifton at once set about building another clipper; and he boldly wrote to the Governor-General of India, Lord William Bentinck, offering to carry the Company's opium to China three times a year instead of once, thus procuring three markets instead of one. Lord William Bentinck saw the force of his arguments and agreed to advance the necessary funds for the first year of the experiment.

The result of this enterprise was the little barque *Red Rover* of 255 tons, which may truly be called the first of the opium clippers.

The *Red Rover* was built by the Howrah Dock Company, being laid down in early September, 1829, and launched on December 12. This launch with the backing of the Governor-General was a much more important affair than that of the poor little *Louisa*.

Let me quote the delightful reporter of that day:

A launch is at all times a very gay and highly interesting scene, and that of the *Red Rover* from the yard of the Howrah Dock Company on Saturday afternoon was particularly so. Numerous boats filled with gay company, amidst which were conspicuous many of the fashionables of Calcutta, arrived at an early hour and at a quarter past three Lady William Bentinck, Lord Combermere and suite landed under the usual salute. Her ladyship having christened the vessel, the dog shores were struck away, and at half-past three the *Red Rover* glided majestically into her new element amid deafening shouts of applause and a salute of thirteen guns from the beach, which was answered from on board.

This beautiful little vessel drew but 9 ft. 6 ins. aft and 7 ft. forward, and we are informed by competent judges that she is, of her kind, perfect in every respect.

At four o'clock Lady William Bentinck, Lord Combermere and a numerous assemblage of ladies and gentlemen sat down to an elegant collation laid out in the most tasteful manner. During refreshment the band of His Majesty's 16th Regiment performed some favourite pieces.

The *Red Rover* was flush-decked with little or no sheer: she had a square stern with a long counter but no quarter-galleries, and her figure-head consisted of a fierce effigy of Cooper's famous character, after whom the barque was named.

Her first owners were Captain Clifton and his own old employers, Alexander & Co.; then, in 1833, Alexander & Co. dropped out and Brightman & Co. (John Brightman and Jonathan D. Gow) took $21\frac{1}{3}$ shares, whilst Francis Mender, merchant, bought the remaining $10\frac{2}{3}$ shares.

In 1846 she was bought by Jardine, Matheson & Co., who clapped some gingerbread on to her in the shape of false quarter-galleries.

She remained in their service until she was lost in the early 'seventies.

The "Prince de Neufchatel."

It may appear surprising that Captain Clifton should have been so confident in the powers of his little vessel to beat all previous records in battling against the monsoon in the China Seas, but somehow or other he had obtained the lines of a very famous American privateer, which lines had been taken off the little vessel when she was dry docked at Deptford on her arrival in England after being captured on the Banks of Newfoundland by three of the finest frigates in the Royal Navy, the *Newcastle*, *Leander* and *Acasta*.

This was the notorious *Prince de Neufchatel*, a brigantine of 310 tons, 17 guns and 150 men.

Her model was exactly reproduced in the opium clipper, though Clifton, influenced no doubt by the prevailing fashion, preferred to rig the *Red Rover* as a barque instead of a two sticker.

The history of the *Prince de Neufchatel* deserves to be recorded in detail, for besides being one of the most successful of the numerous American privateers in the war of 1812, she gave her shape to a whole fleet of opium clippers which were copies of the *Red Rover*.

Seventeen different British men-of-war chased the *Prince de Neufchatel* at various times, but she always managed to escape through her extraordinary speed until overpowered by Sir George Collier's squadron; and even then it is said that she would have escaped had she not buried herself by carrying too much canvas.

It was blowing hard with a rough sea and yet the *Prince de Neufchatel* kept her distance for hours, running with the wind free.

The leading ship of the chase, the *Newcastle*, was logging 13 knots most of the time.

I cannot trace the early history of the *Prince de Neufchatel*, but she is supposed to have been built in New York. She was armed and fitted as a privateer at Cherbourg in 1814, and even then before she had been blooded she must have been recognised as an exceptional vessel, for the renowned Captain J. Ordronaux, of the French privateer, *Marengo*, a well-known scourge of British merchantmen, was persuaded to take the command. Sailing from Cherbourg in March, Ordronaux on one short cruise picked up nine valuable prizes in the English Channel. In June the *Prince de Neufchatel* came out again and in less than a week—between the 4th and 10th—she sent six prizes into Havre.

In August her only victim seems to have been a stubborn brig which she sank with a single broadside in the Irish Sea.

In September she chased, captured and destroyed the brigs *Steady*, *James*, *Triton*, *Apollo*, *Subron*, *Albion*, *Charlotte* and *Mary Ann*, the sloops *George* and *Jane* and the cutter *General Doyle*. She also captured and made cartels of the *Nymph* and the *Barewick Packet*, which was bound from Cork to Bristol with 50 passengers. In addition to all these she sank the transport *Aaron* of 4 guns, bound from Gibraltar to Lisbon and captured the ship *Harmony* of 4 guns. The *Harmony* was the only one of all these vessels thought to be worth preserving. A prize crew was put aboard her but a few days later she was recaptured.

Only one vessel escaped her on this cruise. She had to hurriedly abandon an English privateer, of which she was about to take possession owing to the appearance of a man-of-war over the horizon.

Having swept the seas from Dover Straits to Gibraltar, Captain Ordronaux set his course for Boston where the *Prince de Neufchatel* was given a thorough overhaul and refit.

The Fight with the "Endymion's" Boats.

The *Prince de Neufchatel* put to sea again at the beginning of October. The 11th found her becalmed about half a mile South of Nantucket Shoals, whilst a British frigate off Gay Head was rapidly approaching under a fresh breeze.

Captain Ordronaux had a lately captured merchantman, the *Douglas*, in tow; and as the frigate was still 12 miles away at 3 p.m. when the privateer took the breeze, he hung grimly on to his prize.

At 7 o'clock it fell calm again, and as the current was sweeping her inshore, the *Prince de Neufchatel* was obliged to cast off her prize, the two ships anchoring about a quarter of a mile apart, the prize being nearest to the frigate.

It was quite dark by 8·30 when the *Douglas* signalled that several boats were approaching from the direction of the frigate. As soon as these could be distinguished the *Prince de Neufchatel* opened rapid fire with both her great guns and small arms.

But the boats, which had kept well together, dashed up on all sides. There were five of them—the first two pulled under each bow, the second two hooked on to the main channels and the fifth boarded over the taffrail.

The fight that ensued was as fierce and stubbornly contested as any in the whole war. In the darkness every kind of weapon was brought in to play—pistols, knives and belaying pins against boarding pikes, cutlasses and dirks—Captain Ordronaux himself fired 80 rounds from his sash full of pistols.

Then as the English gained a footing and the fighting grew more desperate, bare fists, teeth and finger-nails came into play. The "Endymions" must have been surprised at their reception, but they did not know that Captain Ordronaux had vowed to blow up his ship rather than strike his colours. And at one moment of the fight he was near putting his vow into execution. His men were showing signs of retreating before the impetuous charge of the enemy when he seized a lighted match from a tub, dashed to the open companionway and threatened to drop it into the magazine below him if any man gave way. In this way he rallied his crew and fought the "Endymions" to a standstill. Though only of 20 minutes' duration the fight was one of the most sanguinary of cutting-out affairs.

Of the 5 boats 1 sank alongside, only 2 men out of 43 being rescued, 3 drifted away empty whilst their men were contesting the deck and 1 was captured, 8 of its 36 hands being killed and 20 wounded. The total of the attackers was given as 120; the

Endymion's first lieutenant, Hawkins, and a master's mate were killed, and her second lieutenant, 2 master's mates and 2 midshipmen wounded.

The *Prince de Neufchatel* seems to have left Boston with a very small crew numbering 37 all told. Out of the whole, 7 (including Charles Hilburn, a Nantucket pilot) were killed and 24 wounded.

Captain Ordronaux found himself severely inconvenienced by 30 prisoners, and with only 8 unwounded men aboard the privateer he was obliged to keep his prisoners towing astern in their boat, the oars, etc., having been removed. The wounded British officers he kept on board.

When the breeze came away the privateer managed to give the frigate the slip, and after landing her prisoners and wounded at Nantucket arrived back at Boston on October 15.

It is interesting to note also that the discomforted *Endymion* on October 31 fell in with the 56-gun ship *Saturn*. The latter was bound for Halifax and the *Endymion's* surgeon and 28 wounded men were sent on board her, a reinforcement of 1 lieutenant, 4 midshipmen and 33 seamen and marines being received in exchange.

The Capture of the "Prince de Neufchatel."

This was Captain Ordronaux's last cruise. The successful privateersman retired and became part owner. He appointed his first officer to the command after making him swear never to surrender the little brigantine to the foe.

We have a most interesting account of the *Prince de Neufchatel's* last cruise and fight by a member of her crew.

His descriptions of his officers are worth transcribing. His captain, it is surprising to learn, was "a Jew by persuasion, a Frenchman by birth, an American by convenience, and so diminutive in stature as to make it appear ridiculous, in the eyes of others, ever for him to enforce authority among a hardy, weather-beaten crew." The first officer was "a man who never uttered an angry or harsh word, made no use of profane language, but was terrible even in his mildness when faults occurred through carelessness or neglect. He knew what each man's duty was and his capacity for fulfilling it, never putting more to the men's tasks than they were able to get through with: but every jot and tittle must be performed and that to the very letter, without flinching, or the task would be doubled.

"While manoeuvring the men, he would go through with the various duties without oaths, bluster or even loud words, and do more in less time than all the other officers on board with their harsh threatenings, profane swearings and loud bawlings through their speaking trumpets. The men honoured and obeyed him and would have fought with any odds at his bidding."

The second officer was passed over as "a mere nobody" without further comment.

The third officer had been a warrant officer in the *Constitution*, who had been discharged for "unofficerlike conduct." He also was a very indifferent seaman.

The *Prince de Neufchatel* slipped out of Boston through the blockading force on the night of December 21. When five days out she encountered a heavy gale; and the morning of December 28 found her tossing in a wild sea, with her decks awash and her upper spars with the exception of the fore and foretopsailyards housed. When the first officer came on deck at 8 a.m. he was disgusted to find no man on the lookout and the deck a raffle of tangled ropes' ends and snarled up gear. It had been the third officer's watch from 4 to 8. The first lieutenant at once ordered the sharpest eyes in the ship aloft and the man had not been at his post ten minutes before he reported three heavy frigates coming up fast. These were Sir George Collier's squadron in search of the *Constitution.* The *Prince de Neufchatel* was squared away, but in the hard wind was gradually overpowered. That she took some catching is shown by the fact that the chase continued all day, and that the privateer had scarcely rounded to in token of surrender than one of the frigates lost her jibboom, and fore and main topgallantmasts and carried away her mizen topsail yard in the slings, whilst another sprang her foretopsail yard, and carried away her main topgallant and mizzen topsail yards.

The sea and wind were so heavy that only one small boat from the *Leander* succeeded in getting safely alongside. If it had not been that the privateer was a wreck aloft, her officers would have made an attempt at recapture during the night, for they had a desperate crew of Americans, French and Portuguese who would have fought to the death.

One man indeed, who had been a prisoner ten times and is described as "a Frenchman by birth, a Calmuc in appearance, a savage in disposition, a cut-throat at heart and a devil incarnate," seized a brand from the caboose and was making for the magazine, when he was caught by the "ever watchful" first lieutenant, who threw the brand overboard and hurled the dastardly Jose "twice his own length" along the deck.

Sir George Collier was so impressed by the little brigantine's appearance that, instead of sending her to be sold at Halifax or Bermuda, he sent her home with dispatches announcing that the American squadron was out and therefore the homeward convoys in danger.

On her arrival in England, the *Prince de Neufchatel* was so much admired that orders were given to take off her lines and preserve her model.

Soon after this had been done, the Deptford Dockyard officials allowed her to get across the dock sill so that her back was broken, and she was thereupon sold for a song.

"Red Rover's" Maiden Voyage.

Captain Clifton, confident that his new vessel would make up for many disappointments, set sail from Calcutta on December 28, 1829, with 800 chests of opium on board. He took his departure from the Sandheads on January 4 in company with the beautiful little *Falcon*, which with her wonderful powers of ghosting along in favourable winds actually arrived at Singapore on January 20 a few hours ahead of the clipper.

The *Falcon* continued her voyage on the 23rd, but the *Red Rover* remained at Singapore until the 26th. Her new rigging and sails had stretched and had to be set up and rebent, besides which there were many other small faults of the riggers to set right, and Captain Clifton wished to be certain that everything was "a-taunto" before he thrust out into the teeth of the monsoon.

The distance between Singapore and Macao is about 1400

miles, but to this must be added from 600 to 800 miles of adverse current. Captain Clifton worked the *Red Rover* tack and tack up the middle of the China Sea, and averaging about 100 miles a day dead to windward, anchored in Macao Roads on February 17, 22 days out from Singapore Strait, a performance which had never been approached before; indeed, the only other vessel that had made the passage against the monsoon, the little *Dhaulle*, had taken a great deal longer.

The *Red Rover* was only 10 days in Canton waters, sailing on February 27, in thick weather with the monsoon growing light and variable. At this date the *Falcon* had not yet arrived. *Red Rover* reached the Sandheads on April 1, having made the round voyage, pilot to pilot, in 86 days. Before she sailed there had been many conflicting opinions about her, and a great many bets were made on the result of her voyage.

Though built expressly for speed, the little clipper had proved herself an easy, well-behaved sea boat, and so well built as to bear comparison with the best productions of the Thames or the Wear.

Besides being the first of the opium clippers, *Red Rover* was one of the least in trouble and the longest lived. When Captain Clifton completed his three voyages in the 12 months, Lord William Bentinck called the Calcutta Chamber of Commerce together, and in a eulogistic speech stating the great boon which Captain Clifton had conferred upon the trade of India and China, said that he was authorised to present the enterprising captain with a lac of rupees (£10,000.)

Nor were the merchants behind-hand, two silver vases, inscribed with the *Red Rover's* performances, were their contribution.

The "Forbes" tows the "Jamesina" from Calcutta to Canton.

That very few shipping people in Calcutta believed that the little *Red Rover* could conquer the monsoon is proved by the extraordinary towing project, which after having been mooted for several years, actually was carried out in 1830.

At daylight on March 14, 1830, the *Forbes* proceeded from Diamond Harbour with the *Jamesina* in tow. The former was drawing between 11 and 12 ft. with 130 tons of coal on board, two-thirds of it being British and one-third Burdwan. This, it was reckoned, would last 12 days. Aboard the *Jamesina* besides 840 chests of opium, there was another 52 tons of coal. It was a much more favourable period of the year than that of *Red Rover's* experiment, the winds being light and variable all the way to Singapore.

The upper buoy of the Gaspar was passed at 5 p.m. and by night the ships were at sea, the *Forbes* chunking along making 17 to 24 revolutions of her paddle-wheels per minute and steaming at an average of from 5 to 5½ knots, but reaching as much as 7 when the wind was favourable.

Without stopping at Penang, the *Forbes* and her tow reached Singapore on March 27. Here a fresh supply of coal was taken aboard and away they went again on the 31st. On the first day out from Singapore the wind was light and variable with fine weather, and the *Forbes* made 17 revolutions and logged 4 to 5½ knots. In the China Sea the monsoon was still blowing, light at first but gradually increasing to a moderate breeze. At first the *Forbes* was able to make 5 knots, but as the wind freshened their speed dropped from 5 to 4, from 4 to 3½, and from 3½ to 2½. Frequent stoppages had to be made to clean the copper boiler and three times a necessary trans-shipment of coal from the *Jamesina* to the steamer caused a delay of from three to four hours each time.

On April 12 the two ships were in Lat. 14° 5′ N., Long. 113° 57′ E., but the wind was still blowing steadily in their teeth and the *Forbes* had only four days more coal; thus she was compelled to cast off and proceed alone. Without the *Jamesina* she was able to make from 4 to 5½ knots against the last kick of the monsoon, but she trusted to her sails for the last half of the distance and made the Lintin Anchorage on April 19, the *Jamesina* arriving on the 21st. This was a passage of 38 days, which was promptly equalled by the *Red Rover* in the spring of 1831. Needless to say the *Forbes* and *Jamesina* experiment was never repeated.

The *Forbes* was the first steamer ever seen in Chinese waters. When she took her Chinese pilot aboard, she was under steam with wind and tide against her. The pilot showed no signs whatever of astonishment, but quietly gave the helmsman steering orders as if the *Forbes* was running before a fair wind.

At last the captain could stand this bland indifference no longer, and he asked the pilot if he had ever seen a steamer before; the latter calmly replied that such a mode of propulsion had once been fashionable in certain ports of the Celestial Empire but had fallen into disuse. He believed that all was safe as long as black smoke came from the funnel, but directly white steam began to show he grew very uneasy.

The Chinese nomenclature in pigeon English for the different rigs of ships were:

A full-rigged ship = three piecey bamboo.
A barque = two and a half piecey bamboo.
A brig or schooner = two piecey bamboo.

That for steamers was as follows:

A paddle wheeler = outside walkee.
A screw steamer = inside walkee.

The *Forbes* was the first "outside walkee," but she did not rouse nearly as much interest or terror as the iron *Nemesis*, which played such havoc with the forts and junks in the opium war that she was known as the "Scourge," the "Mystery," the "Pirate," and even the "Devil."

Captain Robert Bennet Forbes.

If Captain William Clifton was the father of the British opium clipper, it was Captain Robert Bennet Forbes who introduced the famous American pilot-boat model into the trade and was responsible for practically every American-built clipper in Chinese waters. He was one of those live wires who, in an age of heroic pioneering, was the life and soul of every undertaking in which he found himself.

His chief interest was not money-making or even helping on the march of what our ancestors were pleased to call civilization, but in the improvement of ship design. He was a sailor from truck to keel, and even when he was the head of Russell & Co. his heart was on the sea.

Born on September 18, 1804, of Scottish descent on both sides,

CAPTAIN ROBERT BENNET FORBES
Lent by Mr. Allan Forbes

CAPTAIN PHILIP DUMARESQ
National Maritime Museum, Greenwich [*See page* 80

CAPTAIN AUGUSTINE HEARD
Lent by Mr. Allan Forbes

RUSSELL STURGIS
National Maritime Museum, Greenwich [*See page* 90

Forbes was twice a captive of war on the high seas before he was seven years old. The winter of 1811 found him crossing the Atlantic with his mother and brother aboard the tiny topsail schooner, *Midas*, laden with salt fish from Boston for Marseilles, where his father, an American merchant, was experiencing a very difficult time owing to the ubiquitous British cruiser.

We can hardly conceive, in these soft days, the hardships which our travelling ancestors had to undergo. Luckily Mrs. Forbes had a stalwart heart as well as a graphic pen. Here is an extract from one of her letters:

Across the Atlantic in 1811.

Schooner *Midas* at sea, March 10, 1811. I am excluded from almost every object that is pleasant; my drawing room, which contains my sleeping place and that of the children, is about 6 ft. square; a small glass in the deck admits the light which rests dimly on the paper I am scribbling, and everything about me partakes of the same sombre hue. I am as yet undismayed by the prospect before me, and I often call to mind the consoling reflection that God is able to shelter me as well on the wide waste of waters as in the full city.

A few days later she continues her letter—

We had a fine run off the coast, with every prospect of good weather and a short passage; but our flattering hopes were soon blasted, for, shortly after clearing the Capes, it fell calm, and almost all the ropes were covered with ice; the prospect was dismal indeed and the wind began to blow directly against us. We continued much in this situation for several days, when a most violent tempest arose, which lasted almost without intermission for four days. We lay to in the gulf nearly forty-eight hours, the wind a complete hurricane, so that we could scarcely lie in our berths.

We lost our quarter boards, part of the rails, caboose, two casks of water, jib-boom, one anchor; split our sails, stove the boats, broke the tiller; our skylight was torn off and the glass much broken; torrents of water washed over us and came into the cabin; all our fowls and two of our pigs were drowned, which I did not much lament as it put an end to their sufferings.

The morning the skylight was washed away Bennet was quite ill, but had crawled into the cabin to get some air and, if possible, something to eat. We had not been able to cook anything for several days until that morning; the kettle had been boiled and breakfast prepared—he was sitting under the skylight and got completely drenched.

Young Forbes, clinging to a pot of hot chocolate, went to the floor, in an ice-cold flood. At that very moment the mate burst in to snatch up an axe, with the comforting remark: "If we ship such another sea, we shall go to Davy Jones in five minutes."

However the gallant little schooner survived only to be captured by the British frigates *Apollo* and *Resistance*, when almost within sight of her destination.

But in those days they did not make war on non-combatants. Mrs. Forbes was treated with every courtesy by Admiral Cotton and his officers, the two boys were made pets of aboard H.M.S. *Blossom* (Captain W. Stewart), who took some trouble and risk in landing the family on Plania Rock, 6 miles outside Marseilles.

On May 13, 1813, this indomitable family, this time the father included, embarked on the letter of marque *Orders in Council*, a Baltimore schooner, armed with six 9-pounders and a crew of about 20 all told, which sailed from Bordeaux in company with two other American schooners, the *Whig* and *Thistle*, all loaded with silks and wine.

An Old-Time Sea Fight.

Hardly were the three schooners to sea before a British man-of-war cutter hove in sight and gave chase. She was soon joined by another cutter and a schooner. The three Americans scattered on different courses, but the chasers, headed by the cutter *Wellington*, held on after the queerly named *Orders in Council*. The chase continued for days, first one gaining and then the other. Every known method of increasing the schooner's speed was tried, the sails were watered, casks of liquid were hung from the mainstay, stanchions and beams were sawn through, but all in vain. At last it fell calm, the American ran out her sweeps, but the pursuers lowered all their boats in order to tow the *Wellington* into action, which, both towing and sweeping, opened the action with her bow guns on the American's port quarter, just on the bearing which the smallness of the schooner's ports prevented her guns from laying upon, without yawing.

The fight, which began by a shot which whizzed over young Forbes' head, continued for an hour and forty minutes. The Americans, stripped to the waist and wildly excited by the privateersman's tipple, rum and gunpowder, fought like tigers, whilst gusts of deep cheering came across the water from the cutter at every broadside. Then a breeze sprang up and the *Wellington*, with several shot holes between wind and water, dropped astern until she could alter her trim and plug them.

Meanwhile with all hands fishing spars and mending rigging, the schooner drew away, only to run straight into the path of the frigate *Surveillante*, commanded by Sir George Collier, which put a prize crew aboard. Night found the "long-legged clipper schooner with wounded masts and rigging" labouring badly in a Biscay gale. The guns got adrift, the fore topmast went by the board, the main-boom was sprung and the ship's goat fell down the companion-way on top of little Forbes and broke its leg. The only hope was to run before it for Corunna.

From here a second attempt to reach Boston was made in an old brig called the *Caroline*, which was promptly captured on the eighth day out by the *Pomone* (Captain Philip Cartaret) in spite of being protected by a licence from the Admiral. The Forbes' next ship was a fishing boat which landed them in Lisbon.

Finally they embarked in the *Leda* of Baltimore, which after a thirty-six days' passage landed them at Newport.

Forbes goes to Sea in the "Canton Packet."

After such adventures it was not likely that Forbes would rest content with the life in a merchant's counting house. Thus, on October 19, 1817, we find him going to sea in a little barque belonging to his uncles, J. & T. H. Perkins, named the *Canton Packet*.

Before leaving he received much good advice, the most curious being from an old salt named William Sturgis. He said: "Always go straightforward, and if you meet the devil cut him in two and go between the pieces: if anyone imposes on you, tell him to whistle against a nor-wester and to bottle up moonshine."

The *Canton Packet* arrived at Whampoa on March 13, 1818, and was back in New York by November 25.

On his second voyage, when not yet sixteen, he was taken into Mr. Cushing's office whilst the ship lay idle awaiting her cargo.

Cushing wrote to Thomas H. Perkins on November 7, 1819:

"I have omitted in my letter per *Nautilus* mentioning our young friend, Bennet Forbes, recommending his being promoted to be an officer on the return of the *Canton Packet*. He is, without exception, the finest lad I have ever known, and already has the stability of a man of thirty."

To Forbes' mother Cushing wrote: "Bennet has been with me since July. He has become so useful that I really regret to let him go away; but as he has set out to make a sailor it is best to let him persevere; and I will answer for his being at the head of his profession within a few years. He is one of the finest lads I have ever met with, and knows already more than two-thirds of the shipmasters out of the country."

In appearance Forbes was tall and thin, with a dark complexion, and answered to the name of "Black Ben." Being strong and active it was seldom that he allowed anyone to be before him at the weather earing.

On the very next voyage the boy became third mate, and in October, 1824, sailed as master of the *Levant*, 264 tons, considered the favourite and lucky ship of his uncles, but when he arrived out in China Cushing turned the *Levant* into a store ship, and transferred Forbes, his officers and crew, to the brig *Nile*, of 250 tons.

His first passage in the *Nile* was to Manila, and on the way back to Lintin he had his first adventure with pirates.

Adventure with Pirate Junks.

As the brig in the lightest of airs was headed for the Asses'-Ears Channel one morning in May, Forbes noticed that a number of apparent fishing junks seemed all to be making towards the brig. Like all China traders the *Nile* was well armed with four broadside guns and a big arms chest. Presently the nearest junk, being almost within musket shot, sent two men in a sampan with some fish with the evident intention of spying upon the brig. Forbes made no objection to their coming aboard, but when the men stepped over the side there were twenty armed men lying under the bulwarks, matches burning and guns cast loose.

"Hi-yah! Hi-yah! No makey lallylung (thief) pigeon—all ploper pigeon!" cried the first, completely taken aback, and without further pretence he went over the side, calling a warning that made everyone of the junks draw off.

When he arrived at Lintin Forbes was told that these very junks had lately captured many small vessels and murdered their crews.

"Black Ben's" next trip was to California, and it was on his return to China in December, 1826, that he took George Beale and Thomas Dent up the coast in search of a new opium market. In March, 1827, he loaded a cargo worth 100,000 dollars for Buenos Ayres, in spite of the fact that there was a war on between the Argentine and Brazil. However, though captured by the blockading force and actually placed "in limbo" with other unfortunate shipmasters, Forbes' agents by using lots of palm oil not only got him but his ship cleared of most of her cargo.

Forbes takes out a Cargo of Turkey Opium.

On arriving home after a long adventurous voyage, Forbes found a larger and better ship being fitted out for him. This was the brig *Danube*, which he took over on March 12, 1828, sailing for Smyrna with a small cargo of coffee, 20,000 dollars in specie and a credit note on Barings for about £60,000.

In those days the Archipelago was infested with Greek pirates, and it was the custom for traders to be convoyed on from Malta. There being no American man-of-war at Malta when the *Danube* arrived, Forbes put himself under a Dutch brig-of-war which with a galliot was about to sail for Smyrna. Beyond amusing himself by sailing round and round the Dutchman Forbes had no excitement that trip.

Forbes had instructions to buy all the Turkey opium he could without unsteadying the market. His agent was Mr. Joseph Langdon, the principal American merchant in Turkey. The pair of them decided that after buying as much opium as possible with the proceeds of the coffee and the dollars, Forbes should sail for Gibraltar and "await operations on a larger scale."

The *Danube* this time did have a U.S. war vessel to convoy her past the pirates. This was the schooner *Porpoise* of $177\frac{68}{95}$ tons carpenter's measurement, commanded by an old timer named

Bell, with L. M. Goldsborough (afterwards the well-known Admiral) as her first officer.

Forbes made every preparation to keep up with the slippery schooner. On the day they were to sail he turned his hands out early, hove short, mastheaded his yards, cast off the gaskets, making up his sails with yarn stops, and got all his stunsail gear ready.

At sunrise, a gun went aboard the *Porpoise*, the signal for sailing, and within 20 minutes the *Danube* was leaving the port of Vourla with all sail set to stunsails.

The *Porpoise* when the gun was fired still had her awnings bent and a boat in the water. In vain she hurried after the brig, with the wind free the latter had the heels of her. In those days no man-of-war could abide being outsailed by a merchantman, and soon the signal halliards of the *Porpoise* were busy.

"Shorten sail," was the first order.

But as this had no effect, "Heave to and await convoy," was the next hoist.

Forbes was always full of fun and he and Goldsborough became life-long friends after this first brush.

After this encounter Forbes took a delight in working his way up on the schooner's weather, and as the brig began to creep by the voice of the schooner's first lieutenant would boom across the water.

"*Danube*, ahoy!"

"Sir?" answered "Black Ben"

"Keep under my lee quarter, sir!"

"Aye, aye, sir!"

On arrival at Gibraltar Forbes found that he was to transfer himself, crew and cargo to a new ship, named the *Bashaw*, which had just been bought by his uncle for the China trade. After receiving several other shipments of opium, the *Bashaw*, a full-rigged ship of 390 tons, sailed on July 10.

Forbes arrived in the Straits of Sunda in October. At Anjer he fell in with the brig *Leander* of Salem, belonging to Joseph Peabody, which he had met leaving Smyrna, when in the *Danube*.

The *Leander* had opium on board and it was important that her captain should not suspect that Forbes also carried the drug. However,

Forbes was not a man one could forget, and directly the *Leander's* captain came aboard he recognised the late skipper of the *Danube*. Both he and his super-cargo at once tried to find out the truth, but Forbes had given strict orders to his crew to let out nothing.

Captain Smith of the *Leander*, never having been in Chinese waters before, suggested that they should keep company. Forbes agreed so long as the little brig could keep up with the *Bashaw*. It was just at the change of the monsoon, and it was a question whether to go by the Palawan Passage or head for Pulo Sapatu and Cape Padaran. The two ships kept together until they were past the Natunas, and then one squally night with the wind at South-east the *Bashaw* hauled her wind and saw no more of the *Leander*, arriving a week ahead of her.

Forbes' old chief, J. P. Cushing, had embarked for home in the *Milo* and he found his brother Thomas head of the house of Perkins & Co., Canton, and also American Consul. The *Bashaw* and the *Leander* were the only ships bringing Turkey opium, and the total amount from Smyrna was not more than 1000 chests. Forbes, who had seen very little of his elder brother Thomas, was glad of a five months' stay with him, and he little knew that when he sailed from China in April, 1829, that was the last he was to see of this brother.

Thomas Forbes lost in a Typhoon.

That autumn Thomas Forbes left Macao in his little yacht *Haidee* to go to the Lintin Anchorage where the *Mentor* had just arrived from home. Anchoring for the night off the Nine Islands, owing to calm, Forbes was awakened about midnight by a fierce gust of wind from the North. The weather looked threatening and Forbes wisely up anchored and ran back to Macao, where he brought up close to the Praya Grande, and not far from the East India Company's cutter *Louisa*. He would have landed but his chief clerk, Monson, lay ill below. By daylight it was too late, the wind had shifted to the North-east and was blowing along the shore in terrific squalls.

Forbes hoisted his colours union down, but the cutter with only Lascars aboard could barely look after herself. Soon after daylight both vessels decided to try to run round to the inner harbour, but both were compelled to anchor under the point. A full typhoon was blowing with sheets of blinding rain. The cutter's anchors held on, but one after the other the two cables of the little schooner snapped.

Nothing could be seen but rain and spray. The head of the foresail was raised, Forbes took the helm and let her scud. A rock or two were missed by a hair's-breadth. Then the water shoaled and grew steeper and full of mud and sand. A sea broke aboard and nearly swamped her; the next smashed the rudder and broached her to. As she went over, the Lascar Alee (one of two composing the crew, along with one English sailor) pushed the skylight towards Forbes, but the latter sprang for the main rigging and hung on.

The next breaker washed every one of them away; the two Lascars, who could swim like fish, managed to reach the shore in an exhausted condition, Forbes, Monson and the white sailor were drowned.

After the gale a search was made, the masts of the *Haidee* were found sticking up out of the water and presently the bodies were recovered. They were buried in the English cemetery at Macao.

The "Lintin" Store-ship.

The *Bashaw* arrived home in October, 1829, and not long after arrived the news of the death of Forbes' brother, which sent Cushing hurrying out to China again to reorganise the Canton agency, in which the firms of J. & T. H. Perkins and Bryant & Sturgis were equally interested.

At this stage of young Forbes' career, he was only 25, his great ambition was to command the firm's store-ship at Lintin—a very lucrative position, apparently, for her commander.

This job was then held by the ship *Tartar*, belonging to Bryant & Sturgis, with a nephew of Sturgis in command, but before leaving China "Black Ben" had arranged with Sturgis to replace the *Tartar* and relieve him, and this project was agreed to by the home partners in America.

A store-ship was not entirely a receiving ship for opium: she stocked all kinds of goods as well as supplies for the shipping; the best ship for the purpose was naturally one with good cargo capacity.

Forbes found just such a ship on the stocks at Medford almost ready for launching, and he promptly bought her with the financial aid of his friend, Daniel C. Bacon. He sailed for China on July 7, with three passengers, his younger brother John, Captain Augustine Heard and Dr. Jennison.

Naturally with such a tub a slow passage was to be expected. The *Lintin*, according to Forbes, never made over 10 knots in her life. She was 44 days to the Line and another 53 to Java Head. On her arrival in China, she took the place of the *Tartar* at the Lintin Anchorage, where, except for shifting in the typhoon season, she remained for nine years.

Forbes remained in her till 1832, when he sold part of his ship to Russell & Co., gave a share to his brother John, and left F. W. Macondray in charge.

Russell & Co. in 1830.

With the arrival of Augustine Heard in the *Lintin* the old American house of Samuel Russell & Co., known in Canton as the Kee-Chang Hong, was reorganised. Founded by Samuel Russell as far back as December, 1818, up till the middle of 1830 the only partners had been Samuel Russell and Philip Ammidon. It was now reorganised, William H. Low, who had arrived out in the ship *Sumatra* in the previous September, and Augustine Heard becoming partners, whilst young John Forbes joined the staff. At this date Russell & Co. were purely an agency, they owned no ships and they did no trade on their own account, but they were lucky in having much of the business of Baring Bros. and also that of Houqua. Besides this, with two such go-ahead sailors as Augustine Heard and R. B. Forbes interested in the firm, from this date it went ahead by leaps and bounds.

Captain Augustine Heard and the Pirates.

Captain Augustine Heard, who remained a partner of Russell & Co. until the end of the year 1836, was an old shipmaster of resolute character and many adventures. At one time he commanded the famous little *Emerald*, of the Boston Jewel Line of Atlantic packets, after she had been sold into the East India trade along with her sisters.

In the 1820ties and 1830ties it is no exaggeration to say that the Atlantic seas from the West Indies to the Canaries, and from the Cape Verdes to the Bight of Benin, were crowded by European pirates.

In 1829 the *Topaz*, when close to St. Helena, was captured by the Spanish pirate Alcantra of the brig *Macrinarian*, her whole ship's company being made to walk the plank. In 1832 Benito de Soto, in his notorious *Black Joke*, plundered the *Morning Star*. Captain Augustine Heard in the *Emerald* was running down the trades when he encountered another of these piratical gentry, the typical low black schooner, which after circling round him once or twice at a distance, ranged up under the packet's lee bow and fired a round from her long-tom as a signal to heave-to. The *Emerald's* guns had been loaded and her crew kept out of sight. Captain Heard now ran up his colours, and sent his hands to the weather braces, before seizing his one chance of escape.

"They who have seen Augustine Heard in times of danger," wrote Forbes, "and they alone can conceive of the stillness which came over him, when the crisis was at hand, the greater the risk, the more quiet and unmoved he seemed. His dark eye never wavered for a moment and his voice, always low, sank to a hoarse whisper as he softly gave the order."

This was "to hard up the helm and round in the weather braces." The *Emerald* was racing along before the strong N.E. trade; as the quartermaster hove the wheel up she lay down and, increasing her speed, headed straight for the beam of the waiting pirate.

The next moment there was a tremendous crash, some blood-curdling shrieks, and the *Emerald* had crushed in the light hull of the schooner like an eggshell and sailed clean over her.

Captain Forbes, who spun the yarn, for not a word about the incident could ever be got from Augustine Heard's lips, ended up with the verse:—

And as to catch the gale
Round veered the flapping sail,
Death! was the helmsman's hail,
  Death without quarter!
Midships with iron keel
Struck we her ribs of steel;
Down her black hull did reel,
  Through the dark water!

The Affair of the Washing Boat.

Captain Forbes had not been many months moored off Lintin before he was involved in an affray which was actually referred to Pekin.

A sampan containing the newly washed linen of the officers of the ships at Lintin was returning from Macao with a few Lascars and sea-cunnies on board and had almost arrived alongside Forbes' ship, when a long mandarin rowing boat, containing about 40 men, dashed up and demanded money.

The Lascars of course refused, the mandarin boat thereupon attempting to carry them off. A sea-cunny called lustily for help. The crew of the *Lintin* had to be ready for action at any moment; and in a few seconds a manned and armed boat was being lowered whilst her signal halliards were busy notifying the other ships.

The mandarin boat's crew raised their spears, and primed a small cannon. This was quite enough provocation for the Americans, who let fly a volley. A short fight ensued, and before the washing boat could be retrieved one Chinaman had been killed and five wounded.

The Hoppo immediately demanded an investigation from the Hong merchants. They applied to the Select Committee of the Company. The latter replied that they were not concerned as there were no Company's ships at Lintin. The British and American agents and merchants at Canton pleaded ignorance. For some time no more was heard, and then the Viceroy of Canton pronounced the guilt to be upon the following heads:—

Tihtae, the murderous person on an English country ship.

Sampaling, the Englishman who controls the sale of opium on board the foreign ships: he is a Chief Captain and the murderous Foreigner who led on the men that fired the shot.

Tsaemow (Atom), an official Linguist at Canton.

Manyik (Magniac), the head of the business (either Jardine or Matheson). He is always at the Thirteen Factories with Sampaling; a stationary demon, who receives the money for the opium.

Woo Showchang (Houqua junior) is the principal of the merchants who are securities for foreigners; defends and protects the murderous foreigners; a traitorous Merchant who monopolises the fees derived from the sale of opium.

Woo Afoo, a Linguist who remains on board Sampaling's ship selling opium.

This mandate gives a good idea of the insulting way in which the Chinese higher officials referred to all foreigners.

English Merchants in Canton, 1830-1.

The firms outside the Honourable East India Company consisted of Magniac & Co., Thomas Dent & Co., Ilberry, Fearon & Co., Whiteman & Co. and Turner & Co.

The partners in Magniacs were:—William Jardine, Francis Hollingworth, Alexander Matheson, Henry Wright, James Matheson, Thomas Chay Beale and Henry Robinson.

In Dents were Launcelot Dent, Robert Inglis, Thomas Allport and Robert Wilkinson.

There were also some half dozen merchants playing a lone hand, of whom James Innes and Thomas Beale were the best known.

Besides these business men there was George Chinnery, the portrait painter, a watchmaker and four shopkeepers, who would have been more correctly described as the keepers of sailors' grog-shanties.

The Parsees in Canton, 1830-1.

According to the census of foreign residents there were 21 Parsee merchants, with 5 clerks and 15 servants.

The most important of these was probably Dadabhoy Rustomjee, the son of that merchant prince of Calcutta, Rustomjee Cowasjee, who owned the largest fleet of ships trading out of India, which included some of the best known of the clippers.

Dadabhoy Rustomjee arrived in Canton waters in 1830 aboard the well-known *Lord Amherst*, a hardwood frigate-built ship of 506 tons, which had been built in the Blackwall yard in 1824.

Though only a boy of 19, "Daddy Boy," as he was always

called, was entrusted with the disposal of a large cargo of opium and cotton. In 1831 his brother Manockjee, a boy of only 16 years, came out to China, and in 1834 the well-known firm of Dadabhoy and Manockjee Rustomjee was established at Canton, to manage the family business in China.

Rustomjee Cowasjee and his sons were members of the famous Banajee family, which was founded by Banajee Limjee at Bombay about the time Bombay became a British possession.

From the first the Banajees were merchants and shipowners, two of the best known of Banajee Limjee's ships being the *Gunjaware* and the *Prem.* Rustomjee Cowasjee was great-grandson of Banajee Limjee, the Davur; his brothers were Framjee Cowasjee and Cursetjee Cowasjee, whilst Sir Cowasjee Jehangeer and Hirjee Jehangeer Readymoney were his first cousins; another cousin was Merwanjee Jeejeebhoy, who became a partner in D. & M. Rustomjee. A very familiar house-flag in the East was that of the Banajee family, a white pennant with a blue St. George's Cross.

Next to Rustomjee Cowasjee and his sons, the three brothers Bomanjee Framjee Cama, Pestonjee Framjee Cama and Dossabhoy Framjee Cama owned more opium clippers than any other Parsees.

Other great shipowning Parsees were the Wadias, the Lascaris, the Patels, the Readymoneys, and of course, Sir Jamsetjee Jeejeebhoy, the great friend and first business partner of Dr. Jardine.

The Famous Clipper "Sylph."

Of all Rustomjee Cowasjee's fleet, the *Sylph,* though by no means the largest, was probably the favourite. As soon as the astute Parsee saw that the little *Red Rover* had conquered the monsoon, he sent to England to the best ship designer he knew of, Sir Robert Seppings, and asked him to send out the lines and specifications of the strongest, fastest ship of 300 tons that he could devise.

Sir Robert Seppings was then Surveyor of the Navy; he gave way to Sir William Symonds in June, 1832. He will chiefly be remembered for his method of diagonal struts and ties fitted inside the timbers for strengthening purposes, but he could also design a very shapely hull. His larger men-of-war were criticised for their slow speed—they were too bound up with no give in them, complained some officers—yet many of his smaller vessels were by no means slow, and the *Sylph,* tied together as she was with his diagonal bracing, was one of the fastest of the opium clippers throughout her days. She was not considered so rakish looking nor so beautiful to a sailor's eyes as the *Red Rover* type with its long, low hull, its lack of sheer and freeboard and its much cut-away ends, but to the end of her days she proved very hard to beat.

The *Sylph,* though barque-rigged, was not flush-decked like the *Red Rover* but had a low poop and topgallant fo'c'sle. Her stern was square, she had single quarter-galleries and a female figure-head. Below her maindeck the *Red Rover* had only a light movable platform, but the *Sylph* had two laid decks, the height in her 'tween decks being 4 ft. 6½ ins.

The first owners of the *Sylph* were Rustomjee Cowasjee, James Cullen, Robert Browne and Alexander Robertson, all merchants of Calcutta holding the 64 shares jointly.

In 1833 Cowasjee's partners sold out but he retained 24 shares, the firm of Thomas de Souza & Co. buying 24 shares, Brightman & Co. 8 shares, and her commander, Robert Wallace, 8 shares. By 1841 Rustomjee Cowasjee had succeeded in becoming sole owner, but in that year he sold her to John Lyall of Calcutta, who altered her from a barque to a ship. Her last owner was John Johnstone of Calcutta, who bought her in 1846.

The Flying "Waterwitch."

One of the *Sylph's* greatest rivals was the beautiful clipper barque *Waterwitch,* built at Kidderpore in 1831. She also had a small poop and topgallant fo'c'sle and a 'tween decks giving 5 ft. 3 ins. in head room. She was square sterned but with no quarter-galleries and her figure-head was a very finely imagined sea maiden.

Her first owners were Dwarkanant Tagore of Carr, Tagore & Co., merchants of Calcutta, 32 shares; William Storm, merchant, 16 shares; and Captain Andrew Henderson, her commander, 16 shares. In 1841 Dent & Co. held half the shares in this pretty little ship, having bought out Storm and Henderson, and by 1848 all the shares were in the names of Lancelot and John Dent.

The Opium Passages, 1831-1833.

I should have liked to have been able to give details of the best opium passages each season; but at this distance of time such records are no longer procurable and it is only possible to give a very incomplete record of the passages, especially outwards, when the movements of the clippers, up to the time of the first Chinese war, were always kept as secret as possible.

The early English newspapers in the East do, however, give a good many arrival and departure dates; but unfortunately neither the India Office, the British Museum nor any other public library possess the very early numbers of such papers as the Calcutta *Englishman*, the Singapore *Free Press*, or the Canton *Register*.

Besides these sources of information there are the captains' letters and ships' logbooks. Though I have been lucky enough to come across a few captains' letters and abstracts, not an opium clipper's logbook has come to hand.

On her second outward passage against the monsoon, *Red Rover* left Calcutta on December 30, 1830, was off Penang on January 8, 1831, reached Singapore on January 13; here she remained until the 18th, then proceeded to beat up the China Sea against the strength of the monsoon with such success that she took her Canton pilot on February 7, only 20 days out from Singapore and 39 from Calcutta.

That the weather was against her is proved by the fact that H.M.S. *Crocodile*, 28-gun corvette, and the country ship *Penang Merchant*, which attempted to follow her, both had to put back in distress, the heavy weather being too much for them.

The *Red Rover* arrived back in the Hooghly, on March 14, 1831, her round voyage, including days in port, having only taken 76 days.

These details are taken from Captain Clifton's own passage abstracts and an article in the *Englishman*.

The little clipper's performance raised a great stir in Calcutta, for until she showed the way the only method of reaching China during the N.E. monsoon was by Pitt's Passage, a route which usually took from three to four months. Captain Wilson of the

Honourable Company's ship *Pitt* discovered this way of getting to Canton, which became known as the Eastern Passage.

On her third voyage against the monsoon *Red Rover* dropped her Calcutta pilot on January 11, 1832, was off Penang on January 21, anchored at Singapore on January 27 and took her Canton pilot on February 28, 48 days out from the Sandheads.

Still I have no records of any other clippers in the N.E. monsoon; but two remarkable passages were made during the favourable monsoon, by the *Sylph* (Captain Wallace), and the *Waterwitch* (Captain Henderson).

The *Sylph* arrived off Lintin on September 1, 1832, 18 days out from the Sandheads which she had left on August 14, and the *Waterwitch* took 21 days for the same passage.

In 1833 the *Red Rover* again conquered the monsoon in excellent time, but I still have no records of other vessels.

Captain Clifton dropped his pilot off the Sandheads on January 1, 1833, passed Penang on January 9, arrived Singapore on January 15 and took his China pilot on February 10, 40 days out.

Up to this date the only vessels attempting the passage to China during the unfavourable monsoon were the *Jamesina*, *Falcon*, *Red Rover*, *Waterwitch*, and *Sylph*. One other vessel, evidently a clipper, made one trip against the N.E. monsoon, and that was the *Lady of the Lake*, of 243 tons, in 1832. This little country ship, however, did not stay long in the opium trade. In 1836 her captain, James Pearson, who was then sole owner, took her to Hobart, Tasmania, and sold her locally. She continued trading under various changes of ownership until 1877, when she was broken up.

"WATERWITCH"

National Maritime Museum, Greenwich

[*See page* 94

H.M. CORVETTE "MAGICIENNE"

National Maritime Museum, Greenwich

[*See page* 110

CHAPTER IV.

A BOOMING TRADE.

I went aloft one morning
To take a look around,
And there I spied a clipper ship
For China she was bound.

Adventurous Voyages up the Coast in 1832.

WITH the conquest of the monsoon by the clippers and the resulting increase in the amount of the drug coming to China, it became more important than ever to find new markets to the North East, and in 1832 serious efforts were made by the opium houses to supplement the clandestine Canton market.

The first vessel to be despatched to the Northward was Rustomjee's *Agnes*, which sailed from Lintin at the end of January. She, however, only proceeded a short distance up the coast and then brought up off a walled town, called Shin Tsean. Here she lay for a month patiently waiting for the smugglers to come off to her, but though she was supplied with fresh provisions by a local compradore no one showed any desire for her opium, and in March the captain ran back to Macao in disgust.

The next vessel to sail into the unknown was the frigate-built Blackwaller *Lord Amherst*, a smart ship of 506 tons and 70 men, which was chartered by the Honourable Company for 2500 dollars, from her consignees, Whiteman & Co., and loaded with broadcloth, camlets, calico and cotton, but not a single chest of opium. She was commanded by Captain Rees, but an official of the Company named Lindsay was in charge of the expedition.

The "Lord Amherst" Tries to Open General Trade.

Sailing from Whampoa on February 26, 1832, the *Lord Amherst* was much held up at first by the strong monsoon, and it was not until March 26 that she anchored off Namoa. Without charts and on an unsurveyed coast her captain seems to have watched the coasting junks and fishermen and used them whenever possible as pilots. For instance, on March 22, in a gale of wind he followed junks in among the rocks off Breaker Point, and, anchoring where they anchored, thus took shelter for the night.

When off Chinghae on March 26, when the whole horizon was covered with fishing boats, 1200 being counted within sight, Mr. Lindsay sought information not only from a trading junk but from some war junks. Only a short stay was made at Namoa and on March 30 shelter from the usual N.E. gale was taken in a fine bay, opposite the town of Tung-shan-ying. The next day *Lord Amherst* worked along the shore in short tacks, anchoring for the night under the lee of Hoo-tow-shan (Tiger's Head Hill). On April 2 Captain Rees anchored at Amoy, where the ship remained a week, whilst every possible effort was made to open trade.

The next places visited were the Pescadore Islands and Formosa, and April 21 found the *Lord Amherst* off the entrance to the Min River.

On May 3 her log records moving into the river and anchoring opposite the Custom-house near the Five Gates. Here she remained until the 17th whilst Lindsay made every effort to placate the local mandarins.

The next longish stop was made at Ningpo, which was left on June 13.

On June 17 *Lord Amherst* sailed inside the Chusan Archipelago, the passage she used being named Amherst Passage. Here again she followed junks into the Yang-tze. After remaining in the Shanghai River from June 20 to July 8, the voyage was continued into the unknown North. On July 15 *Lord Amherst* anchored at Wei-hai-wei, continuing next day, proceeding very carefully towards the Loktaou Islands with his long-boat sounding ahead, until anchor was dropped on the 25th opposite a large Korean village.

On August 12 the ship was headed South; on the 21st Sulphur Island was passed and on September 5 the *Lord Amherst* came to an anchor in the Cap-sing-moon Passage.

On the whole this endeavour to open up general trading without the added attraction of the drug was a failure. The common people were only too anxious to trade and be pleasant to the foreign devils, but the mandarins everywhere had strict imperial orders that they were not to allow trade or even communication with the great "three piecey bamboo."

The Reverend Charles Gutzlaff.

One of the most remarkable of the early missionaries took part in the *Lord Amherst* expedition. This was the Rev. Charles Gutzlaff, a Prussian, who had arrived in China aboard a junk from Singapore in 1826.

His methods of attempting to spread Christianity were most enterprising but decidedly original. A very clever linguist, he aped the Chinaman to such an extent that even the most highly educated mandarins refused to believe that he was an European, who had only been acquainted with their country for six years; as for the common people, they always took him for one of their own nation in disguise. And this was not surprising for he had a large, round clean-shaven face with small eyes, and when in Chinese dress, as he often was, looked a thorough son of Han. During the *Lord Amherst's* voyage he proved himself quite invaluable. Not only was he able to translate all Chinese proclamations, but he was able to compose counter-proclamations and advertisements in Manchu or dialect for the less talented Lindsay. He posed also as a doctor, and wherever he went ashore he distributed tracts, pills, and Morrison's translation of the Bible to all and sundry.

The tracts against dishonesty, lying, drinking, gambling, etc., which had been printed at Malacca were probably used to light fires, but the pills and balsams in Gutzlaff's medicine case were very much appreciated. The translation of the Bible was the cause of that extraordinary outburst of misguided Christianity—the Taeping Rebellion, which began some twenty years after Gutzlaff's voyage in the *Lord Amherst.*

In character, Gutzlaff was a queer mixture. Though fearless and kind-hearted, he was yet irritable and thin-skinned. Very masterful and self-confident, he was fond of posing as a genius, with the result that many considered him an untrustworthy humbug.

The Chinese certainly relied on him to stand their friend in all dealings with the treacherous Hung-maon or red-bristled nation (British). But the latter were wont to declare that it only needed time to discover that Gutzlaff was just a bubble of self-glorification.

New-comers to China regarded him with awe, and his "specious manner and assumption of omniscience" made a great impression on the young, for whom he delighted to display a kindly superiority. Yet with all this he undoubtedly possessed more intimate knowledge of the Chinese nation than any other European of his time. He seemed to have no scruples as regards the opium trade, for hardly had the *Lord Amherst* returned from the North before he had shipped himself as interpreter aboard the *Sylph* for an opium voyage of discovery to the same parts.

The "Sylph" and "Jamesina" go North.

The safe return of the *Lord Amherst* evidently encouraged the opium merchants to see what they could do.

On June 30, 1832, the firm of Magniac & Co. was wound up, and reopened under the title of Jardine, Matheson & Co. on July 1. The first act of the new firm was to despatch the clipper *Sylph* to the far North and the *Jamesina* (which since her voyage behind the *Forbes* had been acting as a receiving ship at Lintin), to Chin-chew Bay, Amoy and Foochow.

The super-cargo of the *Jamesina* attempted to trade without courting observation, whereas Captain Robert Wallace of the *Sylph* and his super-cargo, Alexander Robertson, behaved in the boldest fashion, even to hoisting flags and firing guns in order to draw the attention of the mandarins to their presence.

Both ships carried woollens and cottons besides their opium. The *Jamesina* returned with 330,000 dollars in specie, the result of successful trading, but her super-cargo wrote in his journal:

"My mind is made up that until some important change in the relation of the two countries takes place, the only chance of pushing English manufactures on this coast is by having them as a small item in an opium cargo; at the same time it must be stated that the population of the country are most anxious to trade if they could escape mandarin vengeance."

The *Sylph*, which sailed from Lintin on October 20, 1832, had a very adventurous voyage, though she was not so successful in trade as the *Jamesina* owing to the extreme poverty of the natives in the North. She went as far North as the Gulf of Liao-tung in Manchuria and experienced terrific weather. The spray froze as it fell on the deck, the rigging was iced up, one of the crew died of cold and the little clipper got aground and very nearly left her bones in the Yellow Sea.

During the voyage of the *Lord Amherst*, whilst Lindsay and Gutzlaff were ashore, Captain Rees and his officers, notably J. Jauncey, were busy surveying and charting the coast. This habit of surveying wherever they went was the cause of some of the official hostility; this was explained by one of the mandarins, as follows:

"We are afraid of you: you are too clever for us. For instance, no sooner does a ship of yours arrive than out go your boats in all directions, you sound, you make charts, and in a week know the whole place as well as we do.

"Now some Koreans were wrecked in this neighbourhood last year; they were placed under no restraint, but were allowed to go everywhere, and were finally sent home through the provinces. We do not fear them; they are stupid, they look at all things, but observe nothing."

The *Sylph* returned from the North with a little over 250,000 dollars as a result of her trading. The only other vessels which went North in 1832 were the Danish brigs *Danesborg*, of 90 tons, and *Kronsberg*, and the Dutch *Carlotta*. The *Danesborg* had the enterprising James Innes as her super-cargo and went to Ningpo, where she remained three weeks, doing quite a trade in opium and English manufactured goods.

Even war junks came and anchored near her in order to buy opium, and it was probably this success of Innes's which induced Jardine, Matheson & Co. to send their brig, the *Colonel Young*, up the coast to take up her station as a receiving ship in 1833.

The First Coaster.

In order to maintain connection with the *Colonel Young*,

Jardine, Matheson & Co. bought a brig of 161 tons in Liverpool, named the *Fairy*. This little vessel arrived at Lintin *via* Singapore on November 27, 1833. On December 15 she left the anchorage with a full cargo of opium for the *Colonel Young* and was back again off Lintin on January 6, 1834. From that date she acted regularly as tender to the receiving ship up the coast. It was not long before the enterprising Charles Gutzlaff took passage in her to act aboard the *Colonel Young* in the same capacity as he had in the *Sylph*.

The Mutiny of the "Fairy."

The little *Fairy*, commanded by a Scotsman named McKay, continued to run successfully between Lintin and the receiving ship *Colonel Young* until the summer of 1836. On June 20 in that year she sailed from Lintin; after transferring her opium and receiving bars of gold besides silver in exchange, she set forth again on the run South.

It appears that the chief officer, Guthrie by name, had been finding fault with the Manila men in the crew and had repeatedly knocked them about. About 4 a.m. on the second day after leaving the Bay of Chinchew—this was about August 21—the weather being dark and rainy, the six Manila men, armed with swords and pistols, set upon the mate, who had the deck, and killed him. They then burst into the cabin, and after a sharp resistance overcame and killed the captain, second mate and gunner, who were thrown overboard.

The rest of the crew, consisting of Lascars, two or three Portuguese and some five Chinese, were asleep in the foc's'le, but being poked awake with swords, they were told to hoist out the long-boat and make for the shore. They made no resistance and leaving the brig about 9 a.m. made the coast about 5 p.m. Unfortunately there was a heavy surf running on the beach and in making a landing the boat turned over and some of them were drowned.

Meanwhile the six Manila men sailed for Luconia, and after a rough passage of twelve days made the land; and, standing along the coast, at length anchored off the village of Cavayan, where they landed with the gold and silver after scuttling the brig. Such was the sad end of the first coaster. There were 14 survivors from the long-boat and they were brought before the magistrate of the Changpooheen district, who gradually extracted the whole story.

The Last Year of John Company's Regime.

In 1833, the last year of the Honourable East India Company's privileged position at Canton, the Select Committee, consisting of William Henry Chicheley Plowden (president), John Francis Davis and James Nugent Daniell, soon found that they were in for a difficult season, for the opium smugglers and free-traders, now that their strict rule was ending, were taking a high hand in every matter in dispute.

Though the Company loaded 22 Indiamen, totalling 26,417 tons, and 3 smaller ships for Canada, there were no less than 22 private traders which arrived at Whampoa with general cargo and 16 with rice. Besides these outsiders, there were 44 ships that did not go further than the Lintin Anchorage.

This is a big total for British ships alone; included in it were the first class Indiamen *Lowther Castle*, 1507 tons; *Thames*, 1425 tons; *Farquharson*, 1406 tons; *Herefordshire*, 1354 tons; *Castle Huntly*, 1353 tons; *Lady Melville*, 1350 tons: *Marquis of Huntly*, 1348 tons, *Buckinghamshire*, 1369 tons; and *Kellie Castle*, 1332 tons.

Five opium clippers were entered as making two trips in the year between Calcutta and Lintin. These were *Jamesina*, *Falcon*, *Red Rover*, *Waterwitch* and *Sylph*.

Amongst the store and receiving ships lying at the outer anchorages were Dent's *Jane* and *Charles Forbes*; Jardine Matheson's *Hercules*, and Russell's *Lintin*.

Of these the *Charles Forbes* was a specially fine Indian-built ship, launched at Calcutta as far back as 1821 for Hormusji Bhicajee, and costing, so it was said, three lacs of rupees.

Besides the big British fleet, trading to Canton in the Company's last year, there were 59 American ships, 8 Dutch, 7 French, 4 Danish, and several odd ships of other nationalities.

It can therefore be concluded that the Select Committee, the Co-hong, the private houses, and the numbers of other people connected with the shipping were pretty busy; nor was it likely that the complicated trade of the great port, both lawful and illicit, could be carried through without some friction.

James Innes, the Stormy Petrel of Canton.

Amongst the British merchants at Canton one of the senior was James Innes, who has already been mentioned as going North in the Danish brig *Danesborg* in 1832.

Innes was one of the most outstanding personalities in those early days; playing a lone hand in the trade of Canton, without ever taking a partner, he held his own by sheer force of character.

He had arrived at Canton in December, 1825, holding a free merchant's indentures from the Honourable Court of Directors.

In 1828 the Select Committee demanded under what authority he continued to be a resident in China. He replied by forwarding them a copy of the indenture with the following outspoken letter:

"If the Gentlemen entrusted with the power for the time here consider the non-residence of any British subject here necessary for the public good, they will enforce that non-residence against about 200 Parsees and 40 born British subjects, equally as against me, and however I may suffer, I shall yield a ready obedience to such authority, and suffer in silence; but as it has been reported to several of the Body of Directors that I came out here clandestinely and secretly, I feel very much gratified in having so direct an opportunity given me of contradicting this in the most decided manner."

The Committee were anxious that he should regularise his position by "carrying in his pocket Letters of Consulship from some independent State," but Innes by sheer pertinacity forced them to give him the following certificate of character:

"We feel it incumbent on us to remark in justice to Mr. Innes, that he has conducted himself with perfect propriety in the capacity of a British merchant, during the time that he has resided in this country."

In 1829, when Innes imported over 100,000 buttons and some 10,000 cotton handkerchiefs, he found himself up against the Customs who rated 74,080 of his buttons as gold and 43,200 as silver, and classed all his handkerchiefs as large. He protested that all the buttons were either copper or brass and all the handkerchiefs of small size. The security merchants for the goods appealed to the Select Committee and in the end Innes won the day.

In the following year we find his name heading a petition by 26 British merchants, protesting against a most insulting Chinese proclamation which amongst other things forbade foreigners from using Sedan chairs. Here again Innes forced the Company to take strong action. But his most resolute action against Chinese pin-pricks occurred in 1833.

Innes hired a hong from Houqua, and in the spring of that year he was much annoyed by Houqua's coolies billeting large quantities of firewood on the granite pavement alongside the hong. Failing to get the nuisance stopped although the Hoppo had forbidden it, Innes, backed up by his friends Jardine and Blenkin, went to the Custom-house to see the officer responsible for carrying out the Hoppo's order. Whilst the three merchants and a compradore were passing along a dark passage in the Custom-house, a man rushed out from amongst a crowd of coolies in the kitchen and wounded Innes in the arm with a chopper. Innes acted with his usual resolution. Barely waiting to have his arm bound up, he proceeded straight to Houqua's hong and announced to the old security merchant that if the coolie that had attacked him was not in custody by sundown—it was then 2 p.m.—he would set fire to the Hoppo's house.

Houqua, well used to the slow progress of most squabbles between Chinese and Europeans, quietly went off to his country house across the water and dined. Whereupon Innes coolly obtained some rockets and blue lights, and by 8 p.m. the great mandarin's residence was burning strongly. Half an hour later Houqua himself was knocking at Innes' barricaded door, ready to grant all the latter demanded, and the next day the coolie was paraded through Canton wearing the cangue or wooden collar, with his offence written upon it. The Viceroy of Canton and the Hoppo both wrote obsequious letters of apology to the triumphant Innes, who reported the matter to the Select Committee with many sarcastic allusions to their frequent failures to obtain redress when grossly insulted.

The Committee were furious, but they could only reply by forwarding a copy of the George III Act giving them authority over their own countrymen but not, as they pointed out, over the Chinese.

Captain Grant of the "Hercules" and the "Red Rover's" Mail Bags.

A few weeks later James Innes again found himself involved in a squabble. This time it was between the Company and the captain of Jardine Matheson's receiving ship.

There had for some time been much dissatisfaction over the Portuguese post at Macao, and a bag from Calcutta containing 118 British letters had recently been discovered at the Macao Custom-house, where it had been lying for three and a half years.

Since the advent of the opium clippers, the mails were now always entrusted to them.

On June 19, 1833, the *Red Rover* arrived at Cap-sing-moon on her second outward passage of the year, and at once sent an officer ashore with the Company's mail bags. These it was customary to hand over to the steward and butler of the Factory, who, when the President was in residence at Macao, took them straight up to his house.

But on this occasion, Henry Skinner, the steward, and John R. Marks, the butler, were not at the landing stage, so the *Red Rover's* officer, with a coolie carrying the mail bags, went to the well-known tavern of Richard Markwick, where he not only found the butler and steward, but James Innes and Captain Alexander Grant of the *Hercules*.

Captain Grant immediately seized the mail bag, cut the string and poured the letters out on the table. Then he coolly proceeded to sort out all the letters addressed either to himself or his firm.

The steward and butler were horrified at this high-handed proceeding and even the innkeeper looked aghast at such temerity. The Select Committee were furious when they heard of this contempt for their fast waning authority, but they soon had further grievances against Jardine, Matheson & Co., for Captain Wallace of the *Sylph* also broke their regulations by turning his refractory seamen ashore.

The Select Committee and the Licences.

There had been a long-standing complaint that the masters of the country ships were very dilatory in producing their licences. The Company considered themselves responsible to the Viceroy, and when these licences expired it rested with them to renew them. Irritated by the high-handed actions of Jardine Matheson's captains, Grant and Wallace, the Select Committee refused to renew the licence of the *Hercules* and even went so far as to stick up a notice on the front of the Factory declaring that the licence was withdrawn. This roused a vehement protest from Jardine, Matheson & Co., who pointed out that this action would jeopardise over a million dollars worth of property belonging to themselves and some Parsee merchants.

The Committee thereupon wrote to the Governor-General in Council at Calcutta as follows:—

"So great has been the desire of Messrs. Jardine, Matheson & Co. and of Captain Grant as commanding their opium ships, to erect themselves into an authority independent of the Committee, that we find on record four years since, Captain Grant to have applied to the Government of Bombay to grant him a licence without the usual forms enacting obedience to our orders, and every procedure of the parties in question has been to shake off all control as lay within their power."

Linked to Jardine, Matheson & Co. in the rebellion against the authority of the Company were James Innes and all the Parsees; only Dent & Co. remained aloof, and refused to take a part in this baiting of the Select Committee over the ship's licences.

The Samarang Affair.

In the end the Committee gave in about the licence of the *Hercules*, but Captain Grant who acted as Jardine Matheson's ship's-husband or marine superintendent—though this last term had not yet been invented—was soon in much more serious trouble.

On August 7 he moved the old country ship *Samarang* into Tsinkeo Bay, and, hauling her up the beach, proceeded to break her up.

On August 17 a crowd of about 100 Chinese, armed with pikes, spears and staves, arrived from the neighbouring village of Keeow and proceeded to carry off some of the iron and copper from the *Samarang*, which was piled up on the shore.

In the melee the English gunner of the Portuguese ship, *Don Manoel*, managed to capture one of the villagers, who was taken aboard the *Hercules*. But Captain Grant released him when he promised to obtain the return of the *Samarang's* material. A few evenings later the villagers made another swoop. This time they attempted to carry off a tindal. The man was rescued, but in the confusion and darkness a sea-cunny disappeared and it was presumed that either he had been taken prisoner or killed.

By this time Captain Grant, who was far from being the most patient of men, was thoroughly roused. He immediately manned and armed the boats of all the opium ships lying at the Cap-sing-moon Anchorage and sent them against the village under Captain Hector of the *Lady Hayes*. The village opened fire with artillery, the boats fired a volley and retired without seeing a sign of the sea-cunny. But a villager was wounded and subsequently died.

Captain Grant advanced the argument, "A life for a life"—the Keeow villager paid for the sea-cunny—and he was ready to let it go at that and call quits.

But this was too simple for the Chinese mind. The matter required more serious consideration. It was not a case to be treated so lightly. The Select Committee were forced to take a hand, the Co-hong became involved, the Hoppo made an investigation and the Viceroy of Canton proceeded to make an interminable report to the Son of Heaven himself. Finally a mandarin, the brother of the Hong merchant Mowqua, was instructed to obtain redress and "save face" in truly Chinese fashion.

Taking with him a considerable sum of money to expend in a bribe, he went to Macao to find a Malay or some other coloured man, who would be willing to play the part of brother to the dead sea-cunny.

This man's story was carefully manufactured. He was to say that, in trying to save his brother, the sea-cunny, he had rushed forward, that his musket went off by mistake and by some dire mischance caused the death of the Keeow villager. Further, he was to plead that his aged mother was awaiting the return of his murdered brother and himself, but that owing to a tender conscience he refused to leave the country without confessing the whole truth and nothing but the truth.

A man was actually found to play this more than risky part. He was taken to Canton for trial and would undoubtedly have been executed but for the firm intervention of the Select Committee. This effort on behalf of its enemies, the free-traders and opium smugglers was the last official act of the great Company before closing its books and its doors in China for ever.

Opium Clippers compared with British Men-of-War.

It was contended by the commanders of the opium clippers that there was not a ship in His Majesty's Navy which could sail as fast as their little flyers.

"Until the arrival of the *Dido*," wrote Keppel from Singapore in 1843, "the handsome and fast opium clippers had it all their own way."

I can find no instances before the 'forties of men-of-war and clippers being in company or sailing against each other. Before the first China war His Majesty's ships were rarities in the China Seas. But in December, 1831, two of the fastest sailers in the Royal Navy appeared in Canton waters with a despatch from the Governor-General at Calcutta. These were the experimental ships, *Challenger* (28 guns) and *Wolf* (18 guns), which had been built in 1826 from the designs of Captain Hayes, R.N., known throughout the Service as "Magnificent" Hayes, owing to his superb seamanship in sailing that ship off a lee shore in a gale of wind.

Then in 1832 the 18-gun brig-sloop, *Cruiser*, appeared. She belonged to that large class of 18-gun brigs, to which the *Jamesina* ex *Curlew* had belonged. They were considered the smartest small craft in the R.N. during the Napoleonic war.

But neither the two experimental ships nor the *Cruiser* could compare with the British man-of-war which came to an anchor off Lintin on November 5, 1833. This was the 24-gun corvette, *Magicienne*, undoubtedly the fastest vessel in the Royal Navy at that date. This beautiful man-of-war certainly could sail alongside

Red Rover, *Sylph* or *Waterwitch*, and I have looked up some of her passages and logs, in order to be able to compare them, for during her three and a half years' commission in Eastern waters she not only made some extraordinary passages but outsailed every ship with which she fell in company.

The Corvette "Magicienne."

This famous man-of-war, a general favourite with both officers and men in her day, was built in 1812 in a merchants' yard as a 46-gun frigate armed with 32-pounders.

In 1831 she was cut down—or razeed, as it was called—from a 46-gun frigate into a 24-gun corvette. This was done in Woolwich Dockyard by the well-known master shipwright, Oliver Lang, on a plan of his own which was so successful that the *Magicienne* became the talk of the Navy, not only for her sailing powers, but her seaworthiness and internal comfort.

Some of the results of razeeing were as follows:—She drew 18 inches less water; carried her guns 18 inches higher; stowed her boats and booms a deck lower; had 100 tons of topweight timber taken off her, besides the weight of quarterdeck and forecastle guns; had 6 ft. more drop to her courses, jibs and spanker; had her topgallant sails and trysails enlarged; she had more stability and less tophamper, yet more canvas though less displacement.

Her lower deck, too, allowed more room for her men and she had more air and light through the introduction of circular tube scuttles, an invention of Oliver Lang's. On her orlop deck she had a thorough ventilation fore and aft and there was plenty of room for midshipmen's chests with the wings left quite clear. She was not crowded out like most men-of-war of her day, yet she could stow five months' bread and six of every other provision.

Here are some reports about her sailing:—Her inclination—a most important factor in our sailing navy—was usually about 10° under single reefed topsails and topgallant sails when close-hauled and going 9·6 knots. On a wind she was able to log 6½ knots in a light wind with skysails set and all reefs out. She could go 10 knots close-hauled in a fresh breeze and 13½ with yards squared.

She was a particularly easy ship in bad weather but like all fast ships very wet on a wind, when she threw a great deal of spray over abaft her fore rigging. She never plunged deep enough to bury her head and unship the lee bumkin, as was the way with 36-gun frigates built on the same draught.

A proof of her strength and easiness on her gear was shown in her 3½ years' commission, when she gave no signs of being strained by the weight of her metal (32-pounders), nor did she carry away a single chain plate. Yet she was very lofty and heavily rigged, her main topgallant mast being 60 ft. long, 16 ft. longer than that of a 46-gun frigate.

Under Captain J. H. Plumridge this beautiful corvette was as renowned for the state of her discipline and the smartness of her drill as for her other qualities.

Early in the commission a corporal of Marines found the forward sail-room on fire: it was the morning watch and the room was right over the magazine. Without saying a word the man went quietly aft and informed the captain. Without staying to dress, Captain Plumridge ran on deck, ordered the helmsman to steer for an imaginary ship on the horizon to leeward. This ruse was to get the ship before the wind. Then he told the officer of the watch to beat to fire quarters. In less than a minute every man was at his post. Only those stationed near the sail-room had any idea that it was more than fire-drill; but they, headed by their captain, worked with such speed and gallantry that the burning sails were smothered and the ship saved when the flames were within 3 inches of the gunpowder.

For comparison with those of the Company's East Indiamen, country craft and opium clippers, I have included a few of the *Magicienne's* passages in an Appendix.

"Red Rover" races "Sylph" in 1834.

There was very keen rivalry between the *Red Rover* and *Sylph* in 1834. Sailing with the new season's opium, the *Red Rover* was first ship away, leaving Calcutta on December 31, 1833, and dropping her pilot off the Sandheads on January 1, 1834. She was off Penang on January 7, anchored Singapore on January 15 and took her Canton pilot on February 11, 43 days out. The

Sylph left the Sandheads on January 5 and took her Canton pilot on February 15, 41 days out.

On the return passage *Red Rover* sailed on March 15, touched at Singapore and Madras and reached Calcutta on April 23, 39 days out. This was a good victory for Captain Clifton, for Wallace took 54 days.

The Schooner "Syed Khan," ex-Slaver.

A new vessel was added to the opium fleet, in 1834. This was the Baltimore clipper and ex-slaver *Syed Khan*, a topsail schooner of 193 tons.

She was commanded and owned by Captain John McKinnon, an old China hand; and on her very first homeward passage left the Canton River on November 11, 1834, and after being detained 24 hours off Penang refitting her topmast, etc., after a carry-away in a squall, reached Calcutta on December 6, only 25 days from China. This was claimed to be the shortest passage to date, with the exception of the *Sylph's* record of 17 days 17 hours.

"The Barbarian Eye."

With the end of the Honourable Company's monopoly in China came a period of trouble and confusion. The British Government appointed Lord Napier to a newly invented post which they called "Chief Superintendent of British Trade in China." As Lord Napier had no more knowledge of the wily Celestial than the British Government itself, Mr. Davis and Sir G. B. Robinson, who had lately been members of the Select Committee of the East India Company, were chosen to act as his assistants.

"The Barbarian Eye," as the Chinese quaintly named the head of a foreign commission or embassy, arrived at Macao with his suite on July 16, 1834, aboard the 28-gun frigate *Andromache* (Captain H. D. Chads, C.B.), escorted by the *Imogene* (18-guns, Captain P. Blackwood).

Lord Napier, though very well meaning, was a proud nobleman, who could ill brook the petty pin-pricks and insults which the Chinese officials delighted in: and when he was so ill advised as to proceed to Canton without the usual chop or permit, he was

"Imogene" Cutter "Louisa" "Andromache" Schooner "Sylph"

FORCING THE BOCCA TIGRIS, 1834

National Maritime Museum, Greenwich

[*See page* 114

CAPTAIN HENRY PYBUS
Lent by Captain H. Pybus, R.N.R.

CAPTAIN JOSEPH PYBUS
Lent by Captain H. Pybus, R.N.R.

[*See page* 124

quite nonplussed when the Viceroy refused to receive any communications from him. Lord Napier's first act was to send Mr. Astell, the secretary to this new trade mission, to the city gate with his credential. There the wretched secretary stood whilst every kind of indignity and insult was showered upon him for three hours, only to be told in the end that all communications should be forwarded through the Hong merchants.

The Chinese were evidently determined to treat Lord Napier in the same contemptuous, insulting way that they had treated Lord Amherst in 1816. Though it was not suggested that he should perform the ceremony of kow-tow and make the nine prostrations in honour of the "Lord of the Azure Heaven and Mother Earth," as Lord Amherst had been asked to do, the treatment meted out to him soon caused him to retire to Macao in despair, and there he died of chagrin and fever on October 11, 1834.

But just as the insults to Lord Amherst had been avenged by the little frigate *Alceste*, at the Dragons Mouth, so those of Lord Napier were avenged by the *Andromache* and *Imogene*.

Ever since the first European ship had traded with China, the Bocca Tigris—or Bogue, as it was often called, the narrow mouth of the Pearl River leading up to Whampoa and Canton—had been the port of entry for the whole Celestial Empire. and for a foreign ship to proceed through the Bogue by force of arms was as great a blow in the face for the son of Han and the Emperor of Heaven as could well be imagined.

H.M. Ships "Andromache" and "Imogene" bombard the Bogue Forts and Sail through the Bocca Tigris.

At 12·30 p.m. on September 7, 1834, the two men-of-war weighed anchor and set sail towards the Bogue.

There were about a dozen war junks in Anson's Bay and these immediately warped up the bay into shallow water, in a great fright.

At the same time the forts at Chuenpee and Tycocktow appeared from a distance to be like disturbed ant heaps. As the ships came slowly on a couple of blank cartridges were fired, but the forts immediately followed these up with round shot. These were, however, too late and fell astern—and the ships passed these forts without replying. But hardly were they within the entrance to the Bocca Tigris, with the forts on North and South Wantong ahead on the port bow and the Anonghoy forts on the high land to starboard, than the wind chopped right round to the North, right in their teeth, and they were obliged to brace sharp up.

They at once split tacks, to use a yacht racing term, the *Imogene* heading for South Wantong and the *Andromache* towards Anonghoy on the port tack. Both ships reserved their fire till the range was almost point blank, and then returned the wild firing of the panic-stricken Chinese gunners with great effect. Huge clouds of dust rose from the forts, many of the shot were seen to hit the parapets or plunge clean through the embrasures, with the result that in a very short time the forts were as silent as death, whilst the order to "Cease fire on the main-deck" resounded aboard each ship. The best shooting against the ships came from Wantong Island, the *Imogene* received several rounds between her hammock nettings and the awnings and one shot came through the side of the quarter-deck, grazed the foreside of the mainmast and knocked down and wounded a bluejacket with splinters.

In the light head wind it took the two ships nearly two hours to make the passage through the Bocca Tigris, and if the forts had had a single gunlayer of any skill both ships must have received damage.

Accompanying the men-of-war was the cutter *Louisa*, belonging to the East India Company, a vessel which played quite an important part in the stirring days of the opium war. At her helm under an umbrella as some protection against the broiling sun sat Captain Charles Elliot, R.N., calmly steering her tack by tack in the wake of the men-of-war. Captain Elliot belonged to Lord Napier's mission, and soon, as we shall read, became the Superintendent of Trade himself.

His cool action on this occasion must have provoked the anger of the flustered Chinese gunners, for several shot were aimed at the *Louisa*, and not a few struck her, wounding her mast, splintering the gunwale of her jolly-boat, and testing the nerves of her Lascar crew, who however behaved extremely well. The small schooner yacht *Sylph*, belonging to Mr. Markwork, of Canton, also followed the British frigates. Soon after the ships had passed the forts the wind became so light and baffling that they were obliged to bring up off Tiger Island. Here they remained until the 9th, whilst the Chinese at the Tiger Island Fort were observed making every effort to prepare for a second affray. Hundreds of matchlock men were seen parading on the ramparts. Numbers of boats appeared with arms and soldiers. It was evident that a warm reception was being prepared.

On the 9th the ships got under way with a fair wind and steered to pass within 200 yards of the fort, so that the parapet overlooked them. As they drew abreast, the crews gave a mighty cheer, and a well directed broadside was opened upon the fort, with grape and canister, whilst the Marines and topmen fired their muskets into the embrasures.

This time the Chinese fired with greater effect. Aboard the *Imogene* the captain of the forecastle was killed and three men wounded. The *Andromache* had a seaman killed and three wounded on the maindeck, whilst several rudely cast grape shot fell spent upon the decks of the two frigates.

The fort suffered severe punishment, much of the stone parapet was shattered and a joss-house fell in a heap of ruins.

The ships had hardly ceased firing before they were obliged to anchor below the Second Bar for want of wind. But a severe lesson had been taught, the Viceroy had lost face and the many insults received by poor Lord Napier had been repaid.

The Wreck and Salvage of the "Sylph."

In 1835 the Calcutta opium sales took place at the beginning of the year, and the clippers sailed for Canton about the middle of January, the *Waterwitch* being first away, closely followed by *Red Rover*, *Syed Khan* and *Sylph*.

The *Sylph*, making a very good run down the Bay of Bengal, reached Singapore at noon on January 29, a day ahead of *Syed Khan* and two days ahead of *Red Rover*, which had left Calcutta on January 16, and passed Penang on January 23. *Waterwitch* apparently was leading the fleet.

The *Sylph* left Singapore at noon on January 30 and with a fair wind and tide had the North-east point of Bintang, from which she was going to take her departure, only a few miles ahead at 7 p.m. Finding that the ship was closer in than he expected, owing probably to the strong current, Captain Wallace ordered a cast of the lead to be taken. The *Sylph* was travelling a good 8 knots. As the deep-sea lead was being passed the ship grazed slightly, and a moment later, with a tremendous crash she ran on a reef of rocks.

Captain Wallace's first action was to throw every sail aback; and on this proving useless he tried to make her pay off. Her head swung inshore with the swell and the wind right aft, and with some very violent bumps the *Sylph* continued to forge more and more over the reef, so that for a while hopes were entertained that she would force her way over the coral into deep water. But after an hour of banging and crashing on the reef Captain Wallace realised that she was hard and fast.

The *Sylph* apparently only possessed one boat besides her long-boat and this was a jolly-boat, in which the second mate was sent off to Singapore, which was about 60 miles off.

All that night the crew and passengers, to the number of sixty souls, were kept hard at it pumping, with the ship filling up fast, her sternpost and rudder having been carried away and her counter burst open. At daybreak a sharp lookout was kept for ships, though the *Sylph* was a good deal inside the beaten track. At length the *Syed Khan* hove in sight, hoisted her colours and seemed as if she would bear down upon the helpless *Sylph*, which promptly hoisted a string of flags. It was not possible to fire a gun as a sign of distress because the *Sylph*, as was usual with the clippers when racing to China with the drug, had all her guns down in the hold and by this time under water.

Hardly had Captain Wallace hoisted his signal than the schooner hauled her wind and sailed away. The clippers were so fond of playing tricks with each other by signalling that it was supposed that the *Syed Khan* suspected the *Sylph* of trying to humbug her.

All that day, though sails were sighted on the horizon, nothing came near the wreck which by nightfall had settled down in sand and coral, completely waterlogged. On all sides the surf roared and foamed. On the jungle-clad shore it was noticed that crowds of Malays had assembled, who were evidently biding their time in hopes of plunder.

The long-boat was now got over the side, and each man served with a little biscuit and a bottle of water. The night was an anxious one. A high sea was running. It was feared that the ship might break up. Fires along the beach told of the Malays waiting for their prey. But with daylight appeared the Honourable Company's sloop-of-war, *Clive*, of 18 guns. It required very fine watermanship for the boats of the sloop to get the passengers off the wreck, but the service was carried out successfully without a single mishap.

Captain Wallace and his crew stayed by the *Sylph*, and for a whole week the *Clive's* boats worked at removing the clipper's valuable cargo in such a big surf, that the greatest care was needed to keep the boats from swamping. On one occasion Captain Hawkins and his white boat's crew did capsize and were three hours in the surf before being washed up on the shore, and one of the men was drowned.

On February 7 the following letter from Captain Wallace appeared in the Singapore *Chronicle:*

> We have delivered up to the *Clive* 540 chests and I have about 150 on deck ready to hoist out. I am also anxious to get some divers off, for the greater part of the men who have been at work in the hold are laid up with inflamed eyes.
>
> The most difficult part is now come, for the people are required to dive under the water to get the opium from under the beams, and on our lee side we have 8 ft. of water, and the difficulty of removing the opium is increased from the guineas and hides of the chests being much swollen.
>
> If it blows at full moon with a high sea, it would be hard to say if she will hold out, but should she hold together these first springs, I have then no doubt she will keep together all the monsoon.
>
> When we get the cargo out we will then be able to find out whether she is bilged and whether we will be able to float her off.

There were 1115 chests of opium on board and these were insured for 14 lacs of rupees.

After a week's work, the *Clive* returned to Singapore with 680 chests, all more or less damaged. She left the brig *Mavis* and the *Sylph's* long-boat standing by the wreck, both well armed to keep off Malay pirates.

The *Sylph* did hold together and presented the most convincing proof of the excellence of Sir Robert Seppings' principle of trussing. She was eventually floated off the reef, when all her cargo was out, and was repaired at Singapore.

Though it might seem that Captain Wallace was to blame for trying to cut corners, this could not have been the case, for he was promoted to the command of Rustomjee Cowasjee's new clipper.

"Lady Grant," "Sir Herbert Compton" and "Cowasjee Family."

There were three new opium clippers in 1835. These were the brig *Lady Grant*, of 239 tons; the barque *Sir Herbert Compton*, of 346 tons, and the barque *Cowasjee Family*, of 431 tons.

The *Lady Grant* was thus criticised in the Calcutta *Englishman*:

> We are informed that the *Lady Grant* is the very extreme of sharpness: indeed, to those unacquainted with the lines of a sharp built vessel, the *Lady Grant* looks as though she had only wings and legs. There cannot be a doubt that on a fine steady breeze her ladyship must clip along in grand style—a regular racehorse: but if the typhoon comes or the wind increases to a gale, all nautical men will say "give us the model of our Calcutta built clippers."

Both the *Lady Grant* and *Sir Herbert Compton* were built in the Bombay Dockyard.

The *Lady Grant* was described as teak-built with a fir bulwark, and square-sterned with topgallant forecastle and sunken cabin abaft. She had six gunports a side but very little gingerbread, having no quarter-galleries and a billet head instead of a figure-head.

Her master was William Jeffrey. All the 64 shares were owned by Kemchund Mottichund, merchant of Bombay.

Sir Herbert Compton was built to the order of Aga Mahomed Rahim Sherazee and her first master was G. J. Simmons. She was built of teak, copper fastened to the wales, with two decks, poop and topgallant forecastle, square stern and single quarter-galleries, and a billet head in the same style as *Lady Grant*.

In 1838 the well-known Captain Fred S. Boulton took command and Sherazee sold half his shares to Cursetjee Cowasjee, Framjee Pestonjee and Muncherjee Framjee. Finally, in 1850, *Sir Herbert Compton* was registered under the Camas house-flag and converted to ship rig.

The *Cowasjee Family* was Rustomjee Cowasjee's new opium clipper. She was built at Calcutta by Mr. Currie from the designs of Sir Robert Seppings, who, by the way, was the Honourable Company's surveyor.

Like the *Sylph* she was strengthened by Seppings' plan of diagonal trussing. In model she was considered an improvement on the *Sylph*, being given more freeboard and more comfort for her passengers. She is described as having a very rising floor with great area at the line of flotation—her lines being perfectly regular and nicely graduated. She had a fine entry with good bearing above the water and what was thought a great deal of in those days, a beautiful run. It was estimated that she would carry 1500 chests of opium. She was launched on Saturday, December 15, 1835, and christened by Lady Grant before a huge crowd. She glided into the water with her topmasts fidded and skysail poles, carrying flags, in place of her topgallant masts.

Built of teak and copper fastened, no fault could be found with Currie's construction. Country built ships were always fond of gingerbread or flim-flammery, as some called it. Let me quote from the newspaper account:—"The carving and gilding are really exceedingly well done. In the centre of the stern is a sun—*splendens micante auro*—in a cerulean-blue field with cornucopias on the right and left, and a wheat sheaf below, over which the God of Day sheds his genial influence. At either side of the stern frame is a shell richly gilt, emblematic of the productions and wealth of Neptune's empire—the whole elaborately designed and tastefully executed: the pretty little false galleries are very neatly fitted. The head is the bust of a male—pater-familias of the Cowasjee, we presume, very well carved and richly gilt."

The *Cowasjee Family* had two decks with topgallant forecastle and poop. The lower deck, or 'tween decks as we should call it, had a platform with scuttles like a man-of-war. She was square-sterned with sham quarter-galleries. Her first owners were Rustomjee Cowasjee, 40 shares; Lawrence de Souza, 16 shares; and Jonathan D. Gow, 8 shares. In 1841 Cowasjee bought out his partners, but in 1849 sold her to Joseph Ezrah, Ezekiel Judah, Rustomjee Nusserwangjee and Pestonjee Dhunjeebhoy.

Finally in 1854, she also came under the flag of the Camas, and like *Sylph* and *Sir Herbert Compton* ended her life ship-rigged.

Her launch went off with all the usual ceremony. As she struck the water, she was saluted by nine guns and loud cheers, and 150 people sat down to a sumptuous tiffin.

That night Rustomjee Cowasjee entertained Calcutta society to the number of 300 to a splendid ball and supper at his "garden house."

H.M.S. "Raleigh" in a Typhoon.

The way in which the heavily-masted, low-hulled opium clippers survived such cataclysms of Nature as the Indian cyclone and the Chinese typhoon is little short of marvellous and speaks volumes for their seaworthiness and the seamanship of their officers.

To show the effect of a typhoon on a perfectly appointed and disciplined British man-of-war, here is a short account of the *Raleigh's* dismasting in the China Sea on her way to Macao in August, 1835.

The *Raleigh* was a 16-gun sloop, commanded by Commander M. Quin. She had left Plymouth on October 12, 1834. On November 28, on her way to the Cape, she overhauled and captured a slaver named the *Rio de Plate* with 565 slaves on board and a great quantity of tortoiseshell. She reached the Cape on December 16, 1834, and on June 17, 1835, arrived at Bombay, from whence she sailed for China.

August 4 found her in the middle of the China Sea with the barometer falling, the weather cloudy, the wind fresh and squally, and a chilling appearance along the horizon which "bore no friendly aspect to man."

The ship was soon snugged down in readiness for a gale, stunsail booms were got in off the yards; topgallant masts were sent down on deck, the jibboom rigged in, the stern boat hoisted in on to the poop; the hatches battened down; and sail shortened down to fore and main trysails and fore staysail.

At 8 p.m. the typhoon began to pipe up in real earnest; with the first squall the fore staysail was blown to ribbons and the ship went over until she was almost on her beam ends.

After a two hours' fight the *Raleigh's* crew succeeded in close reefing and setting the fore trysail and unbending the main trysail. All this time the storm was increasing at every gust with the wind veering and a tremendous cross sea.

At 11 p.m. the ship was making some very dangerous lurches to leeward; the first gig got adrift and was immediately cut away. Alarmed by the way in which his ship lay over on her side at every gust, Commander Quin had the fore trysail taken in. At midnight the barometer was 29·4, still falling with the typhoon steadily growing worse.

At 3 a.m. when the barometer registered 28·30, the master, fearing that the sloop would go down under their feet, recommended that the masts should be cut away. But Quin refused to be frightened declaring that he would hang on until daylight, and then part first with his guns and heavy deck lumber.

That middle watch must have been a fearful experience. The sloop laboured in a terrifying manner. On one occasion she rolled ten ratlines of her main rigging under water.

Daylight only served to show up the awe-inspiring fury of the elements to the *Raleigh's* worn-out crew. The cutter on the larboard quarter now had to be cut away, for fear of the davits breaking and getting adrift.

The spare tiller was shipped and worked with relieving tackles. Commander Quin reluctantly gave the order to let the five lee guns go through the ports along with their shot, the studding sail booms and other spars. But even this did not relieve the sloop, and at each lee lurch she rose with greater difficulty so at 8 o'clock eight more guns were launched overboard.

At 9·30 a.m. the *Raleigh* took a deep lee lurch, at the same moment she was struck by a heavy weather sea, which carried away both wheel ropes. Then down she lay, absolutely on her beam ends with her keel showing between seas and her tops out of sight beneath the wave. Her officers and crew somehow managed to scramble out on to her side, and with a coolness and daring which it is hard to really appreciate, they managed to cut the lanyards of the lower rigging and backstays. How they hung on during the ten minutes that they were hacking at the well-tarred lanyards it is hard to say. But this was not all, even in this moment when each man's life hung by a thread, opportunity was found to cut the lashings of the pinnace and second gig, so as to free them from the booms.

At 9·50 the masts and bowsprit went by the board, the *Raleigh* righted with 6 ft. of water in her hold. As soon as the lee rigging could be got at, the lanyards were cut and the masts and spars along with the pinnace and gig floated clear of the ship. Half an hour later the only boat remaining was blown to pieces.

This was the last effort of the typhoon. It now began to moderate, leaving the *Raleigh* a sheer hulk, with everything gone on deck and absolute chaos below. Only two of her men were lost overboard when she capsized. These were a Marine and a boy. This only serves to show the incredible activity and gymnastic ability of the old time seaman. All hands must have been as sure-footed and quick-grasping as monkeys.

To show how the poor little sloop had been tossed about, her chain cables were found tossed out of the lockers into the carpenter's cabin; the ballast had stove in several of the spirit casks; the pigs of iron being hurled about like cricket balls; fore and aft everything perishable had been destroyed—books, charts, nautical instruments, all mixed up in a sodden mass with clothes and provisions.

But—though little more than a wreck—the sloop had come through it. Jury masts were rigged and on August 11 she arrived at Macao.

"Lady Grant" attacked by Malay Proas.

The schooner *Syed Khan* was the first away from Calcutta after the opium sales in January, 1836. She passed Singapore on the twelfth day out from the Calcutta pilot brig. *Red Rover* dropped her pilot on January 11, passed Singapore on the 23rd, and anchored off Lintin on February 12, only 32 days out. *Waterwitch* followed her on January 13, and took a fortnight reaching Singapore; then came the new clipper *Cowasjee Family*, which under Captain Wallace left the Sandheads on January 14 and made Singapore in one day less time than the *Waterwitch*.

The *Lady Grant* left Calcutta on January 20, with 400 chests of opium, under Captain Jeffrey.

When off the Sambilangs she was attacked by Malay pirates. I will quote from her captain's journal:

> 2nd February, 1836, at 2 p.m. Sambilangs bearing South-east, we passed five Malay proas, one of which was very large, carrying a black flag at the main, and apparently full of men. When on our quarter they shortened sail and rowed to windward until they got into our wake: they then made sail and stood after us, but having the advantage of a breeze we outran them.
>
> We observed they were using every exertion to overtake us; cleared the decks for action. At 6 p.m. the proas nearly out of sight astern. At 7 p.m. it fell calm, kept all hands at quarters. At midnight saw the proas making for us from ahead. When they came within shot, opened fire upon them from the forecastle. But not being in the least intimidated, they gave us three cheers, yelling and shouting and beating the tom-tom.
>
> Let go the kedge with a spring on it and got our broadside to bear on them; opened fire but apparently without effect. Finding they closed in with us very fast, we gave them a second broadside which checked their ardour a little. They were by this time within half a cable's length of us and seemed determined to board, but a well directed fire of grape and canister made them sheer off and pull a little further astern, and lay to for some minutes, we still keeping up a well directed fire. They then pulled inshore apparently very much disabled. I am confident that had we not been all ready they would have succeeded in boarding us as they were close to before they were seen, although all hands were on the lookout.

If the pirates had succeeded in boarding, all would have been over with the brig, for the *Lady Grant* had a Lascar crew who were all paralysed with fright and hid themselves below decks, with the exception of the four European sea-cunnies and the British gunner, who served the guns with great activity, aided by the *Lady Grant's* officers.

New Clippers in 1836.

Four clippers were added to the opium fleet in 1836. The first of these was the Bombay-built barque *Ardaseer*, called after the well-known Parsee Ardaseer Dady, and built for Cursetjee Cowasjee in the upper Bombay Dock. She was launched by Sir Charles Malcolm on June 30, and her dimensions were: Length overall 117 ft.; length of keel 96 ft. and beam extreme 29 ft. 6 ins.; her tonnage being given at her launch as 422 tons.

The famous firm of Green & Wigram built the clipper brig *Antonio Pereira* in the Blackwall yard for her captain, William O. Young, who sold 16 shares to Francis Gunnis and Henry Crighton of London, and 16 shares to the Calcutta merchants, Levington, Syers & Co. The *Antonio Pereira* had, apparently, one and a half decks, a square stern and a bust figure-head of her namesake.

One of the other two clippers was the ex-slave brig *Ann*, which it was rumoured had been built in the Island of Cuba about 1834, though Captain Henry Pybus, R.N.R., the son of one of her owners, believes that she was built in the West Country. She was condemned at Sierre Leone in 1834 as the Spanish brigantine *Tangador*; she was bought by Captain Pybus, and sailed out to China from England.

The Pybus Brothers.

Though Jardine, Matheson & Co. and Dent & Co. had no professional seamen amongst their partners, this was not usually the case with either merchant firms or shipowners in those early days. Nearly every shipmaster ended by owning a few ships, and some of them amassed quite a fleet.

Amongst the owners of opium clippers were the two brothers, Captain Henry Pybus and Captain Joseph Pybus, who, when they retired in the middle 'forties, were the owners of ten smart little ships.

There was a very well-known sailor and politician of the name of Pybus in Nelson's time. This was Charles Small Pybus who distinguished himself when master of a Dover packet by beating off three French privateers of superior force. He became M.P. for Dover and Lord of the Admiralty. It was whilst he was in office that Vancouver's expedition was sent out, and Pybus Bay and Point Pybus, Prince of Wales Island, British Columbia, were called after him.

In 1793 Charles Small Pybus sent out a relative named Thomas to construct barracks for the troops in Canada. This Thomas was one of the first to recognise the possibilities of the Canadian lumber trade and also one of the first men to ship timber home. On his return to England he joined his cousin, Joseph Fletcher in the Union Docks at Limehouse.

Henry and Joseph Pybus were his third and fourth sons. Henry Pybus went to sea about 1816, and when only 22 years old gained the command of the East Indiaman *Windsor Castle*. Joseph Pybus, the younger brother, went to sea in 1819 in the East Indiaman *La Belle Alliance*, and was chief officer of the *Lord Amherst* when he was 20. Contemporaries declared that Joseph Pybus was the smartest seaman they had ever seen, but Joseph himself declared that he was not a patch on his brother Henry.

Both brothers were in the employ of John Company when the China monopoly came to an end. It was Henry Pybus who saw the money to be made in the opium trade; and his first action, when the *Windsor Castle* was thrown out of work, was to go to Lloyd's Captains' Room, where the slaver prizes were sold, and buy the brig *Ann*. This "skimmer of the seas," as she was called, had lately been captured at anchor up an African river, when just about to sail with 250 slaves on board. She was taken by H.M. steamer *Pluto*, when most of her crew were ashore.

On several previous occasions she had escaped from H.M. cruisers, and had with the aid of her sweeps three times got away from steamers, when it was almost calm.

The last slaver that was sold by auction at Lloyd's was the brig *Cazador* in July, 1836. From that date an Act of Parliament forbade the selling of slave prizes. There were then 24 prizes lying at Sierra Leone. The only one of these to be sold was the schooner *Gazita* which had been captured by the *Pylades*. She was hauled up, cut in two and sold for £132.

It is not likely that Henry Pybus got the *Ann* at anywhere near this price, but when he got out to China he was so pleased with his vessel and prospects that he wrote home to his brother Joseph to buy the fastest vessel that he could find and sail out and join him.

The Schooner "Time."

It was just about this time that the fruit schooner, *Saucy Jack*, in turning to windward bound to Corfu, beat H.M.S. *Sapphire* (28 guns), one of the famous experimental corvettes, by a distance of 4 miles in one and twenty. The *Saucy Jack* had good reason to boast of her laurels, as only recently the *Sapphire* had beaten the American squadron in a sailing contest.

This little schooner had been built by Mr. Bally of Shoreham. No sooner had he heard this story than Joseph Pybus hurried off to Shoreham. There he was informed that the smartest vessel in the whole Mediterranean green and dry fruit trade was a schooner of the name of *Time*, registering close on 140 tons, and about 90 ft. in length by 20 in breadth and 10 ft. depth of hold, built by his father's firm, Henry Fletcher, Son & Fearnall at Poplar in 1832. This little heeler was so sharp and had so much dead rise that, when Captain Pybus overhauled her, he found when standing in her hold he had to rest one foot on the keelson and other on the ceiling. After buying her, he made two voyages to the Mediterranean to learn all there was to schooner sailing. He then had her raised 2 ft. all round, as her freeboard was a bit low for the China Seas. He armed her with a brass 12-pounder long-tom amidships, and six 4-pounder broadside guns. She had been ranterpike rigged, but young Joseph Pybus resparred her as a rakish topsail schooner. Shipping a crew of 26 all told, he sailed out to the Cape in 54 days.

Here coasting freights were so attractive that he remained for a whole year before going on to join his brother. During this year he very nearly went to Davy Jones's Locker. The *Time*—which, by the way, had a figure-head of Father Time—was lying hove to in a heavy gale off Cape Recife with the helm lashed. Captain Pybus was below when a heavy sea struck her, the ballast—sand—shifted to leeward and she went over on her beam ends, not quite as far as the *Raleigh* but far enough to send the crew into the rigging. As she went over, a hawser coiled down on deck was washed over the companion hatch, preventing it from being opened and confining Pybus below for 36 hours. The gallant little ship weathered it out till it moderated, when the crew were able to trim the ballast and get her back on an even keel.

The other clipper was a Boston brigantine, which was sent out by Captain Forbes.

Forbes sends out the Brigantine "Rose."

The 150-ton clipper brigantine *Rose* was designed by Joe Lee and built by Barney at Swansea, R.I., to the order of Captain

R. B. Forbes and S. Cabot. She was named after Forbes' wife, Rose Green Smith, whom he had married in 1834. He loaded her pretty deep with flour and sent her out to China by way of Callao under Captain B. T. Foster.

She had very bad weather and poor trades to start with, was 23 days to the Line after leaving Boston in November, 1836; made the land about Cape St. Thomas on Christmas Day, 37 days out; was in 34° S., 51° W. on January 1, 1837, made the Falklands 55 days out on January 12, entered Magellan Straits on January 15 and anchored in Freshwater Bay. She was a week getting through the Straits according to Forbes and reached Callao on February 13, 86 days from Boston. From Callao she touched at the Sandwich Islands and anchored off Lintin on April 25, 66 days from Callao, having had light winds all the way across the Pacific. Her captain was loud in her praises and pronounced her to be the "neatest craft" in the opium fleet.

She became a coaster under Russell's house-flag. Her first trip North is mentioned by W. C. Hunter, who was on board. She left the Cap-sing-moon Anchorage with 300 chests valued at 300,000 dollars on board. The weather was delightful, the wind steady and the sea smooth which was very satisfactory for Hunter and his English guest, for the *Rose's* scuppers were within 2 ft. of the water.

On the third day out they anchored inside the island of Namoa close to Dent's brig *Omega*, and Jardine Matheson's brig *Governor Findlay*.

" All Same Custom " at Namoa.

Inshore of the opium clippers two mandarin junks lay at anchor, both dressed with flags, flown from bamboo sticks in exactly the same way that the Tudors flew their steamers and pendants.

The largest junk proudly displayed the flag of a Foo-Tseang or Commodore.

Until his excellency paid his formal visit to the *Rose* no trade was possible, no Chinese boat dared to come alongside—not even a bumboat or a sampan.

However the *Rose* had scarcely furled her sails and spread

her awnings before the great man was seen approaching in his Admiral's barge, a scow-like boat almost as broad as she was long, rowed by the usual sturdy Chinese boatmen. Aft sat the commodore smoking meditatively in an armchair. He was surrounded by attendants in grass-cloth dresses, conical hats of rattan with long red silk cords attached to the brim. One of these servants held a huge gaily painted umbrella over the commodore's head, others fanned the flies and mosquitoes away.

Captain Foster, attended by the schroff, received this dignified personage at the gangway; and, as soon as the usual etiquette in the way of salaams had been observed, the steward came forward with wine and cheroots. Having partaken of refreshment, the commodore gravely asked the cause of the brigantine's anchoring at Namoa. The schroff, without the flicker of an eyelash, solemnly replied that the barbarian vessel being on her way from Singapore to Canton, and having encountered contrary winds and currents, had been forced to put into Namoa Island for wood and water. The mandarin, after listening to this absurd statement without a sign of astonishment or disbelief in his smooth, round face, stooped down and pulled a long red document from his boot, which he handed to his secretary, who handed it to the schroff for translation. It was an Imperial edict and ran as follows:—

> As the port of Canton is the only one at which outside barbarians are allowed to trade, on no account can they be permitted to wander about to other places in the "Middle Kingdom." The "Son of Heaven," however, whose compassion is as boundless as the ocean, cannot deny to those who are in distress from want of food, through adverse seas and currents, the necessary means of continuing their voyage. When supplied they must no longer linger, but depart at once. Respect this!
>
> Taou-Kwang. 17th year, 6th Moon, 4th Sun.

As soon as this precious document had been read it was replaced in the commodore's boot. His excellency then rose from his chair. This was a signal that business could proceed. His Chinese servants returned to the waiting barge, whilst he and his secretary were invited below.

Directly he was comfortably seated in the brigantine's tiny cabin this double-faced official threw off all pretence.

"How many chests have you on board?" was his first question. "Are they all for Namoa, or do you go further up the Coast?"

"PEARL"

National Maritime Museum, Greenwich

MODEL OF OPIUM SCHOONER (PROBABLY "BRENDA")
in Dunkirk Museum

Lent by Captain Balsen

[*See page* 132

"POPPY" IN CASTLE PEAK BAY, 5th FEBRUARY, 1847

From a Drawing by A. G. Dallas

[*See page* 142

was his next. And he carelessly offered the information that further North the mandarins had to be very strict in carrying out the will of the Emperor of the Universe. He desired all the opium to pay "cumsha" into his coffers. This important question of "cumsha" being settled, a cheroot or two smoked and several glasses of wine poured down his ample throat, the great man said:

"Kaou-tze" (I announce my departure.) He was immediately escorted on deck. The captain and his secretary helped his large bulk over the side, he sank back heavily into his chair of State beneath the silken umbrella; and that was the last seen of his excellency.

A day later several small junks stood out from the mainland, flying an agreed private signal at their mastheads; and in a short while their own boats were busy removing the chests of opium.

This opium had been sold at Canton for delivery at Namoa, and had been put on board ready packed, marked and numbered, so that there could be no mistake. The head compradore aboard the junks brought the order for its delivery aboard the *Rose* rolled up in his cotton handkerchief.

Whilst the opium was being transferred to the junks, he smoked a friendly pipe with the brigantine's schroff, drank a cup of tea, and then with the usual parting words, "Good wind, good water!" went over the side. No time was wasted. The junks had anchored with their matted mainsails aback. As the last bag of the precious drug was hoisted aboard they broke out their ponderous anchors and filled away to the Northward.

Not all the opium was taken by the same parties. Sometimes a coaster had to wait a month or two, disposing of her cargo.

The Schooner "Harriet" loads Treasure.

This was the case with the *Rose*, *Omega* and *Governor Findlay* in 1837. Three weeks went by, they still had some opium to dispose of when a small fore-and-aft schooner came in from the Northward. This was the *Harriet*, 100 tons, commanded by John Vine Hall, one of the few vessels ever built at Macao on European lines.

As the other vessels were not ready, they transferred all the treasure they had received for their opium to this tiny schooner.

This amounted to no less than 430,000 dollars in gold bars and Sycee silver—a large amount to trust to a small, ill-armed, craft with a crew which barely totalled a dozen souls. However, Hunter and his guest were not afraid to trust themselves to such a conveyance, to which they removed themselves with their servants and baggage.

The cabin of the *Harriet* was hardly large enough to house her captain; Hunter was glad enough to camp down on deck, for this cabin was overrun with ants, cockroaches and centipedes albeit it contained a king's ransom.

The run South was a picnic of fine days and glorious nights in which the time was spent in yarning and smoking; with lots of drink, many songs and a practical joke or two. They were lucky, too, for the little schooner anchored under the Kowloong shore, just in time to ride out an unusually vicious typhoon. All the coasters had especially heavy ground tackle and the *Harriet*, with good holding ground and a weather shore, came through it safely.

The "Waterwitch" Weathers out a Typhoon and a Cyclone.

On her second voyage in 1836 the crack clipper, *Waterwitch*, had a very rough time. On her outward passage she encountered a typhoon about 50 miles to the S.S.E. of the Paracels; and on her homeward trip, between Singapore and Calcutta, she was nearly overwhelmed by a cyclone.

The typhoon struck the barque at midnight on the June 20 and came on with very little warning from the barometer. After blowing very hard for four hours, it lulled to a calm, whilst the dreaded centre of the storm was passing. This lasted about 20 minutes, and then the wind came again with redoubled fury from the opposite quarter and laid the *Waterwitch* on her beam ends.

Somehow her crew, like the crew of the *Raleigh*, managed to cut away her main and mizen masts, at which the gallant little ship righted. The next job was to cut the tangled wreck of spars and gear adrift before it damaged the hull. This also was done successfully. Throughout the 21st the typhoon screamed and raged, the air being so full of flying scud that nothing could be seen until 6 p.m. when the weather cleared just in time to show the white line of breakers, hurling themselves on the Discovery Reef dead to leeward under the bow. A providential shift of wind carried the *Waterwitch* clear of the danger. Then it piped up again and blew as hard as ever. But again the barque weathered it out and a calm of three days off the coast of Hainam enabled her crew to get up jury masts. In the end she reached Lintin with neither her cargo nor hull injured.

On her return passage after refitting, the *Waterwitch* made a quick run to Singapore, which she left on November 7. Then her troubles began; with wind and current dead against her she took ten days getting to Penang. On the morning that she made the island, the barque was almost caught in the calm vortex of a water-spout. Light variable winds prevailed until the 24th, when a hard S.W. gale came on. Whilst running under a close reefed fore topsail the *Waterwitch* had another alarming experience. What her crew called a whirlwind came hissing along the surface of the water directly at them. With the heavy sea running this so alarmed Captain Henderson that he ordered men to stand by the masts with axes. Luckily it just missed the little clipper; but on the very next day, November 25, a cyclone came roaring up from the South, the wind quickly shifting round to the West where it blew longest and fiercest.

"We scudded as long as we could to the Eastward," wrote a passenger, "going 10 knots under bare poles, but getting within 70 miles of Cheduba, a dead lee shore, we were compelled to bring the vessel to the wind in the most dreadful sea I ever saw. As it was probable she might be thrown on her beam ends, we had the axes on deck ready to cut away the masts, but she came to in a way that astonished us, rising over the huge seas like a gull; towards sunset the furious gusts increased in violence and the barometer fell to 28.70. The noble little craft still stood out the raging tempest, without shipping any water to windward, but as she rose on the towering waves and met its augmented fury, her lee lurches became fearful and the sea washed in over her lee gunwale."

With night coming on and the cyclone steadily growing worse, Captain Henderson reluctantly gave the order to cut away the topmasts. The gear was cut through, but for some little time neither mast seemed inclined to go—then the fore topmast went over the side taking with it the head of the foremast, the slings of the foreyard and the jibboom.

The main topmast hung on but sprang the lower mast with its working. In cutting away the gear to leeward one man was washed out of the main channels and lost. Everyone was up to their necks at every lee roll, when hacking at the gear. Captain Henderson and his two officers, Venables and Reeves, were ably supported by the British gunner and the four sea-cunnies, of whom three were Europeans, but the Lascars sat down on the deck, wringing their hands and calling upon Allah. Soon after 8 p.m. the barometer began to rise, the squalls to ease up, and by daylight the cyclone had passed on and the little *Waterwitch* had weathered out her second hurricane in the course of one short voyage. But like her outward run her homeward one was spoilt by the weather.

"Cowasjee Family's" Success.

Captain Wallace was delighted with his new clipper. He declared that a child could steer her, that she could carry her canvas longer than the *Sylph*, went 10 knots easy "going large with skysails set" and 9 knots close-hauled "with the leeches of her sails shaking." Indeed, he declared her to be the finest vessel he was ever in.

On her first homeward passage *Cowasjee Family* left Macao on March 3, 1836, reached Singapore in 7 days and arrived Calcutta on March 30, only 27 days out. She easily made her three voyages in the year; on her third she dropped her anchor in the Hooghly on December 13, 29 days out.

New Clippers in 1837: "Rob Roy," "Omega," "Psyche" and "Pearl."

Though the year 1837 was one of commercial crisis everywhere, and the three China houses of Thomas Wilson & Co., George Wildes & Co., and Timothy Wiggin, commonly known as the three W's, all failed in London, the illicit opium trade continued to flourish and several new vessels appeared in the racing fleet.

The first of these was the barque *Rob Roy*, of 352 tons. Built of teak and copper fastened with square stern, sham quarter galleries and figurehead of Rob Roy, she was launched from Ambrose's yard, Calcutta, at 2 p.m. on January 7, 1837, amidst the usual cheers and firing of guns. She was owned by the de Souza family and Captain McKinnon left the little *Syed Khan* to command her. She sailed with the new season's opium in the wake of the *Red Rover*, which, by the way, had been taken over by Captain Wright in 1836, Captain Clifton having gone home to buy a new clipper. Another new commander in the fleet was Reynell, who took the *Waterwitch* from Captain Henderson, who after his two hurricanes considered that he had earned his retirement. Captain Reynell was a very successful opium skipper, and by 1842 he had made enough money to buy the Steam Ferry Bridges at Calcutta in partnership with Captain Hyde, the secretary of the lottery committee, for 80,000 rupees.

Bombay's representative this year was the brigantine *Pearl* of 118 tons, described as teak-built with one deck, a sunken poop, small forecastle, standing bowsprit, square stern, no galleries and a female bust as a figure-head.

She was built for Captain William Edmond and owned by the Bombay merchants, Edmond, Bibby & Co.; but, on her speed proving exceptional, she was bought by Cursetjee Cowasjee and entered the opium trade under the command of Captain Joseph S. Boulton. She remained in the opium trade till the end of the 'forties, when she was sold to Dinshaw Pallonjee and became a Mauritius and Ceylon trader.

Other new clippers were the Cowes-built brig *Omega*, of 178 tons, and the 100-ton schooner *Psyche*. These two vessels raced to China from Singapore a few days behind the *Lady Grant*.

The *Lady Grant*, from Bombay on February 7, left Singapore on March 25, 1837, and made the passage to Lintin in 21 days. *Omega* left Singapore on April 3, and took 19 days, and the little *Psyche*, following on the 7th, made the run in 16 days, which was considered the best passage on record for that season of the year.

The *Psyche* was another condemned slaver, having been captured by a British sloop in 1834 as the Spanish schooner *Indagador*. She was flush-decked, Baltimore built and square-sterned with a bird figure-head. Dent & Co. bought her from

Gardiner & Potts of Austin Friars, and George Kennedy commanded her.

Ahead of these clippers were the *Red Rover*, *Antonio Pereira*, and *Rob Roy* from Bengal; and the *Sir Herbert Compton* and *Motichund Amichund*. This last was not a clipper so far as I know and only took part this season.

"Sir Edward Ryan" built at Moulmein.

The first clipper to be built at Moulmein was the barque *Sir Edward Ryan*, of 320 tons, 15 guns besides swivels, and a complement of 70 men.

She was carvel-built with a square stern, sunk poop and forecastle, two decks, no quarter-galleries and a likeness of Sir Edward Ryan as a figure-head.

She was built to the order of Captain Henry Pybus, and probably on his design—though this is not certain—whilst Captain Pybus was up the China Sea in the *Ann*, Captain McGowan sailed the new clipper, between Moulmein and Calcutta. On his maiden passage he left Burma on July 7, and arrived in the Hooghly on the 19th.

"Ariel" Dismasted.

The clipper barque *Ariel* was launched at Kidderpore in 1837. She differed from most of the previous Indian-built clippers in having a round stern. She also had a high quarter-deck and topgallant forecastle. The height in her 'tween decks was only 4 ft. 1 in. She had a beautifully carved woman figure-head but no quarter-galleries. Before she came under Dent's flag, she was owned by her master, William Warden, and the Calcutta merchants, William Prinsep, John Stewart and George T. Braine.

Commanded by Captain Warden, she sailed from the Hooghly in the fall of the year with 970 chests of opium. On October 24, 1837, she left Singapore for China.

The China Sea was in a very bad mood that autumn. The *Antonio Pereira* arrived off Lintin in December, having fought a constant gale between November 20 and 29 and weathered out two typhoons. The little brig must have behaved wonderfully, for she came through both practically unscathed. In the first, beyond a few sails being blown to ribbons, the longboat was the only loss. A big sea sweeping aboard capsized the chocks, broke the lashings, and took the boat over the side. The second typhoon took the lee rail out of her.

The new barque, *Ariel,* with her gear not yet properly stretched, was not so lucky.

Throughout November 16 she had been battling with a hard gale, which gave every indication of developing into a typhoon. This burst upon the labouring *Ariel* with indescribable fury at 10 on the morning of the 17th. The rain and flying scud made it impossible to face to windward. The sea was heaped up in pyramids, which fell aboard in every direction. The little barque dipped first her bowsprit under, then her counter, then her lee rigging. Often the main rigging disappeared half way up to the top, in a raging flood as the vessel lay down under the squalls. All that night and the following day the fight for life continued.

After each lee lurch she rose again with the utmost difficulty and some of the gusts laid her over till her lower yardarms were dragging in the water, whilst to leeward the sea was often washing over the coaming of the main hatch. In one violent pitch the jibboom and fore topgallant mast were broken off like rotten carrots.

At last it was evident to Captain Warden and his officers that the ship was settling down and recovering with increasing difficulty. So the order was reluctantly given to cut away the mainmast. This, in its fall took the fore topmast with it, and at the same moment the mizen went 10 ft. above the deck.

The *Ariel* immediately righted. As soon as the gear was cut away it was a case of all hands to the pumps for the carpenter announced that there were 3 ft. of water in the hold.

The hull was tight enough, however; the water had only drained in through deck apertures, and the barque was dry by 6 in the evening

All this time the typhoon showed no signs of letting up. Throughout the night the wind veered quickly from point to point, thereby showing Captain Warden that he was very close to the centre of the turmoil. The rain still fell in solid sheets, and as the *Ariel* rolled heavily with nothing left to steady her, an awful sea swept clean over her with hardly a breathing space for her worn-out crew.

On the morning of the 19th it cleared up a little, but by noon the squalls began to pipe up again with a dark threatening appearance to windward. The sky was so thick with rain and spray that visibility was very poor, but at one moment during the afternoon the sudden brick-dust coloured glare, the sure sign of a typhoon's fury, showed up a line of huge spouting breakers less than a mile away. It was the sea surging mountains high over the Scarborough Shoal. And now above the shrieking of the wind a terrifying booming sound could be distinguished—the noise of the breakers on the reef, right on to which the *Ariel* was drifting fast.

Somehow or other a storm staysail was run up, and a clew of the foresail loosed, so that the *Ariel* could be got away before the wind in time to clear the shoal; and she was lucky to find herself out of that dangerous neighbourhood by nightfall.

The night of the 19th was no better than the previous one, the *Ariel* wallowing in the trough of the sea was swept by wave after wave and it was still so thick that at daylight on the 20th not a ship's length ahead could be seen.

It was now a question what to do. To the Westward lay the Macclesfield Bank, 200 miles to the Eastward was the port of Manila, but in her disabled condition it was impossible for the *Ariel* to fetch that port, so Captain Warden thought it wisest to bear up for Singapore, which she reached on November 29.

Though the chests had been under water and so tossed about as to be damaged in many cases, the opium proved to be unhurt—and that was all that mattered in the eyes of the opium dealers.

Nor did it take long to repair the hull and refit the barque after this disastrous maiden passage.

Glut of the Drug in the Spring of 1838.

What with the growing hostility of the Chinese authorities and the ever increasing number of chests arriving in Canton waters, the opium brokers were finding considerable difficulty in disposing of the drug. When the *Antonio Pereira* arrived at Lintin at the beginning of December, 1837, followed by the *Lady Grant* with

460 chests of Malwa from Bombay, the receiving ships already had 16,000 chests on hand, and the Hong merchants complained that the whole trade of the port of Canton was being jeopardised by the continual arrival of opium at Whampoa in lots which often ran to over 40 chests a boat.

Yet the new crop of Patna and Benares was reckoned at 19,000 chests and of Malwa 22,000. How all this opium was to be disposed of in the face of Chinese opposition was a question which was seriously worrying the merchants at Canton.

The first vessel to sail from Calcutta with the new crop was the *Waterwitch*. Twelve hundred chests were stowed in her hold, and more would have been taken if there had been room, the shippers eagerly contending for preference and many being shut out.

This was the largest quantity ever shipped from Calcutta in one vessel up to that date.

She was quickly followed by the *Red Rover*, *Sylph* once more in full sailing trim, and the *Antonio Pereira*, which had made a very quick passage back of 21 days from Canton. She left Lintin on December 9 and arrived Calcutta December 30, 1837. This was the smartest passage of the year, beating that of the *Red Rover* which left Canton waters on December 1 and arrived in the Hooghly on Christmas Day, 24 days out.

The *Rob Roy*, sailing from Lintin on December 2, took her pilot off the Sandheads on the same day as the *Antonio Pereira*, when 28 days out.

Of the Bombay fleet the *Sir Herbert Compton* made a trip to the Persian Gulf and did not get back till the end of March; but *Lady Grant*, *Ardaseer*, and the *Castle Huntly* all took in opium at a freight of 12 dollars a chest.

The *Waterwitch* was the first arrival in Canton waters; she was followed by *Antonio Pereira*, which, sailing from Singapore 5 days behind the *Red Rover*, came in 2 days ahead of her.

Although the trade was still very depressed at Canton in April, this did not prevent the shipment of the drug. By May most of the clippers, belonging to Calcutta, were back, and loading their second cargoes of the year.

Opium Passages 1838.

It was just as important for the clippers to make smart return passages as it was on the outward run. Several of these return passages in the winter and spring of 1838 are worth recording.

Clipper	Captain	Left China	Passed Singapore	Arrived Calcutta	Days out
Ann	H. Pybus	Jan. 7	Jan. 16	Feb. 9	33
Cowasjee Family ..	Wallace	Jan. 13	Jan. 21	Feb. 15	33
Ariel	Warden	Feb. 3	—	Mar. 4	29
Waterwitch ..	Reynell	Mar. 7	Mar. 18	April 7	33
Rob Roy	McKinnon	Mar. 18	Mar. 29	April 17	30
Antonio Pereira ..	Christie	April 15	May 11	June 2	48

The first two vessels away in March were the Pybus clippers, *Ann* and *Sir Edward Ryan.* Captains Henry Pybus and McGowan changed vessels. They sailed in company, their times being:

Clipper	Captain	Left Calcutta	Passed Singapore	Arrived Lintin	Days out
Ann	McGowan	Mar. 16	April 12	May 7	52
Sir Edward Ryan	Pybus	„	„	„	„

This was not very good, but they seem to have been taking it easily, for the *Ariel,* sailing from Calcutta a week later on March 25, left Singapore on April 18 and reached Lintin on May 2, 5 days ahead of them and only 38 days out.

This was again beaten by the *Waterwitch* which loaded at the Esplanade Moorings in rivalry with the *Cowasjee Family. Waterwitch* stowed 1190 chests and the Rustomjee clipper 1469.

The *Waterwitch* was loaded first and, sailing from Calcutta on May 6, made the best passage of the season. She reached Singapore 14 days out, and arrived at the Cap-sing-moon Anchorage on June 4, only 29 days out. *Cowasjee Family* arrived a week later.

" Sylph " Races " Antonio Pereira."

The greatest interest was taken this year in a race between the *Sylph* and *Antonio Pereira,* whose officers wagered a good deal of money on their respective clippers. They got away from Calcutta together on June 16, and dropped their pilots on the 18th.

The following letter from Captain Viall, the commander of the *Sylph*, describes their passage as far as Singapore:

Singapore, July 10, 1838.

I arrived here yesterday afternoon after a passage of 21 days. We had very bad weather with much rain and heavy squalls from the Southward for four days after leaving the pilot, our pumps got choked and we were obliged to get all the chain cables on deck to get down in the pump well, but kept a watch night and day to bail it out, till we got the pumps to work. The vessel makes no more water than she has usually done.

After laying becalmed off Penang five days, the *Antonio Pereira* came up with us in a strong squall, hull up, but as soon as we got the breeze we left her astern again and she is now coming in, after the *Sylph* beating her by 24 hours. I think after this they should put the *Sylph* down as *the* first class clipper.

Sailing again on July 18, the two clippers continued their struggle. The *Sylph* arrived in due course after an average passage. but the *Antonio Pereira* was never seen again. When she did not arrive at Macao, H.M. brig *Algerine* was sent in search of her on August 11.

Then the sloop *Larne* (Captain Blake), taking on board Captain Young, *Antonio Pereira's* first commander and a Chinese interpreter, proceeded first to the Paracels, then to Twin Bay and finally to Tienpak, where a white man was reported to have been cast ashore.

The ship *Orestes* reported seeing the topgallant masts of a foundered vessel a little to the Eastward of the Paracels, and it was generally concluded that these belonged to the unfortunate *Antonio Pereira*.

It is probable that the brig's captain risked cutting through the Paracels and got caught on a reef.

"Cowasjee Family" Dismasted in a Whirlwind.

There were other atmospheric disturbances in the Indian and China Seas besides cyclones and typhoons.

I have related how the *Waterwitch* narrowly escaped a willy-waw or whirlwind. The *Cowasjee Family* on her return passage during the summer of 1838 was not so lucky. She left China on

June 15, and Singapore on July 18; on July 31 she was suddenly dismasted when under all sail.

Her captain's letter makes interesting reading:

Cowasjee Family, Aug. 5, 1838.

I beg to acquaint you we are now in Split Bay, with the loss of topmasts on July 31, and most of our sails in a very bad state from a long continuance of bad weather, as also the crew worn out with fatigue. We were in the latitude of 17° N. and longitude 90° E. when we met with this accident, since which we have made our passage with a foresail, mainsail and mizzen and fore topmast staysails from the time we were dismasted to when we got the pilot off False Point, we have not had an observation one day.

I am happy to say we succeeded in saving a great part of the wreck, topsails and yards, topgallant mast and yard, studding sail booms and a great part of the rigging—the main topmast going, carried all the rest with it: there must have been a whirlwind aloft which we did not feel below: the weather breast backstay parted and the jerk it gave might have sprung the topmast, for nothing else that I can think could have caused it, for I was on deck and looking at a large ship passing on the opposite tack at the time the masts fell.

We were rather unfortunate down the China Sea—came in for all the bad weather which the *Witch* escaped—never once able to set a studding sail and from frequent squalls and rain our sails were constantly splitting, and before arriving at Singapore I was obliged to cut up awnings, boat-sails and a fore topgallant sail to enable me to keep a sail to set.

The *Cowasjee* is as lucky or more so than when we left the pilot outward. We pump every two hours, which adds to our troubles.

The unfortunate *Cowasjee Family* reached Calcutta on August 7, 53 days out.

The captain who wrote this letter was not Wallace but a man named Stavers, Wallace's successor.

Passages to Calcutta—Autumn 1838.

Waterwitch was the heroine of the year. *Syed Khan* had one of the worst passages in her life, and was almost overcome by a terrific typhoon in the China Sea. On her arrival at Calcutta a strict survey was held on her, with the result that she had to be practically rebuilt. Her whole framework was opened up and every timber the least bit affected taken out and replaced with new. Though her model was carefully preserved, there was very little of her old self left beyond the oak timbers of the keel and kelson by the time Messrs. Beauchamp & Co. were ready to launch her from their patent slip. I fear she was never quite so fast after her grand repair, for it is a fact that a loose, leaky, working ship sails faster than a tight bound-up one.

Other return passages to Calcutta worthy of note during the late summer and autumn of 1838 were the following:

Clipper	Captain	Left China	Arrived Singapore	Arrived Calcutta	Days. out
Waterwitch ..	Reynell	June 10	July 6	July 23	43
Rob Roy	McKinnon	June 20	July 25	Aug. 10	51
Syed Khan ..	Ovenstone	July 1	Aug. 22	Sept. 11	72
Sylph	Viall	Aug. 20	Sept. 20	Oct. 18	59
Allalevie	Clark	Oct. 9	Oct. 22	Nov. 13	35
Red Rover ..	Wright	Oct. 27	Nov. 11	Dec. 3	37
Ariel	Warden	Nov. 14	Nov. 22	Dec. 16	32
Cowasjee Family	Stavers	Nov. 22	Dec. 3	Dec. 27	35
Waterwitch ..	Reynell	Dec. 4	Dec. 13	Dec. 29	25
Ann	Grey	Nov. 30	Dec. 8	Dec. 29	29

It is very noticeable how the times vary with the seasons of the monsoons, the favourable monsoon making a difference of quite 20 days on the passage.

The New Clippers of 1838.

A number of new clippers appeared in 1838, the most notable of which were the tiny barque *Nymph*, and the brigantine *Poppy*.

Many fast vessels adventured into the opium trade for a season or two and then wandered off into other trades. They were generally ships which were owned by their captains.

Of such was the *Allalevie*; another was the fast barque *Will Watch* (Captain Bristow), and one constantly finds vessels advertised to load opium in the shipping columns of the papers of Calcutta, Bombay and Singapore, which are seldom afterwards mentioned.

Here is such an advertisement, dated August 28, 1838, in the *Englishman*:

> For Singapore and China, under engagement to sail before the holidays, the fast sailing new clipper-built ship *Chelydra* (Captain Davis Small), 350 tons. For freight of opium or passage, having splendid accommodations, apply to Fergusson Brothers & Co.

A clipper was launched at Kidderpore on September 25, 1838, which almost immediately went missing. This was the *Syren*

(Commander James Alves), which was loaded in November by Lyall, Matheson & Co., sailed for China and was never heard of again.

The little *Nymph* which was intended to cruise upon the coast of China and carry the prohibited drug wherever a market could be found—so report said—was launched at Howrah, from Oakes' dock on Saturday, November 3, 1838.

Here is the typical newspaper report:

> There was a largish concourse of spectators: the day was fine: the folks were gaily dressed: the bonnie bark was sprucely decorated with flags innumerable; the guns were fired at the critical moment; three bottles of choice St. Julien were cracked by three ladies on the joyous occasion: the ways were delightfully long, and all went off; in fact, as glibly as did the clipper to commence her career on the glad waters.

The *Nymph* was built in what was considered the incredibly short time of three months, and registered 157 tons,

She had a sunk poop and forecastle, was square-sterned with sham quarter-galleries and a female bust figure-head.

Her commander was Captain John McGowan and her owners were Jonathan Duncan Gow, Edward William Brightman and Nanjee Tacoran.

The *Poppy* was launched from the yard of the Calcutta Docking Company at Kidderpore on Saturday, December 29. It will be noticed that Saturday was the usual day for launching in Calcutta. The following dimensions were given by her builder, Mr. Bremner:

Length overall	108 ft.
Length between perpendiculars ..	97 ft.
Extreme breadth	24 ft.
Height amidships from lower edge of rabbet to lower side of covering board	14 ft. 1 in.
Tonnage (about)	250 tons

The christening ceremony was performed by Mrs. F. Pereira. Her owners being Dent & Co., no expense was spared in her building she was beautifully finished, with the usual lavish gingerbread ornamentation, her stern being decorated with a carved bunch of poppies with buds in the centre and sprigs extending on either side of the counter.

Other clippers of which we read for the first time in 1838 were the schooners *Attaran* and *Governor Doherty*, and the brig *Moulmein.*

The schooner *Time* (Captain Joseph Pybus), also arrived from the Cape in 1838.

Doctor William Jardine retires.

The head of the great firm of Jardine, Matheson & Co., Dr. William Jardine, retired from business and returned to Britain in November, 1838, having amassed a fortune, so it was said, of over a million sterling.

Before leaving Canton he was entertained to dinner in the great banquetting hall of the Honourable Company's Factory by the entire foreign community, including Indians and Parsees. Over eighty people were present and it was one of the last great social events in the old Factory life. He was succeeded by James Matheson as head of the firm. The proverbial saying that sooner or later dire misfortune would overtake the opium trader was followed out in his case. He had only been in Britain a short time before he succumbed to a most excruciating and lingering disease.

"Rob Roy" Strikes a Rock.

During her passage from China in the summer of 1838 the *Rob Roy* struck on an uncharted reef, and was very lucky to get afloat again and make her port. When she was dry docked at Calcutta it was discovered that the whole of her main keel had been wrenched completely off, both fore and aft, so that the long copper bolts, all twisted and bent, were sticking out through her bottom.

If she had not been well and strongly built of the very best materials she would never have survived. As it was she needed a new keel and some caulking of butt ends and that was pretty well all, and six weeks later she was to be seen lying in the stream off the Esplanade in all her delicate beauty of form.

"Sir Herbert Compton's" Rapid Voyage.

After making two or three trips to the Persian Gulf the *Sir Herbert Compton* loaded opium again, and sailing from Bombay on August 22, arrived Lintin on September 24, 33 days out. Sailing again on October 9 she was back in Bombay on November 29, 51 days out—a voyage of 3 months and 7 days. The *Bombay Gazette* in commenting on the clipper's performance, remarked: "This is not the first instance in which this vessel has proved herself a match for any vessel in this quarter of the world regarding her sailing qualities."

Condition of the Opium Trade in Spring of 1839.

The year 1839 opened with the opium trade in a state of fever and hysteria. Prices dropped ten points at a time. Fortunes vanished in a few hours. The markets were overstocked with the drug and every clipper returning from China spread the most disquieting reports of conditions in that part of the world.

On March 6, 1839, Captain Henry Pybus of the *Sir Edward Ryan*, just arrived from Lintin 39 days out, added to the general gloom by his account of printed placards against the opium traffic posted up in all the main streets of Canton. He also brought a copy of Captain Elliot's order of December 18.

About the same time came a notification from Russell & Co. to their East India constituents that they would not longer take consignments of opium.

One of their Parsee customers failed to stop his shipment of the drug, but he managed to post the following letter by the same clipper:

It is now rest in Almighty's pleasure, who I trust will not put all his creatures in ruinous state: the evil result always rest in his power, but the human continually encourages themselt to do as much as they can for their welfare.

Yourselves are too far from me: I cannot form any idea what will result be but I have all my Patna in Almighty care, which cost me 900 rupees per chest. Please exert your utmost exertion as not to part them at ruinous price but retain it until the prosperous result of this trade. I will not draw, I assure, although the scarce cost put me in inconvenient.

Indian letters and chits have always been notorious for their quaint wording. Here is another business letter written to Russell & Co., by Parsees:

Bombay, June 13, 1833.

Dear Sir,—We avail of departure of *Cornywallis* and thanking your favour of April 19, enclosing 2000£ in small pamphlets (note "bills) suitable our order. Now heavy distress falling upon us through Almighty God, taking from bosom of family and friends

LANCELOT DENT

Lent by R. W. Dent, Esq.

WILKINSON DENT

Lent by R. W. Dent, Esq. [*See page* 158

"TIME"

National Maritime Museum, Greenwich

[*See page* 162

our worthy father, who died, after loitering many days, of chronic diarrhoea of guts, much regretted.

"O grave, where is sting! O death, where is victory!" Nevertheless, resigning to will of Providence, and no change in freights since last advised, quoting 10 rupee maund Malwa 8 to 9 dollars Spanish, best Omravutty 80 rupee Candy, inferior goods proportion and by *Sulimany*, sailing few days, we hand bill lading 20 chests best Malwa. Government inspect it.

Hoping same kindness which to beloved parent extended as heretofore, we look in confidence to same continuation.

Faithfully, your heart-broken

HUKITJEE JIMMYBHOY & Co.

To return to the year 1839, the effect of the news from China was so dispiriting that when the newly arrived clipper schooner *Lulworth*, of 86 tons burthen, was offered for sale by public outcry at the Exchange, Calcutta, on March 15, the highest bid was only 12,000 rupees and she was withdrawn.

Shipbuilding was almost at a standstill. Only two vessels of any note were launched in 1839 and only one of these was a regular opium clipper—that was the *Mary Gordon* of 250 tons, new measurement, built in the Mazagon Dockyard, Bombay, for the Parsee, Furdonjee Limjee. She was launched on July 17, 1839, and Captain John Thomson of the H.E.I.C.S. took command of her. Five days before this, one of the finest country craft ever built was launched from the Kidderpore Dock. This was the *Rustomjee Cowasjee*, of 764 tons, which, like the *Sylph* and *Cowasjee Family*, had been specially designed for her owner by Sir Robert Seppings. *Rustomjee Cowasjee* had the following dimensions:

Length between perpendiculars ..	131 ft. 6 ins.
Extreme breadth	32 ft. 6 ins.
Depth of hold	21 ft. 0 ins.
Height between decks	6 ft. 0 ins.
Light draught of water	12 ft. 0 ins.

Though she occasionally carried opium, we find the *Rustomjee Cowasjee* acting as a hired transport in the opium war.

With so many rumours flying about, many of the captains decided to sail no further than Singapore until the news was more favourable. The *Sylph* was offered to convey the mails to the *Red Sea* in rivalry with the steam frigate *Semiramis* of the E.I. Marine; but this job eventually fell to her great rival *Waterwitch*.

L

When *Rob Roy* reached Calcutta on June 24, having left Canton waters on May 11, the news was still more serious, for she brought the account of Commissioner Lin's doings and the destruction of the opium, but this must be reserved for another chapter. At any rate, the boom of the last few years was definitely over.

Captain R. B. Forbes returns to China.

With the clouds gathering fast, Captain R. B. Forbes determined to return to China. Chartering the barque *Mary Chilton* (Captain George Drew), he sailed in June, 1838, with several large credits from Boston merchants, the promise of several consignments of ships and his brother's power of attorney, the latter then being a partner in Russell & Co. Besides this he took letters from Mr. Cushing to all his Chinese friends.

Captain Forbes' own account of the incidents of the passage give one a good idea of the dangers of even the North Atlantic from the pirate and picaroon. In a privately printed little book, he wrote as follows:

One day, just as we were expecting the N.E. trades, a schooner was seen standing within about 5 miles under our lee.

She was a rakish craft, and we found that she was gradually crawling up into our wake, and I felt very suspicious in regard to her: by and by, when in our wake, she kept directly after us. I advised Captain Drew to prepare the only two guns we had and to make some "quakers" (dummy guns) so as to show a disposition to fight if necessary.

When the schooner was about 3 miles astern we took a breeze from the East, and I suggested setting our port studding sails and keeping off a point or two.

We got our two 6-pounders up on the poop, and not only mustered all hands there but made some effigies. The schooner seeing all this, hauled sharp on the wind and before night was nearly out of sight. I doubt not she was a slaver and would have given us trouble. . . . . .

The captain had never been East of the Cape and was quite green as to the China Seas, so that my local knowledge came into play.

When we arrived on the coast of China one fine moonlight night early in October, a Chinese pilot hove in sight. I felt some curiosity to hear what would pass between him and Captain Drew, and requested the latter to heave to, and when the pilot came on board to come near my window in the poop-cabin. This was done, when the following dialogue took place:—

Pilot—"Missee Captain, you must take in that stun-sail: plenty lock (rock) here: stlong tide.

Captain—"How much do you want to take my ship to Hongkong?"

Pilot—"Olo flen (friend), maskee hundled dollah; welly cheap!"

Captain—"Oh no! I cannot pay so much. Fine night, ship all right."

By this time I had become very impatient and went out on deck and crept up close to the old pilot, whom I recognised as an old friend. He turned round and taking a good look at me exclaimed:

"Hi-yah! Olo Fox! Ten dollah can do, Missee Captain."

And so we went in without finding any of the dangers spoken of and came to an anchor about 8 p.m.

Captain Forbes arrived just in time to play a leading part in the important events of the next few years, which put a finish with the sword to the old Canton life.

The Canton Regatta Club.

There was one very English institution at Canton in the old days which certainly deserves a mention, and that was the Canton Regatta Club, started in 1837 by the younger members of the European community in Canton.

At the Macao Passage end of Honam there was a very clever old Chinese shipwright, who went by the name of Mo-Pin, *i.e.* "no pig-tail," because he was absolutely bald. Besides building a number of wherries and gigs, he built several small yachts. The first of these were the *Mouse* for James P. Sturges; the *Ferret* for W. C. Hunter, and the *Rat* for Edward Elmslie, secretary to the British Consulate. These were tiny fore-and-aft schooners, only 26 ft. long.

One of his finest efforts was the 50-ton schooner *Atalanta*, built on the lines of a New York pilot boat for Paul S. Forbes, Black Ben's brother.

At first Houqua was very alarmed by this "dreadful innovation." He seemed to think that boat racing must lead to fighting.

He sent for young Hunter, one of the chief promoters of the club, and impressed on him the words: "Mus take care! Mus take care!"

At the first regatta, a flower-boat was hired for a committee boat, on which tiffin was prepared by the cook of the Suy Hong, the table being ornamented by the cups, which had been specially made by Cutshing of Old China Street.

Captain Scott, of the *Sir Charles Forbes*, surrounded by all the masters of the ships at Whampoa and Lintin, acted as umpire. The scene must have been a gay one. Ship-boats manned by bluejackets or Lascars in clean whites kept the course. Flags flew from every vantage point. The crowd of tanka boats, sampans, etc., gave the Pearl River the appearance of the Thames at Henley.

The first race was between Warren Delano's six-oared gig, *The-not-so-Green*, and an English boat, manned curiously enough from the American Hong.

The sailing races took place shortly afterwards in the Macao Passage round a mark-boat off the Tee-to-tum Fort. The best matched were the *Rat*, the *Mouse* and the *Ferret* when the *Ferret* won. She won again in November, 1838, with R. B. Forbes at the helm.

The bigger yachts raced in Macao Roads. A famous match was sailed in a northerly gale over a 35-mile course by Forbes' *Atalanta* and the 34-ton cutter *Gipsy* belonging to John Dent.

The speeds of the two yachts were recorded as *Atalanta* $9\frac{3}{4}$ miles an hour, *Gipsy* $8\frac{1}{10}$.

The second race in Macao Roads ended in tragedy; though ten were entered only four yachts started in a very rough sea and hard wind. These were Dent's *Gipsy*; Jardine's *Thistle*, of 33 tons; Campbell's *Dream* of 31; and Livingstone's *Dragon* of 30. The cutter *Fairy* of only 18 tons started also, but capsized and sank before she had gone far. Captain Roper, her owner, clung to the mast till rescued, but his crew, consisting of two Lascars and Captain Haddock of the ship *Glenlyon*, were drowned.

W. C. Hunter sailed the *Gipsy* and won the cup by 9 minutes 10 seconds, covering a triangular course of $25\frac{1}{2}$ miles in four hours.

This was the end of the Canton Regatta Club, the war broke it up, and when it started again after the war Hongkong was its headquarters.

CHAPTER V.

THE OPIUM WAR.

Now cities gather their goods and gold
With ships on every sea,
And the Guilds of Craft wax fat and proud
And every hind is free;
And no man bears a weaponed belt
Save he whose trade is war,
Yet—weaponless men are thralls at heart
As it was in the days of yore.

THE first war which took place between Great Britain and the Celestial Empire has generally been called the Opium war: but if the opium traffic was the main cause of contention, it was far from being the only one.

To begin with, so great was the ignorance of the Emperor and his mandarins regarding the world outside China, that their invariable custom was to treat all foreigners with contempt, to ignore despatches and heap insults upon all emissaries. The British agents in China, with knowledge of the cause, showed the greatest tact and forbearance, but they were continually rebuked for a lack of backbone by the incensed Lord Palmerston. He could not visualise the condition of affairs in Pekin and Canton any more than the Taon-Kwang, the Son of Heaven, could appreciate the power and might of the red-headed devils.

Even the issues on the spot were difficult enough to unravel. Whilst the very mandarins, who were employed to suppress the opium smuggling, owed their living solely to their powers of "squeeze-pigeon," compromise and cumsha, Captain Elliot, the British Superintendent of Trade, who was by no means in favour of the illegal traffic, was compelled by his position to do his best to uphold and protect his countrymen who dealt in the drug.

Whilst opium "was by far the safest trade in China, because you got your money before you gave your order" (William Jardine, Parliamentary Papers, 1840) it also caused the most bloodshed.

Private junks contended with mandarin boats for the "foreign mud" in the holds of the clippers and the smug boats.

Whilst missionaries raved at Exeter Hall against the opium traffic, the Celestial Court were more seriously alarmed by the distribution of religious tracts through Mongolian territory than by the dissemination of the drug.

At the same time the Emperor's finance ministers complained "that black dirt was always coming in and the pure silver always going out." And this loss of specie was probably the deciding factor which induced the Emperor to appoint the implacable Commissioner Lin, with full powers to put an absolute stop to the opium trade.

Commissioner Lin.

Though the opium merchants believed that Commissioner Lin would prove as amenable as the Hoppo as long as he was able to feather his own nest and keep the illicit trade hidden from the public eye, the Chinese opium smugglers were seriously alarmed, for the reputation of Lin as an honest administrator was well known throughout the Flowery Land. Born and bred in a maritime province, he was a man who had earned a high place in the imperial favour through being not only a great scholar and a true patriot, but a ruler who could be depended upon to overcome all opposition. He was, however, quite ignorant of the world outside China and had the usual Chinaman's contempt for the foreigner.

When he came to Canton Commissioner Lin was a man of about 55 years of age, short and rather stout, with a keen dark eye looking out of a smooth, full, round face, which except for a slender black beard was hairless. Though bland like all Chinaman and at times vivacious with a clear authoritative voice, his general mien was thoughtful and he seldom smiled.

Captain Elliot, His Majesty's Superintendent of Trade.

The man who had to deal with Lin as the representative of foreign trade happened to be rather an unusual type of British naval officer.

The winding up of the great Company's affairs in China and the departure of its staff had left a blank that it was found very difficult to fill.

By years of service in the East, the Chief and members of the Company's Select Committee knew China and the Chinaman and made few mistakes in dealing with the wily Celestial; but Lord Napier who was appointed Chief Superintendent of British Trade in China—a post meant to be even of greater dignity than that of the Taipan of the Honourable Company—was quite ignorant of the people with whom he had to deal and actually arrived at the Canton Factories in 1834 without having procured a permit—the passport of those days.

His difficulties proved well nigh insuperable from the start, and when he retired to Macao, chagrined and disgusted, he caught a fever of which he died on October 11.

He was succeeded by Mr. Davis, late Chief of the East India Company. But Davis had already had a long spell of the East and he sailed for England on January 21, 1835. He was succeeded by Sir George Best Robinson, with Mr. Astell and Captain Charles Elliot, R.N., as second and third superintendents.

Sir G. B. Robinson was much criticised for abandoning his official residence at Macao and living aboard a cutter yacht at Lintin. He argued that it was cooler and healthier for himself and staff being afloat, more convenient for the shipping and moreover, being on a British ship, he was on British territory. As against this his detractors complained that he, the representative of law and order, was at anchor in the midst of a swarm of opium smugglers. However, Robinson did not reign for long and on December 14, 1836, he was succeeded by Captain Charles Elliot.

Like all naval officers, Elliot had had experience both of administration and diplomacy in the course of his service afloat.

Entering the Navy as a first-class volunteer on March 26, 1815, his first ship was the *Leviathan* (74), on the Mediterranean station. He then had four years in the East in the *Minden* (74). This was followed by a spell on the Channel station in the *Starling* cutter and *Queen Charlotte*, flagship at Portsmouth.

His next service was slave catching on the coast of Africa in the *Iphigenia* (42), bearing the broad pendant of Sir Robert Mends. Here he gained his lieutenant's promotion, continuing on that deadly coast in the flagship and the *Myrmidon* (20), till March, 1823.

He was next appointed to the *Hussar* (46), on the Jamaica station and here in 1825 he gained his first command, going pirate and slave hunting amongst the Bahama Cays in the tiny schooners *Union* and *Renegade*, as a lieut.-commander. These little vessels usually cruised in company, and had a very exciting time—their commands being much sought after. His next command after a short time in a Port Royal hospital ship was one of the notorious coffin brigs, the *Bustard* (10 guns), and from her he went to the fine 18-gun brig-sloop *Harlequin*.

He was promoted captain on August 28, 1828, and after a spell on half pay found himself out in China acting as a kind of consul in about as difficult a set of circumstances as could well be imagined.

At this date it was only rarely that a British man-of-war showed herself on the Chinese coast, and thus Captain Elliot seldom had any backing behind him. If he issued directions to his own countrymen he had no means of enforcing them; many of the shipmasters engaged in the illegal opium trade were owners or part owners of their commands, and neither they nor the powerful British and Parsee opium merchants were too amenable to the discipline of officialdom; indeed Captain Elliot himself acknowledged that he had no authority "except over the lawful trade, his Government not being acquainted with any other."

His feelings were undoubtedly against the opium traffic in spite of the fact that many of the British opium dealers were his personal friends. As far back as April, 1838, he wrote to Lord Palmerston saying that the English smugglers were "vastly increased" and that "frequent conflicts with firearms" were taking place. But he gained no help from the British Government. Despatch after despatch remained unanswered. At last came the following announcement from Lord Palmerston "that Her Majesty's Government could not interfere for the purpose of enabling British subjects to violate the laws of the country to which they trade."

Captain Elliot published this mild reply in the *Canton Register*, only to find that his friends, the merchants, were more annoyed with him than ever, "being horrified that he should have committed his Government to a knowledge of the opium trade."

Captain Elliot orders the British Opium Ships outside the Bocca Tigris.

On December 28, 1838, Captain Elliot, by now thoroughly aroused by the gathering clouds, issued the following notice:

I, Charles Elliot, Chief Superintendent of the Trade of British Subjects in China, moved by urgent considerations immediately affecting the safety of the lives and property of all Her Majesty's subjects engaged in trade at Canton, do hereby formally give notice and require that all British owned schooners, cutters and otherwise rigged small craft, either habitually or occasionally engaged in the illicit opium traffic within the Bocca Tigris, should proceed forth of the same within the space of 3 days from the date of these presents and not return within the said Bocca Tigris, being engaged in said illicit opium traffic.

And I, the said Chief Superintendent, do further give notice and warn all Her Majesty's subjects engaged in the aforesaid illicit opium traffic within the Bocca Tigris, in such schooners, cutters and otherwise rigged small craft, that if any native of the Chinese Empire shall come by his or her death by any wound feloniously inflicted by any British subject or subjects, any such British subject or subjects being convicted thereof, are liable to capital punishment as if the crime had been committed within the jurisdiction of Her Majesty's Court at Westminster.

And I, the said Chief Superintendent, do further give notice and warn all British subjects, being owners of such schooners, cutters or otherwise rigged small craft engaged in the same illicit opium traffic within the Bocca Tigris, that Her Majesty's Government will in no way interfere if the Chinese Government shall think fit to seize and confiscate the same.

And I, the said Chief Superintendent, do further give notice and warn all British subjects employed in the said schooners, cutters or otherwise rigged small craft engaged in the illicit traffic in opium within the Bocca Tigris, that the forcible resisting of the officers of the Chinese Government in the duty of searching or seizing is a lawless act and that they are liable to consequences and penalties in the same manner as if the aforesaid forcible resistance were opposed to the officers of their own or any other Government in their own or in any foreign country. Given under my hand and seal of office at Canton this eighteenth day of December in the year of our Lord 1838.

Charles Elliot.

At the same time a long warning on the evils of opium smoking and the opium traffic was posted up on printed placards in the streets of Canton, which from its scholarly phrasing was judged to be the composition of Commissioner Lin himself.

This last thoroughly roused the local mandarins to action, and they began taking active steps against the Chinese opium dealers.

A Riot in the Square of the Factories.

In December, 1838, a Chinaman, said to be an opium smuggler was actually executed in the Square of the Factories. This was supposed to make the foreigners "lose face," and they determined to try to stop any future act of justice in front of the Factories. But a second attempt to strangle an opium dealer was made on January 26, 1839. This strangling needs some explaining, for the victim is first of all lashed to a wooden cross, several turns being taken round his neck, and a 5 ft. pole, arrow shaped, passed through the bights and then twisted until the wretched man is dead. The cross had already been set up when the occupants of the Factories realised what was about to take place, through the extraordinary hubbub going on. They immediately mustered all hands, from 70 to 80 all told, and proceeded out into the Square and remonstrated with the mandarin in charge.

He declared that he had orders to carry out the execution in the square which was part of His Celestial Majesty's Empire. W. C. Hunter, of Russell & Co., the best Chinese scholar present, explained that the Square had been leased to the foreign traders as a recreation ground and they refused to allow it to be used for a public execution. So far each side was polite. The prisoner with a chain about his neck and held by too gaolers grinned idiotically, being under the influence of the fatal drug, which was being offered to him in pipe after pipe by the mandarin's servants.

The latter's attendants, chair-bearers and a few soldiers looked on, quietly smiling. The crowd stood round wondering.

All of a sudden things began to happen. The cross was seized and broken in pieces, the canopy over the mandarin torn down, his table with its teapot and cups capsized, and blows began to reign upon the heads and shoulders of the executioners.

That morning a boat's crew from the old East India ship

Orwell (Captain Tommy Larkins), had come up from Macao, and whilst wandering about they stumbled across the disputants and promptly took a hand on the side of their countrymen.

The latter had to intervene to save the mandarin from some rough handling. The gaolers rushed away with their prisoner, and the tars, highly delighted with what they considered "a prime lark," soon found that they had started a riot.

The Chinese guards by the American Factory vainly tried to clear the Square, which soon was filled with a mob of 10,000 people, composed of the worst elements in Canton. This rabble seemed bent on wiping out the foreign devils. Tearing down the heavy posts of the Factory enclosures, they used them as battering rams against the gate of No. 2 Suy-Hong, occupied by Russell & Co., and screeching like fiends hurled themselves against the shuttered premises.

The inmates rolled casks of coal up against the doors, and scattered broken bottles on the steps, to keep off the bare-footed mob. In the Imperial Factory Captain St. Croix of the *Alexander Baring* (Indiaman), headed another party of Europeans, armed with any weapons they could get hold of from fowling pieces to scimitars. Some hotheads actually proposed sallying out on the screaming mob, but wiser counsels prevailed, and about 5 o'clock the Americans, Hunter and G. Nye, offered to try to get word to Houqua.

All the lanes round the Factories were blocked with howling Chinamen, but the two plucky men climbing on to the roof of No. 4 Suy-Hong managed to get across to a shop in Hog Lane, from where they were able to reach Houqua's Hong by means of "Thirteen Factory Street." Houqua at once sent off to the Kwang-Chou-foo or chief magistrate of the city; and at 6·30 a clanging gong announced the approach of mandarins and soldiers with whips. The rioters at once fled in a panic, many flinging themselves into the river, where the boatmen, in real Chinese fashion, calmly allowed them to drown.

The mandarins, seating themselves on chairs brought out from the Factories, calmly camped down in the Square for the night; lanterns were lighted, the doors of the Hongs were unbarred and the barricades removed; finally the hourly beating of the watch gongs so reassured the Europeans that they retired to bed, after thanking their rescuers.

Meanwhile the condemned man, completely drugged by the many pipes he had bribed his gaolers to give him, was strangled with all due ceremony on the public execution ground.

Not long after this episode, on February 26 to be exact, the mandarins did succeed in executing a Chinese opium smuggler in the Square. They chose an hour in the afternoon when most of the Europeans were away boating or taking a walk. The victim was tied up to the cross, strangled, and the body taken away up Old China Street before the rowers landed from their boats.

This insult to the foreign community, for such it was meant to be, was replied to by the lowering of the national flags in front of the Factories, and these were not re-hoisted until March 22, 1842.

Commissioner Lin arrives.

Canton remained outwardly quiet but inwardly perturbed until the arrival of the imperial envoy. All this time Captain Elliot at Macao was under the impression that the opium trade was finished with in the Canton River, and that henceforth the Indian opium would have to be disposed of at Singapore and Manilla. But the storm instead of subsiding was just about to break.

Commissioner Lin staged his own arrival at Canton, with the Viceroy, and all the civil and military officers in his train, with a great deal of prearranged pomp and ceremony. He arrived by water in a large very ornate black and gold imperial pulling-boat at 8·30 on the morning of Sunday, March 10, 1839.

This dragon led a procession of other official boats of the chop-boat description. Each boat had the rank of its occupants painted on its sides in gold letters, and flew a flag in its stern. Their crews were all clad in new uniforms of red trimmed with white, and wore cone-shaped hats of rattan. His Excellency Lin, the Kin-Chae, who, it was said, had once worked as a day labourer in his father's porcelain factory, held himself with great dignity, looking sternly to the front, and seated in solitary state, his nearest attendants, some red and blue button mandarins, taking care to keep their distance.

The whole city gathered on the banks of the river to greet him, every door and window being blocked with people, but an uncanny silence prevailed, not a single gong beat, not a voice was raised, even the yulos of the tanka women were quiet, for every boat except those in the imperial procession was hauled in to the shore. The walls of the Dutch Folly Fort to the Eastward and of the Red Fort opposite the Factories were lined with soldiers in new rainbow-hued uniforms. All the Europeans thought it wise to remain within the Factories with the exception of three Americans, who watched Lin's arrival from the deck of a small schooner lying off the Factories.

On March 17 the Hong merchants, linguists and compradores obeyed a summons to an audience. They went in fear and trembling but Lin's object was to get the names of the foreign opium dealers.

On the next day the Hong merchants were again summoned and thoroughly frightened, being told that their heads would pay for it if the opium trade was not immediately stopped.

"No have see so fashion before," whimpered one of them, and they spent most of the following night deliberating in the "Consoo."

That same day Commissioner Lin, as foreigners always called him, issued a long edict ordering all opium to be surrendered under penalty of death.

The next morning the chief opium merchants, Messrs. Matheson, Green, Dent, Daniell, Whetmoor and the Parsee, Dadabhoy Rustomjee, met the Hong merchants at the Consoo House, to discuss what should be done. It was evident that some of the opium must be given up. It was reckoned that there were 15,000 chests aboard the Lintin receiving ships, 5000 chests at the stations up the coast, worth altogether over 12 million dollars.

Two days later, on the night of March 21, the opium merchants again met the Co-hong in the Danish Factory, and this time it was decided to offer Lin 1034 chests of opium valued at 725,000 dollars. This offer was disdainfully refused.

The Siege of the Factories.

The Factories were by this time in a state of siege. The

gates opening out into Thirteen Factory Street were bricked up by Lin's orders, and soldiers were to be seen at all points; besides which all communication with the shipping at Whampoa was cut off by a cordon of mandarin boats.

Commissioner Lin gave further evidence of his earnestness in further proclamations and decrees against the opium traffic. He even addressed a flowery pompous remonstrance to the Queen of Britain.

Another effort of his was to obtain a hostage. Lancelot Dent was asked to meet the imperial envoy within the city; but his companions in distress persuaded him not to run this risk and he refused to trust himself to Lin's mercies. At this the latter made a fresh move.

On March 23 every Chinaman employed by the Factories, from compradores to cooks, was ordered to leave at once or suffer death. The position of the Europeans in Canton was now extremely serious—they were prisoners in their own quarters with no servants, no food and no fuel. At the same time the guard over them was strengthened. A strong guard was mounted in the Square. Thirteen Factory Street was full of soldiers and a triple cordon of boats stretched from the Creek to the Danish Factory.

On March 24 the brave Charles Elliot flung himself into the breach alongside his countrymen. Hearing rumours of Lin's high-handed proceedings at Macao, he raced up in the launch of H.M.S. *Larne*, burst through the cordon of boats, stepped ashore at the Company's landing and at once ordered the Union Jack to be hoisted at the old Company's flagstaff. His arrival put heart into the besieged. That night there was a full moon in a cloudless sky, but instead of pacing the Square, cheroot in mouth, the inmates of the Factories attacked their menial duties in a truly light-hearted manner.

Captain R. B. Forbes in his autobiography records how they carried on in the Suy-Hong.

In this Hong lived Mr. P. W. Snow, the American Consul, and the members and staff of Russell & Co.

"I was called upon to organise the house for work," wrote Forbes. Lots were drawn to settle who should cook and who play the part of waiters, chambermen, etc. It fell to me to be chief cook. The first thing to be done was to clean out the kitchen, into which no white man had before entered; all hands went at it, and soon made things fit for my new work. My first effort was fried ham and eggs; when the dish came to table it was difficult to distinguish between eggs and ham; all bore the same colour and partook of the consistency of dirty shoe-leather.

It was immediately voted to depose me and to put Warren Delano in my place, and I assumed his duties, which were to look after the glass and silver: to this end I put upon the sideboard a piece of sheeting, and when I required towels I had only to tear off a strip, wipe my utensils and throw the strip into a corner.

W. C. Hunter was lamp trimmer and all had something to do. The live-stock was driven into the rear, and barricaded—pigs, sheep and fowls all mixed up together and making day and night hideous with their smells and noises. Mr. John C. Green, the chief, being much engaged as chairman of the Chamber of Commerce, was exempted from ordinary household duties. Bathing being important, and no coolies at hand to carry water to the upper rooms, we rigged whips and attempted to hoist up the big pails into the verandas: but this proved a failure, the ropes twisted up, and the pails remained suspended in mid air.

Hunter tells of other cooks—of how Green boiled rice till it was glue and how Low boiled eggs till they resembled grape shot.

During the day all sorts of devices were invented to pass the time. Terriers, being almost as abundant as rats, the younger men got up regular rat hunts, which they alternated with foot-races and cricket matches. The sailors—there happened to be several British boats' crews caught in the Factories—when not engaged in menial work like the Americans, took part in every kind of sport, even to climbing the flagstaffs for prizes.

The elders were content with a quarter-deck walk in the Square every day, when they heaped abuse on the heads of His Celestial Majesty Taou-Kwang and his energetic envoy, Lin; speculated as to how the season's tea was to be shipped home; bemoaned the money they looked like losing in opium; and discussed methods of making soup and cleaning silver.

The imprisoned community would undoubtedly have been in danger of starvation but for the good offices of the Hong merchants who, by astute bribery, arranged so that their own house coolies were allowed to keep watch at the gates of the Factories instead of Manchu soldiers; and during the night these coolies managed to pass in provisions and firewood.

Commissioner Lin's next move was to put pressure on the

Co-hong. A day or two after Captain Elliot's arrival, Houqua and Mowqua appeared in the Square with long faces and chains round their necks, and an intimation that their necks were to be forfeit if the opium was not given up, and this broke down all further resistance.

The Delivery and Destruction of the Opium.

On March 27 Captain Elliot demanded all British opium in Canton waters, promising its owners that the British Government would refund their loss. After considerable parley the owners consented to deliver it to the representative of the British Superintendent of Trade, and the Kinchae agreed to accept the amount offered.

Accordingly opium to the amount of 20,283¼ chests, and to the value of two millions sterling, was accounted for chest by chest, mark by mark. The lists from each firm were checked, certificates presented and official receipts issued.

The contribution of the two chief firms, Jardine, Matheson & Co. and Dent & Co., was about 7000 chests each; the Parsee Dadabhoy Rustomjee relinquished 1000 chests, and Russell & Co. handed over 1500 chests belonging to English customers, for whom they acted as agents.

On April 3 Alexander Johnson, the second British Superintendent of Trade, with an escort of mandarins and Hong merchants, was sent down the river with full authority from the merchants to receive the opium at Chuenpee near the Bocca Tigris.

The ships, both receiving ships and clippers, received orders to proceed forthwith to the rendezvous at Chuenpee. These ships were the *Hercules, Austin, Jane, Ariel, Mithras, Mermaid, Ruparell* and *Lady Grant.*

The schooner *Attaran* (Captain Jackson), with 130 chests on board, was wrecked near Nanpang, a few miles S.W. of Macao on January 3, or she would have been included in the list.

There was one other opium clipper on the station at the time—the schooner *Time,* with 20 chests on board had only just arrived—and as soon as he heard of the confiscation Captain Pybus slipped quietly away.

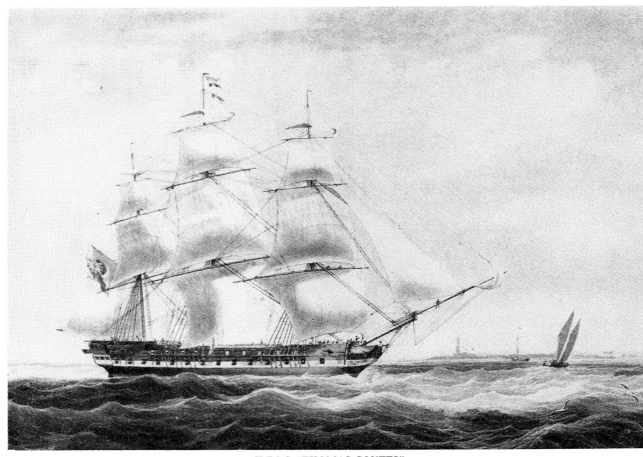

H.E.I.C. "THOMAS COUTTS"

National Maritime Museum, Greenwich

[*See page* 172

"HELLAS"

National Maritime Museum, Greenwich

[*See page* 180

At first Lin offered the whole amount of the opium handed over to the Emperor, but the latter wisely ordered it to be destroyed on the spot.

On April 5 the cautious Lin required that all owners of the relinquished opium should enter into a bond "that they would not again introduce opium into the inner land, and that if such be done the vessel and cargo be confiscated to the use of the Government, and the parties offending should suffer death at the hands of a Celestial Court."

It is not known how many merchants signed this bond. At any rate Lancelot Dent did so and as a consequence retired from his firm. The American firm of S. Wetmore & Co. also gave up dealing in opium.

On April 10 Commissioner Lin and the Governor of Canton proceeded to the Bogue to witness the destruction of the opium in person. But hardly had the imperial envoy arrived there than rumours got about that fresh arrivals were attempting to resume the opium traffic. Captain Elliot at once published a strong remonstrance, urging that any such action might endanger the lives of the people imprisoned at Canton.

It took some time before all the opium was surrendered. The *Hercules*, *Austen*, *Jane* and *Ariel* had all arrived at Chuenpee by April 12, but *Mithras*, *Mermaid*, *Lady Grant*, and *Ruparell* took several days delivering their opium.

The destruction of the surrendered opium was most carefully carried out; about 500 workmen being employed and between 60 and 80 inspectors and overseers. The operation took place within a strong palisade, at the gates of which stood sentinels who would allow no one to enter without a signed pass. Everyone going out of the enclosure was also carefully examined. Within the palisade were several small enclosures where the opium was stored by special officers as soon as it had been unpacked from the chests and its marks verified and tallied.

On the West side three large trenches were dug, 150 ft. long by 75 ft. wide and about 7 ft. deep, flagged with stones and lined with heavy timbers. Water was run into each trench to the depth of 2 ft. The opium balls were brought to the trenches in baskets, the coolies then broke them up by stamping them under foot on the planking and then kicking the remains into the water.

Other coolies were employed stirring up the mess in trenches by means of hoes; a third gang busied itself spreading salt and lime over the surface of each trench. As soon as the opium was sufficiently decomposed, it was drawn off through a narrow sluice and a screen, and so found its way into the creek.

The operation which began on May 3 was not completed until the 23rd, about 1000 chests being worked off each day. Commissioner Lin looked on with a bland face of satisfaction. Once only was he seen to smile, and twice a frown crossed his brow when he listened to accounts of Britain's naval power.

Captain Joseph Pybus Hoodwinks the Opium Brokers.

As soon as it became known that the destruction of the year's opium crop was a fact, the price of opium inside the city of Canton rose to 3000 dollars a chest, whilst along the coast it was fetching 1600 dollars. Yet at this very time holders in Singapore were glad to get rid of the drug at between 150 and 250 dollars a chest.

Meanwhile the schooner *Time* was beating down the China Sea against the S.W. monsoon. For six weeks Captain Pybus never left the deck, sleeping in a "dog's house" without taking off his clothes; and he drove his little schooner so hard that she became badly strained, spurting the water through her seams at every plunge.

However he duly reached Singapore, where he landed his twenty chests of opium in the most ostentatious manner at a time when the Bund was crowded with Moormen, Jews, Parsees and Chinese, opium holders or brokers to a man.

This was the first news to reach Singapore of the happenings at Canton and Chuenpee, for at that date it was only the opium clippers that thrashed their way South against the monsoon, and all the other opium ships in Canton waters were busy delivering their cargoes to the destroyers.

Pybus gave out that he was bound for Calcutta, and quietly up-anchored and slipped away as soon as he had reprovisioned. But he left orders with his agent to buy what opium he could without attracting attention. This was not difficult. The "foreign mud" was dirt cheap, many holders being unable to hold any longer, and the agent managed to secure 700 chests at an average of 250 dollars a chest.

Meanwhile the *Time* disappeared into the blue. Captain Henry Pybus, the son of her commander, is under the impression that she lurked about the Java Sea for a while. The shipping column in the Calcutta *Englishman* states that she arrived in the Hooghly from Mauritius on June 26, 1839, and she was advertised to sail from Calcutta for China on July 3. This does not leave much time for repairs.

After her beat against the monsoon she was leaking like a basket, and Captain Pybus not only gave her a coat of chunam, but had her sheathed all over with 1-inch teak planking. She then sailed for China, and without stopping at Lintin or Macao, carried on up the East Coast where Captain Pybus disposed of his cargo at an average of 2500 dollars a chest.

So much for enterprise and business acumen!

The Embargo at Canton.

As soon as the opium was destroyed, the siege of the Factories was raised, the cordon of boats removed and foreigners given permission to leave the city—this, in the case of British subjects was made compulsory, and Captain Elliot, before departing himself on May 22, was obliged to issue a notice to this effect.

As merchants and brokers wished to know just where they stood and what was the attitude of the British Government, a deputation, consisting of G. T. Braine, partner in Dent & Co. (chairman), Joseph Jardine, partner in Jardine, Matheson & Co., W. Thompson, Wilkinson Dent, W. F. Gray, Dadabhoy Rustomjee, C. B. Adam and Crawford Kerr of Lindsay & Co. waited upon the Superintendent of Trade.

Captain Elliot was as charming and courteous as usual, but as he had not yet had any directions from the home Government he could tell them very little that they did not know already; they were however, quite satisfied with the way he had handled a peculiarly difficult situation, and when he left Canton all the most prominent merchants attended him to the steps as a mark of respect.

By the end of May all the Hongs and Factories were empty with the exception of the American.

John C. Green, the head of Russell & Co., embarked for home at the beginning of June in the *Panama* (Captain Benjamin), leaving the redoubtable Captain R. B. Forbes as chief partner in his place. Forbes, besides being a most capable shipmaster, was an extremely shrewd business man. When Elliot begged him to follow the example of the British and other nationalities and close down in Canton, he replied:

"I have not come to China for health or pleasure and I shall remain at my post as long as I can sell a yard of goods or buy a pound of tea." And he added: "We Yankees have no Queen to guarantee our losses," whereupon Elliot asked him if he was willing to do business with a chain round his neck. His reply was characteristic. He declared that he believed the chain was an imaginary one; at any rate he would only retreat step by step buying and selling as long as there was any trade. However he sent his most important books and papers down to Macao in charge of W. C. Hunter.

No less than a dozen large chop-boats left Canton for Macao on May 29; containing the staffs of Jardine Matheson, Dent, John Shillaber, Dadabhoy Rustomjee, Lindsay, and others, and leaving Captain Forbes and 24 other Americans, the sole representatives of the Fan Kwae in Canton.

On the same day H.M. sloop *Larne* put to sea, thus leaving Elliot without any force behind him with the exception of the well-armed opium clippers. With the Canton River forbidden to British hulls, the season's export of tea and silk to Great Britain was in jeopardy. It was Forbes who saved the situation, for, one after the other, the British firms were obliged to come to him and he soon found himself so busy that he was obliged to make his headquarters aboard a British ship, which had been consigned to his firm, called the *Heroine*; this vessel was lying amongst the large fleet of held up ships at Kowloong.

Owing to the continued hostility of the Chinese Commissioner it was not long before this fleet was compelled to retire to the Lintin Anchorage, and even further, so that by the beginning of August the roads opposite the almost unknown island of Hongkong were for the first time used by the British and foreign shipping.

All this summer, Forbes and his firm carried the Canton trade on their shoulders. Their old receiving ship, the *Lintin*, voyaged up and down the river, with her upper spars down, cotton or tea piled up to the leading blocks, at 5 to 7 dollars a bale, and her holds crammed.

Large Chinese pulling boats assisted her over the 90-mile trip, and she drifted down under bare poles.

The *Akbar*, under the renowned Yankee skipper, Philip Dumaresq, was another vessel doing useful work in this emergency. She brought out a large cargo of tea, raced round to Calcutta with it, ran back to Whampoa with 5000 bales of cotton and again came out again full of tea.

Even the little opium clipper brigantine *Rose* went up the river with her hold full of East India goods, cotton piled on her deck three tiers deep, and casks and her spare spars lashed alongside to prevent her capsizing.

Every ship that could be got hold of was seized upon in this race to get the cotton goods in and the tea and silk out of Canton.

One day a ship flying American colours ran into the Hongkong fleet and anchored far out. Let me here quote Forbes again: "I sent my aid, Captain Gilman, to reconnoitre and to report: he returned and reported the *Navigator* (Captain Bridges), belonging to the Neals of Salem, full of betelnut and rattans. The captain said he was as full as a tick, and not over stiff, and could not make room for anything. I jumped into a 'fast-boat' and went to see for myself. I found the lower hold full of betelnut, the between decks nearly full of rattans. I told the captain that rattans did not count under the present circumstances: that he must pile them on deck, up to the cat-harpins if necessary, and fill up the between decks with cotton. He seemed to consider me out of my mind; but when he came to learn that 7 dollars a bale could be had, and to realise that by getting down all his upper sticks, he would not turn over, he came to believe I was sane, and I think took in six or seven hundred bales."

Captain Forbes, with the loyal help of Messrs. W. Delano, A. A. Low, Edward King and W. C. Hunter, thus saved the tea market. The tea was brought down the river in the *Lintin* and other vessels under the American flag, piled up on the deck, under mat-houses 8 or 10 ft. high, whence it was transferred to the waiting British tea ships.

"Ariel" and "Waterwitch" carry the Mails.

Meanwhile the clipper barques *Ariel* and *Waterwitch* were taken up by the Indian Government to carry the news of these momentous happenings to the Red Sea; this being the quickest way of getting it home.

The *Ariel*, with Captain Elliot's despatches on board, sailed from Macao on May 30, 1839. Captain Warden reported at Anjer on July 6, arrived at Aden on August 5, and after beating the whole way up the Red Sea was compelled to bring up for three days in the Sea of Suez owing to a gale in his teeth. He landed his despatches and mails at Suez on September 1, being then 94 days out from the Canton River.

The *Waterwitch* was chartered for 8000 rupees to take the Calcutta mail. This was a very small freight compared to what this crack clipper earned as a rule, being only about one-sixth of her usual freight when carrying opium. She left Calcutta on July 13 and dropped her pilot off the Sandheads on the 15th.

Captain Reynell, writing from Aden, gave the following report of his passage:

> We arrived here on the afternoon of the 21st instant (August 21, 1839). I had a rough passage down the Bay, carried away a jib-boom and had main topmast sprung, split some sails and lost the serang overboard a week after leaving the pilot: crossed the line on the 29th, got no trade till 7° South, which obliged me to adopt the longest or Southern route: had rather a light trade till in 53° and rounded Cape Guardafui at noon on the 15th (one month from the pilot) having come 250 miles from the previous noon. From here we had dead calm for three days or should have anchored three days earlier. On the 14th off Cape Guardafui we unfortunately lost another man overboard, blowing a gale at the time and no chance of a boat living. On the whole we have been fortunate. Captain Haines and the Marine officers here say we have made an incredibly short passage.

I am happy to state that the *Witch* is in my opinion now a better ship than ever she was in every respect.

The *Waterwitch* would have taken the mails on to Suez, if she had not sprung her main topmast. They were transferred to the schooner *Constance*, of 182 tons, a man-of-war armed with five 12-pounders, built in the Bombay Dockyard in 1838 and belonging to the Indian Navy.

The passages of the *Ariel* and *Waterwitch* compared very favourably with those of the regular ships carrying the mails. From Bombay to Aden the *Constance* took 41 days in June; the *Oressa*, 41 days in July; and the brig *Euphrates*, of 255 tons, belonging to the Indian Navy, "thanks to rats," we are told by the Bengal *Harkaru*, was nowhere. Compared with these the *Ariel* was only 24 days from Java Head to Aden and the *Waterwitch* 36 days from the Sandheads to Aden.

The *Waterwitch* left Aden on her return trip on September 18, 1839, and reached Calcutta on October 16, only 28 days out.

The *Ariel* was only 13 days from Suez to Aden, where she waited for the English despatches and mails, which were expected from Suez on November 12, 1839, by the *Zenobia*.

The Opium Trade during the Canton Blockade.

On March 27, 1839, the *Friend of China* declared: "The unexpected proceedings of the imperial commissioner may be considered as having crushed the opium trade. No merchant possessed of ordinary prudence can justify to himself or his constituents the outlay of any further capital in so forlorn an enterprise." Four months later, on August 1, 1839, that same paper remarked: "It is well known that 20,000 chests, and more, of opium are only waiting the smallest appearance of an opening to be thrown into China."

The captains of the opium clippers were nothing if not enterprising, and even at a time when opium smugglers were being paraded through the streets of Canton in gangs of forty and fifty with "shackles of iron upon their necks and feet," the coasters were busy, as we have already seen in the case of the schooner *Time*.

Another of the Pybus fleet, the brig *Ann*, commanded by Captain Grey, was the first vessel to get into serious trouble with the imperial forces.

About the middle of July she was attached at Tienpack by a fleet of mandarin junks and only beat them off with difficulty. During the action several of her crew were killed or injured through a gun bursting. The brig reached Hongkong on July 16, 1839, and afterwards proceeded to Manila to dispose of her opium.

The *Red Rover* (Captain Wright), and the *Sir Edward Ryan* (Captain Henry Pybus), were both at Hongkong at this date. They appear to have disposed of their cargoes successfully though possibly the receiving ships took it. At any rate they left Canton waters on June 28, 1839, the *Red Rover* being just twelve hours behind the *Sir Edward Ryan.* Both ships reached Singapore on the same day, July 27; and continuing in company, the *Red Rover* took her pilot at the Sandheads two hours in front of the *Sir Edward Ryan*, Calcutta being reached by both clippers on August 15.

Continuing their rivalry, they sailed again on August 28, 1839, the *Red Rover* still maintaining her two hours' lead, which she kept as far as Singapore. From the Straits they both went on to Manila. Other vessels taking opium to the Philippines at the same time were the new brigantine *Poppy* the old East India sloop *Ternate*, belonging to the Parsees, the *Victoria* and the ex-fruit schooner *Hellas.*

Several clippers again went missing in 1839, including the *Syren*, *Young Rover* and *Nymph.*

The Calcutta *Courier* put these disasters down to overmasting. In an article about the missing clippers on January 21, 1840, they remarked:

> We have been assured by authorities on whom we place every reliance that in the instances of the clippers great blame, in nine cases out of ten, is to be attached to those who have the superintendence of the equipment of the vessels in their masts and rigging—their masts being in general considerably too large for the size of the hull and the sails too large in proportion. The consequence of which is, if they are overtaken by sudden squalls or a heavy gale of wind, they are instantly capsized or thrown so much on their beam ends as to preclude the possibility of their again rising, though the masts be cut by the board; and they sink gradually and disappear before the unfortunate officers and crew have time or opportunity to make provision for their escape in the boats. Many

lives have been thus sacrificed to the owners' love of lucre and many lacs of property destroyed and lost.

The famous *Sylph* had to content herself in 1839 with running between Calcutta and Singapore. At the beginning of the year it seemed likely that she would run under charter to the India Government, taking the mails during the height of the monsoon from Bombay to Aden, where a steamer was to be in readiness to receive them and take them on to Suez. However this scheme fell through, probably because her owners were not willing to sacrifice the possibility of high opium freights for the low-cut mail service.

Piratical Attack on Schooner "Black Joke," and Other Outrages.

The destruction of the opium at Chuenpee was considered by the Chinese to be a great "loss of face" for the red-headed devils; and proceeding on the old "tooth and claw" psychology, Lin and his menials conceived that the time had come, when the devil was down, to hit him in every possible way that could be devised.

Outrages began to be reported from every direction. Those firms which had been driven out of Canton and had opened up again in Macao soon found that the enmity of Lin had pursued them there.

The fishermen, the country men, the shopkeepers—all were encouraged to make it as difficult as possible for the Fan Kwae. In driving British shipping outside the Bocca Tigris and then away from the Cap-sing-moon and Lintin Anchorages, Commissioner Lin acted the part of Providence, for the ships all crowded to the deep water anchorage off the Island of Hongkong; and then when the firms were forced to leave Macao the occupation of Hongkong began to be considered.

The ugly word war also began to crop up in conversation. Several collisions between the Celestial and the foreign devil during the summer of 1839 served to still further aggravate matters. The first of these took place in July when a party of British and American sailors ashore on the Kowloon side got into a squabble with natives and, in fighting their way clear, killed one of them.

Then came the attack on the schooner *Black Joke*, which on her way from Macao to Hongkong with a Mr. Mark's personal and household effects, was attacked when lying at anchor off the point of Lantao. Mark, a British subject, gave the following graphic account before the procurator of Macao:

At about 9 o'clock I heard the crew, consisting of Lascars, cry out: "Wy-lo! Wy-lo!" I ran to the skylight and saw three guns fired at us, loaded with charcoal. When I reached the deck, I saw three Lascars cut down and received myself a cut on the left side of the face, on which I ran below. When I heard the Chinese crying "Ta-ta!" putting my head out of the companion, I got a most severe wound on the top of my head from a pike. The Chinese then laid hold of me, stripped me of my clothes and cut my arm in three places as I put it up to save my head. They then proceeded to plunder and break up the boat; and coming down with lights into the cabin, one of them, seeing I had a ring on my finger, attempted to cut the finger off—but I quickly took off the ring and gave it to him.

Another, seeing my watch, took it out of my pocket, and laying hold of my ear, cut it off with a large portion of the scalp on the left side of my head and put it in my mouth, attempting to push it down my throat.

I was then knocked about on all sides by the Chinamen. I saw them bring a barrel of gunpowder with which they attempted to blow up the boat but did not succeed.

I was rendered insensible from the smoke caused by the explosion and nearly suffocated.

Making a last effort I reached the deck and called out the names of some of the Lascars.

Seeing a rope moving astern, I found that the tindal, alone of the whole native crew, had saved himself by hanging on to the rudder under water.

He came up and gave me some water, of which I drank five basins full and felt refreshed.

A short time after this the *Harriet* (Captain Hall) came up. From Captain Hall I met with the tenderest treatment, he dressed my wounds, took charge of the *Black Joke* and brought me back to Macao.

The *Harriet* was a little 100-ton schooner, built at Macao by a shipwright named Hamilton.

The *Black Joke* was an ex-slaver of 113 tons, the Portuguese brig *Esperance*, which was condemned at Sierra Leone in 1836. She was owned by Captain John Miller, of Launceston, Tasmania, in 1838, and was bought by Rustomjee & Co.

After the attack on the *Black Joke* came the kidnapping of Mr. Stanton and the burning of the Spanish brig *Balbaino* in Taypa Harbour, owing to her being mistaken for an Britisher. All these three outrages were considered to have been engineered by a man named Wang Chong, an agent of Commissioner Lin's. Indeed,

ck *Joke* affair, Lin ordered that all British
killed.
nt was the disappearance of the master
Psyche. At this psychological moment
Captain Henry Smith) appeared.
r has solved many mysteries and unravelled
where diplomats have been of no avail.
less, but Captain Smith calmly prepared to
anton. At this the missing shipmaster

uses Excitement.

was at its worst, the well-known East
flying Joseph Somes' flag, arrived on the

1334 tons, which had been built in the
was very well known in Canton waters.
stest of all John Company's Indiamen.
l by Alexander Chrystie, she arrived in
2, only 82 days from the Channel; she
ded 4198 taels of teas and silks, and left
ored in the Downs on March 2, 1827,
voyage to the East ever known, being

roud ship calmly ignored the political
dvice from Captain Elliot, applied for a
nd, and without more ado sailed up to

l by this cool, high-handed proceeding
ying off Hongkong, but when the *Thomas Coutts* came out of the Bogue with a full cargo of tea, loaded by the American Russell & Co., many of the sorely tried shipmasters rushed indignantly to the patient Elliot, who could only reply that the *Coutts* had been playing with fire and bluffed her way through by sheer audacity. He counselled patience, but at length agreed to send a chop to Commissioner Lin.

H.M.S. "Volage" and "Hyacinth" destroy 29 War Junks.

The only two British men-of-war in Canton waters, the *Volage* of 26 guns (Captain Henry Smith), and the *Hyacinth of* 18 guns (Commander William Warren), were sent to the Bogue to deliver the chop. Lin, in his most grandiloquent manner, ordered the 29 war junks stationed at the Bogue to surround and seize the two British men-of-war. The Commissioner was a scholar who had no knowledge of war, and he naturally supposed that 29 imperial junks, crowded both with guns and men, would make short work of the two small Britishers.

The latter fired warning guns as the Celestial fleet approached with flags flying, gongs beating, stink-pots hoisted, and every preparation for a fight plain to see.

Then, observing that the junks were determined to come to close quarters, Captain Elliot, who was present in person—he was one of those leaders who was ever at the post of danger—reluctantly gave the order to fire in earnest.

In a few moments five of the junks had been sunk or blown up, whilst the rest in a severely battered condition did their best to get out of range of the murderous broadsides; and they would most certainly have all been destroyed had not the merciful Elliot ordered the cease fire.

This action took place on October 29, 1839. From this date the two nations were virtually at war—though it was not actually declared by the Chinese until December 6.

The Kidnapping of Captain Gribble.

On January 12, 1840, Captain Smith of the *Volage*, the senior British naval officer in Canton waters, again gave notice that he would blockade the port unless an Englishman who had been captured by the Chinese was delivered up within three days.

This Englishman was the well-known Captain Gribble, formerly one of the Honourable Company's commanders, who had just arrived out in the ship *Thames* with his wife and children, his intention being to start business with a man named Hughes, who had been in Baring's office.

Captain Gribble, who was a big burly man with but very little fear or want of self-confidence in his composition, calmly left the anchorage in a fast boat, manned by about 25 Chinese, in order to pay a visit to the famous Captain Bobby Towns, who had just arrived from Sydney in the *Royal Saxon*, and had brought up near the Bogue. As he was consigned to Russell & Co., Towns intended to make the Whampoa Anchorage.

Captain Gribble got alongside the *Royal Saxon* about 2 a.m., and having finished his business with the Australian captain set out half an hour later to pull back to Lintin. Chinese boatmen are incomparable oars, but Gribble's crew, after pulling all night, were too tired to get away from a mandarin's boat, which they found pulling athwart their hawse just as daylight was breaking. They did, however, manage to reach the shore first, and whilst Gribble calmly opened fire on the mandarin dragon, which was full of men and pulled thirty oars a side, his Chinese boatmen jumped out and scuttled away like rabbits. Luckily for the determined captain he was not too good a shot with a pistol, and though he made play with a weapon in each fist he did no damage. He was speedily captured and stripped of everything of value including a gold watch, gold pencil-case, and his pistols. He was then handed over to a military officer ashore, and carried in a sedan chair to the Viceroy's Ya-mun* at Canton.

This journey took six days and he was escorted by 60 soldiers. His next adventure was a three hours' interrogation by the mandarins. They even made him load his pistols and discharge them at a tree.

When the bullets struck the trunk, the court laughed uproariously with many exclamations of "How-how-ah" (good-good). It is possible that the big sea captain found a difficulty in seeing the joke.

By this time a good deal of the starch had been taken out of his composition as well as his clothes. He had been captured on December 25, and this examination took place on January 2. He was afterwards sent to the Consoo House, when the Hong merchants produced the American, W. C. Hunter (of Russell & Co.), and Captain Bobby Towns to testify in his favour, the chief accusation against him being that he was trying to smuggle opium.

* Public office.

However, two days after Captain Smith's notice, Captain Gribble was released and put on board the *Volage* along with five Lascars, who had been picked up drifting in the sea.

H.M.S. "Druid" arrives at Macao.

On January 24, 1840, H.M.S. *Druid* (44 guns, Captain the Right Hon. Lord John Spencer Churchill), arrived at Macao. As she was very much larger than any warship seen before in Canton waters His Excellency Commissioner Lin and the Viceroy of Canton became more than a trifle anxious, and a mandarin was sent to the American Hong in order to see what he could find out.

He began his questioning of the Americans with some typical Chinese bombast.

"What chance had the red-headed devils in a war with the Celestial Empire, which covers the whole earth. Think of the frowning batteries of the Hoo-Mun (the Bogue). When their terrible engines are opened the remotest corners of the world are agitated."

"Quite so," returned the American uncommittingly.

"Our imperial ruler controls the whole universe. His wisdom is as the five great genii, broader than the four seas is his benevolence, higher than the skies is his clemency."

"Quite so," agreed the American monotonously.

"The red-haired barbarians from a speck in the ocean come to the Flowery Land and reap unheard of money, deluging the 'Roses and Lilies' with poisonous filth. The Yellow Dragon is insulted. He says, 'Drive them forth, cut them off for ever, shower upon them no longer our goodness, our tea, our rhubarb, our sweetmeats. What to us are their buttons and musical boxes, their knives with six blades, their corkscrews and files!' "

"Quite so," droned the American.

Then at last came a tone of nervousness in the Tae-Yay's speech:

"A large vessel called the *Too-Loo-Te* (*Druid*) has arrived. What soldiers has she? What guns? Is it true that she carries two cannon of enormous length—no less than 45 ft. 7 ins.?"

The American—it was Hunter, the great linguist—roused

himself and professed entire ignorance of such cannons, though he admitted that they had such ships as the *Druid* in his country.

The mandarin's questions were now almost whispered, so grave was his subject.

"Is it true that fire-wheel ships are coming, filled with flames and hot water?"

At this Hunter at last let himself go. "Fire-wheel ships are number one curio. They care not for wind and tide, they carry bombs for razing cities and wiping out forts. They eat fire and race the wind—but you will see them up the river."

"Hi-yah! Hi-yah! Not inside the Bogue?" asked the now terrified Chinaman.

"Aye—mighty probable," said the American indifferently.

And so the interview went on until the mandarin at last announced his departure in a quavering voice. He was by now thoroughly subdued. However, he cheered up when presented with a bar of yellow soap and a bottle of Vermont eau-de-Cologne at parting.

Lin's Method of Warfare.

Lin's idea of making war seems to have been chiefly by putting a price on the heads of his enemy. Elliot's head he valued at 5000 dollars alive, but only a third of that sum dead. The same amount he offered for the person of a captain of a man-of-war. For British merchants, whether English or Indian, he only offered 300 dollars alive and 100 dollars dead; and he even proclaimed that he would pay a few dollars for every dead British bluejacket.

His price for captured ships was 20,000 dollars for a ship of the line; 10,000 dollars for a "three piecey bamboo" merchantman; 100 dollars a gun for war sloops; and about the same for opium clippers.

The "Mor" arrives from Plymouth, February 15, 1840.

The first vessel to reach China from the outside in the spring of 1840 was a new clipper, the *Mor*, a little full-rig ship of 280 tons, specially built on the Thames for Jardine, Matheson & Co.

Her passage out was a remarkable one; leaving Plymouth on

October 23, 1839, she reached Anjer on January 12, 1840, only 81 days out. Then she proceeded to beat up the China Sea, against the strength of the monsoon, and actually anchored off Macao on February 15, only 115 days from London at about the worst season of the year. Her commander was Captain W. Young. Jardine Matheson despatched her at once to Bombay, and here again she showed her unusual speed by covering 586 miles in 48 hours, on her way down the China Sea.

At Bombay crowds of people visited the new flyer, which afterwards turned out to be one of the fastest clippers in the Bombay opium trade.

"Waterwitch" and "Lady Hayes" attacked.

Although the two countries were now in a state of war, several of the most daring of the clippers beat up the China Sea on the heels of the *Mor* with their usual cargoes on board.

Some of them, such as the *Sylph* and *Cowasjee Family*, shipped all British crews and mounted extra guns for defence against the fleets of imperial war junks which were hovering in wait about the Ladrones and even further South. As much secrecy as possible was observed, and after the opium sales at Calcutta it was given out by all clippers loading the drug that their destinations were Singapore and Manila.

The first vessels to be attacked were the *Waterwitch* and *Lady Hayes*. They were assailed by a force of 17 gun-boats but fought their way through and reached Macao without damage or loss of men.

The Mate of "Cowasjee Family" runs amuck.

One of the first ships to sail from Calcutta with the new season's drug in 1840 was the *Cowasjee Family* (Captain Dunbar) which left Calcutta on December 2, and arrived in Tongkoo Bay, where all British ships had assembled in February. In the files of the *Englishman* there is a letter from her captain, which explains how Captain Wallace came to be in command of his old ship, a couple of months later, when she was attacked by Chinchew junks to the Northward of Amoy.

"SIR EDWARD RYAN"

National Maritime Museum, Greenwich

[*See page* 182

"FALCON", JARDINE MATHESON'S FLAGSHIP

National Maritime Museum, Greenwich

[*See page* 188

The unfortunate Captain Dunbar writes as follows:

On the morning of March 1, about 2 a.m. awaking and hearing no person moving about the decks of the barque *Cowasjee Family,* which was under my command and then lying at anchor in the Bay of Tongkoo, laden with a valuable cargo and preparing to proceed to the East Coast of China, I went on the poop, which I found to be wholly unguarded, not a single individual being awake.

The sea-cunny was lying asleep close to the mizen mast, although it was his watch. He was awakened by me and after I had reprimanded him for his negligence in being asleep, I inquired of him what officer should be in charge of the deck. He informed me it was the chief officer's watch, whom I found lying asleep upon his chest in his cabin. I then ordered the sea-cunny to call him; and upon his coming on deck I remonstrated with him in a kind manner upon the danger to which he exposed the vessel and crew, in consequence of being asleep when in charge of the ship; more particularly at a time when he was well aware, in consequence of an attempt of that nature having been made the night previously and which we had escaped with difficulty, that the ship and the lives on board were hourly exposed to the greatest danger from the fire-rafts which the Chinese had in preparation to destroy the whole British fleet, then lying in the Bay of Tongkoo.

Instead of his receiving the reprimand in the proper spirit, he became very insolent and I was therefore obliged to request him to go to his cabin, saying that I would speak to him the next morning.

He refused to comply with this order in very offensive language; consequently I told him that unless he obeyed me I should compel him by force.

After some consideration he rushed into his cabin, drawing the door to with great violence, and there he remained about 15 or 20 minutes.

In the meantime I had provided myself with a great-coat, etc., and had seated myself upon a chair on the poop with my feet upon the brass rail, with the intention of keeping the watch until daylight, the second officer having had the first watch.

I was, however, surprised to see the chief mate, Mr. Willins, open his cabin door and rush on the poop. He immediately opened a volley of abuse upon me, demanded redress for being confined to his cabin and tried all that he could to irritate me and make me strike him. But on finding that he could not succeed in inducing me to do so and that I was perfectly cool and collected, he put his fist against my face in a threatening attitude, calling me at the same time a "bloody coward," and following up this aggression with a blow in the mouth. I immediately attempted to rise from the chair, but I was unable to do so in consequence of his placing his knee between my legs and holding me down with his left arm, while he kept assaulting me with his right hand—and from my legs being entangled in the brass railings as well as being confined in a great-coat, I found it impossible to extricate myself from him. I then called out to the serang for assistance, and upon his answering me Mr. Willins immediately released his hold saying: "Wait till I get my pistols," and rushed from the poop to his cabin. Fearing that he might, from the frantic state in which he appeared, be induced to commit some rash act, I followed him down with a view of preventing him, if possible, from perpetrating any further violence.

On entering his cabin I found that his back was towards me, and perceived that he had a pistol in his left hand, his right arm being extended in the act of taking another pistol from the becket in which it was placed. The first thing which I did was to secure the pistol which he held in his left hand, and on doing so he turned round upon me and knocked me down with the pistol in his right hand, cutting my head open and knocking me senseless.

On my coming to myself, I found the blood streaming down my face from the wound in my head and felt very faint and suffered great pain.

On my leaving the cabin I heard the second officer, who was dressed only in his shirt and trousers—and I supposed him in consequence to have just risen from his bed—remonstrating with Mr. Willins on the starboard side of the quarterdeck. I dis inctly heard the second officer say to Mr. Willins: "Why don't you go to your cabin and keep yourself quiet? You see that you have wounded the captain; you will be sorry for this to-morrow."

From the poop I then requested the second officer to secure Mr. Willins, to prevent his doing any more mischief. Upon hearing what I said, Mr. Willins replied:

"Neither you nor he, nor any such —— like you can do it." And rushing into the cuddy, he took from the stand of arms a loaded musket and proceeded with it on deck, snapping at the crew, who had by this time come aft with the view of securing him.

They, on being threatened, ran away and hid themselves, some in the main rigging and others forward, Mr. Willins chasing some few that had remained round the capstan, but fortunately the musket would not go off from the badness of the flint.

Upon his finding the defects, he said: "Wait a little: I will damn soon find one that will go off," and returned into the cuddy to procure another musket.

In the interim, I, considering it high time to bring things to a more decided bearing, went to my cabin and armed myself with a brace of pistols, which were always kept there loaded, and returned to the poop.

Mr. Willins, on returning to the quarterdeck, appeared to be searching for me, saying: "Where is the ——?" And turning round on his heel, discharged the contents of the loaded musket directly at me, the ball passing close over my head.

After this he appeared more frantic than ever, and swore that he would blow up the magazine. Hearing this I became much alarmed, knowing that he had the key in his possession. He then took a light from his cabin and deliberately removed the apron from a 12-pounder, loaded with round shot and canister, and discharged it, the shot passing over the forecastle of the *Royal Saxon* and nearly killing the watch on deck.

Mr. Willins then came upon the poop with the intention of again attacking me, upon which I desired him to go to his cabin several times and solemnly warned him that if he advanced another step towards me I would shoot him.

He, however, persisted in his intention. I fired at him, upon which he dropped the pistol upon the deck, folded his arms across his breast, and said: "Now, I suppose I must go down." He then walked from the poop to his cabin and laid himself in his bed.

Captain Elliot, pre-occupied with weightier matters, apparently did not gather more of the affair than that the captain of *Cowasjee Family* had shot at and wounded his mate. He sent Captain Dunbar down to Singapore to be tried before the Court. Here the unfortunate captain remained in prison for two months; he was then refused a trial and discharged upon his own recognisance. He ends up his letter:

> Such, sir, is the wrong of which I complain, a wrong which has occasioned me incalculable anxiety of mind, the most serious injury to my professional character and future prospects and for which I am entirely without remedy.

He attaches the following curious letter from his obstreporous mate, Nathaniel Willins.

> To Charles Dunbar, Esq.
>
> Dear Sir,—No doubt you are as tired of remaining at Singapore as I am of remaining in China unemployed, I am very sorry to observe, these last two months and upwards, waiting for a conveyance to Singapore to procure your acquittal. Dadabhoy Rustomjee, when I left the hospital, in which place I was 114 days, sent me on board a vessel belonging to himself, where I have remained up to the present time at my own expense. . . . God above knows that I have long and long ago forgiven you and so again both solemnly and sincerely forgive you for what occurred to my detriment on March 1, which I regret to say I shall have cause to remember as long as I exist.
>
> NATHANIEL WILLINS.
> 11th Sept., 1840.

The *Harkaru* and *Courier*, besides the *Englishman*, commented on Captain Dunbar's case; but he does not appear to have resumed his place in the opium fleet.

The "Sylph" and "Cowasjee Family" fight off a Fleet of Chinchew Junks.

It must have been a providential piece of luck which produced her old commander when the *Cowasjee Family* was so suddenly deprived of both her master and chief mate.

Captain Wallace was just the man to restore discipline and take the ship on the dangerous trip up the East Coast, for he was well known for his cool nerve.

He sailed from the Canton River in company with the *Sylph* (Captain Viall), the two clippers intending to keep company up the coast. Nothing happened till they were to the Northward of

Amoy, but off Chimmo Bay a large fleet of Chinchew junks appeared and a regular battle took place. *Cowasjee Family* fired no less than 50 rounds of shot besides grape, and *Sylph* expended a like amount. At last the two captains decided that it was wise, whilst they had the wind, to take advantage of their superior speed and run for it.

This fight took place at the beginning of May; another vessel which had to fight her way clear about the same date and place was the *Omega*, which also came off unscathed.

The "Hellas" makes a Desperate Resistance.

One of the smartest of Jardine Matheson's coasters was the *Hellas*, which was an ex-Mediterranean fruit schooner of 209 tons, built at Waterford at the beginning of the 'thirties and bought by Jardine Matheson in 1838.

On May 22, 1840, she was lying becalmed in the neighbourhood of the Brothers, to the Northward of Namoa. Not far away from her were eight junks and three large pulling boats, which Captain Jauncey of the *Hellas*, a very experienced master in the opium trade, took to be ordinary traders. However, when it was noticed that they were using their sweeps to approach the schooner, suspicion was aroused and every preparation was made.

The enemy evidently knew what they were about. The *Hellas* was not only becalmed but foul of a lot of fish stakes. The junks came up from right astern, so that she was unable to bring her broadside guns to bear. They, on the other hand, had no cannon, though well provided with muskets, hand grenades and stink-pots. As soon as they were within range the Chinese, well protected behind barricades of mats and mattresses, opened a steady musketry fire, which was at once replied to from the decks of the schooner. It was soon found that there were some good marksmen aboard the enemy, for anyone who exposed himself above the bulwarks of the *Hellas* was soon a casualty.

The junks came on by means of their yolos until they were so close on the quarters of the schooner, that they could hurl their stink-pots aboard. These were so skilfully plied that the schooner caught fire several times, but every preparation had been madc for such a contingency, and each time the fire was smothered before either the tarred rigging or sails was reached by the flames.

Matters were looking desperate, when at last a breeze sprang up and the *Hellas* was able to make use of her cannons, but before the junks sheered off, after a fight of four hours, most of the crew of the *Hellas* had been wounded, many of them fatally. Out of a crew of 50, everyone of the Europeans, 15 in number, were wounded besides 10 of the Lascars.

Captain Jauncey, besides a number of flesh wounds about the legs and body, had his jawbone broken by a gingal ball and an eye injured.

All seem to have behaved with the greatest gallantry. When things were looking at their worst for the *Hellas*, just before the breeze came along, junks were bumping alongside the schooner on both sides, stink-pots were being thrown amongst her crew, flames and black smoke hid the combatants, who wrestled and fought hand to hand—but the schooner's crowd were even then attacking as well as defending.

The first tindal, a Malay, flourishing his creese, leapt aboard one of the junks, cleft the head of her captain in twain, just as he was about to fire his matchlock, then after keeping a ring of Chinamen at bay, jumped back aboard the schooner without receiving a scratch.

When the breeze came, whilst the *Hellas* was still foul of a junk, McMinnis, her mate, and a couple of seamen, attacked the latter with such ferocity, that her crew took refuge overboard, many of them being drowned. Again the bold attackers came off safely, though one of them got a scalp wound, from a gingal fired from the hold of the junk.

As soon as the junks and pulling boats were out of range, the *Hellas* made all sail for Hongkong, where two of her wounded men died soon after her arrival.

Captain Jauncey reported that, owing to the numbers of pirates about, the trading junks had been compelled to move in convoys for mutual protection, and that when these junks anchored near him the night before they attacked he took no notice of them, judging them to be one of these convoys. He was so badly knocked about himself that he seized the opportunity of going back to America in the *Niantic*, on which R. B. Forbes, by this time badly in need of a rest, and Dr. Parker were sailing.

There was very little room in the *Niantic* and the wounded man swung in a cot over the dinner-table. The *Niantic* was 54 days to Anjer, and lost most of her sails in the usual squally weather; indeed, if it had not been for the high-spirited Forbes she would probably have come to grief.

The captain, Doty, was struck down by the sun just before sailing, the mate was incompetent, the second mate and five of the crew were down with fever, and it needed all the help of Forbes' partners, Delano and Hunter, and the crew of their sampan to get the old ship under way. However, the *Niantic* managed to get home safely, Jauncey recovered of his wounds and was soon out in China again.

He afterwards commanded Jardine Matheson's *Falcon*, *Warlock* and *Mazeppa* in turn, being considered one of the most experienced captains on the coast.

"Sir Edward Ryan" makes a Profitable Cruise.

If Captain Joseph Pybus showed that he could take advantage of the most difficult condition in which the opium trade was now placed, his brother was no whit behind him. He boldly sailed North with a full cargo, and in the course of a few weeks netted a profit, so it was said, of £50,000. "His voyage," said the *Friend of India*, was a bold and well planned venture, and other vessels have been encouraged to follow in the track." It did not go off entirely without excitement however.

Whilst the *Sir Edward Ryan* was lying at anchor in Amoy Roads the local mandarin sent off his card with the intimation that "he was eating gunpowder and would come out to fight the following morning." He duly appeared at the appointed time with five war junks. Captain Pybus immediately got under way and stood towards them, opening fire with his long-tom. This was quite enough to quench the mandarin's warlike spirit; he immediately hove about and politely withdrew.

Another adventure awaited the ship when lying in the Clipper

Roads, off Swatow. Her gig, with its two boat-keepers, who were Malays, broke away from the stern during the night. It was certain death for the two men if they fell into the hands of the mandarins. Captain Pybus managed to circulate a notice in Chinese offering a reward of 200 dollars for the men and 50 dollars for the boat if they were returned unharmed. Nothing was heard of them for some time and they were at length given up for lost.

However about six weeks later the two men came off to the *Sir Edward Ryan*, dressed as Chinamen, wearing false pigtails and bringing the brass rowlocks and steering yoke of the boat.

A year or so later when Captain Joseph Pybus had the *Sir Edward Ryan*, he, it was, who discovered the rock off Swatow, called the Ryan Stone. This was just after the opium war, when piracy was so rife along the whole stretch of the China coast, that the natives were only able to stay on the island under the protection of the opium ships.

Here, one day, Captain Joseph Pybus sent his long-boat ashore for water in charge of a petty officer. The Chinese ashore had been warned that they were on no account to supply liquor to the crews of the ships. Nevertheless the crew of the long-boat got full up with shamshoo. As a stiff breeze was blowing, they had a hard pull off to the ship, seeing which Captain Pybus veered a barricoe astern on the end of a line, so that they could get hold of it and haul themselves up to the ship. As the barricoe drifted down on the boat, the drunken men all dashed to one side to get hold of it, with the result that the deeply laden boat capsized and two of the men were drowned.

The old-time skipper on the China coast invariably took the law into his own hand and acted resolutely and without a moment's hesitation. Captain Joseph Pybus immediately manned and armed his boats, rounded up a whole mob of Celestials, cut off their cues, and not content with this terrible indignity, carried them off and set them ashore amongst their jeering compatriots on the mainland.

The Singapore Packets.

The Pybus Brothers made so much money by cleverly taking advantage of the disturbed conditions of trade that they had three schooners and a brig built at Moulmein on the lines of the *Time.* These were named *Harlequin, Clown, Columbine* and *Pantaloon.*

There were two *Harlequins* in the China Sea in the early 'forties, not to mention the man-of-war brig of that name. The other *Harlequin* was a vessel of 292 tons, which came across from Mexico with specie and remained on the coast.

No sooner were the four clippers belonging to the Pybus Brothers in the water before they were taken up by J. Mackey & Co. to run with mails, passengers, cargo—occasionally but not always, opium—between Calcutta, Penang and Singapore.

As an example of their good sailing, the *Columbine* (Captain Major), left Calcutta on September 7, 1840, discharged a full cargo at Singapore, loaded another, and reached Malacca on the morning of September 26. Here she took on board a number of passengers and sailed the same evening. This was considered one of the fastest runs on record.

At the beginning of 1841 the Singapore packets, as they were called, extended their voyages to Macao, being advertised to sail regularly at intervals of from 35 to 40 days.

The brig *Pantaloon* was not launched until 1841, and until she was ready Messrs. Mackey chartered the brig *Dido* of 230 tons, which was launched at Calcutta on May 4, 1840, and afterwards became a well-known coaster, under Captain Robert Saunders.

Soon after Pybus Brothers retired, Donald C. Mackey failed, but he started again in a short while and was, I believe, one of the founders of the British India S.S. Co.

The "Falcon"—Flagship of the Coasters.

With the Canton River in a state of blockade, imperial war junks ever on the lookout to catch the unwary, and opium valued at an unheard of figure, many of the regular Calcutta clippers adventured up the North-East coast in *Sir Edward Ryan's* wake.

And it was just at this psychological moment that Jardine, Matheson & Co. became possessed of a vessel which was admirably suited to the dangerous service of smuggling opium in war time. This was the famous *Falcon,* lately the flagship of the Royal Yacht

Squadron, the delight of her owner, the commodore (Lord Yarborough) and the pride of the British yachting community.

The *Falcon* was built at Fishbourne by List of Wootton, but it is probable that Lord Yarborough had more to do with her designing than any one else.

She was a full-rigged ship of 351 tons register and 434 tons displacement. Her water-line length was 102·8 ft., her extreme breadth 27·4 ft. and draught of water 12 ft. 9 ins. forward and 13 ft. aft. She was one of the yachts whose elements are given by Fincham in his *History of Naval Architecture* in the greatest detail.

She was launched on Tuesday, June 10, 1824, amidst the "roar of guns and the hearty congratulations of the populace" and she was christened by the "accomplished Miss Hastings."

The main object of the founders of the Royal Yacht Club was to try to improve the form of the ship and specially the design of the warship; thus, in the early days of the club many of the members built experimental ships which could be easily turned into men-of-war. This was the true *raison d'etre* of the club and considered of much greater importance than the annual regatta at Cowes.

The *Falcon* may be said to have been the first of these experimental yachts. She was designed as a 20-gun corvette.

The commodore's patriotic example was quickly followed by other members. The Honourable George Vernon built the brig *Harlequin*, of 292 tons, as an example of a brig sloop; and the Marquess of Anglesey built the cutter *Pearl*, of 113 tons, as an example of a revenue cruiser.

Then came the Duke of Portland with his famous Symondite brig *Pantaloon*, of 306 tons, launched in 1831, which was purchased by the Admiralty in August of that year. As an improvement on her White of Cowes built the beautiful little brig *Waterwitch*, of 331 tons, for the Earl of Belfast, the vice-commodore of the club. She was bought by the Admiralty in 1834.

To return to the *Falcon*, though Lord Yarborough commanded her himself, he had a naval lieutenant named Cannon as his second in command, and even carried a couple of midshipmen. The *Falcon*, as flagship of the R.Y.S., had a crew of 54 hands, these were picked men-of-war's men under naval discipline, who were paid extra wages in order that they should conform to the regulations of the Service and even to the use of the cat-o'-nine tails. With a broadside of eleven cannons, they were also given regular gun drill; and on October 20, 1827, the little *Falcon* actually took part in the battle of Navarino, when Lord Yarborough flew his commodore's burgee at the fore and his flag as admiral of the Isle of Wight at the main. It is interesting to note that at that date the burgee of the Royal Yacht Club was red with a yellow crown and foul anchor. It was not until 1829 that the Lords of the Admiralty granted the club the distinctive privilege of wearing the St. George's Ensign, as it was then called, when the red burgee was changed to the white with St. George's cross and crown.

Lord Yarborough always joined the experimental squadron in the Channel, and he delighted to lead the squadron of club yachts and even to exercise them in sailing evolutions. A special Royal Yacht Club signal book, on the lines of the Service signal books, was published in 1830. Besides the special code flags of the club and the special naval code for signalling to club yachts, this book contains orders of sailing, with diagrams, which included tacking in succession, wearing in succession, forming line abreast, sailing large in two columns and even forming on a line of bearing.

Many successful cruises were made under the popular commodore especially across the channel either to the French regattas or for the purpose of buying wine.

In 1831 the yachts of the Royal Northern Y.C., headed by Colonel Madden's *Ganymede* and also the *Little Paddy* flying the harp and crown on green of the Cork Water Club, joined the fleet under Lord Yarborough for the trip across the Channel to Cherbourg Regatta.

Lord Yarborough always entertained in regal style, and the *Falcon* was the scene of many an international ball. However her end as a pleasure vessel came in 1836. In 1835 the old commodore received a severe injury to his legs by being thrown across a sea chest in a gale of wind and he was also laid low by a very severe bout of influenza. These were given as the reasons for selling his noble yacht, but the real reason was probably one of finance.

During the race for the King's Cup at Cowes Regatta in 1836 the *Falcon* came out of the harbour and sailed to the Eastward, having been purchased by a London firm for £5500. The crowds on the front, the beach and esplanade watched her go in silence, sorrowful indeed to see the pride of the island sailing away with the red ensign instead of the white at her spanker gaff.

The purchaser turned out to be the astute Captain Clifton, financed by Thomas Baring. In London she was fitted with engines of 48 horse power and paddle wheels. This took time; and it was not until January, 1838, that she sailed for India. The engines were not considered a success, and on her arrival in the Hooghly were quickly removed.

At Calcutta she hoisted the commodore's swallow tail of Jardine, Matheson & Co.

The first free-ship despatched to England at the end of the Company's regime was the *Sarah*, 488 tons (Whiteside commander) in 1833. She, however, only carried silks, nankeens, cassia bark, rhubarb and china root.

According to the records of Messrs. Jardine, Matheson & Co. the first vessel to sail into the port of London with a tea cargo under the free trade banner was the *Falcon*. The date is uncertain, but it was almost certainly in 1838 or 1839, for 1840 found her back in the China Seas.

An officer who served aboard her has left a very interesting description of her as an opium clipper:

> With a bow round and full above the waterline, she was as sharp as a wedge in her entrance below. Her midship sections gave her a long flat floor; whence commenced a clean run aft, that, with her form of entrance, minimised resistance and displacement to a marvellous degree. Her breadth of beam over this long floor enabled her to stand up under a more than ordinary press of canvas, while it afforded quarters for a small battery of guns, including a long brass piece amidships and some pivot and swivels over bows, counter and quarter, that made her a wholesome terror to the swarming fleets of pirates, which then infested the Hok-keen Coasts.
>
> In all cases of bad weather, the heaviest of these were run in and well secured, indeed, there were times and occasions when the whole armament was dismounted and put under hatches, so that nothing should encumber the spacious white flush deck beyond the neat coils of running gear placed in tubs made for the occasion. The *Falcon* was a full-rigged ship, heavily but beautifully masted, as to rake and proportion. Her yards

and spars were of dimensions equal to a ship of, perhaps, twice the size in actual carrying power in the ordinary Mercantile Marine. These were beautifully fashioned and finished—not in the tapered and pointed style affected by traders within the tropics, nor of the dilettante in the summer seas at home, but in a style that savoured rather of massive strength and utility. There was no skysail or moonsail or flagstaff extension. Our masts seldom went more than a few inches beyond the rigging that supported them.

In summer-like weather we sent up topgallant and royal masts in one, but during the strength of the monsoons and in all passages to the Northward—and we sometimes went very far North—short topgallant masts were fidded. We trusted more to spread than hoist; and in going free the show of canvas upon our square yards, further extended by lengthy stunsail booms—in the rigging out of which our topmen had few compeers—would leave an observer in no doubt of the immense pressure under which the comparatively slight and beautiful fabric trembled and vibrated in its headlong career.

Sailors, I fear, do not write about their ships in these days in the lover-like style of these old seamen; let me continue quoting:

I hesitate to touch upon the secondary furnishings and fittings of the *Falcon*, but I remember that they were unusually elegant and substantial and costly; that where metal was employed it was mostly of copper or brass, even to the belaying pins; and that toprails, stanchions, skylights and coamings were of mahogany, whilst the accommodation below for the officers and crew was extravagantly luxurious.

It will better become me to speak of her higher and greater qualities, qualities which made her an object of pride and real affection, as of the tenderest care, of her crew, officers and men. She was easy, handy and smart in every evolution. She swam like a duck and steered like a fish. She was fast, yet dry; lively, yet stiff. Sensitive and responsive to every yard of canvas that could be judiciously spread, as to every touch of the braces, tacks and sheets, and to every spoke of the wheel.

It was in the *Falcon* that I learnt to comprehend and to adopt a singular belief that prevails among seamen; and it was in her and by her, that I was first touched by that strange sympathy which is created by a favourite ship upon the minds of an appreciative crew. If the *Falcon* had been a living being that sympathy could scarcely have been greater. She would resent every neglect in her handling, and rebel at once against any over pressure or any tampering with her trim, so that our common expressions—expressions that could have no meaning to a landsman—that she was complaining or sulking or huffed or offended seemed to us to be rightfully applied.

One felt proud to watch her dealing with opposing forces so persistently and so gallantly. We had been afloat in her for upwards of three years with few losses and fewer changes than could have been expected in so large a crew; and, having watched and studied her pretty ways for so long a period, we had acquired readiness and skill in her management, and had learned to look upon her as a thing to be loved and petted. "She can do everything but speak," was a common remark among the crew.

The Coasters "Audax," "Denia" and "Gazelle."

The *Falcon* was far from being a typical coaster. She was reserved entirely for the most dangerous and difficult duties. Her officers were picked men, picked not only for their courage and seamanship, but for their skill in surveying and hydrography.

Captain Jauncey, when he commanded her, published several charts of the coast, including one of the Cap-sing-moon Anchorage, in which he was helped by Captain Rees, his old commander in the *Lord Amherst*.

The *Falcon's* job was to discover new ports and open up trade. Other coasters had more regular duties; indeed, as soon as the war was over and the treaty ports open some of them did no more than run between the ports of Hongkong and Amoy or Foochow or Shanghai.

These were all smart little brigs and schooners and it was not until the war had begun that there were more than half a dozen of these mosquito craft. The *Nymph* as we have seen was intended for this work, and so were the *Psyche* and the brig *Spy*, of 120 tons, built at Calcutta for Jardine, Matheson & Co., in 1840.

But there were three very beautiful little ships built at home in 1840, which became very well known a few years later on the coast. These were the *Audax*, brig of 151 tons, and *Denia*, schooner of 133 tons, both designed and built by White of Cowes, and the *Gazelle*, one of Hall of Aberdeen's very early schooners. Launched the year after the *Scottish Maid*, which was the first vessel built with the famous Aberdeen bow, the *Gazelle* was a much finer lined vessel.

Fire-rafts through the "Flood Gates."

Before the arrival of the British Expeditionary Force from India, the Chinese made no less than three attempts to burn the shipping lying in the Cap-sing-moon Anchorage.

Previous to the third attempt to smoke the British out of Canton waters, a sampan loaded with small packets of poisoned tea was sent into the anchorage in the hopes that the tea would be bought and prove fatal to the British sailors. But before any harm was done pirates seized the sampan and unwittingly distributed its poisoned cargo amongst their own countrymen, and when many of these died in agony the whole fiendish plot came out.

The night of Tuesday, June 9, was very dark with no moon. The Cap-sing-moon Anchorage was full of shipping, which, however, was pretty much on the alert owing to previous alarms.

About 2 a.m. a noise was heard inshore. This proved to be some mandarin boats attempting to capture the cutter *Devil*, several of whose Lascar crew were wounded. Shortly after the noise of the fighting had not only roused all the small fry inshore but the larger vessels in the outer anchorage, several lights began to show in the direction of the passage called the "Flood Gates." The commander of the ship *Danish King*, which happened to be nearest, immediately fired a gun and hoisted the signal, which denoted the approach of fire-rafts. And hardly had the report of her gun died away before the whole horizon to the Norrard was lit up, disclosing no less than 18 fire-rafts drifting down upon the shipping before wind and tide. These were really old fishing junks, chained together, two and two. Some of these blazed furiously, others exploded, going off like those fire-works known as "flower-pots."

Throughout the anchored fleet trilled the boatswain's pipes and gruff orders to man and arm boats, and in a very short time every available boat was pulling away for the fire-ships on the nasty job of towing them clear of the shipping. But it seemed to most of the captains that the fire-rafts must be amongst the anchored ships before the boats could get to work, so the greater number of the merchant ships slipped their cables and dropped to leeward under headsails alone.

The anchorage, however, was too crowded for this manoeuvre, ship bumped into ship, officers bellowed contradictory orders through their speaking trumpets, the men holloaed and cheered, occasional guns went off with a deafening roar, and the confusion was such that the whole anchorage, lit up as it was by the flaming junks, showed, as a veteran put it, for all the world like the Battle of the Nile. Many a gallant deed was done in the course of the night. Boats never hesitated to make fast to the fire-ships despite the flames and smoke and the unpleasant prospect of being blown sky high; and gradually most of the rafts were towed inshore till they grounded or else were anchored clear of the shipping.

What little fighting there was took place amongst the smaller craft inshore. Perhaps the most daring act was that of the boat's crew of the little schooner *Mavis* (113 tons), a recent addition to the opium fleet. The two Chinese bumboat men, who attended on the *Mavis*, were dragged out of their tanka-boat by a passing mandarin's dragon and carried ashore.

In answer to their cries for help a boat's crew of Malays under a British officer quickly left the side of the schooner and went in pursuit. They were just in time to distinguish the two prisoners being hurried away inland. There had been no time to load their muskets, but they charged after the mandarin party, caught them up and used the butt end to such good purpose that the latter let go of their prisoners and fled. It was a lucky rescue for the sampan wallahs, for they would certainly have suffered a painful death at the hands of their countrymen.

In the midst of all the hurly-burly and confusion H.M.S. *Alligator* (Captain Kuper), the first ship of the Expeditionary Force, found her way into the anchorage, the pilotage being made easy by the flaming junks.

On the following morning some of the burnt out fishing boats, full, now, of dross, were still floating about the bay; and the only result of this effort was to supply the shipping with firewood for a month.

The British Expeditionary Force Arrives.

The *Alligator* (28 guns) arrived in Canton waters from Sydney nearly a fortnight ahead of the main body of the Expeditionary Force, which left Singapore in May 30, 1840, and sailing in regular order, each ship in its allotted station, must have been both an imposing and beautiful sight running up the China Sea before the S.W. monsoon in fine sunny weather with stunsails boomed out and all flying kites set.

Besides the *Alligator*, the Honourable Company's armed steamer *Madagascar* (Captain Dicey) was allowed to go ahead and she reached Macao on June 16

The following ships arrived off the Ladrones on June 21:

Wellesley (74), Captain T. Maitland, bearing the broad pennant of Commodore Sir J. J. G. Bremer.

Cruiser	brig-sloop	16 guns	Commander H. W. Gifford
Algerine	gun-brig	10 guns	Commander T. H. Mason
Rattlesnake	troop-ship		Act.-Commander W. Brodie
Queen	H.E.I. Co.'s steamer		Captain Warden
Atalanta	H.E.I. Co.'s steamer	616 tons	Captain Rogers
Blundell	sailing transport		Captain Traill
David Malcolm	,, ,,		Captain Malcolm
Defiance	,, ,,		Captain Evatt
Eagle	,, ,,		——
Edmonstone	,, ,,		Captain Macdougal
Ernaad	,, ,,		Captain Hill
Indian Oak	,, ,,		Captain Rayne
Isabella Robertson	,, ,,		Captain Cole
John Adams	,, ,,		Captain Eales
Medusa	,, ,,		Captain Purdie
Mermaid	,, ,,		Captain Sedgwick
Rahomany	,, ,,		Captain Landers
Rustomjee Cowasjee	,, ,,		Captain Gallie
Stalkart	,, ,,		Captain Dixon
Sulimany	,, ,,		Captain Macfarlane
Victoria	,, ,,		Captain Potter

Then on the 22nd the remaining transports joined the main force. These consisted of:

William Wilson	sailing transport	Captain Hawkins
Elizabeth Ainslie	,, ,,	Captain Lyster
Futtach Salem	,, ,,	Captain Gillet
Mahomed Schah	,, ,,	Captain Ovenstone

These last ships were shepherded by the *Conway* (28, Captain C. R. D. Bethune) and the *Larne* (20, Captain P. J. Blake).

This list comprises the whole Expeditionary Force. Not one of the transports exceeded 1000 tons, and most of them were queer old country ships of less than 500 tons. Their total tonnage only amounted to 12,000 tons. Aboard of them were the following British regiments: 18th (Royal Irish), 26th (Cameronians), 37th and 49th; besides which there were the Madras Native Infantry (37th), the Bengal Volunteers, Madras Artillery and a detachment of Sappers and Miners.

"NEMESIS" DESTROYING JUNKS IN ANSON'S BAY

National Maritime Museum, Greenwich

[*See page* 198

H.M. CORVETTE "DIDO"

National Maritime Museum, Greenwich

[*See page* 231

The Commander-in-Chief, Rear Admiral the Honourable George Elliot, flying his flag in the *Melville* (72, Captain the Honourable R. S. Dundas), did not reach Macao until June 28, and the China Expeditionary Force, as it was called, was further reinforced during the next few weeks by the *Blenheim* (74, Captain Sir H. S. Fleming Senhouse, K.C.B.; *Blonde* (44, Captain F. Bouchier); *Modeste* (20, Captain H. Eyres); *Pylades* (20, Captain T. V. Anson; *Nimrod* (20, Captain C. A. Barlow); *Columbine* (16, Captain T. J. Clarke); and the Honourable Company's armed steamers *Madagascar* (Master Dicey), and *Enterprise* (Master West), and *Young Hebe*, surveying schooner. A further number of merchantmen were taken up by the Government to carry stores and ammunition, so that the China Seas were soon crowded with a British Armada which filled Lin and the other Chinese officials with consternation.

Following in the wake of the fighting ships came a swarm of opium craft, ready to take advantage of every opportunity. Many of these were new vessels, or at any rate, new to the trade, such as the clipper brig *Kitty* (Captain Willie); the schooner *Lady Wallace*, the barque *Inez*, the barque *Bengal Packet*, the brig *Coringa Packet*, the barque *Amelia* and the schooner *Linnet*.

Some of these we shall not come across again. Any master that could persuade shippers that he had a real flyer of a craft under him was able to get a cargo of the precious drug in those days of wild speculation. During more stable times it was not at all easy for an outsider to get into the trade.

The Armada sails North.

To the astonishment of the Cantonese the whole dreaded British Armada made sail to the North-East on June 23, leaving behind the *Druid*, *Volage* and *Hyacinth* under the command of the energetic Smith, to blockade the port of Canton. Smith had succeeded to the command of the *Too-Loo-Te*, on the death of Lord H. J. Spencer-Churchill on June 3. The latter's is one of the many English graves to be seen in the foreign burial ground at Macao.

Smith very effectually stopped up the port of Canton by posting the *Volage* and *Hyacinth* just outside the Bogue. The last ship to go up to Whampoa was the American *Chesapeake*, lately the British *Cambridge*, a vessel of 900 tons. She sailed through the Bogue with £150,000 worth of British goods piled high above her rails, just as the two frigates were taking up their position off Chuenpee.

Meanwhile the Expeditionary Force sailed away before the monsoon with the object of capturing and occupying the island of Chusan. This was considered to be a more important strategic point then any place further South—owing to being in such a commanding position with regard not only to Ningpo, but to Hangchow and the famous Grand Canal leading into the Yang-tze-kiang, which was the main artery of the Chinese Empire.

We have only space to give the merest outline of the military operations, but this first war with China must have been of the most extraordinary interest to those who took part in it. Strange sights and wonders were the daily portion of our troops and bluejackets. In many ways it was a fantastic war, with comedy ever chasing tragedy, good humour constantly dispersing terror, and devastating loss not infrequently turned into unimaginable gain.

The Chinese were ever ready to supply their enemies with all they wanted at a price, and the British were equally ready to pay that price. Though they could have looted the country of treasures galore, they paid handsomely for every bag of grain or bundle of firewood.

It seemed to be realised on both sides that the war was not against the Chinese people but their rulers; and as soon as John Chinaman discovered that non-combatants were not butchered, robbed or ill-treated he was keen to trade, especially with the carriers of the drug, which not only followed close in the wake of the fighting ships, but often showed them the way into the various anchorages.

The first rendezvous of the Expeditionary Force was off Buffalo Island and by the evening of June 30 every anchor had got a grip.

On July 2 the passage was resumed, *Wellesley* and *Conway* being taken in tow by the *Atalanta* and *Queen*. That afternoon they anchored amongst the islands not far from Chusan, and on the tide ebbing the whole fleet was found to be surrounded by miles upon miles of fishing nets. Soon the fishermen appeared in their boats, and two of the boldest of these were taken as pilots. They were soon dressed up in seamen's clothes to their own great delight and the amusement of the sailors and troops.

The common Chinese exclamation of "Hi-yah!" to express astonishment was speedily adopted by the rank and file of the Expeditionary Force with great gusto, whilst Tommy's pigeon English was a masterpiece of comical imagery; indeed, so much did he delight in such expressions as "makee look see," "walkee topside" and the like, that to a stranger he became almost unintelligible.

The Chusan Archipelago without reliable charts was anxious work for the navigators. The *Atalanta* towing the *Wellesley* whilst attempting a narrow passage between an island and a rock piled up on a sandbank, the battleship, carrying her way, just touched but came off, having removed the steamer's paddle-box in the process.

The *Melville* got on hard and fast, and had to be hove down for repairs, a piece of the higher seamanship which gained great praise.

Jack's first sight of his foe, as the ships slowly ran into the beautiful harbour of Ting-hai, consisted of eleven war junks, such strange engines of war as even in his nightmares he had never imagined, with their flaunting streamers, painted poops, red-muzzled guns and gong-beating bosun's-mates. These formed a line in front of the forest of merchant junks which lined the shore.

At the top of a small hill overlooking the harbour was a joss house. Here some hundreds of Chinese soldiers took their stand about some half a dozen quaint cannon, which were so laid that they could not be trained upon the advancing Armada.

One day, July 5, sufficed for the capture of Tinghai, the capital of Chusan, a walled town entered by four double-arched gateways, as usual with Chinese cities, and surrounded by swampy rice grounds, except where a raised bank, on which some thirty pieces were mounted, kept out the sea.

This action, however, did not draw first blood. This honour was reserved for the *Blonde* (44, Captain Bouchier), who a few days earlier had sent in his boat under a flag of truce in an attempt to get in touch with the authorities at Amoy. But the boat was fired at, whereupon the *Blonde* opened a hurricane bombardment upon the batteries lining the shore, the war junks in the harbour and the Chinese soldiery drawn up on the beach.

As soon as a garrison of troops and a guard of warships had been detailed for Chusan, Captain Elliot, who was now joint plenipotentiary with the Admiral, hurried North in the steamer *Madagascar* to the mouth of the Peiho, below Tientsin. Here he delivered Lord Palmerston's despatch and at the same time met Keshen, the successor of Lin.

The Astute Keshen.

Keshen was a very different man to Lin; he was a thorough diplomat, full of polished courtesy, shrewd in sight and bland cunning. From the first he seemed to have recognised that China's only chance lay in the battle of wits rather than that of weapons, and in his very first encounter with the well-meaning Elliot he seems to have succeeded in bamboozling him entirely.

The fleet had followed the plenipotentiaries to the Peiho, and here, to Keshen's great disquiet, was an irresistible armament, with fire-devils complete, within 100 miles of the imperial palace.

Somehow he persuaded Elliot that negotiations could best be carried on at Canton, and pending these negotiations an armistice was concluded. Captain Elliot was always ready to seize any excuse for stopping this war, which he had done his very best to avert, with the result that whenever the Chinese found themselves in a very tight place the persuasive Keshen proposed a truce whilst peace terms were discussed.

Though some of the British ships went on to the Gulf of Petchèlee, on purpose to see the Great Wall, nothing further was attempted, and by November 20 not only the plenipotentiaries but the greater part of the British squadron were back in Canton waters.

They were soon to learn how far Keshen's truce carried. On November 21, the *Queen*, proceeding through the Bogue with a flag and a despatch, was fired on by the Chuenpee Fort. Contenting herself with throwing a few shells and some heavy round-shot into the fort, she retired to Tongkoo Bay. The wily commandant at Chuenpee at once sent some of the round shot to the Viceroy of Canton as a proof of his glorious victory.

The Opium Trade Flourishing.

Though Keshen had succeeded by his astute diplomacy in moving the war to a safer distance from the imperial palace, affairs were not going at all as the Emperor and his advisers expected.

Besides the occupation of Chusan, Amoy—since the *Blonde* affair—had been strictly blockaded by H.M.S. *Alligator* and other vessels.

CHIEF HOMEWARD BOUND PASSAGES DURING MILITARY OPERATIONS.

Ship	Captain	From Macao	Passed Singapore	Arrived At	Date Arrived	Days Out
Ariel	Warden	April 11	April 29	Calcutta	May 30	49
Waterwitch ..	Reynell	May 14	June 10	„	June 24	41
Kitty	Willie	Aug. 5	Sept. 15	„	Oct. 10	66
Mor	Young	Oct. 15	Oct. 27	Bombay	Dec. 2	48
Sir H. Compton	Boulton	„ 13	„ 27	„		
Sylph	Viall	„ 18	Nov. 2	Calcutta	Nov. 30	43
Rob Roy ..	McKinnon	„ 26	„ 9	„	Dec. 4	39
Amelia ..	Randle	Nov. 4	„ 17	„	Dec. 17	43
Poppy	Ovenstone	„ 6	„ 20	„	„ 21	45
Ariel	Warden	„ 30	Dec. 13	„	Jan. 11 '41	42
Falcon	Pike	Dec. 4	—	„	„ 8 '41	35
Syed Khan ..	Horsburgh	Jan. 6 '41	Jan. 17	„	Feb. 6	31
Bengal Packet	Steward	„ 17 '14	„ 30	„	„ 24	38

An attempt to cut off Macao by building a barrier across the narrow isthmus was upset by the prompt action of Captain Smith. Taking with him the *Larne, Hyacinth, Enterprise* steamer and *Louisa* cutter, he attacked the works, scattered the war junks like chaff, spiked the 12 guns mounted in the field-work and drove the Chinese soldiers away from their parapets and newly built guard-house with the loss of only four men wounded. After everything possible had been destroyed or fired, the landing force was reimbarked and the ships returned to the Macao Roads. Whilst all these military operations were in progress, the opium trade, about which the war was being waged, was flourishing. At this date, August to

November, 1840, there were no less than 16 ships and barques, each mounting from 6 to 16 guns, and carrying from 30 to 90 men, engaged solely in this trade. In addition to these larger vessels there were also 27 brigs and schooners, each mounting from 4 to 12 guns and carrying from 20 to 60 men. At the change of the monsoon it was reckoned that there were 12,000 chests of opium aboard the various receiving ships in China, besides some 28 to 30,000 chests either awaiting transit in India or on passage.

Outward dates of passages to China during the first six months of military operations are not to be had, but the table on page 197 gives the chief homeward bound passages.

The "Nemesis" arrives at Macao.

On November 25, a vessel, which demoralised the Chinese more than all the rest of the British squadron put together, arrived at Macao. This was the shallow-draft, flat-bottomed, iron steamer *Nemesis*.

This little vessel of 630 tons and 120 horse power was a very bold experiment, constructed by Laird at the Birkenhead Iron Works. Beyond the planks of her deck, the fittings of her cabin, and the great paddle-beams every part of her was built of iron, and she was launched within three months of being laid down. Her length over all was 184 ft., breadth of beam 29 ft. and depth 11 feet. When full of stores and provisions she drew 6 ft., but in the Chinese rivers she was easily kept on a draught of 5 ft.

Commissioned by Commander William H. Hall, R.N., she seems to have been chartered by the Government from the East India Company, though that company never included her amongst the ships of the Indian Marine.

It was not long after daylight that the *Nemesis* awoke the inhabitants of Macao by firing a salute right under the windows of the Governor's palace. Her strange appearance and the closeness of her approach to the shore brought crowds of wondering sightseers down to the Praya Grande. Indeed the salute speedily frightened the Portuguese ladies away from their balconies, and the course of the *Nemesis*, which took her right in amongst the fishing craft and lorchas, caused the astonished Governor to send out a warning. But

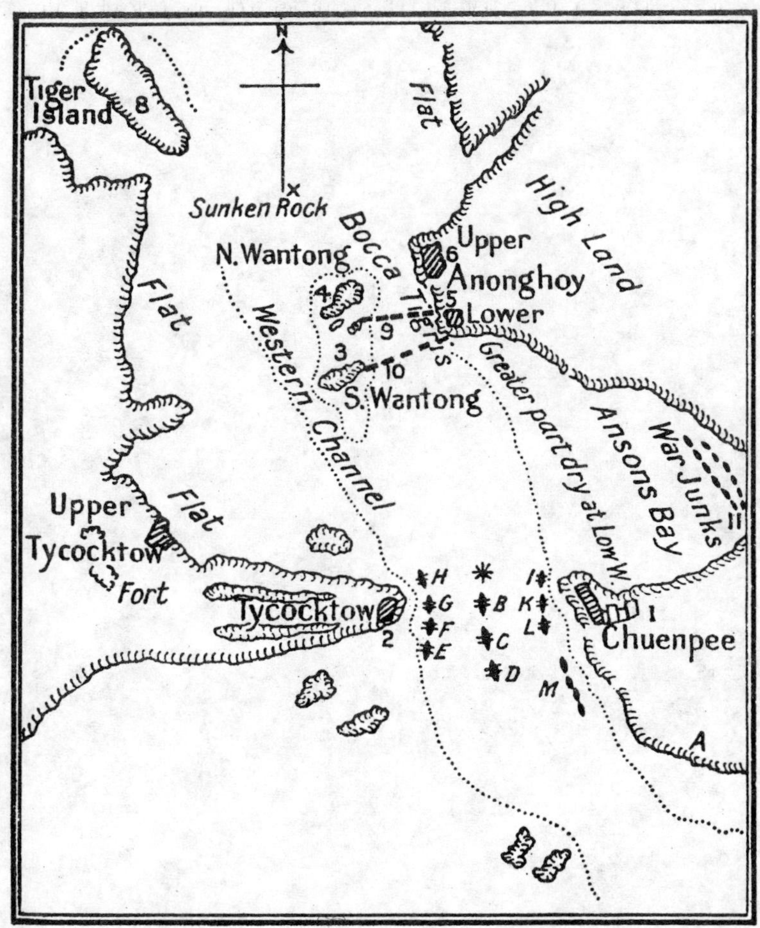

KEY TO BRITISH ATTACK ON THE BOCCA TIGRIS

(1) I K L, H.M.S. *Calliope*, *Larne* and *Hyacinth* attacking Chuenpee Fort.

(2) H G F E, H.M.S. *Columbine*, *Modeste*, *Druid*, and *Samarang* attacking Tycocktow Fort.
B C D, H.M.S. Battleships *Wellesley*, *Blenheim*, and *Melville* in midstream.

(3) British mortar battery.

(4) N. Wantong Fort.

(5) and (6) Upper and Lower Anonghoy Forts.

(8) Tiger Island Fort.
M steamers *Queen*, *Nemesis*, *Madagascar* and *Enterprise* advancing after landing Troops at A.

(9) and (10) Booms of logs lashed together across the channel.

[*To face page* 198

Captain Hall had been serving aboard the *Lyra* in 1816, during Lord Amherst's Embassy, so was perfectly acquainted with the depths in the Typa Anchorage. After landing and paying an official call on the Governor, Captain Hall steamed on to the Tongkoo Roads, where the British fleet were lying.

It was just about this time that Admiral Elliot had a severe heart attack, which compelled him to hand over his command to Commodore Sir Gordon Bremer. As soon as he was able to travel, he sailed for home in the *Volage*, leaving Captain Elliot once more sole plenipotentiary, with the whole responsibility of the war upon his shoulders.

Keshen arrived at Canton on November 29, having instructions to prosecute the war and bring the red-headed barbarians to their knees without any further delay. Though he did his best to throw dust in Elliot's eyes, by his clever temporising and apparent efforts to negotiate a peace, by the end of the year it was clear that further fighting could not be avoided.

The Attack on the Bogue Forts and Destruction of Admiral Kwan's Fleet.

The patience of Captain Elliot being at last exhausted, an attack on the outer Bogue Forts was planned for January 7, 1841. In the usual sporting style of the British fighting man, 48 hours' notice was given to Keshen and his commanders: and the hour of attack was also known to the captains of the merchant ships in Canton waters. Many of these, including the *Time* and *Waterwitch*, got under way and sailed up to the Bogue to watch the engagement.

The troops consisting of detachments of the 26th and 49th Regiments, 500 Marines under Captain Ellis of the *Wellesley*, 137 seamen under Lieutenant Wilson of the *Blenheim*, Royal Artillery under Captain Knowles, the 37th Madras Native Infantry, and a detachment of the Bengal Volunteers, were landed a mile below Chuenpee at 10 a.m. Besides these there were two 6-pounder guns one landed from the *Melville* and one from the *Wellesley*, with 30 seamen to supplement the 24-pounder howitzer of the Artillery. In all the total force, commanded by Major Pratt of the Cameronians, amounted to just under 1500 men.

From the sea side the Chuenpee forts were attacked by *Calliope, Larne* and *Hyacinth* aided by the steamers *Queen* and *Nemesis*, and also by the *Madagascar* and *Enterprise*, directly they had landed their troops.

Twenty-five minutes after the first shot had been fired Major Pratt with two Marines was inside the fort and the British flag was waving over it. So quick indeed were the land forces that the ships had scarcely time to get into position. On the other side Tycocktow was attacked by the *Samarang* (26, Captain Scott in chief command), *Druid* (44, Captain Smith), *Modeste* (18, Commander Eyres) and *Columbine* (16, Commander Clarke).

On shore, bluejackets, led by the first lieutenant of the *Samarang*, spiked the guns, fired the magazines and other buildings, and finally tumbled all the guns into the sea.

After the fighting was over Captain Joseph Pybus landed to inspect the damage; the Chinese had evidently shown no want of courage; many had been killed by the bursting of their own guns; others who carried matchlocks were often found to be badly burnt, through the ignition of the powder in their pouches by their own match.

Several shells, too, from the devil-ship *Nemesis*, had burst in the Chuenpee Fort. These were quite unknown horrors to Tartar troops whose favourite weapons were the bow and the spear. Some of the Chinese soldiers hurled themselves from the battlements into the water and were drowned; others barricaded themselves in the houses belonging to the forts and fought to the last. On the British side the casualties were negligible.

The next service was against the war junks at the head of Anson's Bay. Here the shallow draught *Nemesis* played a great part, assisted by boats from various ships, including two from the *Sulphur*, under Captain Belcher, Lieutenant Kellett of the schooner *Starling* in his gig, and Lieutenant Harrison in the *Larne's* pinnace.

The first rocket fired from the *Nemesis* fell in the hold of a large junk, which blew up with the most terrific explosion and a rush of flame and smoke into the sky for all the world like the eruption of a volcano. This broke the heart of the other 14 junks, which were anchored behind a sandbank in 5 ft. of water, for they all feared a like fate. They mostly slipped their cables and drifted ashore; but their crews dared not leave them until the British sailors came clambering aboard.

Only two small junks escaped—the rest were burnt, and even when the hulls were in flames Chinamen could be seen clinging to the rudder chains or to other parts, being fearful of torture should they be captured. In this way many of them were burnt to death or blown up when the magazines of the junks exploded. Kwan-Teen-Pei, the Chinese admiral, was said to be a lineal descendant of Kwan-Foo-Tsze, the deified warrior of the Han dynasty (A.D. 63-226) who was reputed to have been 8 ft. high, with a beard 2 ft. long, a deep red complexion and eyes like those of the fabulous bird, Fung-Hwang, often to be seen depicted on porcelain and lacquered ware.

Kwan was as brave as his famous ancestor but in the struggle he lost the red button off his cap. This was courteously returned to him through the intervention of Captain Elliot.

Kwan's war junks mounted from four to fourteen guns of various calibres, besides gingals which were provided with pivoting rests on the bulwarks. For defence they not only had rows of round shields, like Viking ships, which were composed of rattans twisted together, but they had fishing nets triced up in such a way that they could be dropped upon any boarders. Their other weapons were spears, swords and matchlocks—which were very little use against shells and Congreve rockets.

Chinese Diplomacy versus British Fighting.

On January 8 the morning was almost calm, but the excitement was great amongst the British ships, for the passage of the Bocca Tigris between the forts of Anonghoy and North Wantong was to be forced.

As soon as it was light the boats of H.M.S. *Sulphur* went ahead to take soundings. They were speedily followed by the *Nemesis* towing a couple of rocket boats; then the battleships in the centre of the stream with the frigates and sloops on either side slowly worked into position, the steamers with the troops on board all ready to land.

It was a glorious winter day and the gaudy Chinese banners waving lazily over the forts flashed their colours in the sun; but hardly had the *Nemesis* and rocket boats begun shelling Anonghoy before every banner was lowered, and up went a signal to cease firing aboard the *Wellesley*.

Then it was perceived that a small sampan, rowed by two old women and bearing an old man in the stern sheets, was rowing off to the flagship from the fort.

It was a "chop" from Admiral Kwan asking for time to communicate with Keshen; and once more a truce interrupted proceedings. Kwan and Keshen were of course playing for time, but though the British sailors and soldiers growled loudly at the way their plenipotentiary was being humbugged, Elliot's chief anxiety was to get the tea and silk for the English market aboard ship and away for home before he carried operations any further in the Canton River. Yet in the end he fell to the wiles of Keshen, and on January 20 preliminary arrangements for peace were concluded, and on the following day the Chuenpee forts were handed over. As the Union Jack came down and the Chinese Dragon went up, the *Wellesley* fired a salute of three guns, which the delighted Chinamen returned from the forts.

The British Flag hoisted over the Island of Hongkong.

The most important clause in the treaty of January 20, 1841, was the cession of Hongkong; yet this was far from being recognised at the time.

In the *Canton Register* of 1836 a far-sighted Englishman wrote the following:

> If the lion's paw is to be put down on any part of China, let it be Hongkong: let the lion declare it to be under his guarantee a free port, and in ten years it will be the most considerable mart East of the Cape. The Portuguese made a mistake: they adopted shallow water and exclusive rules.
>
> Hongkong, deep water, and a free port for ever.

The British merchants in China were not as far sighted as this prophet, for they remarked in a memorial to the Government:

> Such a settlement as Hongkong was never actually required by the British merchants and to them this sudden establishment of a Colony was entirely unexpected.

Possibly Captain Elliot should receive all the kudos, but something of the sort was already in the mind of the British Government, for, on February 3, before the cession of Hongkong was known in England, the Foreign Office had written out to their plenipotentiary.

> You are authorised to propose a condition that if there be ceded to the British Crown an island off the Eastern Coast of China to serve as a commercial station for British subjects, the Chinese merchants and inhabitants of all the towns and cities on the coast of China shall be permitted by the Chinese Government to come freely and without the least hindrance and molestation to that island for the purpose of trading with the British subjects there established.

On January 23 Elliot sent the Hon. Company's steamer *Enterprise* to India with news of the cession of Hongkong. Three days later Captain Belcher, of the *Sulphur*, landed with a detachment of Marines and bluejackets at Possession Point, hoisted the British flag and took official possession, whilst the British fleet made Hongkong Harbour their headquarters.

The old anchorages at Lintin and Cap-sing-moon soon began to look deserted, as merchantmen began to realise the advantages of Hongkong Harbour. To show the rapidity with which this new free port in the British Empire went ahead, the *Chinese Repository* gives a list of 550 merchant ships entering at Hongkong between August 1, 1841, and January 1, 1843.

The first of the British merchants to realise the future value of Hongkong was Alexander Matheson, who bought the whole of East Point and at once started to build substantial houses, offices and godowns, amongst which was the famous Junior Mess of Jardine, Matheson & Co.

The naval and military authorities started their buildings at West Point. The Chinese bazaars and markets sprang up like a growth of mushrooms to the East of Possession Point.

In the map of Hongkong, as it was in 1843, a number of names will be noticed that have since been changed; others, also, were spelt differently.

The only buildings at Hongkong when Captain Belcher took possession were two tumble-down petty mandarin's houses, one at Chek-choo and the other at Shek-pie-wan.

On Tree Island off Shek-pie-wan Harbour there was a Chinese temple. This harbour used to be a great pirates' lair in the early days previous to the British occupation, evidence of this being shown by the number of ruins.

There was soon a rush on the part of speculators to buy land in the new British colony, and as Alexander Matheson remarked: "Men of straw gambled in land and raised the price of it upon those people who were *bona-fide* purchasers."

Chinese merchants and shopkeepers also, and every bad character from the mainland, flocked to the new free port. Within a year of the first sale of land or rather of the annual quit-rents, which was held in June, 1841, not only had stone barracks been built, but commissariat stores, warehouses, wharves and jetties, Protestant, Methodist and Roman Catholic chapels, a Portuguese convent, an Anglo-Chinese college—that of the Morrison Education Society—a roofed-in bazaar, and a road nearly 4 miles long, the Queen's Road, had all been constructed by Chinese labour out of the materials to be had on the island, such as stone from the quarries.

Two small batteries were erected, but Hongkong always relied for defence upon its shipping.

During this first year of Hongkong's life, when Britain and China were at war, not only was the new free port crowded with European and Indian shipping but also Chinese. Junks, lorchas, tanka-boats, sampans and even Canton fast-boats shared the anchorage with men-of-war, Indiamen, receiving ships, country craft, opium clippers, South Sea and Australian sandalwood and beche-de-mer traders, American fur and skin ships from the North-West Coast, and all sorts of mysterious vessels from the Java Seas, whose usual clearance destination was that mythical one of Guam Nor was it long before genuine pirates dared to drop their anchors in the midst of all the other shipping.

Conference between Keshen and Elliot at the Second Bar Pagoda.

On January 26 a conference took place between the plenipotentiary of Great Britain and the High Commissioner of China in a large tent, beautifully ornamented with hanging draperies of the imperial yellow, which was pitched close to the pagoda at the Second Bar.

This pagoda, the usual octagonal, nine-storey building, about 120 ft. in height, was plainly visible from the five-storey hall within the city walls; and many an anxious Canton merchant gazed at its tall, slender shape, towering into the blue vault of heaven, with a heartfelt prayer that its "joss pigeon" should ward off all evil influences from the conference.

This was an historic occasion, for it was the first time that a Chinaman of high official rank had consented to meet a foreigner on terms of equality—and it is probable that this would not have been the case but for Captain Elliot's popularity with the Chinese.

Not only the Co-hong and its head, Houqua, but the outside merchants, the Hoppo and even the Viceroy of Canton himself, always spoke of Elliot as "No one honest man."

And the following anecdote of Keshen gives his opinion. Keshen, for his part in the opium war, was sent as envoy to Lassa by way of a punishment. There he met that famous Frenchman, the Abbé Huc. Whilst talking over the late war, Keshen said sadly: "A dreadful fate—that of poor Elut—he was a good man."

"Ah!" said the Abbé, "I haven't heard."

"Why," returned Keshen, "Elut was ordered to Enge-land when Po-Ting-Che (Pottinger) came out, and was beheaded: a great missee fortune: he was a good man."

Keshen showed great delight when the Abbé told him that his old antagonist not only had not been beheaded but had been promoted.

To return to the conference, it was an affair of great ceremony on both sides.

Captain Elliot, attended by Captains Herbert, Dundas and Maitland, and many other officers, left Macao aboard the *Nemesis*. She was followed by the *Madagascar* with the bands of the *Wellesley* and *Calliope* on board and 100 Marines, picked men from the *Wellesley*, *Druid* and *Calliope*, commanded by Captain Ellis.

As the two steamers passed through the Bogue, each with a large white flag at the fore, they were saluted by the forts on either side with three guns, the regulation number in China. Silken banners were hung out over the forts whose battlements were crowded with spectators as well as soldiers. Captain Hall, as usual, amazed the Chinese by his daring navigation in shallow waters, and when passing the stone battery on Tiger Island actually touched the parapet with his yardarms.

On the arrival of the "devil-ships" at the Second Bar two lesser mandarins were sent on board to welcome the plenipotentiary. A list of the names and rank of the officers whom Elliot would present to Keshen were sent ashore.

Early on the following morning the bands and Marines were landed. To reach the conference place it was necessary to row up a creek; for this purpose some very gaudily ornamented, flat pulling boats were sent by Keshen. The Hong merchants, headed by old Houqua, were also present in their most decorated and handsome boats, but they were not allowed at the conference itself.

At the landing place the guard of Marines was drawn up outside a large reception tent which was covered with many coloured cotton hangings and branches of trees. Here a wildly excited Chinese crowd was kept back by a specially put up railing.

Captain Elliot, accompanied by Captains Herbert and Dundas, and preceded by the two ships' bands playing their loudest, marched up to the outer tent where the presentations to Keshen took place, including, curiously enough, Captain Rosamel, of the French frigate *Danaide*. Dr. Morrison acted as interpreter. No sooner were the introductions over than a *grand dejeuner a la fourchette* was provided for upwards of twenty guests in the outer tent. Many of the officers tasted for the first time such luxuries as bird's-nest soup, shark's-fin, beche-de-mer, roasted snails, and boiled puppy, and drank priceless wines made from green peas, the fruit wang-pe, etc., besides the common rice wine "samshoo"—these all being served in tiny silver or porcelain cups, held in worked silver holders.

After the *dejeuner* Keshen inspected the Marines, the tallest of whom was selected to go through the musketry drill for his benefit. A small bodyguard of Chinese soldiers witnessed these evolutions with complete mystification.

Keshen, kind, courtly, dignified, indeed the perfect Chinese gentleman, had a difficult part to play for he had no authority whatever from the Emperor for the terms which Elliot imagined were *bona-fide*, and he had once more to obtain Elliot's agreement to there being further delay in the opening of trade and final settlement of the peace: this was to be put off till February 2.

When no sign came from the Chinese on that date the patient Elliot grew anxious, and on the 10th he sought out Keshen again in the *Nemesis*.

A meeting took place a little to the North of Anonghoy in Keshen's own covered barge—a meeting this time of urgency and not ceremony. But once again Keshen proved a wonderful diplomat, and managed to gain a further ten days' delay, though in his pocket he held the Emperor's despatch refusing everyone of the terms agreed upon and ordering him to exterminate the foreign devils without further delay or his head would pay the price of failure.

The "Columbine" sails North with Orders for the Evacuation of Chusan.

So satisfied was Captain Elliot with Keshen's honesty that on the very day of the conference, January 26, the brig-sloop *Columbine*, the fastest vessel in the British squadron, was sent North with orders for the evacuation of Chusan in accordance with the terms of the arranged treaty.

The *Columbine*, thrashing her way against the monsoon, tack by tack, arrived at Chusan only 13 days out from Hongkong, a passage which it would have been hard for the smartest opium clipper to equal in like weather. Her despatches directed Brigadier-General Burrell and Captain Bouchier, of the *Blonde*, the senior naval officer, to hand back the island to the Chinese authorities and return with all ships and troops to Hongkong. To the amazement of the Chinese these orders were speedily carried out, and on March 2, the *Blonde*, *Pylades*, *Conway* and *Nimrod*, together with the transports, arrived back in Canton waters.

The Advance on Canton.

It was very soon seen that the acts of the Chinese by no means agreed with their words; active preparations for war were soon visible at the Bogue forts, and when the *Nemesis* was sent up with a despatch for Keshen her boat was fired upon. Once again Elliot had to harden his heart and carry on the war, and the fleet of merchantmen, waiting either at Hongkong or Macao for the season's tea and silk, had to continue swinging idly at their anchors.

On February 19 the light squadron under Captain Herbert, consisting of the *Calliope* (26), *Samarang* (26), *Herald* (26), *Alligator* (26), *Sulphur* (the famous surveying barque of 8 guns, commanded by Belcher), and the *Nemesis*, sailed from Macao Roads for the Bogue, whilst the steamer *Madagascar* was sent for the three battleships, *Wellesley, Blenheim* and *Melville*, which were lying in Hongkong Harbour. Following behind these came the *Druid*, escorting the troopship *Jupiter* and the transports *Sophia, Minerva, Thetis* and *Eagle*.

Both the sailors and troops were as eager as a pack of hounds to get after that old fox, Keshen, who had once more played false. It only needed a few days' reconnaissance and exploring by the *Nemesis* and boats in order to reveal the feverish preparations for resistance that had been going on. Keshen had in fact received the Emperor's orders to root out the foreign devils as far back as February 10, but it was not until the 20th that he actually broke off negotiations with Elliot.

From that date further fighting was certain. On February 25 a mortar battery was landed on the uninhabited island of South Wantung, which at daylight on the following morning began to throw shells and rockets into the North Wantung Fort with great effect. It was a bright sunny day, and as soon as a light wind started to blow at 10 o'clock the warships let fall their topsails and stood into action.

But as soon as the cannonading opened the wind dropped, and at times ships and forts were veiled in heavy wreaths of curling smoke, through which only the flashes of the guns and the glare of explosions could be seen. At 1·30 p.m. the troops were landed from the *Nemesis* and *Madagascar*; and by sunset the whole of the forts were in the possession of the attackers, after an almost bloodless battle from their point of view, only 5 men being wounded.

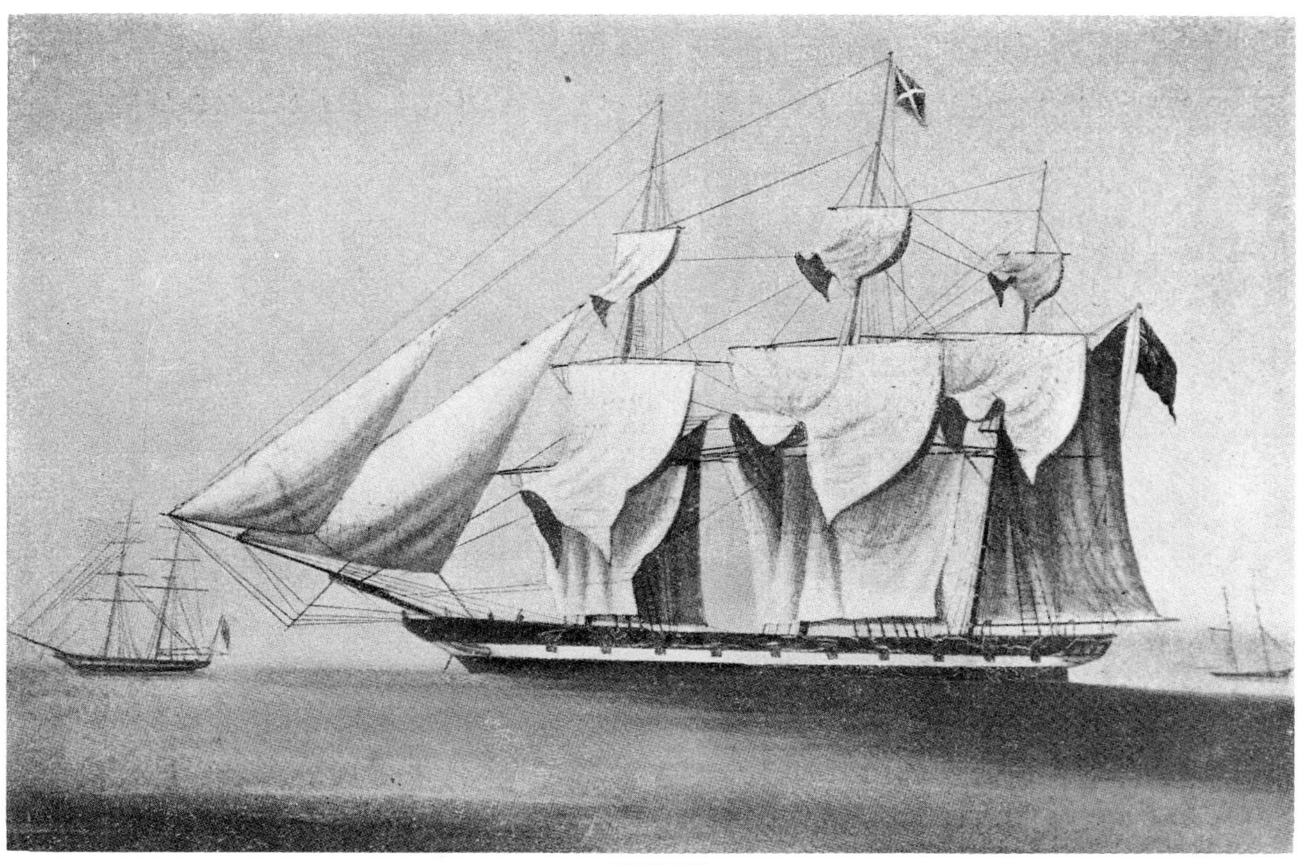

"SYLPH"

National Maritime Museum, Greenwich

[*See page* 236

"ARIEL" LYING IN SHEKPYWAN HARBOUR, HONGKONG

From a Painting

[*See page* 242

It was far otherwise with the Chinese, of whom upwards of 500 were killed and wounded, including old Admiral Kwan, who was bayonetted, as he stood at the gate of Anonghoy Fort.

The "Cambridge" blown up.

On the morning following the capture of the ports the light squadron under Captain Herbert led the advance up the river. Headed by the two shallow-draught steamers *Nemesis* and *Madagascar*, the corvettes slowly sailed past Tiger Island and the Second Bar, on the upper end of which shoal stood the pagoda where the conference had been held. No opposition was encountered until the First Bar came into sight, but behind this a large ship could be seen moored across the river. The squadron immediately anchored whilst the *Nemesis*, with Captain Elliot and Captain Herbert on board, proceeded to reconnoitre.

Just at the Bar itself a strong broad raft of baulks of timber, lashed and spiked together, was discovered extending from one bank to the other, commanded on the left by a mud battery and defended in midstream by a metamorphosed *Chesapeake* ex *Cambridge*. After Captain Forbes had sailed for home in the *Niantic*, Warren Delano sold the old ship to the Chinese admiral, who immediately prepared her in characteristic style to blow every foreign devil who came near her out of the water. Two fearsome looking eyes were painted on her bows. "If no hav eye, how can see?" The words "Courage," "Yang-Yin" and "Pa-Kwa," (emblematic of good fortune) were painted along her rail. Great streamers bearing mottoes and gaudily coloured flags were hung rainbow fashion from her masts. Thirty-four broadside guns of English manufacture were mounted and her decks were carefully prepared for action with fire-buckets filled, neat pyramids of round and stone shot, and everything clean and in order, even to stacks of bows and arrows, matchlocks, and flint and percussion muskets.

As soon as the ships could be moved up the raft across the river, which had been built at the Hong merchants' expense, the mud fort and the *Cambridge* were vigorously attacked.

For a time the *Nemesis* withstood the Chinese fire alone, and was struck several times, one large round shot almost penetrating her steam chest. All this time Captain Elliot stood calmly on the bridge between the paddle-boxes in the most exposed position. He was always present and in the hottest corner when any fighting was going on. At 2 o'clock the *Madagascar* took up a position in support of the *Nemesis*, but it was not until 3 that the remainder of the squadron got into action. Lieutenant Watson, first of the *Calliope*, was the first across the raft, having succeeded in dragging a boat over. He led the attack on the *Cambridge*; the fort was already in the hands of the British, whilst a number of war junks were in full retreat up the river. As Lieutenant Watson, Browne (the master of the *Calliope*), Captain Hall and Mate Galbraith (of the *Nemesis*) with about 10 men swarmed over the port side of the *Cambridge*, her crew flung themselves over the starboard side into the river, where most of them were drowned. Captain Herbert ordered this emblem of Celestial might to be burnt and at 5 p.m., just as it was growing dark, she was set on fire. In an hour the flames reached her magazine and she blew up, her burning timbers being thrown far and wide.

Again the British casualties were negligible, only 9 wounded and 1 killed, whilst the Chinese loss was close on 300.

Operations against the Folly Forts.

In the close neighbourhood of Canton there were four old forts known to Europeans by the names of Dutch Folly, French Folly, Napier's Folly and Houqua's Folly. Besides these there were the Birdsnest Fort, Rouge Fort and Shameen Fort, as well as several field works and sandbag batteries.

The first fort encountered beyond the First Bar was Houqua's Folly, a small stone fort, mounting 30 guns, situated right on the Northern end of Whampoa Island. Here some obstructions were found in the river, a double line of stakes interlaced with bamboos, and some large junks sunk in the stream. Just beyond the fort a masked battery mounting 23 guns was discovered and gallantly carried by Lieutenant Symonds, first officer of the *Wellesley*. Houqua's Folly gave no trouble and was speedily occupied by a detachment of Cameronians and Marines.

The Cantonese, with the mastheads of the British ships showing above the mud flats and rice fields to the North of Whampoa Island, were now in a great state of panic, numbers of the more timid and well-to-do fleeing from the city. Keshen had disappeared in disgrace and there was no one left to treat with Elliot except the Prefect of Canton, who suddenly appeared alongside the *Nemesis* in his barge.

The magnanimous Elliot, ever ready to be lenient to the Chinese, whom he looked upon as misguided and mismanaged children, was persuaded to grant a three days' truce from March 2. But once again his leniency was misplaced. The mandarins plucked up courage and issued an order that no trade or provisions were to be supplied to the British ships; at the same time the opportunity was taken to remove as much of the tea and silk as possible from the city. This indeed did put the Superintendent of Trade's back up, and he issued a proclamation to the people of Canton, in which he declared that "though Canton was at his mercy, the city was only spared in order to show how tenderly the good and peaceable inhabitants were considered, but if the authorities should prevent the native merchants from buying and selling with the foreign merchants, then the whole trade of Canton was to be immediately stopped and the city strictly blockaded."

However, again, all his efforts proved to be wasted, the flag of truce was lowered and operations proceeded.

Napier's Folly on the end of Hanan Island was speedily captured and then another pause took place. By this time Sir Gordon Bremer had arrived up the river with large reinforcements of seamen and Marines from the battleships: Major-General Sir Hugh Gough had also arrived in the gun-brig *Cruiser* from Madras, in order to take over command of the troops. The ships from Chusan, namely *Blonde* (42), *Conway* (26), *Nimrod* (20), *Pylades* (18) and *Columbine* (16) had also arrived in a fever of excitement to take part in the river operations.

For the last phase, the reducing of Canton, it was only possible to use the smallest vessels and even pinnaces and gigs. But a large flotilla of boats gave a chance to some fifty officers alone, whose ships could not get up.

On March 13 the *Nemesis* with Captain Elliot and his assistant

Mr. Johnson, Dr. Morrison (interpreter), Mr. Thom (secretary) and Captain Scott of the *Samarang* on board left Macao in an attempt to reach the advanced squadron by means of the previously unknown Hongshan or Broadway Passage. This notable piece of navigation by which the steamer more than once found herself aground in less than 5 ft. of water and at times had to fight her way against forts and masked batteries was carried out with the greatest success.

On the same day Captain Herbert, piloted by Commander Collinson in the little schooner *Starling*, managed to get the 18-gun sloop *Modeste* round the back of Hanan, where he came upon a fort containing 22 guns. This he named the Macao Fort, and proceeded to capture without more ado.

Canton humbled, March 18, 1841.

It was entirely owing to the strategy and enterprise of Captain Elliot that all the many waterways around Canton were explored as far as possible, thus making it possible to approach the city from more than one direction besides warding against surprise.

The dispositions for the capture of the remaining defences were made by Captain Herbert of the *Calliope*, who, all along, had been in command of the advanced squadron and acquitted himself so well that he was rewarded with a K.C.B. Sir Gordon Bremer did arrive in the *Madagascar* the night before, but he did not interfere and approved all Herbert's arrangements.

Besides the two shallow-draught steamers, *Nemesis* and *Madagascar*, the following ships took part in the final engagement:

Modeste	18-gun sloop	Commander Harry Eyres
Algerine	10-gun brig	Lieut. T. H. Mason
Starling	surveying schooner	Lieutenant Kellett
Young Hebe	surveying schooner	Mr. Quin
Louisa	Captain Elliot's cutter	Mr. Carmichael

In addition to these there was the flotilla of ships' boats, commanded by Captain Bouchier (*Blonde*), assisted by Captain Bethune (*Conway*). This flotilla was divided into four divisions under the following commanders:

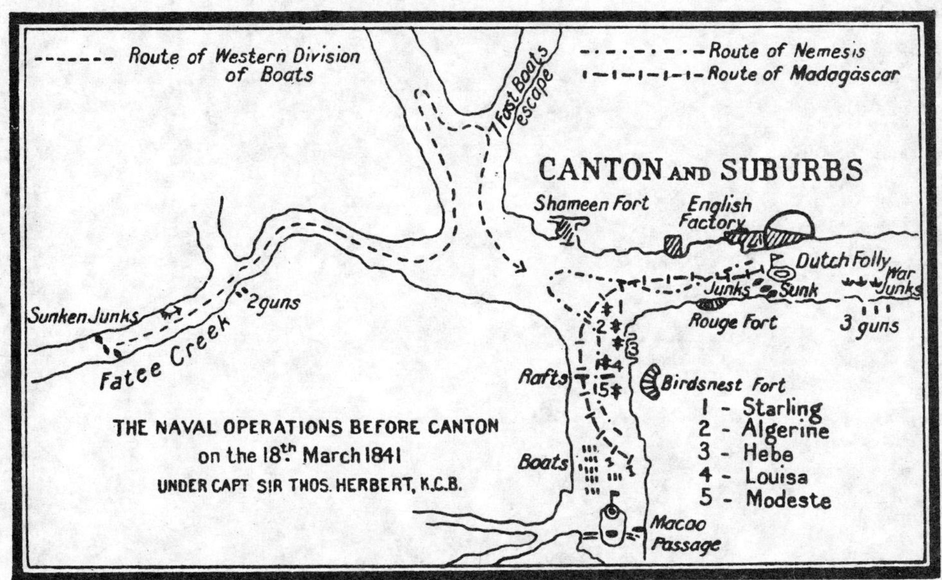

NAVAL OPERATIONS BEFORE CANTON.

[*To face page* 212

1st Division	..	Commander Barlow (*Nimrod*)
2nd „	..	Commander Clarke (*Columbine*
3rd „	..	Lieutenant Coulson (*Blonde*)
4th „	..	Captain Belcher (*Sulphur*), and Captain Warren (*Hyacinth*)

This large fleet of boats was needed to deal with the swarm of fast boats and other small craft which, under the command of a famous smuggler, were drawn up across the Macao Passage opposite the Birdsnest Fort, on the Canton side of a boom of rafts stretching right across the river. The British attack started at 11·30; whilst the *Modeste*, *Nemesis* and *Madagascar* bombarded and silenced the Birdsnest Fort and a neighbouring field-work; the *Algerine*, *Starling*, *Hebe* and *Louisa* forced a passage through the boom, followed by a division of boats, and engaged a sandbag battery and several war junks besides innumerable Chinese boats of every description.

Meanwhile Captains Belcher and Warren with the Fourth Division came through by way of Fatee Creek, dispersing and destroying another fleet of Chinese boats.

After the Birdsnest Fort had been captured by landing parties, the ships moved on through the broken boom and silenced the Rouge Fort, opposite the city. Lastly came the turn of the Shameen Fort and Dutch Folly in the middle of the stream.

The whole operation only took an hour before every defence was in the hands of the attackers, and the ships themselves had anchored right opposite the Factories.

At 1·30 a race took place between Captain Hall from the *Nemesis* and Captain Belcher from the *Sulphur*—which had come up past the Dutch Folly Fort—as to who should be the first to hoist the British flag once more on the Factory flagpole. As the flag ran up, three cheers came from the ships and boats. By tremendous exertions the *Herald* (Captain Nias), and the Commodore, Sir Gordon Bremer, in his gig reached the scene in time to see the Union Jack hoisted.

Only 1 officer and less than 10 men were wounded in the attack though once more the Chinese suffered heavily.

Many ludicrous incidents were recorded. Just before the attack started, a Chinaman came aboard the *Modeste* and asked to see "Miss-ee Kaptan." Commander Eyres took him down to his cabin. Here the Celestial calmly began to argue on the absurdity and madness of the ship and fort (it was the Birdsnest or Swallow's Nest as some called it, and the man was its commandant) fighting one another.

"My show you. My long you No. 1 good flen. What for fightie?" He began. "Large man-ta-le (mandarin) makee fightee, he please. Spose to-molla hav got fightee, you no puttee plum in you gun, my no puttee plum in my gun: puttee fire physic (powder) can do vellee well, makee plentee noise, makee plente smoke. My no spilum you: you no spilum my!" When the bombardment of the fort started, Eyres watching it through his glass, was amused to see his "No. 1 good flen" with his pig-tail tied round his head legging it to the open in championship style.

Another story is told of a sampan wallah who happened to be alongside Dutch Folly when the first British shell struck it. As he sculled madly away with his yulo, he yelled with all his might:

"My chin-chin, you stop littee, my go odder syde!"

Hunter also tells the story of an old China Street porcelain merchant, named Cum-Chong, who happened to be trying to get across the river in a passage boat when a round shot intercepted it.

"My puttee head insi holo," related the merchant, explaining that the odds against a ball landing twice in the same place induced him to poke his head through the torn planking where the round shot had come through.

As soon as the firing ceased, the roofs of the houses and the riverside alleys became black with curious crowds, viewing the two devil-ships and rakish little man-of-war brigs and schooners.

In a very short time the Chinese street venders were selling the most absurd carved-wood representations of the *Nemesis*, *Modeste* and other vessels with blue-coated sailors and red-coated soldiers complete.

A Period of Truce, Trade and Treachery, March 20-May 20, 1841.

Canton was now at the mercy of the British, but those "red-headed devils" were nothing if not merciful. From the moment the cease fire was sounded, Elliot began further negotiations and on March 20 concluded the following truce-terms with a new imperial commissioner, named Yang-Fang:—

(i) Suspension of hostilities.

(ii) Port of Canton to be opened to British trade.

(iii) No bond to be required *re* the opium trade, but British subjects detected smuggling should be liable to penalties as for like offences in Britain.

These terms were far from satisfying the fighting men though satisfactory to the Superintendent of Trade with his eye on the tea and silk waiting for export.

Indeed, so dissatisfied was Sir Gordon Bremer that he issued a notice to the British and foreign merchant shipping warning vessels coming to Whampoa to load that they might find themselves in the midst of flying shot and shell. On March 31 he sailed in the steamer *Queen* for India in order to explain affairs to the Governor-General and at the same time to ask for reinforcements. He left Sir Le Fleming Senhouse in command during his absence.

For a time a guard of Marines was stationed in the British Factory whilst the *Modeste, Algerine, Hyacinth and Herald* remained at anchor off Canton. Captain Herbert with the rest of the advanced squadron anchored at Whampoa, whilst the battleships, transports and supply ships made the new harbour of Hongkong their headquarters.

For a short time all was quiet and trade seized its opportunity; but it soon became only too evident that the Chinese were preparing for further trouble.

At the end of April the Tartar general, Yih-Shan, arrived at Canton with a large body of troops.

On the 30th, 40 boats passed the Factories, troop-laden, and it was reckoned that several thousand were landed beyond Dutch Folly and marched into the city. On May 11, Elliot arrived at the British Factory from Macao, and after a very unsatisfactory and evasive interview with the Prefect of Canton, once more found himself obliged to hand the situation over to the military. Sir Le Fleming Senhouse and Sir Hugh Gough acted at once. Within five days every fighting man was aboard ship, and by the 19th the roads of Hongkong were empty with the exception of the *Druid*, which remained behind as a guardship.

Battleships, frigates, and transports in a mighty procession of white sails were headed for the Bogue.

The Second Battle of Canton.

By the time that Captain Elliot woke up to the truth it was almost too late; day and night for weeks past the Chinese had been preparing to strike a sudden blow which should treacherously wipe out every foreign devil, of whatever nationality, within their grasp.

When the news reached Canton that an interminable line of warships and transports crowded with red coats was passing through the Bocca Tigris and that all the British light squadron which had been lying quietly in Blenheim Reach and the Whampoa Roads were getting under way, a last minute attempt was made to lull the suspicions of both military and merchants.

The Prefect of Canton issued an edict urging foreign merchants to remain quiet in their lawful pursuits, etc. Hardly was this precious document placarded up in 13 Factory Street before the familiar black hull of the devil-ship with its tall thin funnel and monstrous paddle-boxes came puffing up to an anchorage in front of the British Factory.

This was on May 19. Captain Elliot went ashore and found the foreign community all packed up and ready to move at the drop of a flag. They told him that for some days past Tartar troops had been pouring into the city. Some even had appeared in the Square carrying matchlocks and with their slow matches ready lighted in their hands; at the same time the Cantonese in a confusion that was very like panic were rushing away with every valuable that they could carry with them. As the day passed the crisis seemed to be rapidly approaching, and by the morning of the 20th shopkeepers in the neighbourhood of the Factories were putting up their shutters and barricading their doors, whilst guards of Chinese soldiers blocked the streets leading from the Factory location. It was now judged wise to decamp, and all the foreign merchants except two Americans went down to Whampoa in their boats, and before sunset Elliot and his suite and small guard of Marines went on board the *Nemesis*.

By this time Captain Herbert had got most of his squadron anchored in front of the city. The *Modeste* as usual was in the place of honour, at the head of the line and furthest up stream, then came *Pylades*, *Algerine* and *Nemesis*. Elliot's cutter *Louisa* and Dent's little schooner, the *Aurora*, lay in the shallow water near Jackass Point whilst below Dutch Folly were the larger corvettes, *Herald* and *Calliope*.

The sun set sulkily upon a gloomy scene. Instead of the busy hum, the splash of the paddle, and the ripple of water parted by the bows of innumerable passage boats; instead of loud "Hi-yahs," women's laughter, and the chanting undertone and heaving grunts of innumerable oarsmen, the river was silent, stagnant and oppressed. A dull and ominous suspense spread an atmosphere of uncanniness.

The row of black warships seemed to be asleep except for the half-hour tinkle of their bells, yet they were supremely wide-awake with doubled sentries, and all hands ready, fully equipped for instant service. Aboard the *Nemesis* the fires were lighted in the furnaces, so that steam could be raised in a few minutes. On the quarterdeck lay the weary, disappointed Elliot in his boat cloak, whilst on the bridge sat Captain Hall, straining his eyes into the darkness. The night was pitch dark, sultry and oppressive, and aboard the ships not a sound could be heard except the black water lapping against the bends.

Suddenly in the midst of the overpowering silence rang out the cry of a Marine sentry:

"Halt! who goes there?" followed almost instantaneously by the warning sing-song of the seaman on the lookout.

"Bo-o-ats right ahead."

Captain Herbert was aboard the *Modeste*. "Beat to quarters," he said quietly to Commander Harry Eyres, and hardly had he spoken before the roll of the drum and the pipes of the bosun's mates were heard aboard each ship.

"Man and arm boats," was the order, and as each ship resounded with the patter of bare feet and the clump of ammunition boots, the dark mass of fire-rafts, dropping down upon the *Modeste*, suddenly burst into flames and lit up the whole scene.

The attack had been carefully planned, no less than 100 fire-rafts consisting of two or three boats chained together had been prepared, whilst behind them came junks loaded with troops.

Unfortunately for the Chinese, their premature discovery by the wide-awake sentry of the *Modeste*, caused many to be lighted before the agreed zero hour, whilst others were never lighted at all.

The boats of the squadron and the devil-ship, which was under way with anchor at the bow, in 9 minutes, were soon in amongst the flaming rafts with their grappling irons.

The crew of a fire-ship from time immemorial had to be stout fellows; few of the Chinese in charge of the fire-rafts escaped with their lives. Betrayed by their own fires, many of them were shot; others flung themselves overboard and were drowned, others again managed to get their clothing on fire or were blown up by their own stink-pots.

Even Canton itself was not safe, for some of the blazing rafts drifted ashore and set fire to the houses.

Of the British ships the *Alligator* alone by herself off Houqua's Folly had a hard fight to keep clear of the flames; and three days later, at midnight on the 24th, the *Wellesley*, lying at the Bogue, was attacked by twenty boats filled with combustibles and explosives.

Most of her complement were on service with the advanced squadron under Captain Maitland, and for some time her commander, Fletcher, and her few officers and men remaining, with only three boats left behind had a hard job towing the fire-ships clear.

At Canton the fire-ships were only half the programme, for, as soon as the Chinese commanders realised that this attack had failed, they opened fire on the ships from several new batteries, including one with a gun of very large calibre.

Everywhere spurts of fire told of Tartar gunners at work, though the screaming shot went high overhead as a rule. The *Louisa* and *Aurora* were in the most dangerous situation; they dared not lift their anchors till the tide turned, and they would have been blown out of water by the big gun had not they kept altering their positions by veering out and shortening in cable. In this way they managed to escape except for a few grazes.

The wreaths of smoke not only from the burning fire-rafts and buildings but also from the cannonading wrapped the whole fight in mystery. The gun-layers aboard the men-of-war could only lay on the flashes ashore, but that their aim was good was proved at daylight.

As the sun rose it showed the suburbs of Canton in flames, the shore a litter of smoking wrecks, new battery works in ruins and only the Shameen Fort still active. This was soon silenced by a few well-aimed rounds and then captured by a landing party.

Throughout this exciting night the casualties and damage amongst the British ships and boats were almost nil. Captain Hall of the *Nemesis* had his hand and arm badly burnt in gallantly freeing a jammed Congreve rocket, which threatened to blow Captain Elliot, Captain Herbert and everyone on the bridge of the *Nemesis* to Kingdom Come, and he was forced to retire to his bunk through pain and fever.

Fighting continued throughout the 22nd and 23rd. The *Nemesis* and men-of-war boats under Captain Herbert's direction managed to discover the main fleet of war junks, fire-rafts and fast-boats up the creek which led to Tsingpoo. Here they did infinite damage, which though round a bend out of sight of the ships and factories was evident enough from the continuous explosion followed by dense volumes of smoke.

At last the *Nemesis* appeared in sight with the boats in tow. A general cheer went up from the shipping; it was quite a triumphal procession. The devil-ship and boats were all dressed from stem to stern with Chinese flags. Many of the bluejackets had donned Chinese silk garments of the most wonderful colours; some sported caps, others again waved pig-tails.

The British in this curious war much preferred to cut off a Chinaman's pig-tail and let him go in deep disgrace than prog him with a bayonet.

Neither side was anxious to make prisoners. The British always sent them off with a few swift kicks, the Chinese mandarins put them in wicker cages until it should be convenient to cut them in pieces.

No British prisoners were taken on this occasion, but several wounded Americans had been captured as they were trying to escape down the river, and one extremely rash American named Coolidge stayed when everyone else had left the Factories. He and his fellow countrymen spent two extremely unpleasant days in the common prison. At last they managed to persuade the authorities that they were not "red-heads" but the "people of the flowery flag." Whereupon they were taken back to the Factories where they were discovered in great distress by Major Pratt and his Cameronians.

The Looting of the Factories.

A Chinese crowd was not long in taking their revenge for the work of the *Nemesis* and boats. As soon as the Marines were withdrawn the Factories were at their mercy.

Tartar soldiers, sent to search for arms, were the first to begin pillaging; and soon a wildly howling mob of low Cantonese were chasing along the gloomy corridors, throwing furniture down the staircases, and fighting each other for anything considered of special value.

As is the way with mobs, when there was nothing left to loot, there came a ferocious lust for destruction. Doors were knocked off their hinges; panels were burst in and windows burst out; fine oak staircases were hacked to pieces; stone floors were broken up and things smashed to atoms that one would have thought impossible to break. The chief efforts of the rioters were concentrated on the old home of John Company. Here beautiful cut-glass chandeliers were destroyed bit by bit, the great gilded looking glasses were brought down with a crash, the dregs of Canton scrambling for the pieces, and the large marble statue which stood in the hall was hurled over on its side with every imaginable form of insult.

Finally all that would burn was set on fire. Curiously enough none of the Factories on the further side of Hog Lane was touched, the only victims being the Greek, Dutch and British.

At last at the end of the day the Prefect came along with a large body of police who drove off the mob and handed over the wreckage to the Hong merchants and their servants.

Conton Invested and Ransomed.

With the glare of the burning Factories in their eyes Captains Elliot and Herbert steamed away at full speed for Whampoa. The time had come to bring the whole British force, ships, troops and guns against Canton. Everything now depended on the pilots and surveyors—Kellett of the *Starling*; Browne, the master of the *Calliope*; Johnson, the master of the *Conway*; Collinson of the *Young Hebe* and others.

It was at this time that Blenheim Reach gained its name, because that line of battleship was brought up into this channel where, in after years, the largest of the merchant ships loading at Whampoa always lay.

The smaller warships and transports advanced on Canton by way of Browne's Passage, which the master of the *Calliope* declared was the main channel of the river. Beyond a few rounds from some new batteries and half finished forts little resistance was offered. But the small fry of the Navy were busy enough in other directions. All the Canton junk trade was held up—141, including the big salt junks, being rounded up and assembled in the neighbourhood of Napier's Fort. Altogether it was reckoned that 10,000 tons of Chinese shipping and over 1000 water-hands, as Chinese called their seamen, were put out of action.

Captain Belcher had the task of capturing all the fast-boats, lorchas, sampans, tanka-boats, etc., for use in disembarking the troops and stores.

The troops were divided into two parties. The first under Major Pratt, consisting of the Cameronians, a detachment of Madras Artillery with a 6-pounder gun and two mortars and some sappers, were landed at the Factories at 5 p.m. on the afternoon of the 24th by the *Atalanta*.

The rest of the force with Sir Hugh Gough and his staff were towed round to the Tsingpoo landing by the *Nemesis*.

As regards the naval dispositions, which, as usual, were in charge of Captain Herbert, *Nimrod* and *Pylades* attended to the Shameen Fort; *Hyacinth* covered the landing abreast of the Factories; whilst *Cruiser* and *Columbine* anchored by Dutch Folly. Of the ships working up along the North shore of Hanan, only the little

Algerine and *Modeste* succeeded in getting over the bar below Dutch Folly, the latter having to wait till high water before warping over the reef. During the strength of the ebb the *Algerine* found herself obliged to anchor abreast of a sand battery mounting heavy guns (some 10½ inch). Her pop-guns were useless against this obstruction, and no other ships could come to her aid. Captains Herbert and Bethune in their pinnaces tried to reach the brig but were kept off by a heavy fire from French Folly, until 2 a.m., about which time the Chinese loosed a number of fire-rafts.

For a time the fighting round the *Algerine* was hot, then the gig of the brig, under her commander, Lieutenant Mason, aided by the pinnaces of *Modeste* and *Hyacinth*, dashed straight at the sand battery, and after a brisk engagement captured it with the loss of 1 officer (Fitzgerald) and 1 seaman killed and 14 seamen and Marines wounded.

During the morning of May 25, the Chinese arsenal and building slips with 12 war junks just finished and another dozen on the stocks fell into the hands of the attackers. Three of these junks were fitted with mortars and used against the French Folly Fort.

Meanwhile all through the night the troops were being landed at Tsingpoo from the *Nemesis*, *Sulphur* and *Starling* and by daylight all were ashore. They consisted of two Infantry Brigades, a Naval Brigade and an Artillery Brigade, numbering 124 officers and 2271 other ranks.

Troops engaged against Canton, May 25, 1841.

	Officers	Other ranks
Left Brigade, under Lieutenant Colonel Morris		
49th Regiment, commanded by Major Stephens	28	273
37th Madras Infantry commanded by Captain Duff	15	215
Company of Bengal Volunteers under Captain Mee	4	112
Right Brigade, under Major-General Burrell		
18th Royal Irish, commanded by Lieutenant Colonel Adams	25	495
Royal Marines, commanded by Captain Ellis	9	372
Naval Brigade, under Captain Bourchier		
1st Battalion, under Captain Maitland	11	172
2nd Battalion, under Commander Barlow	16	231
Artillery Brigade under Captain Knowles, R.A.		
Royal Artillery under Lieutenant Spencer	2	33
Madras Artillery under Captain Anstruther	10	231
Sappers and Miners under Captain Cotton	4	137

Within half an hour of the advance being sounded the heights overlooking Canton were in British possession and also the forts commanding the city.

Only in a few isolated instances did the Chinese put up a good resistance; but though casualties were small it was a long and tiring day for the troops for the heat was stifling. Gough put off the final assault on the city until the following morning, but unknown to him, through the runner with the message losing his way, Captain Elliot had already agreed to terms by which the city was ransomed.

The ransom which the Hong merchants had to find was six million dollars. The Tartar troops also, to the number of 18,000, had to march out of Canton with banners lowered and without music to a distance of 60 miles. This was not peace with China, but the end of operations in the Canton River.

By the first week in June the British warships and transports had all left the Bogue and anchored at Canton. All the forts had been handed back to the Chinese. Though the victory had been almost bloodless, sickness was fast playing havoc aboard both ships and transports, dysentery, ague and fever being very prevalent. One of the first to succumb was Sir Le Fleming Senhouse, who had shared the fatigues of the troops ashore.

Captain Elliot superseded.

At the end of July the Honourable Company's steamer *Phlegethon*, a sister ship of the *Nemesis*, arrived at Hongkong with the news that the British Government didn't approve of Captain Elliot's treaty of Chuenpee and that Sir Henry Pottinger was on his way to succeed him.

On August 10 the H.C. steamer *Sesostris* arrived in Macao Roads with Sir Henry Pottinger and Admiral Sir William Parker on board. From this moment there was no more hesitation and no more playing at war.

Parker was a veteran of the Napoleonic wars, one of Nelson's most trusted frigate captains. Though an old man with a hard life of continuous service behind him, his energy was no whit impaired, and within a few days he had instilled new life and order into the large fleet of warships, transports and store-ships lying in

Hongkong Harbour, which eleven days after the arrival of its new commander-in-chief was on its way to the attack of Amoy.

Three days after the expedition had sailed, Captain Elliot and his unfortunate fellow plenipotentiary, Sir Gordon Bremer, left China in the worn-out *Atalanta* on their way to England *via* Bombay.

The Second British Armada.

The fleet that left Hongkong at daylight on August 21, 1841, was a good deal more formidable than that which had sailed on July 23, 1840. Including transports it numbered 36 sail, and was divided into three divisions: the centre division was commanded by Captain Herbert, now promoted to the command of the *Blenheim*, assisted by Commander Clarke of the *Columbine*. The starboard division was led by Captain Bourchier in the *Blonde*, and whipped in by Commander Gifford in the *Cruiser* and the port division had Captain Smith of the *Druid* in command, with the *Pylades*, Commander Anson, as his second.

Admiral Parker's flagship, the *Cornwallis* (72 guns), was still on her way out, so the Admiral had hoisted his flag on the *Wellesley*, which also had Sir Henry Pottinger and his suite on board.

Besides the warships which consisted of the two line of battle-ships, *Wellesley* and *Blenheim*, *Druid* (44), *Blonde* (42), *Modeste* (18) *Pylades* (18), *Columbine* (16), *Cruiser* (16), *Algerine* (10), and *Bentinck*, surveying brig, the fleet included the troopship *Rattlesnake*, the four East India Company's steamers, *Nemesis*, *Phlegethon*, *Queen* and *Sesostris*, and 21 hired transports and store-ships.

Captain Nias was left in charge at Hongkong with the *Herald* (26), *Alligator* (26) and one or two other disconsolates.

The Capture of Amoy.

It may be asked why, after Canton had been ransomed, did we go for Amoy, which only ranked in China as a third-class town. Here is what Gutzlaff wrote about Amoy: "Its excellent harbour has made it from time immemorial one of the greatest emporiums of the Empire and one of the most important markets of Asia. Vessels can sail close up to the houses, load and unload with the

HONGKONG IN 1847

From a Drawing by A. G. Dallas

[*See page* 250

"SPEC"

Lent by Director of Peabody Museum, Salem

[*See page* 256

greatest facility, have shelter from all winds and in entering or leaving the port experience no danger of getting ashore. The whole adjacent country being sterile, the inhabitants were forced to seek some means of subsistence elsewhere. Endowed with an enterprising spirit and unwearied in the pursuit of gain, they visited all ports of the Chinese Empire, gradually became bold sailors and settled as merchants all along the coast. Thus they colonised Formosa, visited and settled in the Indian Archipelago, Cochin China and Siam."

Amoy was well defended with forts, as Sir Hugh Gough reported: "Every island, every projecting headland, whence guns could be made to bear, was occupied and strongly armed."

August 26 saw everything in readiness for the attack, the men-of-war were manoeuvring gracefully under topsails, the "devil-ships" were belching out smoke and blowing off steam, the infantry were lined up on the transports in light marching order with coats folded and one day's cooked provisions.

The steamers *Sesostris* and *Queen* led in under heavy fire. Then came the battleships *Wellesley* and *Blenheim*, which at 2.30 p.m. anchored by the stern opposite a long stone battery, the biggest of the lot, and began a crushing fire within 400 yards of the works. Along the front of the town ranged the *Pylades*, *Columbine*, *Cruiser* and *Algerine*, whilst *Druid*, *Blonde* and *Modeste* attended to the defences on the island of Kolingsoo. For perhaps an hour and a half a terrific bombardment, which was echoed back and forth by the hills, took place. Meanwhile the *Nemesis* and *Phlegethon* were going alongside transport after transport and embarking the troops.

The British flag was first hoisted on a small fort on a hill close to the beach. This fort had opened on the *Phlegethon*. Lieut. Crawford, a volunteer aboard the steamer, slipped ashore in a boat, and running round to the back, burst in upon the defenders, so scaring them that they fled down to the beach, so that Crawford may be said to have captured the fort single-handed. (This was the man, Richard Borough Crawford, who, when a middy in command of a prize slaver, beat off a pirate after an action of two hours; he himself having only one man and the Spanish captain of the slaver to help him.)

It was in this fighting that the red coats for the first time came up against the Tartar tiger troops. These wore yellow clothes with black spots or stripes upon them, and as headgear had a rough imitation of a tiger's head.

Captain Hall and a stout-hearted civilian friend, old Mr. Gully, rushed to the attack with such impetuosity that they were nearly cut off, and the skipper of the *Nemesis* fought a desperate duel with a young white-button mandarin whom he succeeded in disabling in the end. By 5 p.m. all the outer defences had been carried and the island of Kolingsoo occupied.

Sir Hugh Gough had issued the strictest orders against looting and the British troops behaved splendidly, but as usual the Chinese suffered from their own rabble, who were almost as great a scourge to the peaceful citizens as the tiger troops, who had been drafted in from distant provinces.

The Opium Clippers "Lyra" and "Ann," and the Devil-ships "Nemesis" and "Phlegethon" take Revenge at Keeto Point.

Leaving a garrison on Kolingsoo and the *Druid*, *Pylades* and *Algerine* as guardships, the Admiral pushed on to the Northward on September 5. The first rendezvous was the Buffalo's Nose, at the entrance to the Chusan Group. Light winds and a heavy swell made progress slow until the 13th, when the N.E. monsoon set in, earlier than usual, with thick fogs and heavy squalls. Under such conditions the fleet became widely scattered. The steamer *Sesostris* was the first at the rendezvous, followed by the *Nemesis*, which, in poking along the shore, worked into the harbour of Sheipoo and shot it up.

Whilst the sailing ships were collecting, *Phlgethon* went on to Keeto Point. Here Lieutenant McCleverty found the two opium coasters, *Lyra* and *Ann*, busily preparing to take vengeance for the murder of an officer and hand belonging to the *Lyra*.

It will be remembered that it was here that Captain Stead of the transport, *Pestonjee Bomanjee*, had been treacherously killed by the natives. The *Columbine* had been sent North from Macao with a despatch demanding satisfaction, but Captain Clarke had to return because the Chekeang mandarins would neither read the despatch nor pay any attention to his personal demands.

Wainwright, the *Lyra's* officer, and one man had been decoyed ashore, under the pretence of offering stock for sale. They were then overpowered and murdered. Lieutenant McCleverty had the dashing Crawford with him aboard the *Phlegethon.* The devil-ship and the opium clippers promptly manned and armed their boats, which, led by McCleverty, Crawford and the two captains, Erskine and Denham, landed and took vengeance on the murderers. A detachment of soldiers was put to flight, their barracks and the village burnt.

Hardly were the sailors back aboard again before the other devil-ship, *Nemesis*, arrived. Captain Hall was a regular fire-eater; he soon persuaded the others to make a second landing. This time the torch was put to everything, buildings, farms, rice-stacks and hay-stacks so that when night set in the whole district round Keeto Point seemed to be in flames.

The Island of Chusan captured for the Second Time.

On September 25 the men-of-war and transports arrived off the little island, called "Just in the Way." The first thing to do was to reconnoitre Chusan, for this old fighting ground was strange not only to the new plenipotentiary but to General Sir Hugh Gough and Admiral Sir William Parker. The two iron sister gunboats, *Phlegethon* and *Nemesis,* were chosen for this duty, and on September 26 they ran in between Tea Island and Guard Island, in spite of the sluicing tide.

The Chinese, it was evident enough, had been doing their best to prepare themselves. On the top of each well-terraced, garden-like hill was a watch-tower, whilst near the landing place on Pagoda Hill were some new buildings which turned out to be specially erected prisons for British captives. Along the embankment overlooking the Devil's Gates Passage was a mud battery with a fortified camp at one end and an unfinished stone fort at its foot. The Chinese evidently considered a frontal attack would be the method of assault, for this long fort held 270 embrasures, the cannon for which were either copper or brass and brand new.

During the following two days, when the weather was very squally, further reconnoitering was undertaken by the *Modeste, Columbine,* and *Nemesis* under Captain Eyres.

In sailing across from "Just in the Way" against a strong wind and sea, which was right ahead, *Columbine* beat *Modeste* with such ease that she had to haul up her square mainsail and even then went away from her. But *Nemesis* managed to keep station with the saucy *Columbine* under sail and half steam. The three ships bombarded the entrenched camp with shot, shell and rockets and knocked down all the new buildings.

This was just a foretaste of what was to come. On October 1, Tinghai and the island of Chusan were once more captured. *Cruiser* and *Columbine* anchored within 200 yards of the beach, whilst *Modeste,* towed in by the *Queen,* brought up off the Pagoda Hill battery and the *Wellesley* off Guard Island. The troops were landed by the shallow draught steamers and all went according to plan, except that the tidal stream was too strong for the heavy *Blonde* to be towed into the harbour.

Chin-hae taken.

On October 10 Chin-hae was most gallantly captured by the troops, the 49th having the post of honour and the *Cruiser* covering the landing, whilst *Wellesley, Blenheim, Blonde* and *Modeste* helped a Naval Brigade under Captain Herbert attack the citadel. *Columbine* and the little *Bentinck* on the South side of the river protected another landing party.

It was practically the first time that the British had come up against China's best troops and it proved a terrible day for the Flowery Land. For the first time the mandarins realised that they could not stand up against the despised foreign devils. Yet their Tartar troops fought bravely enough, and many rather than turn tail threw themselves into the river and were drowned.

When Yu-keen, the imperial commissioner, saw that the day was lost, he walked to the river bank, performed the ceremony of kow-tow towards the imperial city and then calmly leapt in and was drowned. Scores of high officers followed his example. But 500 Celestial soldiers surrendered and numbers who were

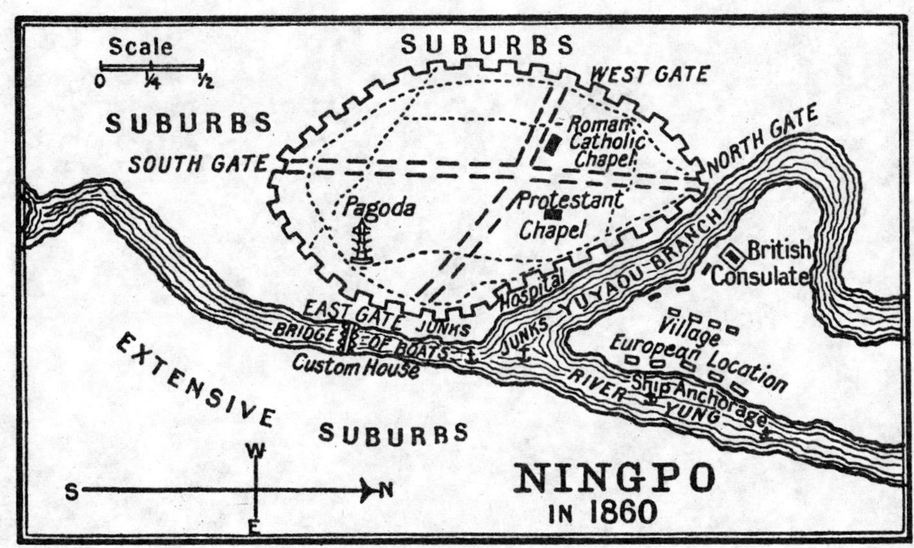

NINGPO IN 1860

[*To face page 228*

fleeing panic-stricken were purposely mowed down by their own batteries.

After the city was captured the bodies of Captain Stead and Mr. Wainwright were discovered on the common criminal burial ground, rolled up in stout mats. They had been beheaded, but besides this there was evidence that they had been barbarously tortured.

Ningpo Falls.

On October 13 the four steamers, *Queen, Sesostris, Phlegethon* and *Nemesis*, packed with troops and followed by the sloops, *Modeste, Cruiser* and *Columbine.* and led by the little surveying brig *Bentinck,* proceeded up the Yung River and brought up alongside the Bridge of Boats. As soon as the devil-ships were recognised by their black smoke chugging up the river, mandarins, Tartar troops and numbers of the civilian population fled the city, and those that remained opened a way for the British troops so that the first class city fell without any fighting.

Beyond a small skirmish at Yuyow, in which only the shallow draught paddle-wheelers and boats took place, there were no more hostilities that winter.

The Last Phase of the Opium War.

An excellent account of the last phase of the opium war, described in doggerel verse by an officer of the flagship *Cornwallis,* was published in the *Nautical Magazine* of the date. This bard, who signs himself "Tom Bowline," begins by recording the line of battleship's passage up from Hongkong against the monsoon.

The month was December, the day twenty-eight,
When we sailed from Hongkong at a deuce of a rate.
Four days took us into the Batuyan Isles,
When a gale drove us back about three hundred miles.
The ship is crammed full of shot, rockets and bread,
And dived down so deeply she stove in her head:
To our caterer's joy, the pigs were all out,
For, if one had been lost, he'd have set up a shout.

At last through the haze Formosa was seen
Or Tai-ouan (an isle off the coast of Fokien)
The ship was then shoved 'twixt Gadd's Reef and Tobago,
Where, if you have luck, in safety you may go.

And so he goes on till he brings his ship *via* Patch-the-cock to the anchorage at Chusan.

Tobago, by the way, is a spot off the South-east end of Formosa, to which this rhyme refers:

There was an old man of Tobago
Who lived on rice gruel and sago
The doctor one day
Unto him did say,
To a roast leg of mutton you may go.

The Attack on Chapoo.

It was not until the middle of May that hostilities were resumed; meanwhile the surveyors had not been idle.

For taking the ships so close in to Chapoo
We're indebted to Kellett and Collinson, who
By dint of hard work, perseverance and sounding,
Anchored all of us close to the shore without grounding.
The currents are rapid, the water quite shallow
And so full of mud that the colour is yellow.

And here is "Tom Bowline's" story of the taking of Chapoo.

Before four o'clock on the eighteenth of May
The troops were beginning to land in the bay,
Some three or four miles from the walls of the town,
The *Columbine* anchored not quite so low down;
With the *Algerine*, *Starling* and *Bentinck* (now *Plover*)
And the steamers, all destined the landing to cover.
Tenasserim took the *Cornwallis* in tow
And we very soon found ourselves anchored below
The fort in the town—where the *Blonde* and *Modeste*
Had been placed—the *Cornwallis* reserving the rest.
As soon as the *Bentinck* a signal had made
That the troops were ashore, on the batteries we played:
This did not last long, for the troops now let loose,
Carried hill after hill—running on like the deuce.
They were met at the first mentioned gingal stockade
By a terrible volley. But the Tartars afraid

Of the fury, with which our brave troops went ahead
Turned their tails and ran off, leaving numbers of dead.
The red coats now close to the ships hove in sight
So we landed our boats, the Chinese in full flight.

In spite of the humanity with which this war was fought by the British troops, terrible sights were seen in Chapoo, not only canals but the drinking wells were found to be crammed with the bodies of women and children. Yet Sir Hugh Gough would allow no looting and the greatest attention was shown to Chinese prisoners and wounded, and when our forces left the town prisoners were released and each of the wounded Chinese presented with money (about 3 dollars per man).

Yet Elepoo, the high-minded Lieutenant-General of Chapoo, was punished and disgraced by the Emperor for giving up Captain Anstruther, Mrs. Noble and Lieutenant Douglas.

The Fight at Woosung, June 16, 1842.

The *Cornwallis*' bard certainly has the gift of describing clearly with a minimum of words; for instance, here is his account of the defences of Woosung:

For a length of three miles on the right as you enter
Was a long line of guns, with a fort in the centre:
At one end of this line was a creek well defended
By a fort of ten guns, on which Woosung depended.
At t'other end of the line where it joined the Yang-tze
Was the town Paou-shan, hidden under its lee.
On the opposite side of this line of defence
Was another fort—shewing they spared no expense
To make it impregnable: yet in two hours,
From the time the ships anchored, the whole place was ours.

At dawn each ship had a steamer lashed alongside her, *Tenasserim* to *Blonde*, *Sesostris* to the *Flag*, *Nemesis* to *Modeste*, *Phlegethon* to *Columbine* and *Pluto* to *Clio*.

It is worthy of notice in this late transaction
'Tis the first time that steam has towed ships into action.

Only the little *Algerine* worked into position under sail. The *North Star* and eager Harry Keppel in his beautiful *Dido*, with every possible flying kite set, arrived just too late to take part in the action.

The Panic at Shanghai.

When the ships and steamers went on to Shanghai they found no one to resist them, the Chinese troops being in full retreat and the civilian population fleeing as if from a plague. Indeed the whole river was crowded with boats of every description piled up with household goods and furniture.

Columbine and *Medusa* sailed on beyond the city with orders to try to turn back the panic-stricken inhabitants, whilst the rest of the ships anchored opposite Shanghai.

The huge trade of this great port was somewhat of a surprise. Both banks of the river were thick with junks, many of them of great size and laden with very valuable cargoes. Stone-built warehouses full of sugar, salt and provisions, timber yards and building slips with large junks on the stocks, all testified to Shanghai's commercial importance. It was reckoned that there were 1000 large South China junks in the port at the time of its capture.

Yet all this rich city with its vast store of every kind of provision and merchandise was surrendered without a shot being fired. No less than 171 cannon were found, many of them new, along with 9 tons of gunpowder, and any quantity of small arms.

The Advance up the Yang-tze-Kiang.

The British Armada, as is our way, now that the final blow was to be struck, had assumed vast proportions. On July 6 it got under way to sail up the Yang-tze, in the following order:—

ADVANCED SQUADRON.

H.M.S. *Starling*	6 guns	surveying schooner	Commander	Kellett
H.M.S. *Plover* ..	6 guns	surveying brig	„	Collinson
H.M.S. *Modeste* ..	18 „	sloop	„	R. B. Watson
H.M.S. *Clio* ..	16 „	brig-sloop	„	T. Troubridge
H.M.S. *Columbine*	16 „	brig-sloop	„	Morshead
H.M.S. *Childers* ..	16 „	brig-sloop	„	Halsted
H.C. Steamer *Phlegethon*		.. ..	Lieutenant	McCleverty, R.N.
„ *Pluto*		.. ..	„	Tudor, R.N.
„ *Medusa*		.. ..	„	Hewitt, R.N.
„ *Nemesis*		.. ..	„	W. H. Hall, R.N.
„ *Proserpine*		.. ..	„	J. J. Hough, R.N.
H.M.S. *Cornwallis*	72 guns	flagship of Vice-Admiral Sir William Parker, G.C.B.		
			Captain Richards	

FIRST DIVISION.

H.M.S. *Calliope* .. 26 guns .. .. .. Captain A. S. Kuper, C.B.
H.M. armed steamer *Vixen* .. .. Commander H. Boyes
Marion, transport, with Lieutenent-General Sir H. Gough and staff.
7 Transports with sappers and miners, followers, etc.

SECOND DIVISION.

H.M.S. *Blonde* .. 42 guns .. .. .. Captain T. Bourchier, C.B.
H.M. Steamer *Auckland* .. .. Commander Ethersey, I.N.
10 Transports, conveying Artillery Brigade, horses and guns.

THIRD DIVISION.

H.M. Troopship *Belleisle*, Captain T. Kingcomb, with Major-General Lord Saltoun and 98th Regiment.
H.M. Troopship *Jupiter*, master commanding G. Hoffmeister, with 26th Regiment.
9 Transports, conveying Bengal Volunteers and Flank Companies, 41st M.N.I.

FOURTH DIVISION.

H.M.S. *Endymion* 44 guns .. .. .. Captain Hon. F. W. Grey
H.C. Steamer *Sesostris* .. .. Commander H. A. Ormsby, I.N.
13 Transports, conveying 55th Regiment with 2nd and 6th Regiments Madras N.I. and the Madras Rifle Company.

FIFTH DIVISION.

H.M.S. *Dido* .. 20 guns .. .. .. Captain Hon. H. Keppel
H.C. Steamer *Tenasserim* .. .. .. Master Commanding P. Wall
H.M. Troopship *Apollo*, Commander Frederick, with 49th Regiment
H.M. Troopship *Rattlesnake*, Master Commanding, James Sprent, with 18th Regiment
8 Transports conveying remainder of 18th and 49th Regiments and 14th M.N.I.

The *North Star* (Captain Sir E. Home, Bart.) was left behind at Woosung to blockade the river and detain and examine junks.

The moving of such a large fleet of sailing ships, many of whom were by no means clippers, up an absolutely unknown river speaks volumes for the pilotage and seamanship in the Royal Navy at that date. The surveyors and masters of the fleet did their best to buoy all the most difficult passages, but the steamers, especially the shallow-draught, again proved of great use in helping the sailing ships, when the tide was at its strongest.

The *Cornwallis's* poet was often enthusiastic about scenery, but Golden Isle or Kinshan specially pleased him:

And here let me pause for a while
To describe if I can what a beautiful view
Met our sight as the Squadron approached Ching-kiang-foo.

The reach of the river (on the left fringed with rushes)
Is here four miles long—at the end the stream gushes
Past a beautiful green, wooded island, by name
Silver Isle, or a Chinese term meaning the same.
Rounding this, at the top of the reach, one then sees
In the midst of the stream, Kinshan, covered with trees
And yellow-roofed palaces in the sunshine
Glittering like gold, and then a long line
Of houses and turrets, and curious old towers
At the base stretch along; and small ladies' bowers
From the trees seem to peep, while, surmounting it all,
Is a fine old pagoda with bright golden ball
And bells hung to the roofs—to our greatest delight
The British flag waved from its top before night.

Chin-kiang-foo taken by Assault.

British troops have seldom had a stiffer day's work than when they took Chin-kiang-foo by assault.

In a sun which actually struck down and killed 1 officer and 16 rank and file, walls had to be scaled by means of ladders, gates had to be blown in and then street by street the Tartars had to be driven back. It was a terrible business, for directly they realised that they were being worsted the Tartars began cutting the throats of their women and hurling their children down the wells.

Often our men caught them red-handed at this wholesale butchery and once or twice were in time to pull the children out alive.

Gutzlaff, the know-all, had assured the Admiral that the Tartars would retreat without fighting, so old Billy Parker landed and actually came in for some of the street fighting, in which a small body of sailors managed to get into the town ahead of Captain Pears of the Madras Engineers, who had the blowing up of a gate as his job. The ships themselves had nothing to do, though the advanced guard were pretty busy holding up junks in the canal.

Here for the first time the beautiful Soochow women and wonderful Soochow craft were seen.

A Chinese proverb says, "To be happy on earth, one must be born in Soochow, live in Canton and die in Lianchan." Those born in Soochow are remarkable for personal beauty, those in Canton enjoy the greatest luxuries in life, and those who die at

Lianchan easily obtain very fine coffins owing to its great forest trees!

As for the Soochow craft, passing up and down the canal, they were as varied and numerous as those at Canton. But none was allowed to pass by the saucy British gun-brigs, not even the gorgeous mandarin junks with their huge umbrellas on top and their gong-beating flunkies at the cabin entrance. And it was this stoppage of the junk traffic, of the commerce of the country, as well as the capture of Chin-kiang-foo which finally brought the Emperor to his senses.

With the canal blocked, that grand canal, which was like the country's life-blood, and that wonderful river, the Yang-tze-kiang, in the hands of the British fleet, he was obliged to stop storming and blustering at his commissioners.

The Termination of the War.

Yet it was not until all the British ships were in position before the walls of Nankin, and three hours before their bombardment was due to begin, that Sir Henry Pottinger's terms were accepted. This was on August 14.

The treaty was finally signed on August 29 in the after cabin of the *Cornwallis*, the venerable, sick and very infirm commissioner, Elepoo, being carried on board. Besides many high mandarins, all the British officers of field rank were present, and there was one uninvited guest, Captain Cecille of the French frigate *Erigone*, who insisted on being present, though his reception was not very cordial. It was not until the middle of November that the British Armada finally reassembled at Hongkong.

The two sloops, *Modeste* and *Columbine*, which had probably seen more of the war than any other two vessels, were granted the honour of bringing the war indemnity home.

The last duty of the *Nemesis* was to hurry off to Formosa in the hopes of being able to save the survivors of the *Ann* and *Nerbudda*, but only those reserved for special torture were still alive.

CHAPTER VI.

THE CHINA COAST IN THE FORTIES.

This is the Law without excuse
For all the Lords of the Sea,
That each must hold his ship from harm
Whatever the odds may be.

IF the opium war was waged with a total lack of war sense on the part of the Chinese and with more than a slight endeavour on the part of their opponents to give them a fresh chance after every round, these methods had this advantage that they did not interfere with trade as much as might have been expected.

Elliot's truces—if they drove the captains of flash frigates frantic, if they set the commanders of natty corvettes to gnashing their teeth and sent the gun-room of every gun-brig to the rum bottle, if they threatened red-faced colonels and loud-voiced majors with apoplectic fits—were yet the means of keeping the trade alive.

Wideawake masters snatched cargoes during the halt after each British success. Freights soared to the skies and dipped to the depths, thus giving a man with a head on his shoulders a chance to make a fortune in a few hours.

As for the opium trade, war made not the least difference to that—the smuggler knows no nationality. The drug merchant juggled with his chests of Malwa or Patna and his boxes of Sycee silver. If the market sometimes rose giddily to heights where perspiring brokers first lost their voices and then their heads, it as often dropped like a deep sea lead as clipper after clipper sailed in with its cargo of the forbidden mud.

Clippers continued to be built in India and to come out from

Britain; at the same time the optimistic Ben Forbes busied himself on the other side of the Atlantic in interviewing the best designers in America with the object of building suitable flyers for the China Coast.

As each new ship entered the lists, the keener became the racing. Whilst the captains of the new clippers loudly proclaimed the marvellous sailing powers of their beauties, those of the old favourites pointed proudly to their past records and defied the newcomers to beat them.

"Sylph" and "Poppy."

In the spring of 1841 a newspaper admirer of the *Sylph* wrote as follows:—

> The good old *Sylph*, the first clipper in the construction of which Mr. Seppings essayed his talents, still wears the belt for a clean pair of heels. Far prettier vessels have been built here, but none that can show her stern to the *Sylph* in a race. The beginning of the year is not the best time to make a quick passage to Singapore (from Calcutta) yet the tight little clipper left the pilot on January 27 and reached Singapore on February 9 only 13 days and a few hours in going from port to port.

Hardly was the ink dry on this letter before the *Poppy* came sailing into Singapore only 12 days out from the Sandheads.

"This speaks well for the youngster," wrote another shipping correspondent, "and we shall expect she will keep pace with her senior in future however difficult the *Poppy* found it on three several occasions to keep pace with the *Sylph's* graceful progress. I am told, however, that 12 days can bear no comparison with 9 and a few hours—the time in which the *Sylph* has done the trick."

There we see the rivalry showing itself in the public news-sheet. At this distance of time it is quite impossible to reach any conclusions as to which of the chief cracks "should be awarded the belt," as those sporting early Victorians had it. If full records were procurable it would be another matter, but they are not.

Racing down the Hooghly.

These letters to the newspapers give one a very good idea of the keenness and partizanship displayed for favourite ships not only by officers, crews and passengers, but by people ashore in those days before the machine.

Here is another letter, this time put aboard the pilot at the Sandheads by a passenger aboard the new frigate-built ship, *Prince Albert* (Captain R. Richards):—

> Yesterday morning while at anchor waiting for water to enter the Auckland Channel, the *Waterwitch* came down with a fair breeze; she anchored about noon and got under way early on the flood and passed over. She was in light sailing trim. The *Prince Albert* could not weigh until 3 p.m. The *Waterwitch* was then a large half league ahead: we soon made sail and stood after her: the wind was a point afore the beam, both ships with their starboard studding sails set, the *Witch* having the advantage of royal studding sails and staysails. At 6 p.m. we came up with and passed ahead of her, took in our studding sail and kept the lead until 7 when both ships anchored with a transport in tow of a steamer. After this the *Prince Albert* may fairly claim the name of the fastest sailing ship in India: this is the third clipper she has passed. Last voyage, sailing two days after the *Red Rover*, she came up with her and passed her eight points in eight hours, both vessels on a bowline with a fresh breeze; she afterwards passed that *ne plus ultra*, the *Mor*, a quarter of a point an hour, both close-hauled; and on her passage from Galle to Bombay gained one day on H.M.S. *Larne* hard thrashing against a North-wester.
>
> I have known the *Waterwitch* since she was built, but have no proofs of any ship passing her before. I have always looked on her as the *prima donna* of Indian beauties. On this occasion she did all she could and was in fine trim: the *Prince Albert* is laden 2 ft. beyond her proper waterline.
>
> What a ship this would be with her spacious and high gun deck for a trip to Suez or to beat up to Chusan when no other merchant ship could attempt it.

The Schooner "Linnet" launched at Chittagong.

The opium trade was a great incentive to the shipbuilders not only in India but in Burma. On March 8, 1841, a very nice little schooner of 90 tons was launched from Captain Marquard's yard at Chittagong for Rustomjee Cowasjee & Sons. In the account of the launching we are told that she was named by Mr. Ricketts, the Commissioner, and that she was "intended for the China trade and from all appearances was well calculated for a smuggler." Her agents were Smith, Mackie & Co.

The Unlucky "Sea Queen."

Most of the Indian and Burma built clippers and country craft were designed by sailors, sea captains as a rule who were either building on their own account or had persuaded one of the lesser firms amongst the Indians and Parsees to order a ship to be built on their model.

Not all these shipmasters' models were a success. A barque was launched from Oakes' yard at Howrah on April 7, 1841, which it was confidently expected would beat all the cracks; this was the *Sea Queen*, designed by Captain Syme and owned by Fergusson Bros. and her commander, Captain C. Smith. She was built of teak and iron fastened throughout except for the upper deck. She was not flush-decked like most of the clippers but had a full poop and forecastle.

Her dimensions were as follows:—

	ft.	ins.
Length between perpendiculars	113	6
Length of the keel	102	0
Breadth extreme	27	10
Breadth moulded	27	0
Height between decks	6	0
Height from rabbit of keel to lower part of gunwale	18	3
Height from ceiling to lower part of upper deck beam	16	4
Height wing transom	18	0
Tonnage	413¾ tons	

The *Sea Queen* left Calcutta on May 18 and put back to the Hooghly on May 25 with the loss of her topmasts. She was evidently overmasted. There was not much speed in her either, and after a couple of voyages Captain Smith handed her over to Captain Harvey. During the summer of 1842, she caused some anxiety by being some time overdue; at last news reached her owners that she had put into Manila with loss of her masts. After this she dropped out of the lists.

The Schooner "Anglona"—a New York Pilot Boat Model.

The first clipper despatched to China by Captain R. B. Forbes was the *Rose*, which foundered in the great July typhoon of 1841.

As soon as Captain Forbes arrived home in the *Niantic* at the beginning of December, 1840, he began looking about for fast schooners suitable for the clipper and coastal services in China.

His first purchase was the New York pilot boat *Anglona*,

which he bought off the stocks at Brown & Bell's yard. She was a 92-ton, flush-decked, fore-and-aft schooner, which he decided would be just the right thing for a despatch boat between Hongkong, Macao and Whampoa, such a vessel being badly needed by Russell & Co.

She was not the only American pilot boat model sent out East in the 'forties. Besides the *Zephyr* and the *Spec*, which were both built on the New York model, three Boston pilot boats were sent out to Shanghai soon after that port was opened to foreign trade. These were the *Golden Gate* (90 tons), *Siren* (90 tons), and *Daniel Webster* (75 tons); these acted as pilot boats in the Yang-tze.

The *Anglona* sailed for China under Captain Turner within a week of Forbes purchasing her.

The following details were taken from her captain's abstract on the voyage out:—

New York to the Equator	31 days—logged	3757 knots
„	Cape	61 „	„ 7680 „
„	Java Head	95 „	„ 13030 „

Her daily average to Java Head was 137 sea miles; best 20-day average 162; and best 24 hours 216.

This is not bad work for a little 90-ton schooner. On her arrival out in China, she was put on the Canton River by Russell & Co., until the new treaty ports opened, and then she went coasting.

Poor Captain Turner did not last very long; he was knocked overboard by the sudden gybing of the mainboom and drowned. After this tragedy her captains changed rather frequently. In 1843 first Abbot and then Adamson had her, then in 1844 we find her in the hands of Captain Macfarlane.

Opium Passages, 1841.

On the outward run to China during 1841 many of the clippers landed chests at Singapore, before going on to Macao, then Hongkong, and then perhaps up the North-east Coast.

The records of the Hongkong Harbour Board evidently began being kept from August, 1841, when the *Chinese Repository* begins giving a list of all ships entered with their cargoes, number of crew and tonnage.

"MAZEPPA" HOVE DOWN, HONGKONG, 18th APRIL, 1847
From a Drawing by A. G. Dallas

"MAZEPPA" LEAVING WOOSUNG
From a Drawing by A. G. Dallas [*See page* 258

"ANN"

National Maritime Museum, Greenwich

[*See page* 262

Amongst the clippers which landed opium at Singapore were:

Sri Singapura	150 chests on	January 29
Columbine	208 ,,	,, 31
Rob Roy	420 ,,	February 5
Eliza	8 ,,	,, 8
Sylph	138 ,,	,, 9

The *Falcon* passed through the roads on February 9 without stopping.

The arrivals at Hongkong from August 1 to end of the year were:—

Aug.	3	*Privateer*	from Macao	256	tons bound to	—
,,	6	*Waterwitch*	,, ,,	265	,, ,,	—
,,	6	*William* ..	,, ,,		,,	—
,,	12	*Omega* ..	,, —		,,	—
,,	16	*Manly* ..	,, Macao	200	,, ,,	—
,,	17	*Harriet* ..	,, ,,		,,	—
,,	17	*Lyra* ..	,, ,,	165	,, ,,	—
,,	17	*Caroline* ..	,, ,,	85	,, ,,	—
,,	18	*Lynx*	,, ,,		,,	East Coast
Sept.	13	*Rob Roy* ..	,, Calcutta	375	tons bound to	—
,,	20	*Anglona* ..	,, Macao	108	,, ,,	East Coast
,,	23	*Harlequin* ..	,, Mexico	292	,, ,,	Macao
,,	25	*Omega* ..	,, Macao	178	,, ,,	East Coast
,,	27	*Red Rover* ..	,, Chimmo	250	,, ,,	Macao
Oct.	14	*Sri Singapura*	,, Macao	85	,, ,,	Whampoa
,,	14	*Harlequin* ..	,, ,,	292	,, ,,	East Coast
,,	24	*Rob Roy* ..	,, East Coast	375	,, ,,	India
,,	30	*Cowasjee Family*	,, Macao	439	,, ,,	—
Nov.	3	*Black Swan* ..	,, Namoa	150	,, ,,	Macao
,,	3	*Red Rover* ..	,, Amoy	250	,, ,,	,,
,,	19	*Island Queen*	,, Macao	193	,, ,,	Whampoa
,,	22	*Lady Grant* ..	,, ,,	280	,, ,,	Namoa
,,	30	*Falcon* ..	,, ,,	386	,, ,,	—
Dec.	1	*Spy*	,, ,,	120	,, ,,	—
,,	2	*Anglona* ..	,, ,,	108	,, ,,	—
,,	19	*Lady Grant* ..	,, ,,	280	,, ,,	East Coast
,,	30	*Salopian* ..	,, ,,	290	,, ,,	—

All these vessels had either opium or specie except *Rob Roy* on September 13, general; *Anglona* on September 20, rice; and *Lady Grant* and *Falcon* on November 22 and 30 respectively with saltpetre.

It is interesting to note that "'saltpetre" was generally used as ballasting when clippers had a clean hold.

Here are a few of the return passages in 1841.

Clipper	Captain	Left China	Singapore	Arrived Calcutta	Days Out
Waterwitch ..	Reynell	March 1	March 27 (Madras)	April 2	32
Time	Pybus	„ 19	April 2	May 9	51
Sylph	Williams	„ 29	„ 15	„ 13	45
Rob Roy	Hunt	„ 30	„ 16	„ 14	45
Falcon	Pike	„ 26	„ 7	„ 15	50
Poppy	Cole	May 2	June 1	June 19	48
Cowasjee Family	Durham	„ 5	—	July 6	62
Waterwitch ..	Reynell	Aug 9	Sept. 8	Sept. 30	52
Kitty	Willie	„ 8	—	Nov. 4	88
Ariel	Burt	Nov. 16	Nov. 26	Dec. 18	32
Red Rover ..	Wright	„ 11	„ 20	„ 20	39
Cowasjee Family	Durham	„ 25	„ 30	„ 24	29
Falcon	Pike	Dec. 13	Dec. 26	Jan 13-42	31

As usual, *Waterwitch* maintained a record which it was difficult to beat. *Sylph* and *Rob Roy* did some very even sailing. *Kitty* seems to have been the slow-coach of the fleet, as her passages are generally very poor.

A number of vessels are not mentioned, but numbers of smugglers were up the Coast, often held up for some weeks in their efforts to dispose of the drug.

The Capsizing of the Schooner "Ariel."

When Captain R. B. Forbes bought the *Anglona*, old Lee —who had designed the *Rose* for Forbes—wanted to know why the captain had not come to him for a clipper schooner.

Forbes was just about to sail for Europe with his uncle T. H. Perkins, in the Cunarder *Columbia*, on a business visit to the Barings and Rothschilds. He hurriedly agreed to take a half interest in a schooner designed by Lee, provided she should beat the *Anglona* in a fair and square trial of sailing. When he returned to America in the summer of 1841 Lee took him to see the new schooner, which had been built by Sprague & James at Medford, and was then lying at the Lewis Wharf, Boston. Forbes saw a long low topsail schooner with very long hardpine masts, the foremast stepped right in the eyes of her; her hold was so shallow that an ordinary sized man could stand on the keelson and look out over the coamings of the main hatch.

"Well, what do you think of her?" said old Lee, squinting anxiously at Black Ben.

"I am of opinion that she can't carry those masts," said Forbes in a slow deliberate tone.

The way he looked at the schooner and the cocksureness of his voice nettled the designer.

"Try her," he said irritably," and if you can capsize her, I will give you my head for a football. She is ballasted and all ready for sea."

Forbes waited for an opportunity to try her against the revenue cutter *Hamilton* (Captain Josiah Sturgis). There was a moderate breeze outside and directly they hauled on a wind the *Ariel*, as she had been christened, proved so crank that they dared not set the foresail.

Old Lee pulled out his memorandum book and did some figuring; finally he said: "I have made a mistake; put 20 tons of lead into her and try again; and mind you wait for a good breeze."

This was done and on a day when a fine nor-west breeze was blowing, the *Ariel* got under way to try her paces against the schooner yacht *Breeze*.

The *Breeze* was a nice wholesome 30-ton schooner with no great pretensions to speed, which had been built for Captain Forbes, Daniel C. Bacon and William H. Boardman. When Forbes went to China in 1838 he dropped out of the partnership. On board the *Ariel* were Captain Forbes, Captain Cleveland, Captain Macondray, Captain Poor, W. C. Fowler, the pilot and Forbes' brother, J. M. Forbes, as well as 7 riggers, making the unlucky number of 13 all told.

Starting at 10 a.m., on the run down to Minot's, it was found necessary to take in a snug reef fore and aft. When near the point they hauled close on a wind on the port tack, heading for the Graves. The wind was very fresh and unsteady, *Ariel* lay down gunwale under whilst the *Breeze* under full sail was quite dry. Forbes was doubtful whether *Ariel* would weather the rocks, but she managed to crawl by and headed for Nahant.

Forbes then proposed to take in a second reef, but Fowler declared it would moderate as they got into the harbour. However it continued to freshen in hard puffs, and whilst in stays off Sound Point Beacon, with the flood tide cutting under, the *Ariel* quietly laid down before she could gather way for a tack towards Long Island and sank in 7 fathoms of water.

As the man stationed at the foresheet was nervous, Forbes had taken his place and was very unwilling to let it go when she went over. Forbes had warned his brother to keep shifting the painter of the boat towing astern to the weather side every time they went about; this had not been done, so that when she went over the painter was fast to a cleat that was deep under water. Forbes coolly walked out along the mainboom, got hold of the bight and cut it adrift, then hauled up the boat.

If everyone had kept as cool, no one would have got wet feet, but in "the confusion" some went overboard and Captain Cleveland, who had been round the world ever so many times, slipped off the cabin trunk into the lee scuppers and was pulled out wet to the skin by Captain Fowler, the pilot. When the *Ariel* sank the *Breeze* was close on her port bow to leeward, and a fishing schooner on her weather bow. Sturgis put the helm of the *Breeze* hard down, someone let go her jib halliards, which went aloft all snarled up; Nick Berry, Boardman's skipper, jumped into the boat and sculled across; at the same time the fisherman sent his dory to the rescue. Everyone was picked up and put aboard the yacht. As the *Breeze* headed back to port she met the yacht *Northern Light* coming down. This was one of the smartest schooners of her day, built by Wetmore & Holbrook in 1839. Her topsides were scraped and varnished with black rails and a crimson stripe; her crew were dressed in red shirts and white trousers. As she ran past the *Breeze*, Colonel Winchester, her owner, sang out: "Where's the *Ariel*?"

"Down the harbour off Long Island," called Forbes.

"I'm just going out to give her a trial," announced the Colonel.

"Give my respects to the crabs and lobsters," roared Forbes, as the boats separated.

When the *Ariel* went down, the signal station near Hull telegraphed to the city: "*Ariel* sunk off Long Island."

The consequence was that when the *Breeze* arrived alongside the wharf they found a crowd of anxious friends. Captain Forbes and his wife were staying at the Dorchester and Forbes asked his brother to stop there on the way home and report his safety. Young Forbes was as full of fun as his brother. When Mrs. Forbes met him at the door and asked what sort of a day they had had, he replied: "Oh, a very pleasant day and the *Ariel* went down beautifully." With that he passed on.

Captain Forbes went straight to his house in Pemberton Square, changed his wet clothes and drove off to the Dorchester with, as he put it, "an excellent appetite."

Whilst doing every justice to his supper, he told his wife rather a racy account of the day's happenings, but Mrs Forbes, being used to his jokes, listened unmoved thinking that he had made it all up to amuse her. But when she read the papers in the morning she came running to her husband in a state of intense excitement.

Forbes' first duty that morning was to go and see old Lee; the latter, who had already devoured the exaggerated accounts in the newspapers, received his friend with open arms and tears on his cheeks. "Thank God! you are safe," he cried.

Forbes broke in at once with wise advice about improving the schooner directly she was refloated. He recommended reducing the masts, shifting the foremast further aft and adding 6 inches to the iron shoe on the keel.

At which the overwrought Lee burst out: "Cut the masts off at the deck, put the foremast down the main hatchway, give her a foot more keel if you like, but don't mention the damned thing again."

It proved an easy matter to raise the *Ariel*; the changes recommended by Forbes were made and she was dispatched to China under the command of William Poor.

Sailing from Boston at the worst season of the year for a quick passage South, on July 21, 1841, the *Ariel* crossed the line in 29 days, having sailed 3933 miles, her best 24 hours being 210 miles. She was 57 days to the meridian of the Cape, her best day since leaving the equator being 226 miles. This run was beaten in 38° S., 57° E., when she ran 245 miles under reefed fore and afters and square sail. Her time to Anjer was 80 days at an average of 160 for the 14,102 knots on the log. This is extraordinarily good work for a little 92-ton schooner.

The "Anglona" and "Ariel" race round Lintin.

It will be remembered that Captain Forbes had promised to take a half-share in the *Ariel* on condition that she beat the *Anglona*. As soon as the former had refitted after her voyage, a match between the two was arranged, the course being from Macao Roads round the island of Lintin and back, a distance of about 40 miles. The stakes—a most important feature in all sailing contests in those days—were 1000 dollars.

The first part of the race was a dead beat to windward with a run home. Though the *Ariel* with 8 ft. off her masts and 8 ins. on to her keel was no longer the topsy-turvy vessel she had been, her forte was not in going to windward, but in running, owing to her shallow draught; thus the *Anglona* had easily the best of it until the island was rounded, when the *Ariel* set her big flying square sail and a topsail above it. These sails sent her racing ahead of the *Anglona*, which had no ballooners, and when she crossed the finishing line she had a lead of 17 minutes.

William C. Hunter wrote a graphic account of the race to Black Ben, in which nothing was omitted or understated.

Forbes, as full of fun as usual, went off to old Lee, and putting on a very long face proceeded to read him the letter. As the superiority of the *Anglona* to windward was recounted, old Lee wore a thundercloud upon his brow, though he was evidently doing his best to keep cool; his quick temper, as Forbes could see, was very nearly beyond his control. But the cloud cleared off when the run home came to be described and hardly had Forbes read the last word before he burst out: "I knew it would come out so. If you had not cut off those beautiful sticks and put on that extra shoe, she would have beaten your schooner a d—d sight more." But this is not the end of the story.

Amongst the many onlookers at the race was that keen young skipper, Joseph Pybus, who was quite convinced that his *Time* could beat the winner, and he at once offered to race *Ariel* for the stake she had won. Captain Poor, however, objected to race against a schooner which had topgallant and royal yards aloft and stunsail booms on her yards, and the story goes that in the end the two captains agreed to race under their fore and-aft-sails, and that the *Time* won.

After this the *Ariel* was sold at a good price to Jardine, Matheson & Co., and Captain Poor returned to Boston, where he took command of a twin screw schooner, *Midas*, a vessel built at Sam Hall's yard to Captain R. B. Forbes' order.

The Hongkong Typhoon of July 21, 1841.

During the summer of 1841 one of the worst typhoons that ever visited Hongkong began at daybreak on July 21. There had not been a "great wind" since August, 1835, when the *Raleigh* was dismasted and a typhoon was thus long overdue.

July, 1841, set in with some truly ominous weather. Day after day the thermometer stood at 90 and over, and there was hardly a breath of wind. Every evening at sunset immense dark masses of wild-looking clouds gathered about the summits of the high hills to the N.E. These had every appearance of being violently agitated by wind yet not the faintest air reached the anchorage, though a distant moaning seemed to utter a distinct warning and kept watch officers on the *qui vive.* This warning was further accentuated by the curious behaviour of the barometer and by the stifling sultriness of the air.

The Chinese boatmen, tanka women and provision compradores were plainly uneasy, and their morning salutation never varied: "How do, Capen sahib, what typhoon pigeon glass makee talkee."

"Typhoon pigeon glass" was the Chinese sailor's term for that mighty joss—the barometer.

If asked their opinion on the weather, the reply would be

something like this: "Me no savee, tinkee weather velly qui si, tinkee for sure we catchee typhoon this piecey moon."

And, if asked for a reason, the answer would come: "Maskee, no savee, tink him so."

Yet every morning the sun came up in a blaze of glory, in spite of the fact that all through the night the thunder had been growling and the lightning playing ceaselessly about the lurid cloud banks with every form of pyrotechnic display—sheet, chain, zigzag and forked.

This weather did not vary till July 19 when a strong N.E. breeze set in with fine clear weather. This did not last, however, and on the 20th the wind was veering all round the compass until it fell calm at 2·30 p.m. with the sky gloomy and lowering, especially in the N.N.W. to N.N.E. sector, the sun obscured, the air heavy and unnaturally stagnant, and a few heavy drops of rain falling out of a pent-up sky.

At 7 p.m. these drops became a waterspout, and a distant roar of wind could be heard. Then at 8·30 p.m. the rain suddenly ceased and all was still. The mercury, though, had now begun to tumble down. The night set in calm with stalks and flashes of lightning and long tremendously grand and impressive rolls of thunder, which went clattering and banging amongst the hills with hardly a pause.

At 2 a.m. a light breeze sprang up from the N.W. At 4 a.m. squalls from the N.W. by N. with heavy rain were coming every few minutes with gradually increasing force.

The anchorage was crowded with shipping; all the men-of-war, transports and store-ships were in the harbour, getting ready for the descent upon Amoy. In addition, there were a great number of merchant ships—Indiamen and free-traders from London and Liverpool; country craft from Bombay and Calcutta; opium receiving ships, clippers and coasters; American fur traders and South seamen; sandalwood and beche de mer brigs and schooners from the Fijis; one of Bobby Towns' decrepit Sydney-side island traders; and several nondescript traders of various nationalities, which had come "seeking" to the new free port.

Though the anchorage is a spacious one, many of these ships

were anchored so close together that there was scarcely room to veer cable.

Daybreak found nearly every ship preparing for the worst, furling awnings, sending down yards, housing topmasts, veering cable, putting on extra lashings, etc., etc.: though even at 6 o'clock there were still a few slack ships with royal yards across and awnings blowing about.

Several transports, which had been busy transhipping stores, etc., alongside each other, now hurried to cast off and find clear berths, whilst hundreds of tanka boats, lorchas and junks were busy getting under way in the hopes of being able to get across to the Kowloon shore, where they would find shelter and smooth water.

On the high stern of every junk stood a man beating a gong with all his might in an attempt to appease the storm-fiend; others of the crew were busy letting off crackers.

In the midst of these unnerved Chinamen, a daring little schooner stood away for Macao. She had treasure aboard—100,000 dollars so it was said—and two or three passengers. She was never seen or heard of again.

Ashore, whilst the bewildered British troops were wondering what all the Guy Fawkes doings were about, the beating of gongs, the firing of crackers, and the explosion of small bamboo petards from one end of the native quarters and bazaar to the other considerably added to the din and confusion. Besides this, all through the night the Chinese had been busy putting up outside their shops and houses the most grotesque looking figures suspended from 30 ft. poles: these were considered a protection against the wind devils.

Up above the growing town of Victoria, on the brow of the hill, was a hospital, built of bamboo and palmyra leaf, 200 ft. long by 18 ft. broad, which was crowded to overflowing with officers and men from the 37th Regiment, some with fever, some with wounds, some with dysentery: indeed there was only one officer out of 18 and 100 men out of 600 still fit for duty. The doctor, MacPherson, was halfway through his rounds when this whole hospital was picked up by the storm and removed several feet away from its foundations. One can hardly imagine the terrifying scene; the shrieks and groans of the crushed patients, the crash of breaking beams, the howling of the wind, the splash and hiss of the rain, all combined to stun the senses of those who were striving to rescue the unfortunates pinned under the uprooted building. Barrack after barrack was levelled to the ground like the hospital, the wind even tore up the wooden flooring: officers' quarters fell, and the wreckage was picked up and hurled along by the storm-fiend, so that it was dangerous to stay in the lines and there was a general *sauve qui peut* into the bush. Along the shore the sea was soon flooding in far beyond high-water mark, until it met the cascades of rain water which was pouring off the hills. The breakers, a mass of drift wood, wreckage, bilged sampans and tanka boats, and mangled corpses, swept the beach, whilst masses of loose stone, rolling down the mountains, destroyed shops and godowns, whose inmates ran out into the storm, shrieking for help from their indifferent gods.

Out in the harbour many of the smaller trading junks and lorchas, which had chosen to trust to their ground tackle, were driving by 8 a.m., by which time the wind was coming in gusts from the N.N.W. and North. An hour later the wind was N.N.E. and many of the merchantmen and even men-of-war had begun to start their anchors and drag.

Time	Bar.	Wind	Remarks
4 a.m.	29·46	N.E.	Strong breezes; commenced raining hard; got the topgallant masts on deck.
6	29·30	N.E.	Fresh gales; struck lower yards and topmasts; let go second anchor.
8	29·20	N.E.	Hard gales and heavy rain; let go sheet anchor; ship dragging small bower, till brought up with 80 fathoms best ditto, and 50 sheet.
9	29·10	N.E.	Tremendous squalls and rain; merchant ships all driving.
10	29·04	East	The heaviest of the typhoon, with very heavy rain; blowing a tremendous hurricane in the squalls.
10·30	29·02	East	
11	29·10	East	
12	rising	E.S.E.	Wind moderating.
12·30		S.E.	
3			Strong gales; rain ceased.

Perhaps the best account of this typhoon was sent to the *Nautical Magazine* by Captain Coldbeck, of the Liverpool ship,

Bencoolen, which, with topmasts housed, jibboom run in, lower yards on the gunwale, etc., hung on without moving a yard about half a mile from the battery occupied by the Bengal Volunteers. Only H.M.S. *Druid* lay inside her; the rest of the men-of-war were further to the S.W., including the *Pylades*, whose first lieutenant, John Hay, kept the log of the typhoon which is given on p. 250.

Here is the captain of the *Bencoolen's* description:

The wind at 10 o'clock blew tremendously from N.N.E., the squalls rapidly increasing in violence; great numbers of vessels driving fast; the harbour now began to exhibit all the horrors of shipwreck; planks and spars were blown about like feathers; ships' boats lifted by the wind and torn away from the davits; the heavy launches which were afloat and veered astern of the vessels either broken adrift or swamped, in many cases with unfortunate men on board, sent to bale the water out.

The destruction of the Chinese boats was terrible, some going down thwart hawse of the ships and others fairly riven to pieces by the violence of the wind and all having several men, women and children on board.

The number of unfortunate beings driven past the shipping and clinging to pieces of wreck, the remains of their only homes, was almost incalculable.

One sinking fast-boat, which drove past our vessel, presented a harrowing spectacle. To the forepart were holding, with the grasp of those struggling for life, a woman and three small children; a fourth was slung at her back according to the native custom. The mute terror painted on their upturned faces and the glance of helpless despair can never be effaced from our recollection. In the arched mat cabin in the middle of the boat were crouched three or four men. When close to us they looked out; a rope was hove on board them, which, however, they made no attempt to catch. There was an apathy in their faces quite unaccountable, whether occasioned by the excess of terror or intoxication of opium, we were at a loss to say.

We heard on making enquiry that such cases of apparent disregard of life were not uncommon during the day. This boat, we were informed, went to pieces a few minutes afterwards, close to one of Her Majesty's ships, lying some little distance astern of us.

At 11 a.m. the typhoon was raging in all its fury, the wind had now veered to N.E. by E., mercury by our instruments (barometer and sympiesometer) being at its minimum 28·50. The roar of the gale was appalling and its violence irresistible. It was impossible to stand on the deck without firmly grasping something, and the gusts, catching the ship on either bow, laid her (although deep in the water and everything struck) gunwale under to every squall.

The view was limited to 30 yards at farthest; the harbour being shrouded in a thick cloud of spray, the summits of the waves being borne aloft in a white shower of salt as high as the tops of a line of battleship. Although great numbers of ships were driving, it was impossible to see them until almost athwart hawse. Many drove nearly as fast as if no anchors had been attached to the cables; their hulls and outlines of spars dimly seen for one moment looming through the haze and the next whirled from view by a furious squall.

We ourselves were continually in apprehension of some of the large ships getting foul of us as they were swept by; fortunately we escaped without injury.

The damage done by this typhoon was reckoned to be 9 vessels totally lost, viz., 2 barques, 1 ship, 1 brig, 4 schooners and H.M. cutter *Louisa.* Four were driven ashore but afterwards got off; 10 were totally dismasted including H.M.S. *Sulphur*, *Royalist* and *Young Hebe.* 11 came off with loss of bowsprits or one or more masts; 2 ships lost their rudder, and several had damage to their hulls only. Nearly every vessel had lost one or more boats and in some cases all the boats had gone.

Several large prize junks were driven ashore and wrecked; one of these, laden with guns and artillery stores, piled up on the island of Cawee-chow. The conductor and gunners were saved, and some time afterwards the guns were got up out of very deep water.

Great numbers of Chinese cargo boats, fast-boats and tanka-boats were destroyed.

Besides the hospital and temporary barracks, all the houses and the bazaar were blown down and the Government wharf much injured.

The typhoon was of small circumference, for it did not blow so hard at Macao and was only a strong gale at Whampoa.

Captain Fraser rescues a Junk's Crew and a Sea-cunny of the Brigantine "Rose."

Captain Fraser, of the ship *Good Success*, belonging to Jamsetjee Jejeebhoy, Sons & Co., one of the most experienced of country captains, ran into this typhoon to the Southward of the Grand Ladrone. On the 21st he encountered such a heavy gale from the S.W. with such a tremendous sea that he had to remain hove to under a close-reefed main topsail for nearly 18 hours.

At noon on the 22nd, when 29 miles S. ½ W. of the Grand Ladrone he succeeded in saving 46 Chinese from a sinking junk. A short while afterwards he picked up, clinging to some wreckage, an unfortunate Portuguese sea-cunny. This man turned out to be the sole survivor of the brigantine *Rose* which had foundered on the previous day with specie on board to the amount of 180,000 dollars.

The Loss of the "Louisa."

That historic little cutter, the *Louisa*, which had a peculiar knack of finding herself in the thick of everything, was wrecked in this typhoon.

Both the plenipotentiaries, Captain Elliot and Sir Gordon Bremer, were on board of her and barely escaped with their lives. They were on their way across from Macao. Soon after sunset on the 20th, it being calm and the tide against them, it was decided to anchor about 3 miles S.E. of the S.W. point of Lantao.

A mile or two away the little surveying schooner *Young Hebe* (Commander Collinson) was also brought up. Both vessels hung on well until the typhoon was at its worst; then a furious squall laid the *Young Hebe* on her side and Collinson was obliged to cut away her masts in order to right her. Soon after this both vessels began to drag. The *Young Hebe*, after driving for about 5 miles, suddenly during a lull discovered that she was within half a cable's length of the island of Chungchow-sye; somehow or other Collinson managed to get his ship in under the lee, where he brought up in safety till the gale abated.

The *Louisa*, being more to the Southward, had a far worse time, being more exposed to the sea. Finding they were drifting down on to Tchow, Captain Elliot ordered the cable to be slipped and a shred of the mainsail set. It was in the strain and stress of raising the head of the mainsail, with every wave sweeping the cutter from stem to stern, that her commander was knocked overboard by the boom and drowned.

Captain Elliot at once took the helm and succeeded in steering the *Louisa* through the middle of the Luna islets, escaping rocks which could only be seen at the very last moment by a hair's-breadth.

However when the island of Myloo appeared right ahead, it was seen that the only chance was to anchor: but they were already in breaking water and no anchor could hold in such heavy surf, so that in a very short time the *Louisa* had bilged herself on the rocks and filled.

In various ways, everyone managed to get ashore, some crawled over the rocks, other swam, and a few were hauled by means of a rope.

For the rest of the night they crouched in a fissure in the side of the cliff, down which a torrent was pouring. At daylight they were discovered by fishermen who had come down to pillage the wreck. They had hardly bargained to be landed at Macao for 1000 dollars when another lot of fishermen arrived; these last stripped them of all their clothing including a star of the Hanoverian Guelphic Order.

By this time bodies of dead Chinamen, some lashed to spars, some horribly lacerated, were being washed up on the shore, and for a time black looks were turned upon the Europeans as if they were the cause of the typhoon.

Luckily Captain Elliot happened to know two of the fishermen, and with them he bargained for the shipwrecked crew to be taken to Macao for 3000 dollars. But their trials were not over.

On their way they were hailed by an armed mandarin boat, looking for wrecks. Luckily the fishermen had made Captain Elliot, Sir Gordon Bremer, Lord Amelius Beauclerk and one other hide in the bottom of the boat under the floor mats, for there was a reward of 50,000 dollars offered for either plenipotentiary alive and 30,000 dollars dead. But the fishermen remained staunch; and presently Captain Elliot stepped ashore at Macao clad in a pair of striped trousers and a monkey jacket without a shirt, the commodore being even further disguised in a blue worsted frock.

In this plight they were recognised by the Portuguese officer of the guard, who would have liked, but tactfully refrained, from turning out the guard in their honour. That was the end of the *Louisa*; the *Young Hebe* came into the Typa Anchorage under jury masts.

Meanwhile at Hongkong the gravest anxiety was felt for the little surveying schooner *Starling*, and the *Nemesis*, which had steamed across and sheltered under the high land on the Kowloon shore, was sent in search of her. Captain Hall came upon the *Starling* beating up through the Cap-sing-moon Passage, on her way back to Hongkong.

Captain Kellett had saved his ship by superb seamanship. As soon as one of her cables parted, he slipped the other, ran through the Cap-sing-moon Passage during the worst of the storm and finally brought up under the lee of Lintin by means of a boat's anchor and two of the *Starling's* broadside guns fast to the cable. She was lucky to be able to ride it out, for no vessel that went ashore came off again, being broken up in a few hours through the fury of the storm, so that every shore and islet was lined with wreckage.

The superstition about the captain's wife being always signalled out for destruction was borne out in this typhoon. The merchantman *Prince George* broke adrift and was soon ground to matchwood on one ot the many small islands off Hongkong. Her whole crew was saved except the captain's wife, who was drowned when the vessel struck.

On July 26 another typhoon swept over the Hongkong Anchorage, but this one was not so severe; at the same time both the shipping and the people ashore were more experienced in how to deal with such a cataclysm of Nature.

"Ardaseer" Twice Dismasted.

With the exception of the *Ardaseer*, which was twice dismasted, none of the regular clippers from Bombay and Calcutta came to grief in 1841 in spite of it being a year of typhoons.

Whilst bound out to Lintin from Bombay with the first season's Malwa, *Ardaseer* was first of all dismasted in the Caramatta Passage, losing her foremast from the deck up over the side along with the jibboom. She put back to Sourabaya on this occasion, where it was found that both hull and cargo had escaped injury. She was refitted and completed the voyage without further incident.

On her second voyage to China in 1841 she left Singapore on November 2. At 2 o'clock on the morning of November 16, the barometer gave warning that something was coming, by a sudden drop. Immediately every preparation was made to resist the battering that was evidently in store for the little barque.

By daylight it was blowing a typhoon with the sea rising in pyramids, that made a clean breach over the *Ardaseer*. The clipper was almost on her beam ends; and, as an old sailor used to say, "when things begin to go, it's time to stand by for Davy Jones' locker." The *Ardaseer's* decks were soon swept clean, both quarter-boats, davits and all, being the first to disappear. Captain McIntyre tried to get his vessel off before the wind but she was too far over to feel the pressure of her helm. Then he gave orders for the lee guns to be sent overboard, but the crew only succeeded in getting one of them over; they then broke in a port to let the water run off.

About 8.30 a.m. a particularly severe squall laid the *Ardaseer* right down, so that the sea came up to the mast-coats. The forecastle was under water, the dead-lights beaten in, and with the cabin half full of water she seemed to be going bodily down.

"Cut away the masts! Axes to the lower lanyards!" shrieked the captain through his trumpet. In those days sailors were like cats, they hung on by their toes and eyelids whilst they worked with hands and teeth. To cut the three masts away seemed a task of sheer impossibility, yet it was done, and so skilfully that they fell together at just the right moment.

Slowly the gallant ship struggled up on to an even keel; and the next job was to cut the spars clear before the hull was damaged—this also was done and the little barque, still as tight as a bottle, weathered it out. Captain McIntyre, having rigged jury masts, tried to make Manila, but, finding it impossible to make headway against the monsoon, he bore up for Singapore, where he arrived on December 9.

Joseph Pybus buys Commodore Wilkes' Tender "Flying Fish."

The American circumnavigator, Commodore Wilkes, arrived at Singapore at the end of 1841. Amongst his little squadron, the ship that did as much useful and hard work and probably a greater mileage than even his flagship was the little tender *Flying Fish.*

When he sailed from America Commodore Wilkes took with him two New York pilot boats, the *Seagull,* of 110 tons, and the *Flying Fish,* of 96 tons (American measurement). These were beautiful little fore-and-aft schooners about as smart all round for their size as any ships ever built, being good sea boats, good

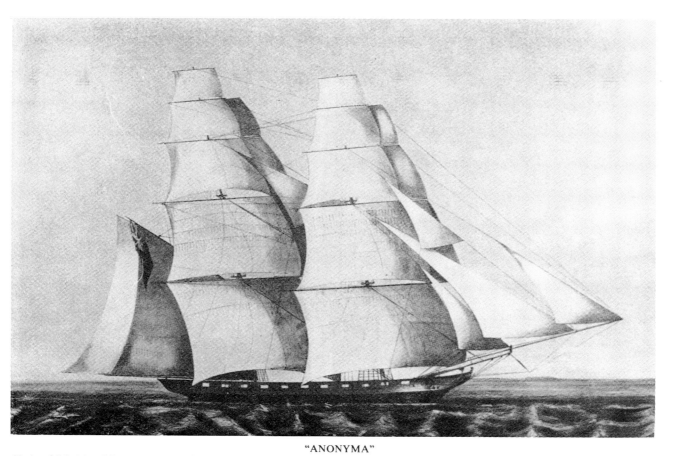

"ANONYMA"

National Maritime Museum, Greenwich

[*See page* 266

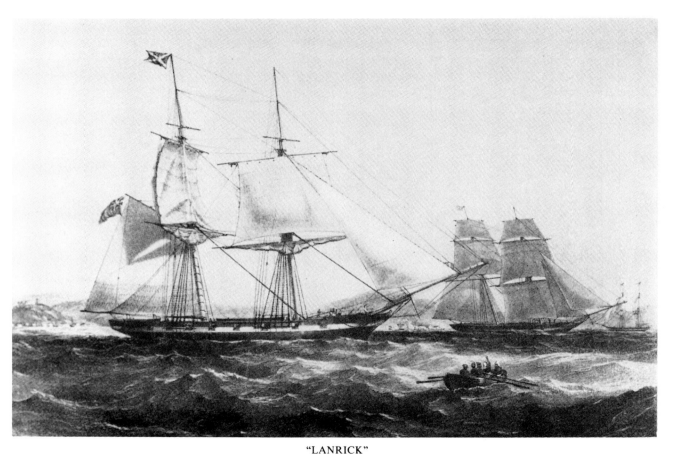

"LANRICK"

National Maritime Museum, Greenwich

[*See page* 268

sailers, and so handy that they could be made to do anything but speak.

The *Seagull* disappeared without leaving a trace during a very hard passage to the Westward round the Horn, but the *Flying Fish* became the commodore's pet, and was given a great deal of tricky and dangerous survey work in the different island groups of the Pacific.

However, when Wilkes and his squadron arrived at Singapore she was so worn out by hard usage that, after getting a very exorbitant estimate for having her repaired, he reluctantly decided to sell her. She was put up for auction in January, 1842, and knocked down to Joseph Pybus for 3700 dollars. Captain Pybus had the little schooner sheathed with teak and put a coat of shunam in between the sheathing; this made her as tight as a bottle.

He renamed her the *Spec*, not because she was so small, but because she was a speculation, which he had entered into on the spur of the moment.

Until well into the 'seventies the little *Spec* was a very well-known vessel on the China Coast, and her adventures, could they be exhumed from the past, would make exciting reading.

When the Pybus Brothers sold her in 1843, she fell into rather disreputable hands and she was seized by H.M.S. *Childers* for attacking a trading junk. Her captain's defence was that he was pirate hunting on his own account, but unfortunately his papers and log showed that the *Spec* was guilty of habitual infraction of the navigation laws. The *Spec* escaped being branded as a pirate, through the simple means of getting rid of the witnesses, who, with their pockets lined with dollars, decamped before the case came on. After this the *Spec* fell into more reputable hands and during the 'fifties was employed convoying trading junks. On one occasion in 1852 she was very nearly captured, being riddled with shot, and in the end she was compelled to abandon her charges and escape by superior sailing.

The pirates who attacked the *Spec* were afterwards destroyed by H.M.S. *Rattler*, one of the early steam gun-boats. After this one finds the *Spec* running between Ningpo and Shanghai until the 'seventies.

I am not certain of her end; Lanning in his *History of Shanghai* says that she was eventually captured by pirates who had their headquarters at Wenchow; Captain Henry Pybus, on the other hand, says she was lost in a typhoon.

Local Nomenclature in India and China.

I should perhaps have explained before the local geographical nomenclature of the country captains, opium skippers and other seamen trading out East which was often rather confusing to newcomers.

The whole of the Western Coast of Hindostan was simply known as "The Coast," whilst the Bay of Bengal lying to the Eastward of the Andamans and Nicobars was always called "the Gulf of Martaban." Then the Coast of Sumatra was known as "the West Coast," whilst that of China became "The East Coast."

The American Schooners "Zephyr" and "Mazeppa."

Two of the smartest schooners on the East Coast during the 'forties were the *Zephyr* and *Mazeppa*, both sent out on spec by Captain R. B. Forbes, and the first bought by Dent and the second by Jardine, Matheson & Co.

The *Zephyr* was a topsail schooner of 150 tons designed by Sam Hall of East Boston on the pilot boat model and built as a yacht to the order of Daniel Burn of Canton and Captain Forbes. Beautifully constructed of American oak and elm, she was very heavily sparred and armed with four 18-pounders a side, all brass, a long 18-pounder brass pivot gun on the fo's'le and a 68-pounder pivot Armstrong amidships.

Launched on April 12, 1842, she sailed for China on May 15, and made the passage out under Captain Thomas M. Johnson of Salem in 112 days.

The following is an extract from a letter which Captain Johnson wrote to Forbes, dated June 8, 1843:

> The *Zephyr* is now in the Raypa, with loss of mainboom, fore-gaff and jib. I was caught off the Grand Ladrone in a gale at North-East; she did well till the jib was lost, and we beat from the Ladrone to here under double-reefed sails and storm jib quicker than anything in China could have done it. None of the vessels I have met could beat

her. On the wind I do believe there is not anything can beat her. When in ballast she is as dry as any of them. We sprang our bowsprit 16 days out of Boston; the double topping lifts cant the boom so as to break the jaws. In smooth water, on a wind, her equal is not to be found in China or elsewhere in my opinion. Properly ballasted, she is the easiest vessel I was ever on board of.

On the passage alluded to by Captain Johnson, the *Zephyr* beat the new schooner *Emma* in a race from Bombay. Both vessels arrived at Singapore on May 20, the *Emma*, which had come by the more direct route, being a few hours in the lead.

The *Mazeppa*, a clipper schooner of 175 tons, was built by Brown & Bell at New York for A. A. Low and Captain Forbes. She sailed from New York on June 21 and Captain Forbes went down the Bay in her.

The Low brothers also went as far as Sandy Hook in her, and when they wished to leave in the tug young Charles Porter Low (afterwards a very famous sea captain in the China trade) was missing. Suspecting that he was trying to stow away, his brothers had the schooner searched and he was eventually found half suffocated in one of the bread lockers.

Captain Forbes discharged the pilot, John Magin and said good-bye, so that every one concluded that he was going the voyage.

A fine whole sail breeze was blowing and soon the *Mazeppa* began to overhaul a sail, which turned out to be the U.S. surveying brig *Washington* (Captain Gedney). Seeing that he could not keep ahead of the schooner, he reefed his topsails. As the *Mazeppa* ranged up alongside, going two to his one, Captain Forbes sang out that he was a passenger on a trial trip and would Captain Gedney put him ashore somewhere. The *Washington* picked Forbes up, and whilst the *Mazeppa* filled away on her course the brig tacked in towards the Highlands, where she put the adventurous Forbes aboard a schooner with a deck-load of Georgia pine. The schooner turned out to be infested with some kind of fever, so when she was approaching quarantine station about 3 a.m. Forbes slipped away in a shore boat. Then after a nap in a "flea-bitten hotel," he took the first ferry-boat to New York, where he met the astonished pilot Magin on the street.

James Matheson leaves China.

On March 10, 1842, one of the great characters of Canton in its early days, James Matheson, left China for good, sailing from Macao for Bombay in the clipper barque *Tartar* (Captain Luce).

The early success of Jardine, Matheson & Co. was in great part due to the charm of manner of young Matheson, as well as to his level-headed Scottish shrewdness. Born at Shiness in the parish of Lairg, Sutherlandshire, on November 17, 1796, he was only 19 years of age when he arrived in Calcutta and scarcely 20 when he left his uncle's counting house and plunged into the unknown, as China was in those days to anyone outside the Company's employ.

Matheson was one of those wise men who studied the people amongst whom he came to live. He did all he could to help the poorer Chinese; he was one of the chief supporters of Morrison's Educational Society for teaching young Chinese English, and it was owing to his friendship that that strange missionary, Gutzlaff, with his tracts and his pills, found himself aboard the *Sylph* and other opium clippers.

In 1827 Matheson imported the first printing press into China, and it was due to him that the *Canton Register*, the first English paper in China, came to be printed.

If his straight dealings and benevolent heart made him a *persona grata* with the Chinese, the Parsees and Indians for whom his firm acted as agents were equally enthusiastic about him.

When the *Tartar* landed him at Bombay on his way home, an address was presented to him by 80 of Bombay's most distinguished native merchants, headed by Sir Jamsetjee Jejeebhoy, Framjee Cowajee, Bomanjee Hormusjee, Cursetjee Ardaseer Selt, Jagonette Sunkersett and Dackjee Dadajee.

In addition to this address they presented him with a piece of plate valued at £1500.

James Matheson never returned to China. He settled down in the Highlands, became M.P. for Ashburton in 1842, married in 1843, was created a baronet in 1850, and died at Mentone on December 31, 1878. His place in the great firm was taken by his nephews Alexander and Donald Matheson.

It is interesting to note that when, after the opium war, the firm of Jardine, Matheson & Co. made Hongkong their headquarters, the partners consisted of Alexander Matheson (representing the firm in England), Donald Matheson, David Jardine (representing the firm at Canton), William Stewart, Joseph Jardine and A. Grant Dallas (representing the firm in Shanghai). B. A. Baretto was head of the Macao branch and Duncan Forbes was head at Amoy.

Terrible Treatment of the Shipwrecked Crew of the "Ann" on Formosa.

The island of Formosa, at the time of the opium war, was a *terra incognita,* even to the experienced masters of the opium clippers.

If Amoy imported great quantities of rice, sugar, camphor and tobacco from Formosa, Formosa had a great attraction for all the bad lawless characters in Amoy, who, joining up with the wild treacherous natives, made the island a particularly unpleasant place to be wrecked upon. As a rule any vessel that got ashore on Formosa was posted as missing, nothing ever being heard of her or her people again.

But during the war there were two wrecks upon the island of Formosa from which some of the survivors did escape to tell the tale.

The first of these was that of the *Nerbudda* in September, 1841. The *Nerbudda* was a small transport on her way to join the Expeditionary Force with some 250 Indian camp-followers on board. When she struck the beach her captain, 28 other Europeans, 2 Manila men and 3 Indians managed to slip away in the ship's boats immediately after she had stranded, leaving 240 terrified Indians behind on the wreck. The boats were lucky enough to be picked up by the schooner *Black Swan,* one of the opium coasters on her way down to Hongkong.

The camp-wallahs seem to have behaved with spirit. They managed to construct rafts, in which most of them reached the shore, though some perished in the surf and others apparently were murdered by plundering Formosans. The survivors were imprisoned by the mandarins and subjected to the most cruel treatment.

The brig *Ann*, under the command of Captain Denham, was on her way to Macao from Chusan, with specie, when she ran ashore on Formosa in March, 1842. Her complement consisted of 57 souls all told; there were 14 English or Americans, including several passengers, 4 Portuguese sea-cunnies, 5 Chinese schroffs and body servants, and 34 Lascars. They all safely got ashore from the wreck at daylight, and marching along the beach for about 2 miles came upon two junks lying windbound in a creek.

The junk-men would have taken them across to Amoy had not the gale still continued; but this being impossible, the want of food compelled Captain Denham to surrender to the authorities that same afternoon. They were all immediately stripped and marched along the beach in a biting wind and sleet. Barefooted, with their feet cut by the sharp shells on the beach, many fell out from sheer exhaustion and two actually died from fatigue and exposure. The rest were presently carried in baskets or sedans. They were fed on salt fish, greens and occasionally a little rice. Each man had a ticket round his neck like a common criminal, and through every village that they passed every sort of abuse and indignity was heaped upon them, and they were crowded into the local gaol at each town or village, where they stopped on their fortnight's march to Ty-wan-foo, the capital. This tiny prison often did not exceed 8 ft. by 7 ft. in the villages, but in the larger towns the gaols had separate cells, like wild beast cages with wooden bars.

For the first 12 days of the march the shipwrecked men were not allowed to wash even their faces, but then the mandarin in charge of them as a great favour allowed them to bathe in a muddy pool by the wayside.

A few days before reaching the capital, every man was compelled to wear leg-irons as well as handcuffs, and the captain's Chinese servant, for some reason or other, had a chain put round his neck.

They arrived at Ty-wan-foo on March 24, 14 days after the wreck. Here the mandarins and soldiers had great difficulty in keeping the curious mob at bay, and for a short while the unhappy prisoners were put into a small temple. Afterwards they were shut up in a small prison in the courtyard of the chief mandarin's house. Here they were questioned for hours on end; besides wanting to know the names, ages and duties of everyone on board the *Ann*, the mandarin asked many questions about the country of the red-haired barbarians, also where the poppy grew and what money they used.

The Chinese carpenter of the *Ann* was made to act as interpreter, and he and the other Chinese members of the crew were more severely treated than the others, being often cruelly beaten with bamboos.

Fever soon began to attack the unhappy prisoners; they were then divided up into separate dens.

Ten of the white men were shut up for two months in a black hole 11 ft. 6 ins. by 7 ft. 6 ins. Here they speedily became like wild beasts, sick, sore, verminous, and indescribably wretched.

It depended entirely on the particular mandarin and gaoler as to how each party was treated. The highest or red-button mandarin was most humane. But one unfortunate gaoler, who was actually kind enough to allow his prisoners to be shaved, received 50 strokes of the bamboo.

Captain Denham and Mr. Gully, a passenger, were lucky enough to gain favour and friends among the Chinese owing to their skill in drawing, and their sketches of ships, etc., were eagerly bought. Mr. Gully, however, nearly died of dysentery—the Chinese prescribed two cures, both of which did good. The first was to eat the skins of mangoes, the second to eat opium.

It was noticed everywhere that not only the mandarins but their servants and soldiers, all carried their opium pipes at their girdles, and were in the constant habit of smoking opium.

Though the head mandarin gave his prisoners a treat on the Emperor's birthday and even reclothed the Lascars, presenting each with a fan, cruel orders from Pekin caused him to change his attitude. Both Captain Denham and the Chinese carpenter were tortured, and about August 12 or 13 all the shipwrecked people except six white men, amongst whom were Captain Denham, and three Indians, were beheaded. It was believed that the nine survivors had been reserved for the purpose of being sent to Pekin, where they were to undergo the terrible death of being slowly cut in pieces.

However the treaty of peace saved their lives and they were taken across to Amoy, where they were handed over to the senior British officer.

A detailed account of this terrible experience was written day by day on common rice-paper with a piece of bamboo by a young English passenger, who was one of those who fell by the executioner's sword. It was found concealed in his cell.

The Salving of "Christina's" Treasure.

Besides the *Ann,* two other members of the opium fleet were lost in 1842. The first of these was the *Christina* (Captain Birkett), bound from Macao to Bombay with specie. She struck on the London Shoal in about 9° N., 112° E., on the night of July 1 and became a total wreck.

Nothing was heard of her for two years, and then a Spanish schooner, fishing amongst the shoals in the China Sea, discovered a chain cable leading over the coral reef on the East London Shoal. On landing to make a closer examination the Spaniards came upon a sextant and chronometer, and close to these instruments what they at first took to be lead, but which turned out to be sycee silver.

Here was a find such as any poor fisherman would dream about! In a very short time 150,000 dollars worth of solid shoe silver was discovered piled up on the reef.

The Spanish captain, who must have been a real hidalgo, stowed the sycee silver aboard his schooner and headed North for Macao. Here he delivered the whole of the treasure to the insurance agents, who rewarded him with a gift of 50,000 rupees. The bullion turned out to be the cargo of the missing *Christina* which was identified by the names and numbers on the sextant and chronometer.

The other vessel lost was the brig *Mavis* (Captain Jones), also loaded with sycee silver. On July 31, 1842, when near the Grand Ladrone, she was struck by lightning and instantly blew up. Evidently the flash penetrated her powder magazine; however, though the brig was torn in pieces her crew somehow managed to save themselves.

Tiger Island swamped by a Cyclone.

Until the cyclone at the Sunderbunds in May, 1842, Saugor Island, which was known to sailors as Tiger Island, was always given a wide berth by ships' boats, owing to the number of wild beasts upon it, specially tigers, leopards, hyenas and jackals.

Every ship that sailed up the Hooghly had some gruesome yarn or other to tell about Tiger Island. The most generally told was the one about the burial party. They were busy interring a comrade in the sand above high water mark when with a terrific roar a tiger leapt out of the jungle, for a moment sniffed disdainfully at the corpse sewn up in its hammock, and then seized upon the most fleshy seaman and disappeared with the screeching man in his jaws.

Another story told is of two natives paddling by in their dugout at a time when food was very scarce on the island. A tiger actually swam out to the boat, swamped it with a blow of his paw, and bore off one of the men to his lair in the jungle.

A similar experience happened to the long-boat of the schooner *Time*. Captain Pybus arrived at Saugor with some very important news of the opium market, which he wished to get to his agent as quickly as possible. To save time he lowered the long-boat, and putting her in charge of the second mate told him to track the boat up the river, going night and day. But whilst they were tracking along the shore of Tiger Island, a tiger sprang out and carried off one of the Lascars. The second mate and his boat's crew were so scared that they all jumped into the boat and rowed up to Calcutta, taking care to keep well out in the stream, especially at night. The result of this cowardly behaviour was that the second mate took ten days delivering his captain's letter at Calcutta and the *Time* lost her market.

There was no chance of anyone being able to sleep aboard a vessel that brought up for the night off Tiger Island, for the howling of the jackals, the scream of the hyenas, and the earth-shaking roar of the tigers as they prowled the jungle in search of food, not only stopped all slumber but gave everyone a strange feeling of nervous disquiet and horror.

Then in May came the cyclone and inundation which at the

Sunderbunds penetrated 17 miles inland. The whole of Saugor Island disappeared under the flood and the wild beasts drowned in their thousands. The story is told at this time of a tiger entering the hut of a native, and acting like a well behaved dog. The Indian and his family were at their meal. The tiger made no attempt to harm them, but famished and worn out as he was, crept into a dark corner of the hut and quietly laid down. He was actually taking refuge with his enemy man from the terrors of the elements.

After the waters had subsided there were no more tigers and no more leopards on Saugor Island and the old name gradually lost its significance.

Opium Passages, 1842.

The *Sylph* was the first opium ship of the season in 1842. She arrived at Hongkong on January 25, 54 days out from Calcutta.

Besides the regular coasters such as the *Falcon*, *Ariel* (schooner), *Psyche*, *Young Queen*, *Black Swan*, *Lyra*, *Zoe*, *Corsair*, *Vixen*, *Aurora*, *Hellas*, *Kelpie* and *Island Queen*, many of the clippers made trips up the East Coast, the presence of British men-of-war seeming to have the effect of heartening the Chinese opium smugglers.

The following list shows the clippers that cleared for the East Coast with opium.

January	*Lady Grant*	.. 33 men	.. 236 tons
February	*Red Rover*	.. 35 „	.. 250 „
March ..	*Rob Roy*	.. 28 „	.. 380 „
May ..	*Pantaloon*	.. 40 „	.. 200 „
June ..	*Red Rover*	.. 35 „	.. 250 „
July ..	*Sylph* ..	.. 70 „	.. 304 „
October ..	*Syed Khan*	.. 25 „	.. 126 „

It is rather bewildering to find how some ships always seem to be changing captains. This was specially the case with the coasters; being small vessels, their captains were always looking for promotion.

These lists are, I fear, very incomplete; but at this distance of time this must be expected.

There is only one new name in the ranks, and that is the *Anonyma* (Captain Hicks).

The following were the chief homeward passages in 1842:

Clipper	Captain	From Hongkong	Singapore	Calcutta	Days Out
Waterwitch ..	Reynell	Jan. 4	Jan. 17	Feb. 6	33
Black Joke ..	McFarlane	Feb. 8	Feb. 18	March 9	29
Cowasjee Family	Durham	April 4	April 19	May 9	35
Anonyma ..	Hicks	„ 10	—	Bombay	—
Ariel	Burt	„ 20	May 9	June 11	52
Mor	Methven	May 12	June 7	„ 23	42
Waterwitch ..	Reynell	July 28	Aug. 20	Sept. 11	45
Anonyma ..	Hicks	Aug. 28	—	Oct. 26	59
Poppy	Cole	Nov. 9	Nov. 17	Dec. 15	36
Rob Roy	Boyd	Nov. 1	„ 15	„ 17	46
Ariel	Burt	Nov. 8	„ 16	„ 19	41
Kitty	Willie	„ 19	—	„ 22	33
Red Rover ..	Wright	—	Dec. 2	„ 22	—
Cowasjee Family	Durham	Nov. 30	„ 9	„ 26	26

The Brig-yacht "Anonyma."

The *Anonyma* was built by William Camper at Gosport in 1839. She was a yacht of 427 tons Thames measurement, 257 tons register, built regardless of expense and with very fine lines for Lieut.-Colonel the Hon. R. F. Greville to take the place of his famous little slave brig *Xarifa,* which after a severe dusting off Brighton when she managed to claw off a lee shore in a March cyclone was found to be badly strained. The *Xarifa,* by the way, had been built at Philadelphia and under the name of *Theresa Secunda* had been captured by H.M.S. *Pelorus* on her first trip.

In 1840 James Bennet Moore bought the *Anonyma* and sold her a month or so later to Captain John Vaux of London. He intended to sail her himself, but, on arrival in Bombay, he was persuaded to part with her for a very large sum to Sir Jamsetjee Jejeebhoy, Robert Crawford and Alexander Matheson, and from the beginning of 1842 she sailed either on the Bombay or Calcutta run with Jardine Matheson's house-flag at her main-truck.

As can be seen from her portrait, she was very heavily rigged with skysails and every kind of flying kite; and Captain Hicks did his very best to keep his end up with the Bombay and Calcutta clippers.

Two Famous Brigs—" Lanrick " and " Antelope."

Two of the fastest merchant brigs ever floated were sent out to China in 1843—these were the *Lanrick* for Jardine, Matheson & Co., and the *Antelope* for Russell & Co. Both were intended for the India run, on which there were very few of the clippers that could stay with them either on a wind or going free.

The *Lanrick* was built at Liverpool to the order of Andrew Jardine, and though only registering 283 tons cost £13,000. Her name came from Jardine's Scottish home, Lanrick Castle.

Here is a testimony to her qualities, made by R. Montgomery Martin, H.M. Treasurer and Member of Council at Hongkong in the 'forties. He wrote:

> The *Lanrick* is superior in sailing on a wind to any man-of-war. I made a voyage in her down the China Seas to Java in 1845, in the teeth of the monsoon, when she was under the command of one of the most skilful and daring seamen that ever sailed. Frequently we were running 8 and 9 knots close-hauled and carrying royals, when a frigate would have had reefed topsails and courses.
>
> Like the other vessels of her class, the *Lanrick* was fully armed with long 9-pounders, musketry, etc. In one of her voyages she carried 1250 chests of Bengal opium, valued at £200,000 sterling.

The captain he refers to was Captain T. B. White. Her armament consisted of five guns aside and a long-tom on a pivot amidships.

On her maiden voyage she went out from London to Bombay in 106 days.

It was just about the same date in 1843 that the American brig *Antelope* arrived at Bombay from Boston in 94 days under Captain Philip Dumaresq, one of the best known in after years of American clipper ship captains.

Antelope was built by Sam Hall to the order of Captain R. B. Forbes, and it seems that her designer thought her big for a brig—she was 370 tons burden—for he put steps in her for the barque rig. On her way out to China with her first opium cargo, *Antelope* had a chance to try her paces with the U.S. frigate *Brandywine*, which had been 80 days from Rio de Janeiro to Bombay.

The two ships fell in with each other in fair weather. It was not the *Antelope's* best point of sailing which was to windward, but she outsailed the crack frigate and beat her into Hongkong by several days. Caleb Cushing was aboard the *Brandywine* and Fletcher Webster, his secretary of Legation, was aboard the *Antelope.*

"Marsdeu" beats "Cowasjee Family" and "Ariel."

Amongst the new clippers in 1843 was a smart Indian built barque of 247 tons named the *Marsdeu.* She was owned by D. Burjorjee and commanded by Captain Dare.

In June of 1843 she beat down to Singapore against the monsoon in 20 days, arriving on June 23, having beaten *Cowasjee Family* by 5 days and *Ariel* by 7 days.

The Schooner "Celestial," first Vessel built at Hongkong.

On February 12, 1843, the first vessel ever built at Hongkong was launched; this was the teak-built fore-and-aft schooner *Celestial,* of 50 tons. This little vessel made a remarkable record in her first year afloat when she sailed from Bombay to Hongkong in 23 days.

It may have been on this occasion that Captain Methven commanded her. He was afterwards a celebrated Blackwall frigate captain after he had commanded the opium clippers, *Celestial* and *Mor.* I give a portrait of all his commands as a frontispiece in *Blackwall Frigates.* *Celestial* will be noted in the foreground and *Mor* away to port.

Rajah Brooke's Yacht "Royalist" bought for an Opium Clipper.

It is easy to get confused by the vessels called *Royalist,* out in China. According to Commander Collinson, the famous surveyor, the *Royalist* which was dismasted during the Hongkong typhoon of July 21, 1841, was an ex-opium clipper, which had been lately bought by Commodore Sir J. Gordon Bremer.

This vessel may be the little *Royalist* which did so much surveying in Eastern waters afterwards, and which on November 19, 1844, arrived at Singapore from Port Essington under Second Master Parkinson, three commanders having died within 12 months, both her masts being sprung and all her gear being in the most dilapidated condition. It was a curious case. The little schooner had apparently been forgotten, no orders having reached her for a year and a half.

Parkinson had to promote himself to keep the pendant flying and proceeded to Singapore without orders, the vessel being in a woeful condition for want of repair.

But she was not Rajah Brooke's yacht, which was bought by Boustead & Co. of Singapore and Hongkong in 1843 and became an opium clipper; finally ending her life as Syme, Muir & Co.'s receiving ship at the Six Islands near Amoy.

The celebrated James Brooke, Rajah of Sarawak, was descended from Sir Robert Vyner, Bart., Lord Mayor of London in Charles II.'s reign.

The father of James Brooke was Thomas Brooke, one of those eighteenth century East India Civil servants whose supposed fabulous wealth and picturesque Indian bearers and khitmutgars earned them the name of Nabob in England. James Brooke was born in 1803, went out to India in his father's footsteps and distinguished himself in the Burmese war, where his reckless bravery earned him a bad wound which compelled him to give up the Service. This was in 1830. He went to China in search of health, and the sight of the coasts of Borneo and other islands of the Asiatic Archipelago first gave him the idea which became the ruling passion of his life and for which he made careful preparation.

When his father died and as his only surviving son he succeeded to what was a handsome fortune in those days, he immediately set about putting his long matured plans into execution.

His first important step was the ownership of the schooner *Royalist*, of 142 tons, with which he entered the Royal Yacht Squadron. For over three years he trained the crew of the *Royalist* before setting out for the East. Here are his own words about the little schooner, which was to add North Borneo to the British Empire:

> She sails fast, is conveniently fitted up, is armed with six 6-pounders, a number of swivels and small arms of all sorts, carries four boats and provisions for four months.
>
> Her principal defect is being too sharp in the floor, which, in case of taking the ground, greatly increases the risk, but I comfort myself with the reflection that a knowledge of this will lead to redoubled precaution to prevent such a disaster.

She is withal a good sea boat and as well calculated for the service as could be desired.

Most of her hands had been with me for three years and upwards and the rest were highly recommended. They are almost without exception young, able-bodied and active, fit in all respects for enduring hardship and privation.

In 1838 the *Royalist* sailed for Singapore, after a year's testing out in the Mediterranean. Taking his departure on December 16, Brooke did not hurry out. Staying some time at Rio, he inspected three slave-ships, prizes to the British squadron. "A most loathsome, disgusting sight," was his comment. He also tested his schooner in sailing against H.M.S. *Calliope* and the brig-sloop *Grecian.* He left the Cape on March 29 in a south-easter, was six weeks to Java Head and reached Singapore on June 1, 1839.

One of his first friends in these waters was Joseph Pybus, who in the *Time* spent a month with Brooke at Sarawak. This was not on his first trip, when Brooke left Singapore for Borneo on July 27, 1839, but his second at the end of August, 1840. Brooke also bought the old East India Company's cruiser *Zephyr*, a schooner of 90 tons, which had been renamed *Swift*, to share the work of the *Royalist.*

In January, 1842, the *Royalist* was hired by the Indian Government to look for the missing boats of the Indiaman, *Viscount Melbourne*, which had been wrecked on the Luconia Shoal. Both she and the *Swift* did as much life-saving as fighting with the Dyaks. In the summer of 1842 Brooke settled down as Rajah of Sarawak, when he had no more use for his old yacht, and she was sold to Edward Boustead in June or July, 1843.

Boustead and his partner Schwabe were amongst the pioneer British merchants in Singapore, and in 1843 they also opened branches at Hongkong and Manila. The *Royalist* seems to have been one of the few ships owned by them; owing to her speed she was very suitable for the opium trade, and under Captain Lees she became very well known in the China Seas.

"Young Queen" and "Anna" at Tongarron.

Not every British pioneer of Empire was as successful as Rajah Brooke, but then few men had his qualifications. Here is a contemporary character sketch of the English Rajah:—

> Of most enlarged views, truthful and generous, quick to acquire and appreciate, excelling in every manly sport and exercise; elegant and accomplished; ever accessible; above all prompt and determined to redress injury or relieve misfortune, he was of all others the best qualified to impress the native mind with the highest opinion of the English character.

In November, 1843, the Honourable James Erskine Murray sailed from Hongkong with the two little opium clippers, *Anna*, brig of 150 tons, and *Young Queen*, schooner of 85 tons. Rajah Brooke had been successful in North Borneo, Murray hoped to be as successful in South Borneo. His idea was to obtain land for settlement and to open a trade with the natives. But his disposition was so adventurous that he must needs attempt to tame the biggest old pirate in all Borneo, the Rajah of Tongarron, who in 1828 had killed Major Mullins, a Dutch officer and 30 Javanese soldiers; and since then had become still more noted for his hatred of all foreigners, and his treachery on every possible occasion. Against this notorious Dyak, Murray pitted himself and the crews of the *Anna* and *Young Queen*, consisting of 35 and 30 men respectively. For trade he carried salt and tobacco and possibly opium, for which he hoped to barter antimony and gold dust.

Tongarron lay 80 miles up the Cote River, which runs into the Straits of Macassar. The dauntless Murray sailed straight up to the old Sultan's capital and calmly anchored, or rather moored, with great deliberation abreast of the Sultan's house. The latter declared that he was most gratified by the visit and only too willing to trade.

But the days passed and no one came off from the shore to trade, except in the dead of night, and this the armed watch of both ships were wise enough to prevent. It was soon evident to Murray and his officers that the Sultan of Tongarron was making careful preparations to capture the two ships. Large bodies of armed men were continually seen round the Sultan's compounds, large prahus with long brass guns began to arrive at Tongarron, and it was noticed that masked batteries were being prepared that commanded the anchorage.

On February 16, 1844, these batteries and the prahus began the attack. Murray and his crews were all prepared. Slipping

"ANTELOPE"

National Maritime Museum, Greenwich

[*See page* 268

"NYMPH"

From a Water-colour [*See page* 286

their moorings the ships began a running fight in an attempt to break their way through. Luckily the prahus kept out of range of the swivels with which the *Young Queen* and *Anna* were armed, but their long guns did severe execution. At every turn in the river a fresh battery had to be contended with—the wily Rajah had made careful preparation—but steadily the two ships fought their way.

At one critical moment the *Anna* got on a mud bank, but her consort bore up and covered her whilst she hove herself off.

During the night which was without a breath of wind the two vessels lashed themselves together, and with a couple of boats ahead drifted down on the strong ebb. A curious incident here was that the men in the boats declared that they heard English voices hailing them from the shore.

After 36 hours' continuous fighting, during which the *Young Queen* fired 550 rounds and the *Anna* a like number, the two vessels found the open sea ahead, but right in the mouth of the river a large fleet of prahus blocked their way across the bar. In this last desperate fight young Murray, who was the life and soul of the expedition and had aroused the most loyal devotion in both officers and men, was killed. He was fighting the *Young Queen's* midship gun when a 2-pounder struck him on the breast and he fell dead.

Besides him, Thomson, the boatswain of the *Anna*, and Dance, one of her seamen, were killed. Two of the officers of the *Anna*, Hart and McNyles, were wounded as well as her gunner and a boy, and the *Young Queen* had her gunner's mate wounded.

Having at last won clear of the fatal Cote or Gote River, provisions now ran short and the two ships actually bartered their guns for rice with a friendly Rajah further along the coast. The piratical prahus, which the *Anna* and *Young Queen* fought in crossing the bar of the river, were well known for their habit of pouncing down upon becalmed ships off the Macassar Straits. Reports also were very common of European captives having been seen by native vessels in many parts of the Sultan of Tongarron's dominions, so that the English voices may not have been fancy on the part of the boat's crews.

Pirates and Robbers at Hongkong.

In the first few years of its life as a British colony the Island of Sweet Waters, as the Chinese poetically name Hongkong, was so plagued by robbers on land and pirates by sea that many British merchants preferred to live at Macao.

Bad characters from the mainland, glad to escape from the Manchu code of laws, discovered Hongkong to be a happy hunting ground for any professional outlaw. Gangs of robbers and pirates concealed themselves in the rookeries of the native town; and it was soon unsafe to take a walk after dark.

In April, 1843, thieves actually broke into Government House, and two days later the new premises of Jardine Matheson, Dent and Gillespie were all burgled on the same night. It was after this experience that Jardine, Matheson & Co. instituted 12 armed chokidars to guard their houses, godowns and compounds at East Point. Then on May 9 the Morrison Institution was attacked by robbers.

It was not until July 18, 1844, that the streets of Hongkong were lighted; until this date the colony not only suffered after dark from the scum of Canton's criminal population, but also from riotous sailormen.

In July, 1843, amongst the new British arrivals was that famous sailor, Captain Harry Keppel, in his beautiful little corvette, the *Dido*. Keppel happened to be the only naval commander in the port at the moment. He was dining one night with Captain Joseph Pybus aboard the schooner *Time*, when the news was brought off that heavy fighting was going on ashore between Moormen and Chinamen.

Keppel immediately hurried off to take charge of the situation and Pybus lent his aid with a couple of armed boats. On the shore the commander of the *Time* found some scared missionaries, who asked to be taken off along with all their household effects. Possibly they had come from the lately-burgled Morrison Institution.

Whilst Pybus rushed off to help quell the riot, he left the missionaries with his boatkeepers, who were ordered to keep their boats afloat, so as to be ready for use at a moment's notice.

When he at length returned, after giving his help to Keppel's bluejackets, he found his boat-keepers calmly smoking their pipes with the two boats hauled up on the beach. To the missionaries' horror, immediately he was back aboard he ordered his boat-keepers a couple of dozen with the cat-o-nine tails. One of the missionaries tried to interfere, and nearly found himself put over the side by the irate shipmaster.

Tanka-Boat Woman's Fortune from Smuggling Opium.

Keppel does not mention this incident in his reminiscences, but he makes two interesting notes in his personal log under July, 1843.

The first was that his little *Dido* was causing a sensation amongst the "handsome and fast opium clippers" and a little later on he remarks: "There is pleasure in a fast sailing ship. Until the arrival of the *Dido* the opium clippers had it all their own way."

His second note stated that an old tanka-boat woman had made 40,000 dollars smuggling opium at Whampoa.

The tanka-boat women, like the laundry women, were peculiar to Canton waters; they made their livelihood out of the foreign ships at the anchorages at Macao, Whampoa and Hongkong.

Here is what an experienced opium clipper sailor writes of these "amphibious creatures" in the 'fifties:

> The tanka girls live an almost entirely aquatic life—they are actually born, live and die aboard their floating homes. Their time seems fully occupied in rowing or sculling with a large oar over the stern of the boat; and this incessant labour makes them strong and well-figured.
>
> Until married it cannot be said that they are either paragons of virtue or modesty, but when married they seem far less amiable to the exiled Fan Kwae. Their personal charms are by no means so contemptible as Europeans generally imagine.
>
> Long intensely black hair, brilliant and merry though oblique black eyes, light yellowish brown and often beautifully clear complexion and lithe, robust figures constitute a charming and singular variety of feminine attractions. They are a gay, thoughtless set, these boat girls. By constant exposure to the sun they are tanned to a regular alabaster gipsy hue, and wicked little gipsies they often are, especially when making a young greenhorn pay six times the proper fare.
>
> Tanka girls are free in all things unconnected with their work, but as many are purchased by aged individuals, owners of boats, they are slaves in so far as their occupation is concerned.

Very different is it with their unfortunate sisters, the slaves of the washerwomen who are bought quite young and trained to an evil life.

It is a usual thing to see, the moment a ship has anchored, several old laundry hags, each with an attendant retinue of fascinating nymphs "taking charge" and establishing themselves in possession of all quarters of the vessel, from the skipper's cabin to the black cook's galley. Of course these little witches make sad havoc of the sailor's hearts and generally of their clothes. Upon pay day the number and affection of these pretty damsels seems to increase surprisingly, and by a very perceptible metallic clinking, when they take their departure by the gangway, it would appear that their sweetness of disposition had not been exerted unsuccessfully.

These tanka girls and laundry girls spoke in expressive pigeon English with their patrons, the "yang guitzo" (foreign devils).

"Hi-yah! missee! wantchee go ashore!" was the usual hail for a tanka boat.

But to those whose duty kept them aboard, especially to fo'c'sle-hands, a tanka girl would call out from under the bows:

"You no wantchee go ashore?" Perhaps the answer would be "Belong ship—no can do."

Then would come in a hissed whisper: "Spose you look see belong shih tim cheong (ten o'clock) mi catchee samshoo."

This peddling of liquor and opium smuggling were paying side lines in the tanka woman's trade.

No picture of Southern China in the bad old days would be complete without her cheery presence.

The Port of Shanghai opened.

On November 17, 1843, the port of Shanghai was opened to foreign trade in accordance with the treaty of Nanking. Captain Balfour was the first British Consul, but in June, 1846, he was succeeded by the better known Alcock.

By December 31, 25 persons had been enrolled as British subjects of Shanghai, amongst these were A. G. Dallas (of Jardine, Matheson & Co.), T. C. Beale (of Dent & Co.), John D. Gibb (of Gibb, Livingstone & Co.), and John Wise (of Holliday, Wise & Co.)

Lot No. 1 of the Shanghai land rent list had the name of Jardine, Matheson & Co. against it. No. 3 was Gibb Livingstone's; No. 4 belonged to Holliday, Wise & Co., No. 5 to Wolcott, Bates & Co.

(Wolcott was the first American Consul); Nos. 8 and 9 belonged to Dent & Co.

During the first six weeks of the new treaty port's existence, only seven ships entered, the largest being the *Eliza Stewart*, of 423 tons and the smallest the opium schooner *Mazeppa*, of 175 tons.

Before the port had been opened three months an opium case occurred. Opium was contraband by Chinese law but not by British.

The manifest of the brig *Amelia* showed one chest of Turkish opium. The Consul's suggestion was that it should be thrown overboard. The very next day the *Maingay* arrived, and it then leaked out that both ships had transhipped opium to the old Indiaman, *William the Fourth*.

On further investigation Captain Balfour discovered that instead of one chest the *Amelia* had had 128 on board. Each of the culprits was fined 500 dollars for transporting or discharging cargo without a permit. Another 500 dollars was demanded from each opium clipper, *Amelia* and *Maingay*, for having false manifests. The *Maingay* had to pay still another 700 dollars for breaking bulk before her permit was issued and for irregular papers.

Finally the *William the Fourth* was sent down under arrest to Canton, and the other two detained pending the decision of the Minister.

One of the *Maingay's* fines was remitted, but the others were enforced and paid over to the Chinese, who made a law that opium whilst it was aboard British ships was under British law, but directly it was landed was liable to Chinese law.

No receiving ships ever moored off Shanghai; they all lay off the village of Woosung in the muddy waters of the Yang-tze-kiang; at first there were only three, but the number was soon increased to six, representing Jardine Matheson, Dent, Burn, MacVicar & Co., Gilman & Co., Rustomjee & Co. and Russell & Co.

The Opium Cutters.

The coasters rarely came up to Shanghai itself; and as soon as they had discharged their cargoes into the Woosung receiving ships and received their due of specie, they were off again for Hongkong. Connection was maintained between the receiving ships and Shanghai by means of what came to be called the opium cutters. These were really sloops of about 50 ft. in length and 12 ft. beam, rather flat bottomed with shallow draught, straight stemmed and with handsome counter sterns. They were rigged with a foresail and Chinese battened lugsail. Being very shallow they had centreboards, the casing of which took up the whole length down the centre of the cabin, which had a raised coach roof with sliding windows, and just aft of it a sunk steering cockpit. Forward there was a tiny fo'c'sle for the crew. Each of the big firms maintained one of these cutters, and the racing between them up and down the Shanghai river was always very keen.

Occasionally in the early days they used to go outside the Woosung bar and meet the coasters coming in. When the bar was dredged open and steamers came into fashion the old cutters were often turned into yachts.

The Opium Passages, 1843.

By 1843 many more vessels were sailing from Bombay than during the 'thirties though one of the vetarans went missing this year—the *Lady Grant*, which sailed from Bombay on April 15 and was never heard of again. Unfortunately very few complete passage times are to be found.

Of the Bombay ships, *Anonyma* sailed on March 20 and arrived Hongkong May 4, 45 days out; *Mor* arrived out from Bombay on June 19; *Falcon* on June 22; *Sir H. Compton*, *Corsair*, *Amelia*, *Petrel* and *Ardaseer* were also from Bombay.

Of the Calcutta ships, the following all arrived out prior to March 16; *Red Rover* with 680 chests; *Poppy* with 330 chests; *Ariel* with 400 and *Rob Roy* with 490. *Waterwitch* had a close race with *Pantaloon*; she left Calcutta on May 5, a day behind the schooner, and they both reached Singapore on the same day, May 30. *Sylph* left Calcutta on her first passage of the year on February 21. Another vessel on the Calcutta run was the brig *Audax*.

The Bombay ships by this date had stopped touching at Singapore on the homeward run, but reported at Anjer instead. Here are a few times to Anjer made against the S.W. monsoon, which were taken from the Resident's report book.

Clipper	Rig	Captain	Left China	Reported Anjer	Days Out
Sir H. Compton	Barque	Boulton	May 25	June 30	36
Anna Eliza ..	Brig	Grainger	June 15	July 21	36
Mor	Ship	Baxter	July 4	Aug. 8	35
Emma	Schooner	Dawson	,, 18	Aug. 20	33
Corsair	Brig	Fraser	Aug. 12	Sept. 21	40
Petrel	Schooner	Pruen	,, 19	,, 22	34
Syed Khan ..	Schooner	Horseburg	,, 19	,, 22	34

Of the return passages to Calcutta I have the following:

Clipper	Captain	Left Hongkong	Arrived Singapore	Arrived Calcutta	Days Out
Waterwitch ..	Reynell	March 2	March 13	April 3	32
Red Rover ..	McMurdock	,, 15	,, 27	,, 30	46
Ariel	Burt	April 22	May 21	June 8	47
Sylph	McDonald	May 29	June 26	July 12	44
Waterwitch ..	Reynell	June 28	July 22	Aug. 8	41
Rob Roy ..	White	Sept. 26	Oct. 19	Nov. 18	53
Red Rover ..	McMurdo	Oct. 16	,, 31	,, 22	37

The *Sylph* on her homeward passage during January and February, 1843, made a very fine run between Singapore and Calcutta. Leaving Singapore on January 28, she reached Saugor on February 11, only 14 days out, having caught up with the *Harlequin* which had left Singapore on January 23. This was Captain Guy's last passage, he being succeeded by Captain Donald MacDonald.

The Pybus Brothers retire.

The Pybus Brothers retired from the China trade at the end of 1843. Henry paid the price of dabbling with the sinister drug for he never lived to enjoy his fortune, dying at Madras on his way home. Joseph Pybus settled down at the Cape.

Their ships were sold to various owners, *Sir Edward Ryan* fell to the command of Captain Holt, who, I believe, was the man who founded Holt's Line of steamers. The little barque under

Captain Holt found herself racing home with a cargo of tea instead of up the China coast with opium in her hold.

Time ended her days as an opium hulk at Woosung, being lost eventually in a typhoon. *Clown* was lost under Captain Lacey in September, 1855; *Pantaloon* succumbed to the typhoon of September 21, 1858. She was wrecked on the rocks off Otao village, and plundered by the Chinese. The *Harlequin* with treasure on board caught fire off the Sandheads on September 20, 1847. She burnt to the water's edge and then sank.

The American Barque "Coquette."

In the spring of 1844 the clipper barque *Coquette* was launched from Sam Hall's yard at East Boston. The model of this 450-ton opium clipper was whittled out by Captain R. B. Forbes with tools borrowed from Hall, and we may gather that the merchant captain was very proud of his handiwork. Intended for Russell & Co., the *Coquette* sailed from Boston under Captain Oliver Eldridge on June 29, 1844.

The following is Eldridge's account of his passage out, written to Forbes from China:

After you left us off Block Island, July 1, we took a fine breeze from the S.W.; went off very fast under studding sails; on the 4th took in studding sails, weather squally, made that day 286 miles, fresh wind abeam and sometimes before it, with a sharp sea. July 6—Passed a schooner going the same way; she was in sight just six hours. July 8—Tacked to S.W.; as we could not go better than East by North on the other tack.

July 14th—For six days we have had light winds South of East. July 15th—Fresh breezes and squally; ship quite stiff, and during the squalls goes like a locomotive: we have trimmed her more by the head as she was inclined to carry a little lee helm. July 28—We have now the South-east trades; had hard luck in the doldrums and lost the N.E. trades in 9° North: on crossing the Line had a visit from Neptune. Made to-day brig *Eveline*, of Newburyport, made her ahead at 9 a.m. and at 3 p.m. she was out of sight astern. July 30—For two days have had fine trade, going pretty close-hauled.

August 4—We have had a good run down the Brazil coast, making a South by East course. August 7—Found our mainmast sprung, owing to 6 large knots near each other. It must have been injured before being put in, as we have had no wind to do it; fished it with a spare topmast.

August 12—For four or five days have made good progress, and had to reef for a short time; I think she is almost too stiff for heavy weather; I find a reefed lower studding sail is handy as she rolls some.

PANORAMA O[illegible]

National Maritime Museum, Greenwich

I IN 1850

[*See page* 276

August 22—For ten days we have had a fine run: we have to-day the first East winds in these latitudes, and are now under double-reefed topsails and whole courses, and but for our sprung mast our topsail halliards would not have been started. I never saw a vessel bear her canvas as she does, and with good spars could carry double reefs as long as any frigate; always dry under full sail. When we come to double reefs she makes the water fly, most ships would be going 5 or 6 knots, we go 9 and sometimes 10. At sundown we could just see a ship to windward, 3 points before the beam, at midnight we tacked and at 1 o'clock passed about a quarter of a mile to leeward of her.

August 26—Yesterday hove to in a South-east gale, but might have carried close reefs but for our mainmast. It is not possible for any vessel to behave better, and but for rain our decks would have been dry; her motion was so easy that in the cabin one would have thought there was only a moderate breeze. When we filled away against the old sea with a South-west wind, she pitched away the flying jibboom. I have a poor crew and there is a ready sale for slops.

August 31—For five days we have had a good run, but not so good a chance as I could wish for; I know she can make 300 in the 24 hours with a stronger breeze. I have seen her take 13½ off the reel; before the glass was out she took all the line off. September 2—Came up with St. Pauls, and sent a boat into the basin, they returned soon without any fish.

September 7—I think we now have the South-east trades. September 9—Strong breezes from the East for a day or two and squally: braced up sharp; by going forward we can get big shower baths, but she goes easy. 13—Rather light trades; we have only four good men among the crew. September 15—At daylight made Java Head, and at 6 p.m. came to at Anjer Roads. 16—Left at 2 p.m. with a light air and strong head current. 18—Passed the Brothers. 19—Passed Gaspar; at 6 p.m. came up with ship *Avalanche* of Philadelphia bound to Canton. The captain was not sociable because we passed so fast; five sick men from imprudent eating at Anjer. 21—Light winds; passed St. Barbs. 22nd—Beating.

October 1—It has been almost calm for seven days. 6—We have finally got a light breeze. 9—Made the Ass'es Ears and at 2 p.m. came to in Macao Roads. The *Coquette* can and does answer expectations. So far we have had the shortest passage to Java.

The *Montauk* was 77 days and 87 to this place: *Houqua*, 78 and 90; we 76 and 99. Captain Palmer of the former wants more canvas and Captain McMichael say he has none too much. Neither has made so much by log as we have at any time. Our mainmast made a difference to our passage.

After replacing her sprung mast, the *Coquette* sailed from Macao Roads on December 3, 1844, and reached Singapore in 9 days, her best 24 hour run being 242 and distance per log 1425. She left Singapore on December 13 and arrived at the Sandheads on the 23rd, her best day up the Bay of Bengal being 164. This was a good passage even for the most favourable time in the year.

New Names in the Opium Fleet, 1843-4.

Every year new names crop up in the opium fleet, but not all of these ships stay in the trade; if they did not prove their sailing powers in a couple of voyages, they soon disappeared from the lists, having gravitated into trades where speed was not such a necessity.

In 1844 amongst the new ships was the *Dhur* of 300 tons, built at Calcutta for Buydnauth Dhur and commanded by William Cumberland.

Another new name was that of the *Magpie*. I know nothing about this clipper beyond the fact that there was a clever theft of specie from her in the spring of 1844. The bags of treasure were attached at intervals to a buoyed line, but this unusual trot was discovered and all the silver secured except one bag, the rope of which broke so that it sank into the deep mud at the bottom.

The schooner *Nutcut* (Captain Lonsdale) appeared in the lists for the first time in 1844; and a schooner of the New York pilot-boat type was sent out to Russell & Co. by Captain R. B. Forbes. This was the *Don Juan* of 175 tons.

In November, 1839, H.M. brig *Pelorus* came ashore in a hurricane at Port Essington, her boatswain and seven bluejackets being drowned. For a while she lay on her beam ends in the mud but was eventually floated and sent to Singapore in a very dilapidated and leaky state. Here she was sold out of the service by Sir J. Gordon Bremer and the little *Bentinck* (brig) bought in her stead for £6000. *Pelorus* was a brig of *Curlew's* class, registering 380 tons. She was bought by one of the opium firms, and under Captain Triggs arrived at Hongkong with a cargo of opium on June 27, 1843. However she did not stay any time in the trade. I believe Pybus Brothers bought her; if so, she had to be sold again within a few months.

Amongst the smaller clippers appearing on the coast in 1843-4 were the *Petrel* (155 tons), *Corsair* (137 tons), *Prima Vera* (202 tons), *Royal Exchange* (130 tons), *Will o' the Wisp* (101 tons), these were mostly schooners or brigantines; then there were the *Mischief*, a big schooner of 221 tons, the still bigger two-topsail schooner *Warlock* of 291 tons, and the American brig *Frolic* of 212 tons, which last was one of Russell's clippers, running from India with the drug.

Opium Passages, 1844.

Of the outward passages, records in 1844 are very scanty. From Bombay the little *Celestial's* was the best, then came the *Mor*, arriving Hongkong on May 25, 37 days out.

This year the *Red Rover* arrived at Macao on March 10, leaking after having had a rare buffeting by the N.E. monsoon.

Again we have some interesting records against the S.W. monsoon taken from the Resident's report book at Anjer.

Clipper	Captain	Left Hongkong	Reported Anjer	Days Out
Anna Eliza ..	Grainger	April 15	May 16	31
Mor	Baxter	June 3	July 6	33
Emma	Dawson	May 27	„ 8	42
Sir H. Compton ..	Boulton	June 17	„ 23	36
Ardaseer	McIntyre	July 11	Aug. 15	35
Louisa	Forgan	Aug. 5	Sept. 11	37
Lanrick	White	„ 19	„ 15	27

Of completed passages to Bombay I have three:

Anonyma (Captain Hicks) left Hongkong March 10, arrived Bombay on April 25—46 days.

Sir H. Compton (Captain Boulton) left Hongkong, June 17, arrived Bombay, August 15—59 days.

Marsdeu (Captain Philips) left Hongkong June 4, arrived Bombay, August 16—73 days.

The Calcutta return passages are more complete.

Clipper	Captain	Left Hongkong	Arrived Singapore	Arrived Calcutta	Days Out
Audax	Vaux	Jan. 6	Jan. 15	Feb. 4	29
Poppy	Cole	Feb. 8	Feb. 17	March 8	29
Sir Ed. Ryan ..	Anderson	„ 14	„ 25	„ 17	32
Sylph	McDonald	March 3	March 16	April 6	34
Waterwitch ..	Reynell	„ 8	„ 19	„ 17	30
Roy Roy ..	White	„ 5	„ 19	„ 8	34
Lanrick	White	„ 30	April 19	May 10	41
Cowasjee Family	Durham	„ 26	„ 13	„ 14	49
Ariel	Burt	„ 28	—	„ 14	47
Nutcut	Lonsdale	„ 29	April 20	„ 15	47
Red Rover ..	McMurdock	April 24	May 19	June 5	42
Audax	Vaux	May 23	June 20	July 4	42
Sylph	McDonald	July 7	July 30	Aug. 16	40
Coquette ..	Eldridge	Dec. 3	Dec. 13	Dec. 23	20

Typhoon at Chusan.

There was a severe typhoon at Chusan in 1844, in which the ships *Moira* and *Ino* were blown ashore. The *Cacique* managed to ride it out hove to, but the little opium brig *William* ran away before it, and arrived safely in Hongkong after a passage of nine days.

The Schooners "Torrington" and "Enigma."

In 1845 two very famous little schooners were built for the opium trade. The first of these was the *Torrington*, the 150th ship built by Alexander Hall of Aberdeen. Many early shipping writers have described her as the first of the Aberdeen clippers; this is not correct, for this title is deserved by the little *Scottish Maid*, launched in 1839. The *Torrington*, however, was the first of Hall's ships to make a great reputation in Chinese waters, and it has generally been said that her success induced Jardine, Matheson & Co. to go to Hall for their tea clippers, *Stornoway*, *Cairngorm* and *Flying Spar*.

Her first captain was Niell and during the 'forties she ran between Hongkong and Shanghai under Jardine Matheson's flag. She disappeared from the shipping lists in 1849, but whether she was captured by pirates, was lost in a typhoon or sold out of the trade, I cannot say for no further trace of her have I been able to find.

If the *Torrington* had but a short life, this was far from being the case of the *Enigma*, which was by far the longest lived of all the opium clippers.

The *Enigma* was built at Calcutta, she was built of teak and copper fastened. Her figure-head was evidently meant to represent her name. It was a curious looking bird covered with fishscales. It is possible that she was called after the little cutter yacht *Enigma*, which on June 8, 1843, won the Grand Challenge Gold Cup of the Royal Thames Yacht Club.

The *Enigma*, like all the coasters, was heavily armed with seven guns on a broadside and two long brass pivot guns. One of her broadside guns is now in the Manx Museum.

After a long career on the China coast the *Enigma* sailed to

London from Calcutta with a general cargo. She left the Thames with a cargo for Glasgow, but running into some very bad weather on her way round the coast she at last put into Peel. Here she was arrested for debt, put up for sale by auction and bought by Thomas Karran, a member of the well-known family of that name at Bailingan, Marown.

This happened in 1860. Captain T. W. Karran commanded her for some years in the Baltic and Spanish trades. Then in the 'seventies she was bought by Joseph Qualtrough of Castleton and under Captain T. Corkill took her place in the British coasting trade. Finally, in March, 1913, she was sold to Thomas Wilson & Co., of Whitehaven, who kept her running to the Manx ports with cheap coal.

In December, 1922, when 77 years of age, the little *Enigma* left Whitehaven for the Isle of Whithorn, Solway Firth, and was lost with all hands in a hard winter gale. Wreckage, supposed to have been hers, was washed up on the Cumberland coast, but it was not actually identified and she was posted missing in 1923.

To modern eyes she appeared a somewhat bluff-bowed tubby little craft above water, and many of our smart coasting schooners could wipe the eye of the one-time crack opium clipper.

The ex-Slavers "Nymph" and "Kelpie."

Two very smart ex-slavers joined the coasting fleet about this date—these were *Nymph*—the second opium clipper of that name—and *Kelpie*.

Nymph was a two-topsail schooner, condemned at Sierra Leone in 1831. She was bought by the Earl of Harborough and turned into a yacht. In 1845 Captain Thomas Horsburgh became her owner, and taking her out to China almost immediately sold her to Dent & Co.

Kelpie was a Spanish brigantine, the *Isabella Estrella*, condemned as a slaver in 1836. She was bought for the opium trade by Alexander Grant.

Both these vessels were exceedingly speedy. They were described as foreign-built, which meant in all probability that they came from the building slips of Baltimore, where most slavers came from. Each had a square stern and scroll figure-head without any false galleries and gaudy gingerbread work, so beloved by the Indian-built cracks, but they were very handsome, thoroughbred looking vessels for all that.

Gambling in Opium.

In 1845 the sale of opium was legalised in Hongkong by Sir John Davis. The trade was in no need of this filip. At Calcutta the bidding at the opium sales was a matter of wild excitement, bulls and bears fighting for the mastery in a feverish market where the price see-sawed in the most giddy manner, soaring and then dropping, only to soar again higher than ever. About five nationalities contended for the drug, English, Scottish, American, Parsee and Hindoo. The opium sale on November 30, 1845, was stopped through two Hindoos bidding against each other till the price rose to 130,995 rupees per chest! Previous to this date there had already been five opium sales, as follows:

Date	Patna sold	Benares sold	Total chests
Jan. 6	4000 chests	1800 chests	5800
Feb. 10	1800 "	850 "	2650
April 21	3600 "	1500 "	5100
May 26	1800 "	850 "	2650
June 29	3685 "	1641 "	5326

This adds up to 21,526 chests from Bengal, to which must be added 18,321 of Malwa opium from Bombay, making an export for the year of 39,847 chests.

"Waterwitch's" Return Cargo.

It must not be supposed that the clippers only brought treasure back to India.

Here is an example of a return cargo per *Waterwitch* (Captain Reynell), which was landed at Calcutta on March 21, 1845.

1793	bags of allum	50	chests—camphor.
3	boxes (contents unknown)	100	boxes of tea
224	whole and half-chests of tea	1	box—musk
126	cases of sago	16	boxes—trunks
1	box of fans	1	box—snuff boxes and treasure
2	boxes (contents unknown)		

Opium Passages, 1845.

The following is a complete list of the outward passages from Bombay until the end of September:

Clipper	Left Bombay	Arrived Hongkong	Days Out
Antelope ..	Jan. 4	Mar. 9	64
Anna Eliza ..	Feb. 6	April 19	72
Mor	„ 16	„ 21	64
Corcyra	Mar. 5	May 14	71
Sir H. Compton	„ 17	„ 12	56
Island Queen ..	April 10	„ 28	49
City of Shiraz ..	May 6	June 9	34
Frolic	„ 8	„ 13	36
Anonyma ..	„ 13	„ 20	38
Black Dog ..	„ 17	„ 26	40
Ardaseer	„ 18	„ 26	39
Denia	June 28	July 29	31
Sidney	July 18	Sept. 6	50
Antelope	„ 27	„ 1	36
Mor	Aug. 7	„ 6	30
Anna Eliza ..	Sept. 11	Oct. 29	48
Frolic	„ 13	„ 27	44
Sir H. Compton	„ 16	Nov. 7	52
Lanrick	„ 20	Oct. 24	34

The outward passages from Calcutta have not been so easy to get hold of. The new American clipper barque *Coquette* left Calcutta after the first sales and discharged her pilot on January 22. She was 15 days to Singapore, sailing 1779 miles, her best day's work being 165 miles. She left Singapore on February 7 and reached Macao on the 28th, beating up the western side of the China Sea in 23 days, her best being 135 miles and her total mileage from Singapore 3021. This passage was beaten by one day by the veteran *Red Rover*, which left Calcutta on February 21 and reached Hongkong on March 29, 36 days out.

Three other passages from the Sandheads to Hongkong were:

Clipper	Left Sandheads	Left Singapore	Arrived Hongkong	Days Out
Rob Roy	Aug. 22	Sept. 17	Oct. 6	45
Mischief	Sept. 4	„ 20	„ 6	32
Coquette	„ 8	„ 20	„ 4	26

Of the homeward passages *Coquette* again made one of the best. She left Hongkong on March 10, and arrived at Singapore on the 16th, only 7 days out, having logged 1445 miles, averaged 206 miles and made 256 on her best day. She left Singapore on the 17th in company with the *Lanrick*, and the two clippers stayed together for 10 days, and eventually arrived in the Hooghly on the same day, April 9. The *Coquette* was 31 days from China, having logged 1838 miles from Singapore, her best day being 184.

The Bombay homeward passages for 1845 were:

Clipper	Left Hongkong	Reported Anjer	Arrived Bombay	Days Out
Black Dog	Jan. 12	—	Feb. 21	40
Island Queen	" 26	—	March 13	46
Zoe	Feb. 18	—	April 14	45
Anonyma	March 6	—	" 22	47
Antelope	" 19	—	May 5	47
Sidney	" 30	—	June 6	37
Mor	May 4	June 6	July 1	57
Anna Eliza	" 22	" 24	" 20	59
Sir H. Compton ..	June 12	July 18	Aug. 11	60
Kelpie	" 13	" 11	" 4	52
Frolic	" 27	" 26	" 17	51
Lanrick	July 9	Aug. 6	Sept. 3	55
Ardaseer	" 15	—	" 23	70
Island Queen	Aug. 14	—	Nov. 25	103
Anonyma	" 30	—	" 5	67
Gem	Sept. 27	—	" 25	59
Denia	" 28	—	" 28	61
Antelope	Oct. 5	—	" 29	55
Will-o'-the-Wisp ..	" 12	—	Dec. 7	56
Mor	" 29	—	" 6	38
Sydney	Nov. 6	—	" 18	42
Frolic	" 17	—	" 22	35

The brig, *City of Shiraz*, sailing from Hongkong in company with *Ardaseer* on July 15, foundered in a typhoon near the Island of Negroes, one of the Philippines. The twin screw steamer *Midas*, which had just been sent out to China by Captain R. B. Forbes, under Captain Poor, was chartered in April, 1846, to go to try to salve the *City of Shiraz*, but no trace of the wreck could be found.

These long lists of Bombay passages are included as up till this date I have given few examples of Bombay runs. In future only the best passages of the year will be given.

CAPTAIN DONALD MACDONALD
National Maritime Museum, Greenwich

CAPTAIN ALEXANDER RYRIE
Lent by Joseph Greaves, Esq. [*See Page* 300

"OMEGA", "MAZEPPA" HOVE DOWN, AND HULK "BAMANJEE", AT HONGKONG, 18th April, 1847

From a Drawing by A. G. Dallas

[*See page* 308

The Stranding and Looting of "Warlock."

On September 7, 1846, the *Warlock* (Captain Bell), left Hongkong in company with the *Poppy*, in dirty squally north-easterly weather. At 6.30 p.m. she anchored in Mirs Bay, proceeding at daylight on the 8th. On the night of the 10th she brought up off Namoa, sailed again on the 11th with the wind at S.E., squally, but on the morning of the 14th the wind veered to the North and began to increase rapidly. Captain Bell reefed down and sent his topgallant yards on deck. Daylight on the 15th found the *Warlock* off Pyramid Point, the gale still increasing and a tremendous sea running. Captain Bell now thought it advisable to bear up and run for the anchorage off Chinchew, and at 7.30 a.m. he brought up between the Islands of Tat-toi and the Main with both anchors down in 5 fathoms.

This spot was reckoned one of the best places of refuge by the coasters. At 3.30 p.m. it was blowing a hurricane. The lower and topsail yards were sent down and both cables veered out to the clench. The ship rode well through the night in the midst of heavy rain. At daylight the wind hauled to East and blew harder than ever, and in less than an hour the barometer fell four-tenths. At 7 a.m. the wind swung into the South with a furious squall which brought in a heavy ground swell. The *Warlock* was now pitching and labouring very heavily and in a short time her port cable parted 50 fathoms from the anchor. Another anchor was at once bent on and let go, but at 10.30, by which time there was a tremendous sea running in, the ship again parted her port cable, and dragging the other anchor, drove on shore.

Luckily the tide was ebbing and at low water the *Warlock* was high and dry. The Chinese gathered round the ship in thousands, and were evidently intent on loot; however the determined behaviour of the captain and crew, who remained on board, kept them off. But when the flood came in again the huge surf broke clean over the little vessel and she began to break up, so that on the next ebb it was decided to leave her in spite of the uncertain attitude of the Chinese, but these latter allowed the crew to force their way through their crowded ranks without molesting them. The captain, however, had scarcely put foot on the beach before the Celestials had begun a rapid and systematic plundering of the vessel. After an 8-mile walk the crew of the *Warlock* arrived opposite the receiving ships stationed at Chinchew. These took them on board and gave them every attention.

Best Passages, 1847.

In 1846 Captain Oliver left the brig *Audax* in order to follow Captain McMurdock in the command of the *Red Rover.* He was succeeded by Captain Sullivan who distinguished himself in his first voyage up the coast, first by discovering a small islet near the Loochoo Islands, which was not laid down on the chart, and secondly by running from Silver Island to Hongkong in 94 hours, which was a record.

On July 20, 1847, the *Audax* had a narrow escape in a typhoon. She anchored just outside the Ly-ee-moon Passage, and when it was blowing its worst a huge Siamese junk, drifting before the storm, almost collided with the brig and then was dashed to pieces in the furious surf under the high cliffs.

Shortly before bringing up, the *Audax* had passed seven of these junks from the Straits, great unwieldy vessels, which it was feared were all lost.

The best outward passages to China in 1847 were:

Clipper	Captain	From	Date Left	Arrived Canton River or Hongkong	Days Out
Red Rover ..	Oliver	Calcutta	Aug. 19	Sept. 11	23
Waterwitch ..	Forgan	,,	July 7	Aug. 2	26
Ariel	Burt	,,	June 1	June 28	27
Antelope ..	Watkins	,,	July 20	Aug. 17	28
Sylph	MacDonald	,,	July 1	July 30	29
Kelpie	Sime	,,	May 19	June 19	31
,, ...	,,	,,	Sept. 18	Oct. 20	32
Red Rover ..	Oliver	,,	April 6	May 12	36
Mischief	White	,,	,, 3	,, 10	37
Poppy	Cole	Bombay	July 8	Aug. 12	35
Lanrick	White	,,	May 5	June 13	39
Coquette	Prescott	,,	April 18	May 27	39
Emma	Hartley	,,	June 12	July 25	43
Mor	Alston	,,	Oct. 4	Nov. 19	46
Sir H. Compton	Browne	,,	March 28	May 24	57

CHAPTER VII.

OPIUM SCHOONERS, GUN BRIGS AND PIRATE JUNKS.

I am fevered with the sunset,
  I am fretful with the bay,
For the wander thirst is on me,
  And my soul is in Cathay.
There's a schooner in the offing
  With her tops'ls shot with fire,
And my Heart has gone aboard her,
  For the Island of Desire.
I must forth again to-morrow,
  With the sunset I must be
Hull down on the trail of Rapture
  In the wonder of the Sea.

—(*The Sea Gipsy.*)

Hongkong Ordinance against Piracy.

IT was not until the "Ordinance against Piracy" was passed by the Hongkong Legislative Council in March, 1847, that any serious attempts were made by British men-of-war to extirpate the fleets of pilongs which, ever since the opium war, had been scourging the China Coast.

The chief clauses in this Ordinance, which was due to Sir John Davis, the Governor of Hongkong, were:—

(i) The right to board and search.

(ii) Offensive weapons called fire-pots or stink-pots to be deemed proof of vessel being a pirate.

(iii) Any offensive weapons found in a junk, lorcha or fast-boat render her liable to forfeiture.

(iv) Trading junks, lorchas, fast-boats, etc., belonging to Hongkong to be registered and licensed, and to carry a flag, with their registered number in large white figures upon it.

(v) Fifty pounds fine for any vessel not hoisting her number.

Receiving Ships in Chimmo Bay Surprised and Captured.

It was not until this Ordinance had been accepted by the Chinese Imperial Commissioner that British gun brigs began pirate hunting in earnest. It was time that the Royal Navy took a hand, for, secure in the knowledge that they had squared all the ill-paid mandarins along the East Coast, the pirates were not only preying upon the junk trade but attacking any European vessels which were unwise enough to let them get to close quarters.

During the war coasting junks were allowed by the Chinese Government to arm themselves as privateers; and, when peace came, many of these were unwilling to go back to the humdrum life of a humble trader, so they either joined up with one of the big pilong fleets under some such notorious piratical Admiral as Shap'ngtzai, or sailed in twos and threes with the main object of waylaying unsuspecting sugar junks and the like.

As these pirates were generally quite indistinguishable from the usual trading junks, it often happened that a junk captain, suspected of or even caught robbing in the high seas, would blandly produce his old war licence as an excuse for his guns and stink-pots.

Surprise attacks were the most effective tactics of these pirates who masqueraded as innocent traders, but they were ready to take great risks where opium clippers formed the object of their attack, and in 1847 they were unusually successful in this direction.

First of all the receiving ships lying in Chimmo Bay were completely surprised and their crews massacred. After this it was thought advisable to moor them in a more frequented anchorage and they were removed to the Bay of Chinchew, a few miles further to windward up the coast. It was soon after this that the schooners *Omega* and *Caroline* were caught napping, whilst lying at anchor near Amoy, and their valuable cargoes were carried off after most of their officers and crews had been killed.

The Gun-brig "Scout" and Pirates.

The first British man-of-war to go into action against Chinese pirates was the brig *Scout* (14 guns, Commander Loring).

It was not long after the opium schooners had been attacked that the *Scout*, on her way to Foochow and when opposite Chimmo

Bay, was boarded by a fishing boat which pointed out two junks standing off the land, which, he stated, had only that morning attacked some traders working up the coast. The *Scout* at once gave chase after the suspicious craft. The smaller of the two junks tacked inshore, but the wind being light three boats under the first lieutenant, E. G. Blake, were sent after her and speedily captured her.

There was no doubt about her being a pirate. She was armed with a 2-pounder, gingals, matchlocks, fire-pots, etc., and carried a crew of 32 men, many of whom jumped overboard and were drowned rather than face the cutlasses of the *Scout's* bluejackets. In her hold four men who had been taken out of a fishing boat two days before were discovered, cruelly bound hand and foot.

The larger pirate was not so easily secured. For three hours a running fight was kept up, the *Scout* firing her fo'c's'le guns which were returned gun for gun by the pilong. At the end of three hours the wind dropped, upon which two boats under Lieut. Josling were sent in chase. As the boats pulled alongside they were received by a hot fire from gingals, matchlocks and stink-pots, which wounded Lieutenant Josling, a midshipman and four seamen and killed one seaman. Luckily the breeze again sprang up and enabled the brig to get way on her; as she ran alongside the pirate, a shower of stink-pots fell upon her decks, wounding the commander and two seamen; however, after a sharp hand to hand engagement she also was carried.

This pirate was a large one with a crew of 120 men, and four 6-pounders. Soon after she was captured a lot of loose gunpowder exploded aboard her, and she fell over on her beam ends and sank. Most of the pilongs were drowned in her, but 36 were saved and handed over to the mandarins at Amoy.

These two pirates had been lying in wait for the Amoy sugar junks, which every day were passing Chimmo Bay on their way North.

The Chinese Junk Trade.

The junk trade extended from Java, Singapore and Siam to the South as far North as Korea. The largest junks ran to several hundreds of tons and were great unwieldy craft with broad cutwaters, painted on either bow with glaring black and white eyes. They had high open sterns, often brightly ornamented and carved. Their masts were tremendous spars, supporting immense battened sails of matting and baggy topsails.

Their cargoes consisted of salt, white and brown sugar, bones, nut-shells (for manure), dried lichis, flints and stones, flour, white pepper, sandalwood, sugar candy, Japan wood, mangrove bark, rattans, cloves, peacocks' feathers, ebony, redwood, swallow's nests, ivory, seaweed, buffalo horns, sweetmeats, dried orange and lemon peel, peas, pea cakes, tobacco, trepang or sea slug, Bombay cotton, deer sinews done up in bundles, betelnut with leaves, rice and lastly opium.

Besides their crews, which seldom numbered more than 20 men, they carried often as many as 60 or 70 passengers.

Many of the finest junks were built in Siam and were called "Pih-tow-cheun" or "white-headed vessels." These were generally manned from the Eastern part of Canton province.

To European eyes these big trading junks appeared to be all dirt and confusion, yet as a matter of fact each man on board had his duties. The buying and selling of the cargo was either done by the owner or his representative, acting as a super-cargo. The ho-chang or pilot was responsible for the navigation of the junk, whilst the to-kung (helmsman) attended to the steering and sails. The petty officers, called tow-muh (headmen) had charge of the anchor, rigging and all deck gear. The seamen, called ho-ke (comrades) were supposed to obey the orders of the tow-muh, but they were usually very ill-disciplined, very independent and very ignorant of their duties. This was due to each man possessing a share of the cargo and having the right to trade on his own account.

The bigger junks also had a compradore and two clerks, who kept the accounts and bought the provisions.

Lastly there was the priest or heang-kun who attended to the joss, burnt incense and gold and silver paper in honour of the goddess of the sea, Ma-tsoo-poo, before whose image a lamp was kept burning day and night aboard every junk. The portly queen of the ocean, sitting on her throne, was often surrounded by minor gods of hideous shape and mien. Every morning the priest appeared before her with carefully washed face and made his prostrations. He then filled a censer with joss sticks of burning incense, which he carried to every part of the ship, even into the cook's galley. His duties were by no means the least important, and began before the junk set sail, for always before weighing anchor the goddess was taken in procession to the nearest joss-house, where, after offerings in the shape of food had been placed at her feet, the priest recited prayers whilst the ho-chang and to-kung in their best clothes kow-towed solemnly. After the prayers came feasting, music and dancing and even acting. Finally the old queen—often much worn by much voyaging—was carried back to the junk preceded by the minstrels and an indefatigable gong-beater and followed by the now uproarious crew.

At sea, if held up by head winds, the priest made an offering to the "spirits of the air." Pigs and fowls were killed, some fruits and samshoo produced, gilt paper burnt; and finally, after several prostrations, the priest would cry out: "Follow the spirits." This was a signal for the crew to rise up from their prostrate positions and set to on the viands which had been prepared.

In a calm the first act of the priest was to send afloat a quantity of little gilt paper junks. If these had no effect in bringing up a wind, he then stated that Ma-tsoo-poo was out of humour, and recourse must be had to the demons of the air. These spirits or demons had to be conciliated on every imaginable occasions, even when sail was set or furled.

The priest had other duties connected with the rudder, the compass and the cable. Offerings of gilt paper were thrown overboard round the rudder, especially when sailing out of a river. Round the compass there was always tobacco, a lighted lamp and a pipe, of which any man might take a whiff. Joss sticks also were burnt in honour of the spirit in the compass, who showed the ho-chang his course, and as if these were not sufficient, much gilt paper twisted up into tiny paper junks was also burnt before this important lesser deity.

The priest also saw to it that both rudder and cable were tastefully decorated with tags of red cloth, a coat of which was made to cover the compass. The compass itself differed from the European compass in having three circles, the first divided into 24 parts, the second into 8 and the last into 4. A sailing directory of the China Coast, the result of centuries of experience, was marked with compass courses, which the pilot made use of whenever his own knowledge was insufficient, and these courses were never far wrong.

The Schooner "Spec" accused of Piracy.

If Ma-tsoo-poo, goddess of the sea, and the demons of the air were efficient in regard to all ordinary emergencies, the trading junks soon found that they were quite useless as a defence against piracy, and at last they were compelled to sail in convoys, guarded by the swift-sailing, well-armed schooners of the British. Two of these schooners were the *Spec*—which the Pybus Bros. had sold to Captain Cole—and the *Dido*; and in this convoy duty both had some exciting adventures. But in October, 1848, the *Spec* was seized at the Rugged Islands and brought to Hongkong on the charge of piratically attacking a junk belonging to Ningpo.

The case put to the Grand Jury by Chief Justice Hulme was a curious one. The charge against Captain Cole rested principally on his own evidence, which had been given without his being warned not to incriminate himself. None of the junk's crew appeared as witnesses against him nor any of those stated to have been wounded in the affray. After examining the *Spec's* log book the Grand Jury after two hours' consultation brought in a finding of "no bill." So Captain Cole and his crew were discharged.

The Trial of Eli Boggs.

In 1848 European adventurers on the China Coast were not as common as they became half a dozen years later when Ben Pease and Bully Hayes were operating in these waters. Neither of these worthies was brought to book, but an American named Eli Boggs was the next Westerner to be tried for piracy at Hongkong. This was in 1856. The following account, taken from the *Hongkong Gazette*, gives one a hint of a story which would have made a Hollywood film producer's fortune.

An American, named Eli Boggs, was tried at Hongkong on Wednesday, July 1, for piracy and murder. His name would do for a villain of the Blackbeard class, but in form and feature he was the hero of a sentimental novel: he was a great dandy as well as a cut-throat. As he stood in the dock, bravely battling for his life, it seemed impossible that that handsome boy could be the pirate whose name had been for three years connected with the boldest and bloodiest acts of piracy. It was a face of feminine beauty—not a down upon the upper lip, large lustrous eyes, a mouth the smile of which might woo coy maiden, affluent black hair not carelessly parted, hands so small and so delicately white that they would create a sensation in Belgravia—such was the Hongkong pirate, Eli Boggs.

He spoke for two hours in his defence, and he spoke well without a tremor, without an appeal for mercy, but trying to prove that his prosecution was the result of a conspiracy wherein a Chinese bum-boat proprietor and a sub-official of the Colony (both of whom he charged as being in league with all the pirates on the coast) were the chief conspirators. The defence was of course false. It had been proved that he had boarded a junk and destroyed by cannon, pistol and sword fifteen men; and that having forced all the rest overboard he had fired at one of the victims who had clutched a rope and held on astern. No witness, however, could prove that he saw a man die from a blow or shot struck or fired by the pirate. The jury, moved by his youth and courage and straining hard at their consciences, acquitted him of the murder, but found him guilty of piracy. He was sentenced to be transported for life.

At the time of the trial, the *Hongkong Gazette* goes on to remark there were 200 junks lying in the harbour, every one of them armed with at least two heavy guns and some with twelve. Probably one quarter of these were pirates, who adopted the coasting trade as a cloak to their real profession.

Captain MacDonald of the "Sylph" describes his Passage.

The last captain of the famous *Sylph*, Captain Donald MacDonald, was twice married. By his first wife he had three daughters, of whom the youngest Jemima alone reached maturity. She married Captain John Ryrie, the eldest of the three Ryrie brothers.

Captain MacDonald's second wife was Helen, eldest daughter of Captain Donald Aeneas Mackay, Royal Horse Artillery.

On May 5, 1848, the *Sylph* left Hongkong with treasure for Bombay, and reached Anjer on May 28, after a smart run of 23 days. The rest of the passage is very vividly described in a letter from Captain MacDonald to his wife, which luckily has survived and is here transcribed.

I will give you, my dearest Helen, a brief sketch of my trip, from the time we anchored at Anjer until we left it and then thence to Bombay. It will help to while away a little of my time in writing it, and perhaps for the five minutes it will take you to read it, it may amuse you a little, although I fear you will find little in it to amuse. However, it will give a faint idea of my mind and thoughts during the trip and also of my loneliness, not having exchanged a dozen words with any of my officers since I left China up to the present moment. You must not infer from this that we are on bad terms. No, all is right so far, but I am in very low spirits and am not in the humour to converse with them, as they cannot enter into my feelings nor yet sympathise with me. I therefore smother all within my own heart, which, I fancy, helps to make me the more unhappy—so much for an introduction.

Now for my visit on shore to the "very noble Dutch Governor" of Anjer on the evening or rather the afternoon of the 28th when I gave him a letter to your address according to promise, which, I trust, my dear Helen, you received, as it would give an account of my safe arrival at Anjer.

Well, then, I went on shore about 5 p.m. and paid my respects to the noble Dutchman who kept me waiting a little longer than I thought was civil; and I was just on the eve of leaving when His Excellency thought proper to make his appearance, with a cigar in his mouth, Dutchmanlike. He did not ask me into a room but we sat down in the veranda where the sun was beating very strong and insufferably hot, which in consequence made my visit very short.

Our conversation:

"I understand you are a Company's cruiser?" I said: "No! but a clipper."

"Na clepar, clepar na smogglers?"

"No, not a smuggler but an opium clipper!"

"Hum!"

I then asked when our wood and water would be alongside as I was most anxious to be off.

"Ah, I tink to-morrow morning."

That, I said, would not answer the purpose of a smuggler as we must leave to-night at midnight; so I asked him to go out with me and see about it and have it hurried off, which he did.

I dare say he thought as little of me as I did of him—the idea of making a Governor look after wood and water! However, I was not mistaken in my man, as he spoke more about the dollars and the price of the wood and water than anything else. He said it was very "dare."

I said: "It matters not to a smuggler. Time and dispatch are everything."

"Hum! " he said: "it will cost you 18 dollars."

I said if it cost 50 dollars I must have it and that this very night, and immediately I went on board I would send him "de dollar."

At parting he said: "Take care of de casks and not *broke* them."

"I will nurse them as a new born baby," I answered. "Only let me have the water alongside," I thought, "and your casks may go to hell." So I parted and went on board of my little ship, disgusted with the Dutchman and the shore and I care not if I never see the place again; I had not been there for nine years.

At midnight of the 28th, weighed, with a light air off the land; throughout calm light airs and rain, made little progress.

29th—The same weather with a threatening appearance to the westward. Annoyed and perplexed at the continuance of the calms. I fear a long voyage.

30th—Light airs and calms with a heavy confused sea. Hard squalls occasionally. Split all our old sails to ribbons, unbent them and bent others. I feel anything but happy two days out and no progress, land still in sight, surely the calms cannot last much longer. Being in latitude 7°, we ought to have fine S.E. winds.

31st May—Still perplexed; light winds and a nasty sea, the ship rolling prodigiously making everything most uncomfortable, I lost all patience.

1st June—Little wind, a nasty sea on, our progress very slow indeed, I fear a long passage. I dreamed of Mr. A. Matheson last night. I do nothing but dream night after night, my mind must be in a strange state of anxiety.

2nd—To-day light airs and calms, sea still keeping up making the ship most uncomfortable—out of all patience.

3rd—We at last have got a fine steady breeze, thank God, going 8 knots. I trust it may continue.

In better spirits to-day than usual. I wonder if those dear to me (my wife and children) are thinking of poor lonely me buffeting it out by myself. Oh! for a quiet nook in some place or other.

4th and 5th—Out of spirits!

6th—Steady breezes and fine. How I do long to see this trip at an end. I never in my life entered on a voyage with greater dislike from the moment it was decided I should go to Bombay; that moment I got the blues and cannot recover my spirits do what I may, and I fear will not until I am again moored at Singapore, if God spares me so long and nothing happens to the old ship.

10th—Although this day has dawned on us cheerfully with a fine breeze, the ship is rolling most fearfully and taking in water right and left, still we are getting on at a goodly pace.

But, my Helen, the day closed, I am grieved to say most melancholy. A heavy sea struck the larboard quarter boat and carried away the foremost davit; and in trying to save my fine boat I lost one of my best men; in fact, the best in the ship, overboard. To save him was impossible, the ship going at 10 knots and under a heavy press of sail with a fearful sea on. To have launched my other boat would have been madness, as I am sure I should have lost her with her crew. I had nothing for it but to let my poor fellow sink to rise no more. We lost sight of him in 5 minutes we were going so fast. So, lost my man and boat; ah, my heart. Would that I was housed in some little cottage of our own with our dear little ones about us.

11th—To-day most melancholy and unhappy, strong fair winds, but the weather most unsettled, a man missing—supposed to have been washed overboard during the night.

Since we left China, my mind was impressed that something fatal was to happen to myself or ship, I know not how it is to end. I am in God's hands. I am now most thankful that my dear wife and child did not join me at Anjer (although at the time a great disappointment) they would have been most wretchedly uncomfortable in consequence of the very unsettled state of the weather since we left Anjer. It has indeed been a most unpleasant trip from first to last.

12th—Fine steady winds to-day, we have done 450 miles last two days, passed vessels steering as ourselves and lost sight of them in a very few hours.

13th—Still our fine breeze continues, but at best accompanied with constant squalls and rain. Must not repine, we are making good progress, having run during the last four days 900 miles.

The man reported as being washed overboard on the 11th was found comfortably stowed away in the ship's eyes, fast asleep. I pretended great anger, but I can assure you, Helen, I felt happy to find the man was safe. I promised him a little castigation but he got off scot free to his great comfort—I was too glad to find the man.

14th—Our fine breeze remains with us still but the ship is rolling most fearfully. Hauled this day 3 points to the Northward. I am glad to say. I wish her head was now N.E. we would then be drawing near our destination. I shall indeed feel happy when this trip is over, I cannot tell what has given me so much aversion to Bombay.

27th—I am happy, my dearest Helen, to tell you we anchored here this morning, after rather a long voyage from Anjer; but on the whole I consider it a good voyage, 53 days from Hongkong.

I feel sorry this morning, as we were running in the *Antelope* was leaving, that I could not send this scroll by her as you would have had it, I dare say, 10 or 12 days sooner. However a vessel is sailing, the *Kailblai*, by which opportunity I take advantage. I am happy to say we will be able to get a cargo here so will not have to go to Calcutta; the day is not fixed for our sailing but I should think about the 12th or 14th of July. I trust you received my hurried chit from Anjer. I have no great faith in the Dutchman sending this by the first opportunity, but I trust he has, it would be a relief to your mind to find I was well.

DONALD.

The *Sylph* left Bombay again on July 17, 1848, and arrived at Hongkong on August 25, just in time to come in for a very nasty typhoon which began on August 31 at 10 p.m.

The "Sylph" and "Eagle" in a Typhoon.

The *Sylph* was brought up in the Cum-sing-moon Passage when this blow started, not far from Russell's brig *Eagle*. The roads were evidently crowded and it was not long before most of the ships had started to drag. The *Eagle* was one of the first to go. At 11 p.m. she drove down upon the U.S. man-of-war *Plymouth* and hooked up the latter's best bower. Captain Gedney, of the U.S. frigate, had begun to pass his stream cable out through a stern port and on over the bow of the *Eagle*, so that the latter might slip her cables and ride by his ship, but before this could be accomplished the *Isabella Robertson* drove down on top of the *Eagle*, carried away the little opium clipper's foremast and bowsprit, tore off her bulwark rail on both bows, forced over her cutwater and started the ends of her planking. After this the *Isabella Robertson* swung clear and shortly afterwards sank, only three Lascars being saved.

The *Eagle*, in company with the *Sylph*, drifted up on to the beach in a deep sandy bay on Cum-sing-moon Island. The former stranded but the latter was able to bring up before reaching the beach, and rode it out in safety though she had all three masts blown out of her.

At noon on the 1st the *Plymouth* sent off boats to their assistance, the *Eagle* begged for an anchor and chain, but Captain MacDonald declined all assistance.

It is possible that it was on this occasion that Mrs. MacDonald gave birth to twins in the midst of the typhoon. She was only a girl of 19, there was no doctor on board, only her Chinese armah, so, when the event occurred, she sent for her husband.

The story Helen MacDonald used to relate in her old age was this: When the captain came into the little cabin, all dripping, and a face furrowed with anxiety, he exclaimed:

"I can't stay below, Helen, my place is on deck." The result was that the twins died through MacDonald's hurry.

And when in after years her grandchildren asked: "Grandmama, wasn't grandfather a fine sailor?"

She would answer: "A very fine sailor, my dears, but no midwife!!"

After refitting, the old *Sylph* left Macao for Calcutta on December 15, 1848.

Logs of Opium Clippers in October Typhoon, 1848.

At the beginning of October, 1848, a very severe typhoon travelled down the China coast and played havoc with the shipping.

It is interesting to read how small heavily rigged schooners, which had been specially built with racing lines, were able to weather out such a convulsion of Nature as a typhoon

The two illustrations from sketches by A. G. Dallas show the little *Mazeppa* having a grand overhaul and refit at Hongkong, in 1847. She sailed for the East coast on October 6, 1848, and ran straight into this typhoon.

Here is an extract from her logbook.

Friday, October 6—5·30 a.m., cast off from *Bomanjee Hormusjee* (Jardine Matheson's hulk at Hongkong) and made sail for East coast of China. Fresh N.N.W breeze and fine weather. 6·30 a.m., sent down royal yard and studding sail booms. 10 a.m., fresh breeze in topgallant sail and one reef in topsail. Noon, moderate and fine, *Kelpie* hull up on lee quarter. Bar. 29·70. Sunset; strong breeze and fine weather. 8 p.m., increasing; in one reef in topsail. Midnight, strong breeze and fine with heavy swell from E.S.E.

Saturday, October 7—A.M., strong breeze and fine with heavy swell. At daylight, Breaker Point bearing N.N.W., wore ship and stood on shore towards Cup-chee. 8 a.m., bar. 29·60, increasing breeze, passed close to Breaker Point. 3 p.m., bar. 29·40 and falling, sent down main topmast and fore topgallant mast. Sunset, strong breeze and fine weather with heavy sea. Cape of Good Hope (near Swatow) bearing N. by E. ½ E. 10 miles. 7 p.m., increasing, reefed foresail and double reefed mainsail. Barometer varying from 29·40 to 29·30. 8 p.m., ditto weather. Midnight, strong gale, in foresail and jib and hove to on port tack. Pumps constantly attended.

Sunday, October 8—A.M., strong gale from N.N.E. with very high sea. Schooner pitching and labouring heavily and shipping a good deal of water. At daylight, bar. 29·35, split the fore trysail. Gale increasing with tremendous cross sea. Noon, still increasing with thick rainy weather, split balance-reefed mainsail, bent close-reefed trysail and set it. Midnight, bar. 29·30 to 29·28, blowing furiously with dark, thick and rainy weather, shipping large quantities of water, pumps constantly going, schooner making good deal of water.

Monday, October 9—A.M., gale increasing to nearly a hurricane. Schooner labouring greatly and shipping large quantities of water. Wind steady at N.E., lee rail and deck completely under water. Bar. 29·25. Daylight, same weather. 10 a.m., bent fore trysail for mainsail going to pieces; unbent remnants and bent fore staysail luff to gaff. Bar. from 29·21 to 29·15. 11·30 a.m., most fearful gusts, schooner nearly on beam ends, hove lee guns overboard and cut away topmast and topsail yard; lightened the decks as much as possible. Sunset, a little more moderate but tremendous sea. Midnight, same weather, ship making good deal of water. During the whole of this day the barometer rose and fell nearly a tenth, occasioned perhaps by the rapid motion of the vessel.

Tuesday, October 10—A.M., decreasing gale with heavy cross sea running. Barometer gradually rising. Daylight, moderating fast, unbent staysail and set it, forestay repaired, and set double reefed mainsail. Noon, bar. 29·50, moderate and cloudy, no observation, wind N.N.W. Made all sail we could to North-eastward. Lat. by dead reckoning 20° 42′, Long. 116° 3′. During night moderate breeze from N.W.

Wednesday, October 11—Moderate breeze and fine weather sent up fore topmast and bent fore topsail and set flying-jib. Noon, spoke *Viscount Sandon*. Pratas Shoal bearing S.S.E. 32 miles. Observation Lat. 21° 12′, Long. 116° 10′. During this day barometer steady at 29·65. During night fresh breeze steering for Hongkong. During the gale, from Saturday night at 6 p.m. until Tuesday at noon the schooner drifted S. by W. ½ W. 133 miles, being 2 miles per hour, the wind veering from N.N.W. to N.E., where it remained steady during the strength of the breeze, but went back to N.W. as soon as it moderated.

The writer of this well-kept log was Captain Mordaunt who had succeeded Captain Jauncey in 1847. The *Mazeppa* only arrived at Hongkong on October 3, 23 days out from Singapore with a valuable cargo, not of opium, for a change, but of sandalwood.

Now let us see how the little *Audax* came through it. Here is Captain Sullivan's log:

October 7—Commenced with heavy N.N.E. gale and confused sea. Bar. 29·50. 8 a.m., blowing very hard; furled close-reefed mainsail and staysail; sent down main topmast and fore topsail yard. Bar. 29·40 and falling. 9 a.m., close-reefed foresail. Noon, Lat. by bad observation 22° 34′ 40″ N., Long. by account 117° 20′ E. Midnight, blowing furiously hard with fearful sea running, furled close reefed foresail. Bar. 29·30.

October 8—1·30 a.m., blowing furiously hard, schooner under bare poles. 3·30 a.m., a sea broke on board carrying away bulwarks on both sides from fore-rigging to quarters, also gig and long-boat, also stripped the copper off from weather bow to quarter, carried away skylight and after hatch from their coamings; one European killed and one Lascar washed overboard, also one man's thigh broken and barometer smashed; guns and caboose only left on deck. Daylight, blowing a hurricane, hands employed clearing decks, securing skylight and after hatchway, pumps kept going, schooner having shipped much water down skylight and after hatch. Noon, same fearful weather, threw guns overboard to ease schooner. Midnight, blowing harder, wind roaring like thunder, sea one sheet of foam, fearfully high and confused.

October 9—Daylight, blowing harder if possible with same high and cross sea; quite impossible to look to windward. Hands pumping and bailing, schooner lying over very much but making little water. 10 a.m., blowing harder than ever with same sea. Schooner thrown on her beam ends but righted a little before cutting mainmast away, which we did as soon as possible to save the ship. One European washed overboard and never seen afterwards, sea making a clean sweep over us. Noon, weather worse than ever. Schooner very much pressed with her foremast only; hands lashed to the pump; schooner tight still though quite under water. 4 p.m., wind moaning and roaring like thunder, and so thick that we could hardly see the foremast at times. Sea much less. 6 a.m., wind shifted to North, and began to moderate. 10 p.m., moderating fast but blowing hard in gusts, wind N.W. Midnight, hard N.W. gale with much less sea, weather clearing up fast.

October 10—A.M., decreasing gale at N.W. 6·30 a.m., set double reefed foresail with head to N.N.E. 8 a.m., moderate breeze at W.N.W., set whole foresail. Noon, fine weather, wind West but very light with high sea. Lat. by observation 19° 55′ 56″ N., Long. by chronometer 116° 15′ E. We drifted from noon of 7th to noon of 10th during the hurricane, while lying to, 172 miles to S. by W. ¾ W. The gale commenced at North, veering to N.N.E. during the first 12 hours, then steady at N.E. up to 4 p.m. on 9th, when it backed round to North and N.W. by midnight, when it began to moderate. We were continually on port tack hoping to reach out of the storm, but owing to our great drift we were in my opinion carried with the gale. I much regret not having a barometer during middle and latter part of the hurricane, as no doubt the mercury would have been very low.

It will be noticed that *Audax*, which came out as a brig, was now evidently rigged as a topsail schooner.

The third vessel to have a bad time in that October typhoon was the brig *Antelope*. This time the record is taken from a letter of Captain Watkins to Captain R. B. Forbes, which runs as follows:

I regret to inform you that we have been totally dismasted. We left Woosung on October 5, 1848, with fine weather. On the 6th blowing fresh from the East, the brig going large 12 knots; at 6 o'clock, we double-reefed the topsails and furled the mainsail. At midnight, took in close reefs, the barometer at 29·35. At 4 a.m., furled the fore topsail and sent down topgallant yards, the wind and sea increasing, washed away both quarter boats and part of the hammock rails. I was compelled to keep running so as to get sea-room to heave to; the wind shifted to North and blew a perfect hurricane. Bar. 29·30. At 3 p.m., the foresail blew away, a dangerous cross sea running. At 4·30 p.m., prepared to heave to, every aperture was carefully battened down and all spare spars and the launch carefully secured. At 5, rounded to. At 5·20, a furious squall and she went over on her beam ends; the helm being no longer of use, she fell off in the trough of the sea. I knew that if she remained so she must go down and I ordered the masts cut away. By 7 a.m., we were all clear of the wreck, and the sea making a complete breach over her. Bar. 29·10.

On the 8th at 7 a.m., let go the stream anchor and the kedge in 21 fathoms, in order to try to get her head to the wind. We soon drifted into 12 fathoms on the Formosa Banks: still blowing heavy and the sea worse than yesterday. At 3 o'clock drifted into 19 fathoms. At 8 p.m., the stream and kedge were lost and she fell off, bringing the wind

H.M.S. "COLUMBINE"

From a Drawing

[*See page* 312

CLIPPER "JOHN BUNYAN"
Form a Drawing from A. G. Dallas

"TORRINGTON"
From a contemporary Drawing by A. G Dallas [*See page* 322

on the starboard quarter. I dared not let go a bower anchor for in the event of a shift of wind I might want the anchors. At 9 p.m., still blowing a heavy gale. At midnight, the wind came round to South-east. Bar. 29·40. On the 10th, at 4 a.m., the wind came out at S.W. and moderated fast. Bar. 29·80. At daylight commenced to rig jury masts. At noon, calm; and by 9 p.m., we had the brig under snug working canvas. I am satisfied that if the *Antelope* had not been one of the best built vessels afloat she must have gone to Davy Jones' locker. When we left Shanghai she was a perfect picture: we arrived (at Hongkong) on the 13th and since then seven others have arrived in similar conditions, and some will never be heard of.

When the *Antelope* came out, she was fitted with mast partners, channels and even a mizen mast so that she could be easily changed from a brig to a barque: and on refitting at Hongkong Captain Watkins, owing to the great demand for spars, etc., after the typhoon, decided to make use of his barque gear and so the *Antelope* emerged from the rigger's hands as a barque, and she was never the vessel that she had been as a brig.

Best Opium Passages, 1848.

Clipper	Captain	Port Left	Date Left	Arrived Canton River or Hongkong	Days Out	Remarks
Red Rover ..	Oliver	Calcutta	Oct. 7	Oct. 24	17	Taken from *Canton Register* Shipping Report
Poppy ..	Cole	„	June 6	June 28	22	
Lanrick ..	White	„	June 26	July 21	25	
Antelope ..	Watkins	Bombay	June 28	„ 24	26	
Waterwitch ..	Forgan	Calcutta	July 3	Aug. 2	30	
Kelpie ..	Sime	„	Aug. 17	Sept. 18	32	Lost fore topgallant mast and main topmast in gale
Cowasjee Family	Durham	„	June 1	July 4	33	
Mor	Alston	„	Aug. 21	Sept. 23	33	
Coquette ..	Prescott	„	May 7	June 11	35	Ran foul of ss. *Pekin* in China Sea, some damage
Red Rover ..	Oliver	„	„ 7	„ 11	35	
Lanrick ..	White	„	1847 Dec. 16	1848 Jan. 24	39	Strong N.E. gale after leaving Singapore
Sylph	MacDonald	Bombay	July 17	Aug. 25	39	Rode out typhoon off Cum-sing-moon Island
Rob Roy ..	Francis	Calcutta	April 12	May 24	42	

By 1848, some of the clippers were sailing from India direct to Woosung without putting into the Canton River or Hongkong on the way. Here are a few of these passages:

Clipper	Captain	Left Bombay	Arrived Woosung	Days Out	Remarks
Zoe	Miller	Feb. 1, '47	April 13	71	
Gem ..	Watson	April 8, '47	June 8	61	Brig of 226 tons
Nymph ..	Landers	Mar. 1, '48	May 13	73	
" ..	Burt	Nov. 30, '48	Jan. 30, '49	61	
Ariel ..	Burt	Jan. 7, '48	Mar. 26	79	Dent's barque

The smartest passage on the coast in 1848 was that of the schooner *Zephyr* (Captain Wilson), which in September came down from Lookong to Hongkong in 82 hours, which was claimed to be a record.

The schooner *Nymph* had the credit of making the smartest voyage, Hongkong to Woosung and back. She left Hongkong on the night of August 11, 1850, and reached Woosung on the 15th, out 4 days and a few hours. After discharging opium and taking in specie, she was back in Hongkong on August 26, the whole trip totalling only 15 days, a record, the next best being 17 days by the *Lapwing*. Captain Wilson had only lately taken over the *Nymph* from Captain Burt, having surrendered the *Zephyr* to Captain Brown. He was evidently a great passage maker.

The Loss of the Schooner "Omega."

Jardine Matheson's *Omega* came to a sad end in January 5, 1849, when bound from Amoy to Hongkong. During a very dark night she was standing in towards the low coast lying just South of Breaker Point. A strong breeze was blowing. At about 2 am., Captain Anderson suddenly recognised that the schooner was running into a big surf; he immediately sang out for the helm to be put down and the jib sheets to be let go, but as the *Omega* was rounding into the wind, she struck. An effort was at once made to get her off before the wind, but though they got her head off-shore, the wind blew her broadside on to the sandy beach. The mainmast was cut away, but this did no good, and with the surf making a clean breach over her, all hands were obliged to take refuge in the fore weather rigging. The schooner lay on her broadside about 200 yards from the shore.

At daylight the wreck was discovered by the Chinese and in a short time thousands had collected on the beach. One of the sea-cunnies now managed to swim ashore with a rope, but he was immediately seized by the Chinese and stripped, finally escaping without a shred of clothing and swimming back to the wreck.

It was low water about noon, when the quarter boat was successfully got over the side and brought under the lee bow. Captain Anderson, Hutchinson the mate, Thomson the second mate, a missionary passenger, the gunner Alexander Sivewright, six Chinese and six or eight Lascars got into the boat, it being arranged that the rest of the crew who were good swimmers should hang on round the gunwale.

But some of the Lascars in jumping into the water from the rigging were swept up against the boat, and clutching at her, capsized her. In this way twelve of the *Omega's* crew were drowned including the mate and missionary. As the survivors struggled out of the surf, they were immediately seized by the Chinese and stripped, the unfortunate captain being thrown down and his head held under water until he drowned, a fate which the others narrowly escaped.

The first to get away were the second mate, the gunner and one of the sea-cunnies, all as naked as the day they were born. They were presently joined by six of the Lascars, and after a three hours' walk along the coast reached a village where the natives gave them a few rags to cover themselves with and some raw sweet potatoes. One of the Lascars spoke a little Chinese, and by this means they obtained a guide, who took them to the large town of Kup-che where the mandarin supplied them with a sleeping place and one mace to purchase food. From Kup-che on the following day they went on along the beach to a big fishing village, where they tried to obtain a boat to take them to Hongkong.

Again the mandarins gave them supper and a lodging, but no boat could be obtained. The next morning after being provided with a mace to buy food, they were sent on to Luhong with a guide. Here they were detained until to their astonishment they were joined by twelve more of the shipwrecked crew, and on the following day three Chinese and one Malay, who had come all the way by himself, overtook them, making up the survivors of the *Omega* to 25 men.

On the morning of the 12th, they left Luhong where they had been kindly treated and provided with food and clothing. After walking all day they reached Hae-hang about 8 o'clock, and were locked up foodless in the jail for the night. They were sent on the following morning in charge of two soldiers, each man receiving 40 cash for food. This had to last them for three days, at the end of which at 6 p.m. the worn-out crew reached Pinsing. Here they were provided with 32 cash each and put into a canal boat, which, travelling all night, landed them at a place called Kweising at about 8 in the morning. The canal boatmen rested until 1 p.m., and again the mandarin of the place provided the 25 men with cash for the purchase of their food, this time about 50 a piece.

The next stopping place was Hwuichan, where they arrived at midnight, but remained in the boat till daylight, when they went to the local mandarin, who supplied each man with 80 cash. At 8 p.m. they again pursued their journey in the canal boat and finally reached Canton on the following morning, January 18.

This was, on the whole, a better experience than most shipwrecked people received at the hands of the Chinese. Before the opium war such unfortunates seldom came off with their lives.

When the *Kite* (transport) was wrecked at the beginning of the war, it will be remembered that the survivors of her crew, including Mrs. Noble, the captain's wife, were confined in cages, with irons on their hands and feet. The cage which contained poor Mrs. Noble for some ten days in bitter winter weather is now to be seen in the Royal United Service Institution.

Captain Forbes comes out by the Overland Route.

The year 1849 saw the return of Captain R. B. Forbes to China. He came out by the overland route across Egypt and compared it very unfavourably to the ordinary sailing ship voyage.

It was, however, considered the most up-to-date and luxurious form of travel possible in 1849 and so a short account of his journey is worth recording.

He sailed from Southampton on July 20 in the famous P. & O. flagship *Hindostan*, of 2017 tons and 520 horse power, commanded by Captain Soy. Gibraltar was reached on the 25th, Malta on the 29th and Alexandria on August 2. Forbes' chief complaints on this part of the voyage were total absence of ice, good water and good bread; the coal dust was also not to the taste of the old sailing ship skipper. At Alexandria the yelling donkey boys with their "Come my donkey, master," gave him a thorough distaste for the sights of Egypt.

The journey from Alexandria to Cairo by means of an iron canal boat was an indistinct memory of broken sleep amongst passengers' trunks and bags, of a heavy wetting dew under a glaring full moon, of dogs barking, of some 70 to 80 overland travellers snoring or cursing the mosquitoes, of fleas and bugs, and a speed in tow of a little iron steamer of some 7 knots against a tortuous, muddy, smelly stream, for a matter of 122 miles. This made the rest at Shepherd's Hotel seem like paradise.

Two-wheeled van-like carriages, driven by Arabs and drawn by two mules, with two horses in the lead, conveyed the overland passengers to Suez. Leaving Cairo at 3.30 in the afternoon, these vehicles with six passengers apiece, in very cramped quarters, rattled at a hard gallop through the dust and heat until 10 a.m. the following morning, when their worn-out contents were bundled out into a heat of 95° and the "worst managed hotel in Egypt."

At Suez Forbes embarked on the *Haddington*, P. & O. steamer of 1647 tons and 450 h.p., a vessel which in her old age was very well known, with her engines out, as a sailing ship. The *Haddington* coaled at Aden, which Forbes contented himself with viewing through a spy-glass. The run to China by way of Ceylon, Penang and Singapore was the most comfortable part of the journey, which was accomplished in 55 days from Southampton to Hongkong.

Forbes, after his experience of the so-called overland journey, in which he declared one ran "a fearful risk of being disgusted with Scripture history, human nature in general and the clergy in particular," advised taking a good sailing ship with a good captain and going out round the Cape in the good old way.

Forbes asks for his Coffin to be made from the "Lintin's" Mast.

Arrived out at Hongkong, Forbes fell a victim to the climate and became so ill that he desired Dr. Parker to have his coffin made from the mast of his old ship *Lintin*, which was lying sunk below Dutch Folly.

After the Emperor had refused Elliot's first treaty, Russell & Co. had sold the *Lintin* to the Chinese, which was anchored off Dutch Folly, having been unrigged to her lower masts, had two great eyes painted on her bows, and the usual zigzag thunder and lightning lines and figures of dragons swallowing moons around her bends and quarters. In this guise with a fat mandarin smoking his pipe comfortably in a bamboo chair, a large silk umbrella over his head and a peacock feather in his cap—as a substitute for Captain Endicott—and a noisy gong in place of the brass fo'c'sle bell, the transformed *Lintin* felt her disgrace so much that at the first fresher she sheered over on to the rocks close to the Folly Fort, holed herself and went down in deep water, only the stump of her foremast showing some 7 feet above the water. On this stump, which Captain Forbes desired for his coffin, a diminutive Chinese lantern of paper was placed, whose faint glimmer was the first navigation light in Canton waters.

Thirty years later the old *Lintin's* foremast with its penny dip still showed the way up and down the Pearl River; for, needless to say, tough old Black Ben did not succumb to his fever.

Seven Opium Clippers go missing.

The year 1849 was a disastrous one for the opium fleet, for no less than seven of the best known clippers went missing, besides other vessels, such as the brig *Grace Darling* and the schooner *Amoy Packet*.

The clippers were *Sylph*, *Coquette*, *Kelpie*, *Greyhound*, *Don Juan*, *Mischief* and *Anna Eliza*.

The *Sylph* left Hongkong for Singapore on July 11, 1849. The *Cowasjee Family*, sailing from Hongkong on July 13 and the *Rob Roy* on the 17th, duly arrived at Singapore on August 17 and 15 respectively, but there were no signs of the *Sylph*.

Messrs. Jardine, Matheson & Co. concluded, as there had been no bad weather, that she had fallen into the hands of the pirates, who lurked in wait off the island of Hainan; indeed, it was reported that a Chinese junk had given information of her capture.

On September 5, H.M. steam sloop *Medea*, with an extra complement of men from the frigate *Amazon*, sailed in search of the missing clipper, but never found a trace of her. The loss of the other ships was also put down to the pirates with possibly the exception of that of the *Coquette*.

Captain Prescott sailed from Shanghai on August 30, 1849, with river mud as ballast, and it is probable that the *Coquette* capsized through her ballast shifting in the typhoon of September 13, as she was reported not far from Hongkong and right in the track of the typhoon. This explanation of her loss did not, however, satisfy her owners, for Captain Prescott was a very experienced commander. They chartered the P. & O. *Canton* and sent her out in charge of Captain Watkins to look for their lost barque, but the *Canton* had no better success than the *Medea*.

The "Pilot" makes Prize Money.

In 1849 there were two large fleets of pirates under admirals of unusual daring. The first of these had headquarters in Bias Bay, which even at the present day is still the breeding place of every piratical venture in the neighbourhood of Hongkong.

The other fleet and the more powerful of the two operated along the Western shore of Kwang-tung and even to the Southward of the island of Hainan. This fleet was commanded by the notorious Shap'ngtzai. Many claimed to know for a fact that the *Sylph*, *Greyhound* and *Anna Eliza* were amongst his captures.

The first vessel to tackle the Bias Bay fleet was H.M. brig-sloop *Pilot* She was a fast little brig of 12 guns and given any wind had no difficulty in overtaking the pilong junks.

The first pirate that she attacked, she captured by ranging alongside and boarding. The flashing cutlasses were too much for the pilongs, and ten of them leaped overboard rather than face the cold steel, and were drowned.

Her second pirate she drove ashore and burnt. The third was a tougher customer, and as the *Pilot* came up alongside 20 stink-pots full of loose gunpowder were hurled on to the decks of the brig. Luckily all hatches were closed so not much harm was done. Headed by Second Lieutenant Hallowes, the bluejackets then boarded, and after a sharp fight during which ten long-tails were killed drove the remainder of the pirates overboard.

Three more junks were destroyed on this occasion, though the commodore in a junk of 16 guns escaped.

At this time British men-of-war were awarded prize money for every pirate killed, and the crew of the *Pilot* received as much £250 for their first capture alone.

Occasionally the naval mandarins went out for a cruise along the coast under the pretence of pirate hunting. They made a great display with 20 or 30 gaudily beflagged war junks, but never made any captures for the simple reason that before setting sail they had taken the precaution to send a warning to the pirates to keep out of the way.

H.M.S. "Columbine" destroys the Pirate Fleets.

It was the famous little *Columbine* which came out to China again and wiped out the pirate fleets.

The first years of her commission, however, under Commander Grey, were spent in attending to the Malay and Borneo gentry of the piratical persuasion; and it was not until Dalrymple Hay succeeded Grey that she appeared in the China Sea. Leaving England on August 22, 1846, with the mails for Madeira, the Cape and Singapore, the *Columbine* did not arrive in Borneo waters until February, 1847. Her first adventure was in Santabony Roads at the mouth of the Sarawak, where she had a narrow shave from shipwreck, and if she had not been a wonderful sea boat and an exceptional sailer in light winds she would have been lost; as it was she clawed off the land in the lightest of airs against a tremendous breaking surf, a feat few ships in the Royal Navy or any other were capable of doing.

From Sarawak she sailed to Pulo Labuan where she found the *Wolf* acting as guard ship and the schooner *Royalist* surveying. On being relieved by the *Columbine* the *Wolf* sailed for home.

At the end of May, our old friend the *Nemesis*, taking Grey of the *Columbine* and Lieutenant Gordon, commander of the *Royalist* on board, proceeded to Bruni where on the 28th the Sultan ratified the treaty with the British.

It was on her way back to Lubuan with the *Columbine's* cutter in tow that the *Nemesis* fell in with a fleet of Balamini or Suloo pirates, who were chasing some fishermen off the island of Moarra. Directly the steamer appeared the prahus, to the number of 11, pulled inshore, and anchored in line, about 10 yards apart with their heads to the sea and sterns in the surf, with warps fast to the trees ashore above the sandy beach. The prahus were crowded with men, who were well armed, and had their bows protected by ampilans of musket-proof planking.

The action began at 1.30 p.m. at a distance of about 200 yards, the *Nemesis* being in little more than 2 fathoms water and rolling heavily in the ground swell. For two hours the pirates kept up a heavy fire, but by this time their prahus appeared much damaged, so Commander Grey took his cutter and the two cutters of the *Nemesis* and dashed at the left of the line of prahus whilst the steamer poured grape and canister into the centre and right. Immediately the pirates cut loose and pulled away to the Eastward, leaving two prahus in Grey's hands. Six of the prahus ran ashore and landed their men, but as the steamer went off in chase of the other three, five of them launched again and attacked the boats. At this the *Nemesis* turned back. Grey managed to capture a large prahu after a fierce resistance, but except for two taken by the *Nemesis* the others escaped in the darkness. The Suloos fought desperately, and lost between 80 and 100 killed and double that number wounded, the British loss was 1 killed and 7 wounded. Of the pirate prahus two were of the largest size, with crews of over 50 men, the rest having about 40 men apiece. The 42 captured pirates were taken to Bruni Town, where on a public holiday they were cut to pieces, the Sultan of Borneo starting the execution by hurling a spear, which pierced the heart of the first pirate. In the prahus were found over 100 Chinese prisoners, 15 cannons, 10 being of brass, from 9 to 6-pounders, and the rest iron, whilst it was reckoned that there were at least 500 men in the eleven prahus.

It was not until September, 1849, that the *Columbine*, now

under Dalrymple Hay, sailed from Hongkong in search of the Bias Bay fleet of pirates. On the evening of September 28 she sailed into Harlem Bay, found that the people of Pinghoi had just paid a ransom and that a fleet of fourteen pirate junks had gone on to attack Tysammee. At 11 p.m. the glare of a burning village caused the brig to crack on every stitch of sail, and soon afterwards the pirate fleet was sighted heading to the South-west before a light wind in two well-formed lines of seven junks each.

At 11.45 the *Columbine* came up and passed under the stern of the third junk from the rear of the leeline. Mr. Caldwell of the Hongkong police, acting as the interpreter, hailed; the junk replied that he was an honest salt trader bound to Hongkong but knew nothing about his companions. He was then ordered to heave to. It was a bright moonlight night. Captain Hay and Mr. Caldwell stood on the *Columbine's* fo'c'sle with all hands at quarters, tompions out, and shot racks full. The junk could be seen tricing up his stink-pots and boarding nettings and clearing his guns for action, of which he mounted 19.

The *Columbine* commenced the action with three rounds of quick firing from her starboard broadside. This was at once returned and the nearest junks joined in. The *Columbine* had to wear round to avoid being raked, and as she came round fired her port broadside into the first junk's second astern. In a short while three junks were wrecks, but as the wind fell calm the other eleven drew off by sweeping. At this the *Columbine* also got out her sweeps.

At daylight the pirate fleet was a mile and a half ahead of the pursuing brig, then a light easterly air sprang up and they hauled to the wind on the starboard tack. At 11.30 a.m. the P. & O. steamer *Canton* appeared round a point of land. With Captain Watkins on board, she was in search of the missing *Coquette*. The *Columbine* at once signalled: "All in sight are enemy."

The *Canton* took the *Columbine* in tow, and between them another junk was sunk, but then a shot through her "steam chest" obliged the *Canton* to sheer off for repairs.

Having no chart of the coast, for it had not yet been fully surveyed, the *Columbine* in chasing her nearest antagonist inshore round Fokai Point grounded on a reef. Hay at once sent his pinnace, cutter and gig away in chase. As the boats boarded the junk, a pilong rushed below with a lighted joss stick and blew her up, Lieutenant Bridges, who was in command of the boats, recognised the pirate captain's intention and roared, "Overboard for your lives." But he was too late; young Goddard who was chasing the pirate below, along with a seaman and two marines, was killed outright whilst three marines and two seamen were severely wounded. Bridges and Captain Watkins, who had deserted the *Canton* to take part in the boat attack, were blown into the sea unhurt.

Meanwhile the little *Columbine* was in a critical position, striking heavily on the reef. The *Canton* came as near as she dared and anchored about 80 fathoms away. She then sent a hawser aboard. This was taken to the *Columbine's* capstan and with all on board at the oars—commander, doctor, purser, idlers and sick—she was at last hove off.

The ten remaining pirate junks had by this time run into the long natural harbour of Fan-lo-kong or the Ram's Horn, at the head of Bias Bay. As soon as he had his vessel afloat, Hay sent the *Canton* off to Hongkong with his wounded and a report of his actions.

At midnight on Monday, October 1, H.M. gunboat *Fury* arrived on the scene, bringing a detachment of seamen and marines from the *Hastings* under that well-known officer, James Willcox. who had led the stormers at the capture of the Bogue Forts.

With Hay's gig taking soundings ahead, the *Fury* towed the *Columbine* in until on rounding a point the wind came fair for the brig and she cast off and made sail. A little further and there lay the whole Bias Bay pirate fleet numbering 23 vessels, each of which mounted 18 or 19 guns. Here also were their repairing slips and arsenal.

A short, sharp engagement ended in the burning of all the pirate junks and their arsenal. Commander Hay standing alongside the quartermaster who was steering the *Fury* had a narrow escape. A round shot struck the deck in front of the wheel and passed between Hay and the quartermaster, doubled up the latter's cutlass and forced its point into the calf of his leg. The quartermaster,

Thomas Flintham, calmly bound up his leg with his neckerchief and went on steering.

On her return to Hongkong after this exploit, the *Columbine* received a public letter of thanks from the Admiral, Sir Francis Collier, who at once decided to send her off after the dreaded Shap'ng-tzai. Commander Hay sailed on October 8, 1849, with the steamers *Fury* and *Phlegethon* under his command.

On the 11th the three ships anchored off the North end of Hainan Island, where they found eight junks of the Chinese Navy under a very intelligent Admiral Wong, who had only recently been wounded in an action with Shap'ngtzai, when the latter passed through Hainan Straits about three weeks before.

With the *Fury* towing the *Columbine*, and followed by the *Phlegethon* and mandarin junks, Hay proceeded into the Gulf of Tong-king to the island of Guei-chow or Guie-chew, where the flotilla anchored for the night. Here Wong consulted the oracle at a famous shrine on the island and discovered that only recently Shap'ngtzai had also consulted the oracle, which told the pirate chief that if he survived the 20th of that month he would have two more years of success.

On the N.W. shore of the Gulf there is an archipelago of islands, 60 miles square. The pilong hunters went through it like hounds drawing a cover, and put up the lookout ship of the pirate. She was speedily captured and burnt by the *Phlegethon*, only two men being saved from her, one a pirate and the other a captive.

Wong and Caldwell interrogated them. They announced that Shap'ngtzai with 64 sail was anchored in fighting formation about 800 yards above the bar in the Tonquin River. He had moored 27 of his best ships in a curved line extending about a mile and a half with their broadsides bearing on the entrance of the river.

The difficulty was to get across the bar to attack him. But Hay was informed that the pirate junks drew 18 feet of water and were yet afloat at low springs so he boldly determined to attempt the bar. At 4 o'clock at the top of high water he led his little flotilla across in the *Phlegethon* without mishap, and as luck would have it, just as they came in range of the pirate a drain of ebb put a strain on their springs so that their broadsides were diverted slightly. The *Phlegethon* with Hay on board attacked the South end of the line, the *Columbine* took the centre, where Shap'ngtzai's flagship was easily distinguished by her bright red flag bordered with gold which sparkled brilliantly as the rays of the setting sun glinted upon it. The *Fury* took the North end of the line.

When the *Columbine* was a bare 600 yards away the whole pirate line of 240 cannons let fly. Thirty-nine round shot struck the *Columbine* and 41 the *Fury*, but the rest went wide, splashing into the water to starboard like a flock of wild fowl. *Columbine* anchored and proceeded to deal with the Admiral, which an hour and a half after the action had begun blew up, and in a blaze of fire burnt through her rope cables and began drifting down on the war-brig, which with all her boats busily engaged was obliged to trip her anchor. For some minutes the little pirate fighter was in dire peril, drifting without wind down on to the bar, where the ebb was roaring, and with the blazing junk close under her bows.

At the critical moment *Phlegethon* with *Columbine's* anxious commander on board forced her way between the burning junk and the bow of the brig, getting the paint all scorched off her iron side in the process. But the brig was saved and quickly towed into safety.

By this time the pirates had begun deserting their junks, many of which were drifting about on fire, having burnt through their cables like the flagship.

It was the anniversary of the battle of Navarino. As night fell, the whole sky was lit up by the flames from the 27 junks and the victors wondered if the Bay of Navarino had presented such a sight. The next morning, Sunday, was the anniversary of Trafalgar. At 6 a.m. before proceeding to the attack of the remaining pilongs, which had fled up the river, the pious Hay read prayers and returned thanks. That day 24 more junks were destroyed.

One large junk, moored in a narrow creek with her stern gun laid on the entrance, was approached by the *Phlegethon*, which would have got it at point blank range had that gun gone off, but on boarding the junk Commander Hay found the gunner dead with the lanyard in his hand, killed by a round of grape from the steamer just as he was about to fire.

On October 22, 7 more pirates were destroyed, and the Cochin-China authorities came down from Haiphong to thank the expedition, which then sailed for Hongkong.

Wong, who had proved a good pilot and loyal comrade, said goodbye at King-chou-foo, and the three ships anchored at Hongkong on November 1.

Both Hay and Willcox were made captains, besides being presented with services of plate by the mercantile communities. Bridges and Hancock were promoted commanders and Chambers and Close lieutenants. It was recognised as the smartest work ever done against those pests of the China Sea, the pilongs.

It was the "Saucy *Columbine's*" last commission. She sailed from Hongkong on November 29, left Singapore on December 26, touched at the Cape January 28, 1850, left Capetown February 4, anchored St. Helena February 16 and Ascension February 25, and was finally paid off at Sheerness, after being inspected and complimented on her good order by Admiral Sir Edward Brace.

In 1854 she was fitted as a movable coal depot and served as such at Sheerness until 1891. Then in 1892 she was sold to Messrs. H. Castle & Sons, the Thames ship-breakers.

I mention these details of her after life because it was commonly said in China that after her last commission she was sold out of the Service, bought by China merchants and ended her days as an opium clipper. No doubt she was mixed up with Pybus' little schooner of the same name.

"Gazelle" in the September Typhoon, 1849.

The following was the little Aberdeen clipper *Gazelle's* experience in the September typhoon which was supposed to have done for the *Coquette*:

September 12—4 p.m., blowing a stiff gale from N.W.

Thursday, September 13—At noon, strong gale at North. Bar. 29·50. 4 p m., hard gale; blew away sails from yards. 10 p.m., blowing a hurricane, lost fore topmast. Vessel buried in the sea; cut away mainmast but could not get at lee rigging from being under water; wreck of mainmast got under stern, carried away rudder and stove in part of stern frame. Shipping large quantities of water through the cabins: everything nearly washed off the deck including compass. Pumped and bailed ship, trying to keep water down, 6 ft. in hold. Barometer fallen to 27.

September 14—At 4 p.m., blowing its hardest. At 6, moderating; wind began to blow at N.W. veering to N.E. At commencement vessel was 10 or 12 miles to Southward of Pedra Branca, drifted in gale about 120 miles to Southward and Eastward of Great Hemma. Barometer remained at 27 for two hours.

The Dent barque *Ariel* was also in this typhoon on her way to Hongkong from Calcutta, but her experience was not as bad as the *Gazelle's* and she came through unscathed, arriving Hongkong on September 17. On the 18th the *Poppy* arrived, also from Calcutta. She recorded:

September 14—Lat. 17° 56′ N., Long. 114° 15′ E. Bar. 29·55. Wind W.N.W. blowing hard, hove to with head to South-westward. At 6 p.m., strong gale from Westward, ship's head Northerly. Bar. 29·50.

She also weathered it out unhurt, as did the *Ardaseer* which left Hongkong for Shanghai on September 15, and had a heavy typhoon from N.E. veering to S.E. The *Red Rover* just missed the typhoon, as she arrived at Hongkong from Calcutta on September 12, having made the round trip from Hongkong to Calcutta and back in 85 days. This including stay in port was smart work, though by no means her best record; for in 1850 she left Hongkong on March 10 and was back again on May 28, only 78 days on the Calcutta round.

CHAPTER VIII.

THE CHINA TRADE IN THE 'FIFTIES.

In dreams the fleets of childhood,
  Sail back a thousand years,
To coasts of strange old fancies,
  And strangely sweet old fears;
And, bound for fair Atlantis
From out the port of chance,
For poet, child and woman,
  Still sails the ship Romance.

—E. J. Brady.

Yankee Clippers enter the China Trade.

BY the beginning of the 'fifties the big shipping firms in China, such as Jardine, Matheson & Co., Dent & Co., Russell & Co., Turner & Co., Gibb, Livingstone & Co., Augustine Heard & Co., MacVicar & Co., Murrow & Co., Lindsay & Co. and the Parsees were finding business about equally divided between the opium and tea trades. The opium trade had always been purposely kept out of the limelight, but the tea trade was widely advertised and public interest which had never been aroused by the fine performances of the little opium clippers was very keen when racing started in the tea trade.

This was mainly due to the stimulus of international rivalry.

During the later 'forties a new type of Yankee clipper with hollow lines and spars that raked the skies appeared in Chinese waters; such world-renowned vessels as:

Houqua	(1844)	706 tons	Captain	Nat Palmer
Rainbow	(1845)	750 „	„	John Land
Samuel Russell ..	(1847)	940 „	„	Nat Palmer
Architect	(1847)	520 „	„	Captain Potter
Sea Witch	(1847)	907 „	„	Robert H. Waterman
Oriental	(1849)	1003 „	„	Nat Palmer

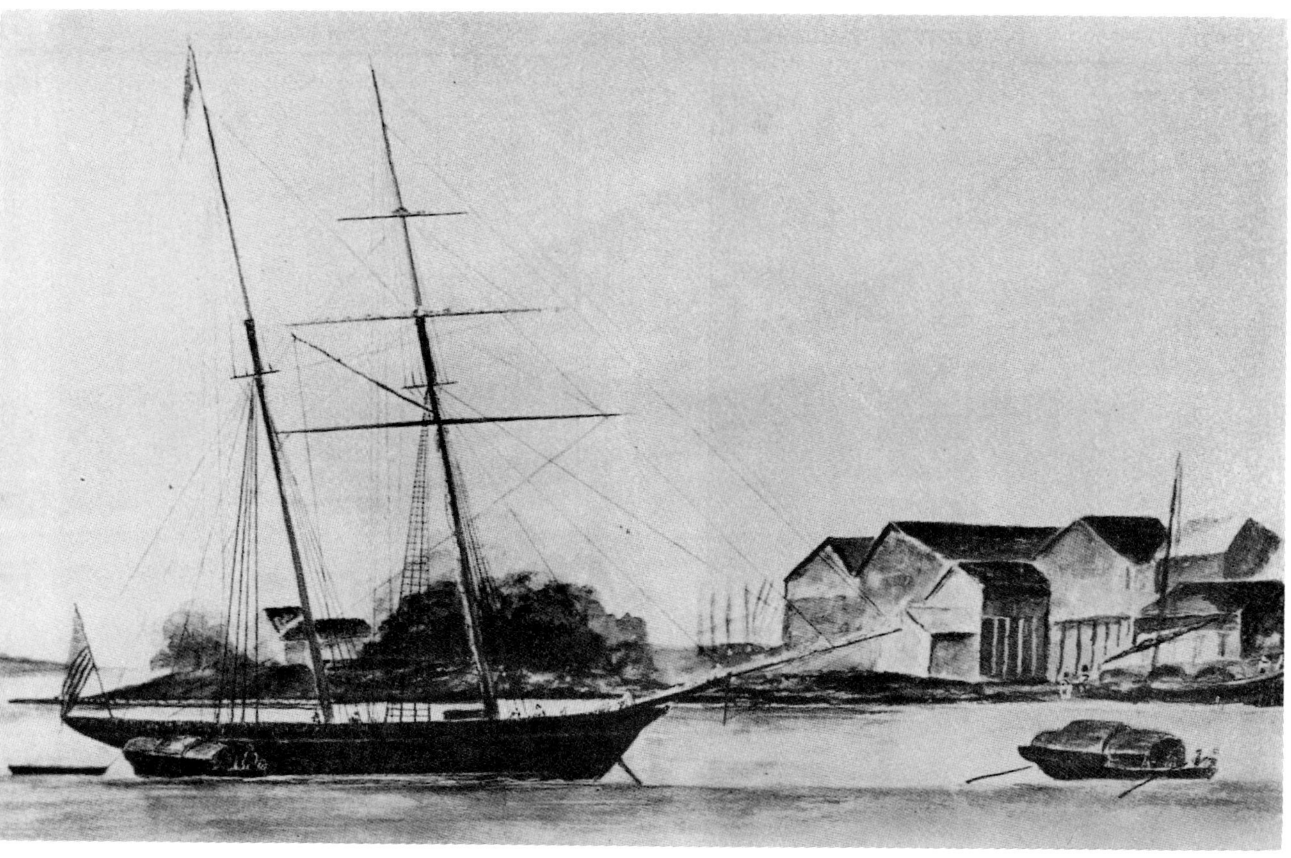

"BRENDA"

National Maritime Museum, Greenwich

[*See page* 334

JOHN DENT

Lent by R. W. Dent, Esq.

BRODIE A. CLARKE, the Last of the Old Hands

See page 338

Here is a significant letter written from Whampoa on September 1, 1850:

There is a fine show of shipping here now. In Blenheim Reach a magnificent old 1400-ton ship, called the *Charles Forbes*, painted like a two-decker, appears to claim superiority over all other craft, and fires a gun at daylight, sunset and 9 p.m.

Next to her in appearance, if not in size, come the *Sea Witch* and *Samuel Russell*, American clipper ships which have astonished the world by their performances. The latter had tailed on a mudbank below the Second Bar and was taken into dock at Messrs Cowper's yard to be examined.

Anything more beautiful than her form it is impossible to imagine, but so weakly constructed, being without diagonal fastenings of any kind, that although she was flying light when she took the ground her back was evidently broken.

The Famous "John o' Gaunt" and Captain John Robertson.

Up to 1850 the most famous vessel in the tea trade was Gladstone's *John o' Gaunt*, which was commanded for many years by Captain John Robertson. She was built as far back as 1835 at Liverpool and registered 449 tons. In the *Nautical Magazine* of 1843 is the following statement: "The *John o' Gaunt* under the command of Captain Robertson has been long famous for her quick and regular voyages to China and the East; so much so that Captain Robertson has been lately requested to furnish his charts of the China Seas for the inspection of the Admiralty."

She was considered so lucky that Canton merchants were fond of labelling tea chests "per *John o' Gaunt*" even when sent by other ships, with the idea that the glamour of her name would increase the price of the tea. Beyond the *John o' Gaunt*, there were no ships with any reputation for speed in the British tea trade until Hall of Aberdeen launched the *Reindeer*, 328 tons, and Hood of Aberdeen the *John Bunyan*, of 466 tons, in 1848. In 1843 a new ship, the *Emperor*, commanded by a naval officer, Lieut. Keane, raced out to Hongkong from Liverpool against the *John o' Gaunt* and there was some heavy betting on the two ships, but the old flyer found no difficulty in beating her new antagonist.

But in 1849 Captain Robertson went to Hall of Aberdeen with an order for a new clipper, that was to be the fastest thing possible for her size. This was the *Stornoway*, which went into the tea trade under Jardine Matheson's flag, and was generally considered the first of the genuine Aberdeen tea clippers. The old *John o' Gaunt* gravitated into the India trade in her old age, but she was still going strong at the end of the 'sixties.

Opium Clippers in the First Tea Race.

When it was announced in 1850 that the *Oriental* was ready to load new teas for the London market, shippers at once offered her £6 per ton freight, about £2 above the rate being given to British ships.

Indeed there were no vessels on the berth that could be compared to her except her own countrymen. This lack of British clippers tempted vessels to enter the lists, which had recently come out to China in order to enter the opium trade, for which they were specially built.

The first of these was the barque *Sea Witch*, commanded by Captain Reynell of *Waterwitch* fame, a clipper of 401 tons, built in London in 1848. This smart little barque ran out from Gravesend to Shanghai in 95 days, a passage which was worthy of the later cracks, *Thermopylae*, *Sir Lancelot* or *Cutty Sark*. Her dimensions were 121.5 ft. by 26.7 ft. by 16 ft. This ship, I believe, has sometimes been confused with the American *Sea Witch*.

The second opium clipper to load tea was the *Astarte*, a beautiful brig of 328 tons, built by White of Cowes in 1846. She loaded at Whampoa at the same time as the *Oriental* and sailed close behind her, being heavily backed to beat the American by numbers of patriotic Britishers.

The *Oriental*, with a freight amounting to nearly three-quarters of her original cost, sailed from the Canton River on August 28, beat down to Anjer against the monsoon in 21 days and hauled into the West India Docks 97 days out. This was too much for the little opium clippers, as well as for the *Reindeer* and *Countess of Seafield*, which were both under 110 days. *John Bunyan* sailing in the favourable monsoon had already arrived home in the very good time of 99 days from Shanghai.

This, the first of the international tea races, over-shadowed every other event in China in 1850. I do not think either the *Sea Witch* or the *Astarte* returned to the opium trade; at the end of the 'sixties Taylor & Co. sold the *Sea Witch* to Captain R. McCully, who took her into the South American trade. The *Astarte*, after being captained and owned by Captain Tom Crossley through the 'sixties, went to F. & A. Swanzy at the beginning of the 'seventies and became a West African palm-oiler.

It was the success of the *Oriental* that brought Alexander Hall further orders for clipper ships, such as the little *Chrysolite* for Taylor & Potter, which under Captain Anthony Enright was to be a keen rival of John Robertson in the *Stornoway*.

But 1850 was the only year in which such a small vessel as the *Astarte* raced home with tea.

The Destruction of the "Ardaseer."

On the morning of April 4, 1851, the *Ardaseer* left Singapore for Calcutta, having the usual China cargo on board including an amount of specie.

At 8 p.m., when Captain Henry Lovett and his chief officer Rogers were on the fo'c'sle-head taking the bearings of Pulo Bouton which lay 10 miles to the N.W., the gunner and his mate rushed up out of the after hatch and reported that the gunroom was full of smoke. No fire could be seen but a dense smoke was coming from the after part of the barque.

Whilst the captain and mate superintended the handing up on deck of the copper powder magazines, the second mate, Chapman, with the rest of the hands was passing water below. As the smoke continued as thick as ever, the carpenter was ordered to cut holes in the deck, through which hoses were passed and water poured down as fast as it could be hoisted up by the primitive means of buckets on the end of a line.

After an hour's frenzied water throwing without any lessening of the smoke, the captain ordered all apertures and hatches to be battened down fore and aft and covered with wet sails. The ship was then headed towards Penang, the long-boat and quarter-boats got ready and some of the treasure got on deck.

Before the cabins could be cleared, the after hatch burst open and volumes of smoke poured out, at the same time the whole after part of the vessel below was filled with smoke and Captain

Lovett was only able to save one of his three chronometers. Within two hours of the smoke being reported the *Ardaseer* was in flames fore and aft and her crew had to take to the boats so quickly that they were only able to provision them with a small keg of water and a few pounds of biscuits, none of the personal effects of the captain, passengers, officers or crew being saved.

Each of the boats had a portion of the treasure, the captain with most of the crew being in the long-boat, the mate in the gig and the second mate and passengers in the cutter. For a while they lay off watching the burning ship which was soon in one blaze to her mastheads, then the captain set a course for Penang. After sailing and pulling until noon the next day, when they were within 50 miles of Penang, and suffering very much from the heat of the sun and want of water, the boats, which had kept together, sighted a sail.

Unfortunately it had fallen a flat calm, and it took three hours of hard pulling before they reached the Bremen ship *Leibnitz* (Captain Wieling), which landed them at Penang on the afternoon of the 12th.

This was evidently a case of spontaneous combustion, the inflammable part of the cargo being stowed aft, where the fire broke out.

The King of Great Peace.

In the year 1851 an unbalanced visionary of a Chinese school teacher, named Hung-Sew-Tsenen, a native of Kwang-Se, who had passed his Sew-tsai examination, that of the lowest degree of literary merit, made his way to Canton and attended a school kept by a Methodist missionary called Roberts.

After a while he returned home and proceeded to evangelise, first his own family and then his neighbours, who were mostly poor peasants and farmers. He was either subject to epileptic fits or was able to fall into trances at will, and this had a great effect on the ignorant Chinese, who soon began to deify him and he took on the name of Tai-Ping-Wang, "King of the Great Peace." Though his Christian teaching was founded on the Ten Commandments and the Lord's Prayer, copies of which were hung up in a prominent position in the houses of his converts, who called themselves Taipings, this school teacher with his languid air and half-closed eyes had not sufficient strength of character to carry through the true Christianising of China, in a Christian spirit. He began as a sincere enthusiast for a noble cause, but there is no doubt that his astonishing success unhinged his brain and turned him into a cruel fanatical despot.

The Battle of Whampoa Reach.

In a very short time Hung-Sew-Tsenen and his Taiping followers began to proselytise by force of arms, and this at once attracted to them all the ruffians and criminals of Kwang-Se and Kwang-Tung. In 1852 these so-called Chinese Christians began plundering and burning the towns and villages on the islands and delta of the Pearl River to the Southward of Whampoa, and the whole valley between the North Wall of Canton and the white Cloud Mountain, some 2 or 3 miles in breadth, became filled with Taiping rebels, who skirmished daily with the "Yung" soldiery manning Gough's, the Bluejacket and other North Wall forts.

The Southern approach to Canton by the Macao Passage had to be protected from the "Red Flags," as the Taipings were also called, from their revolutionary colours, by three tiers of heavy men-of-war junks moored right across the river just below the Tee-To-Tum Fort.* A few miles further down the river was crowded with sampans, lorchas and trading junks, which had been captured by the Taipings. Day and night a desultory firing went on between the Taipings and the mandarin junks, but the former made no attempt to interfere with the Fan Kwae shipping which sailed up to Whampoa through flights of arrows and flying slugs from fizzing matchlocks with complete indifference.

The young bloods from the Factories even made a practice of sailing down from Canton to take tea with the Canton admiral and watch the daily battle.

The schooner yacht *Atalanta*, belonging to Paul S. Forbes, one day got into rather closer quarters to the fighting than was altogether pleasant. On entering the passage between French and Dane's

* So called by the British and Americans of Canton owing to its circular shape and tall central tower.

Islands, with Hunter and another American on board, she encountered a fleet of about 70 double-banked fast-boats, flying the red flag and crowded with Taipings, all wearing long hair and red sashes. These had come from Tsang-Poo, which was then in the hands of the rebels, and were after a big coast junk, which was just working into Junk River on its way to Canton.

As the channel was too crowded with rebel boats to give the *Atalanta* a passage, she came about and sailed in to Whampoa Reach in the midst of the Red Flags. Here stray bullets and even round shot had already begun to fly, and the little schooner found herself in considerable danger. In this dilemma she ran alongside the Peruvian ship *Carmen*, which had just arrived from Callao with a cargo of guano.

This vessel was commanded by an Italian shipmaster, who was very well known and very popular with all the English, Scotch and Americans on the China Coast. His name was Garibaldi! Hunter and his friend climbed to the mizen crosstrees of the *Carmen* and watched the fighting with the future liberator of Italy. They saw the junk being boarded and her hapless crew and passengers being speared by the Red Sashes. Shrieks came to them mingled with the boom of cannon, the crack of muskets and the fierce yelling of the Taipings. Stray shot hummed by, more than once uncomfortably close, even to passing between the *Carmen's* main and mizen masts.

Garibaldi watched this savage battle with a light in his eye and a resolute pursing of his bearded lips, completely indifferent to the sing of the bullet and the roar of the round shot.

Horrid sights were witnessed by the spectators. On the shore abreast of the guano ship a fat Chinese merchant, begging for his life on his knees, began to squeal like a pig as the ruthless spears of the Taiping braves were plunged into his corpulent body. Hundreds of bumboats and washgallees, of tanka boats and sampans, which were attending on the shipping, fled screeching from the Red Flags.

Many a vessel at anchor was struck, and non-combatants unexpectedly wounded; even the U.S. frigate *Macedonian* received a couple of stray rounds in her hammock nettings.

Towards sunset the unfortunate junk was run on the mud, her cargo transferred to the boats of the Red Flags, and the affray brought to an end by the marauders rowing away to their headquarters, the town of Tsang-Poo on the island of Tsang-Poo.

Admiral Drinker and his Fleet.

At Tsang-Poo the leader of this Southern rebellion which menaced Canton had some 8000 or 10,000 followers collected, who by constant plundering expeditions had amassed a great store of booty including, so it was said, some 20,000 chests of tea.

The British Consul and Hunter of Russell & Co. paid this rebel chief a visit in Warren Delano's six-oared gig. Ho-a-luh, the chief and his officers received their visitors with tea, pipes and civility. He was a fine-looking man, dressed in the heavy silk garments of the old Chinese regime, his long hair gathered in a bun on the top of his head and secured with a gold pin. His followers wore the red sash and were armed with three-pronged spears, swords, shields, and muskets or matchlocks. They all pretended great friendship with foreigners, and Ho-a-luh declared that his chief aim was to overthrow the Manchus and restore the last Chinese dynasty. Yet he was undoubtedly an offshoot of the Taiping Wang, and what with his plundering of the whole countryside and his steady increase in power and followers, the authorities at Canton were at last obliged to seek the aid of the Fan Kwae against him.

An extraordinary force for attacking Tsang-Poo was gathered together under an American adventurer, named Drinker, who received an admiral's commission in the Chinese Navy. This force consisted of run-away bluejackets, American and British shellbacks, Lascars and Manila men from the opium and country craft, Macao lorcha men, Portuguese sea-cunnies, and the dregs of the seafaring population of Hongkong.

The flagship was a lorcha, bought at Macao, whose name was changed from *Hesus-Maria* to *Hornet*; a sloop of 80 tons, named the *Vigilant* was the second in command. Captain Creasy, of the *Pathfinder*, left his ship at Hongkong, and threw his traps into the sloop's cabin, being at once appointed second to Drinker. The remaining ships of the fleet were two half-decked boats of about 20 tons apiece well named the *Rough and Ready* and the *Rough and Tough*.

W. C. Hunter and the Hong merchant Kingqua were the brains of this wild gang of adventurers. Creasy, as soon as he had settled down, summoned the *Rough and Ready* and the *Rough and Tough* alongside and proceeded to make a quarterdeck speech.

"You know what you're shipped for?" He began.

"No, sir," called out an old shellback, "but that don't make no difference."

"All right! When we run alongside the town—"

"Run alongside a town," grunted the fire-eaters. That sounded like good plunder, and broad grins of delight began to show through their bushy whiskers.

"You will bundle ashore, artillery to the front," went on Creasy.

"Aye, aye, sir."

"Noise is what we want. Small arms men blaze away right and left. Cheer hearty and all the time. Don't stop to loot (groans), go right ahead. Don't shoot the mandarin sodgers if you can help it—they're our allies—"

"Three cheers for our allies."

"They wear red coats—they're there to help us. Don't hurt the people—they're harmless. Bosun pipe down! Steward, serve out one glass rum to all hands!"

The steward, Sam Cock by name, served out one glass of rum per man and then the little squadron weighed and ran up the reach.

As the *Vigilant* led the *Rough and Ready* and the *Rough and Tough* past each ship at anchor in the roads, cheers were exchanged. All seemed confident that Drinker and his gallant band would speedily capture the rebel city of Tsang-Poo.

Even three river steamers were holding themselves in readiness to transport the looted tea from Tsang-Poo to Canton. These were the *River Bird* (Captain De Vol), the *Canton* (Captain Soames) and the *Spark* (Captain Castilla). Also a 6-pounder gun was bought, for which a carriage was made by Quishing in Carpenters' Square and hidden in Number 1 Mingqua's Hong. Finally zero hour was fixed for midnight. But, alas, at 11 a.m., just when the sun was over the foreyard and Admiral "Bibus," as he was nicknamed, and Vice-Admiral Croessus and their merry men were splicing the main brace, "one piecee chit" was handed Hunter by the compradore of the Sug Hong. This proved to be from the Hon. Robert M. MacLean, the new United States Minister to China, who sternly ordered the disbanding of the whole expeditionary force, with the threat that its leaders might otherwise be incarcerated aboard the U.S. store ship *Supply*, which was anchored off Sha-Ming.

Drinker immediately set off for Whampoa by way of Lob-Lob Creek; but on the way he was set upon by river bandits who robbed him of everything but an old pair of breeches, in which the unfortunate admiral arrived aboard Hunt & Co.'s *Chop*, a floating ship chandlery at Whampoa. Here he lodged a complaint with Cook, Hunt & Co.'s partner, and the U.S. Marshal for unruly Yankee sailors at the anchorage.

The mandarins subsequently managed to wipe up the rebels at Tsang-Poo without the assistance of any European mercenaries. These, however, were to be required a few years later when the Manchus called in the aid, first of all, of the American, Fred Townsend Ward, and after his efforts had failed, of that clever engineer officer, who by his success gained the name of Chinese "Gordon."

The Ryrie Letters.

There is nothing to equal old letters for being able to bring back the past, and the following letters from the Ryrie brothers to their mother and sisters bring the days of the opium clippers very much closer to the reader than any amount of description.

The eldest of the three Ryries was John Mackenzie, who, before commanding the tea clippers *Cairngorm* and *Flying Spur*, had Messrs. C. W. & F. Shand's Liverpool ship *Marian*.

Alexander Ryrie, the second son, after serving his time in Gladstone's ships, became an officer in the opium schooner *Sidney* before being appointed to the *Mazeppa*.

Phineas Ryrie, the youngest, went into the employ of Turner & Co., merchants of Hongkong and owners of the tea clipper *Chaa-tze*.

They were the sons of Lieutenant William Ryrie, of the

Royal Marines, a veteran of the Napoleonic wars, who died about 1828.

Here is the first letter, dated Hongkong December, 20, 1850:

LETTER No. 1.

My Dear Mother,—I have been so very busy since I joined the *Mazeppa* that you must excuse my long silence, for we have not been more than two days in harbour till this trip and when they do give us a day or two, we don't know the moment we may be ordered away.

Jardine, Matheson & Co.'s employ is far before any other in China, but I am afraid I shall have to wait some time before I am promoted to captain. However, I don't mind that when I know that they always promote their own servants to that rank in preference to giving it to strangers.

My captain (Dowman) and I agree very well as yet; he is rather hard to please, but I think we will continue to do so.

Phiney (Phineas Ryrie) had a letter from John (John Mackenzie Ryrie) yesterday; he was about to leave Bombay for Cochin and Ceylon. I intend writing him to-day as this is the first slack one I have had for a long time; I am sorry he is not coming here as I missed seeing him last time.

I suppose Robertson's new ship the *Stornoway* is not far from Bombay by this time.

(The Ryries, by the way, were born at Stornoway, their widowed mother sailing from Stornoway to Liverpool in a small schooner in order to send her three sons out into the world. She was a Mackenzie and came of stalwart stock.)

I left a few dollars with Phiney to send you by last mail, the exchange would be about £12. It was all I could spare as the six weeks of idleness which I spent after leaving the *Sidney* reduced my funds considerably. You know, my dear Mama, that if I had it, you and my dear sisters should share it. I have been misfortune's child ever since I have been afloat and wonder when my luck will change—I don't care how soon.

Phiney is quite well. I see him every day while here. It is a great comfort to me as I was beginning to feel tired of this country.

McDonald of the *Sir H. Hardinge* sailed yesterday for Singapore and Bombay. There is nothing for British shipping to do here now and I am glad on that account that John has not come on.

Cameron of the *Hugh Walker* is here also; he called to see me the other day.

George McAlister is still in his old situation. He is a very nice lad and is of very great service to all the officers in Jardine Matheson's employ.

Now I will tell you what I want and I know you will take a pleasure in getting them for me—that is a dozen pair of good worsted socks and two or three pairs of gloves worsted) for next winter, as I bought some the other day, paid half a dollar a pair for them, and some of the socks were so rotten the first time I put them on they tore across the heel. Send them by some sailing vessel in a month or two so that they will be out here by August.

I have no news to give you but I suppose Phiney will be writing and he is more accustomed to scribbling than I am, so that you will get it all from him. I must now conclude with love to Maggie and Lex (his sisters). Believe me, my dear Mother, to be

Your affectionate son,

A. Ryrie.

P.S.—A merry Christmas and a Happy New Year to you all.

Letter No. 2.

Whampoa, *April* 22, 1851.

My Dear Mother,—I just write you a few lines in haste as the mail leaves here in an hour or two, to let you know of my arrival a day or two ago. I saw Phin at Hongkong. He is well and looking well also. I also saw a glimpse of Alick. The *Mazeppa* was going down the river as I was coming up. He is also well. He is now at Hongkong and no doubt both will be writing to you by this mail. I do not know what I am going to do as yet, there is nothing doing here except California business. I shall write you a longer letter by next mail. Give my love to the girls and believe me, my dear Mother,

Your affec. son,

John Ryrie.

Letter No. 3.

Hongkong, *July* 12, 1852.

My Dear Maggie,—I received your letter from London per last mail and was happy to see by it that John was at home all right. I saw Phiney a few days ago. We had a trip to Whampoa.

I also saw Captain Robertson; poor fellow, he has been very ill and was very much pulled down. He sailed the day before yesterday for England.

(*Stornoway* left Whampoa July 9 and reached the Downs on October 25, 107 days out, after a great race with the *Chrysolite*.)

He told me that when he went to Liverpool last year he only remained there two hours, which was the reason he did not call upon you, but next time he may have more time.

I have been acting captain of the *Mazeppa* for two trips, but cannot say whether I'll retain it or not. There are two senior to me in the employ so that I can't expect it; however it will not be many months I hope before my turn comes on. I may continue in command as I am starting to-night on my third voyage and they have had plenty of time to send for either of those who are senior to me, but I am nowise sanguine about it and am prepared for the worst.

How did Mama enjoy her trip to London? I suppose John has sailed again by this time. I hope if he is coming out here, he won't forget to bring me a pea-coat as the winter is coming on and I have not got one yet.

Lex wrote Phiney last mail and it came to me by mistake so I opened and read it. I see she has forgotten all about me; not a scratch have I had from her for many months. I must now conclude with love to you all and remain yours very affectionately,

A. Ryrie.

LETTER No. 4.

Hongkong, *February* 11, 1853.

My Dear Mother.—I received a letter by last mail from Maggie and one the mail before from Lex, for which give them my thanks and I'll answer them as soon as I can.

I suppose you have heard that John has arrived at Sydney all right and we expect him here shortly.

Another piece of good news for you; I have been confirmed in the command of the *Mazeppa* by way of a New Year's gift from Mr. Jardine.

I have not heard from Phiney for some time. They seldom send us to Whampoa now, so that I have not seen him for nearly six months.

I enclose you a bill for £30; give the girls £5 each to buy their spring dresses with my love and please pay for the last flannel. I'll send money to pay for the coat when I receive it. I must now conclude as I have only half an hour to catch the mail but will send a long letter next mail.

I remain,

Your affectionate son,

A. RYRIE.

LETTER No. 5.

Hongkong, 27th *October*, 1853.

Dear Mamma and Girls,—I have just a moment left to acknowledge receipt of Maggie's letter of the 19th August, by which I was glad to see that John had at last arrived.

I enclose the 2nd of exchange of the Oriental Bank bill for £30, first of which I sent last mail.

I see by the papers that Shanks have built a new clipper barque intended for the Eastern trade. I hope to goodness they will give the command of her to John.

I see (through the telescope) that the *Mazeppa* is in. She has been away nearly a month up at Foo-chow-foo. I have not been able to go off and see Alick—a tremendous mail this—I went to bed at half-past three this morning and was at my desk again at about six o'clock.

Love to all. Your affectionate son and brother,

PHINEAS RYRIE.

I am very much in want of shoes and my flannels have gone to rags. You appear to have forgotten flannel for me this year. I require a new set of singlets every October.

LETTER No. 6.

Hongkong, 22nd *April*, 1854.

Dear Mama and Girls,—I received Maggie's letter of the 19th February on the 13th of this month.

I quite agree with what you say about the absurdity of John remaining in the *Marian* these times—but he is so wedded to old world notions that there is no driving them out of his head. I only wish he would come on here; I think Alick and myself together would succeed in convincing him.

Alick is to be removed to a vessel, called the *Audax*, and will run between this and Shanghai. I shall in future only see him once a month in consequence. He is very averse to the change himself, as it is probable that he will not make near so much money as between this and Amoy, but Mr. Jardine thinks it is promotion for him and he is afraid of offending him by refusing.

You will be glad to hear that he is a prime favourite with Mr. Jardine—indeed, so much so that he (Mr. Jardine) speaks publicly of the high esteem in which he holds Alick—this from a man who is proverbially reserved in his communications is something to be proud of. I hope Alick won't hear of it though, it may make him vain.

There is really no news here at present except what you will find in a newspaper which I send *via* Marseilles.

Your affectionate son and brother,

PHINEAS RYRIE.

These six letters are just a selection out of a large packet.

The Jardine alluded to was probably Joseph Jardine. Poor Alick Ryrie would have done well to have refused promotion into the *Audax*, for she was lost with all hands, when bound to Hongkong from Shanghai in 1855.

The staid old-fashioned elder brother, John Ryrie, evidently consented under pressure to give up the command of the old *Marian*. When old Captain Robertson retired from the sea and took up shipowning and broking, Jardine, Matheson & Co. offered John Ryrie the command of the *Cairngorm*, their big tea clipper.

From her John Ryrie went to their new clipper, *Flying Spur*, in 1860. He commanded this beautiful little vessel until he retired from the sea; he owned a good many sixty-fourths in her and made money with her. It is interesting to see how old Eastern hands were linked together; for instance, John Ryrie married the daughter of Captain Donald MacDonald of the *Sylph*.

Russell's Schooners, "Minna" and "Brenda."

In 1851 George Raynes built two very beautiful little sister ships at Portsmouth, New Hampshire. These were the 300-ton topsail schooners, *Minna* and *Brenda*, belonging to Russell & Co.

For some years these two American clipper schooners were well known on the China coast though they were not kept entirely to the opium trade. Besides plying across the Pacific to the Golden Gate and Callao, they also took a hand in the opening of up Japan, and as early as the summer of 1853 we find *Brenda* under Captain Stone taking coals from Hongkong to Nagasaki. On her previous voyage she had sailed from San Francisco on February 26, 1853, and arrived at Hongkong on April 16, 49 days out. Leaving Hongkong on June 16 for Japan, she anchored at Shanghai 20 days later, in ballast from Loochoo.

Minna, commanded by Captain Pulsipher, left Whampoa for Callao on April 27, 1853, and was back at Hongkong by way of San Francisco on January 26, 1854. She then made a trip to Melbourne and back, before going on the 'Frisco run again until March, 1856, when she went coasting. She was very nearly lost in the famous typhoon of September 21, 1858, when she was driven up on the South bank of the Shanghai River.

Murder aboard the "Arratoon Apcar."

One of the best known shipping firms in Calcutta was that of Arratoon and Gregory Apcar. They did not confine themselves entirely to the opium traffic but traded all over the East. Before they went into steam one of their fastest ships was the brig *Arratoon Apcar*. She was a very regular ship on the Calcutta-Singapore-Hongkong run.

On August 6, 1853, she left Hongkong for Calcutta; besides Bengalees, her crew consisted of 8 Chinese and 2 Chinese carpenters. Her master was Captain Lovett, chief mate J. H. Skirving and second mate a man named Woodburn. Besides these white officers she had Dr. Thompson (late of the P. & O. *Lady Mary Wood*) and Mr. Smith (late of the clipper *Red Rover*) as passengers.

At midnight the pilot left and the second mate relieved the chief mate on watch.

Soon after the change of the watch the Chinese members of the crew, assisted by two Chinese passengers, came aft, armed with long knives. Springing upon the second mate, they speedily stabbed him to death and threw the body overboard. A Portuguese sea-cunny named Augustin was at the wheel; he took refuge in the rigging along with the Lascars of the watch. But paying little attention to them, the murdering Chinamen descended the companion-way into the cabin, where the captain, mate, Dr. Thompson

Mr. Smith and steward, an English boy named Charlie, were sleeping. What happened in that cabin will never be known, for the only survivor was the captain's bull-dog, which was found severely cut across the nose and hip, but there was evidence to prove that the dog had put up a good fight, and fastened its teeth deeply into the calves of the murderers' legs. Of the other occupants of the cabin only the captain remained. Smith, the Lascars declared, had jumped overboard unhurt and when last seen was swimming strongly for Green Island. The others, it was feared, were thrown overboard, badly wounded, for the cabin was like a shambles with blood everywhere. Two Malays on deck also put up a good fight but were killed and thrown overboard.

The murderers then fired the hold, cut the topsail halliards, spiked the guns and finally went off in the two quarter-boats.

The Lascars then aroused the English gunner of the brig, who was asleep forward. On hurrying aft, he came upon Captain Lovett crawling along the deck.

"Give me a drink of water," gasped the captain. The gunner brought it to him, but, after taking a gulp the captain drew a long breath and fell over dead. He had been stabbed in the abdomen.

The gunner at once put the brig about and headed back to Hongkong. He could not explain the behaviour of the Chinese, there was very little treasure on board and the eight seamen had been two voyages in the brig. They had taken nothing of value with them yet they had evidently made an attempt to blow the brig sky high.

The Schooner "Neva" robbed on the High Seas.

A very similar case took place four years later—on October 30, 1857. The little schooner, *Neva*, belonging to Gibb, Livingstone & Co. sailed from Hongkong to the Eastward with about 30,000 dollars in specie aboard and a number of Chinese passengers. At midnight, when about 40 miles up the coast, the passengers, led by the Chinese carpenter, set upon Captain Sinden and two of the watch, all of whom were speedily killed and thrown overboard. The mate, hearing the noise overhead, dashed up the companion-way and bravely attacked the murderers with an unloaded musket:

but, receiving a violent blow on the back of the head, he only managed to save his life by clambering somehow up the main rigging. He was the only European on board besides the captain, the crew being Manila men; two of these were severely wounded, one having his cheek cut through and the other one of his eyes divided in two. The rest of the watch were below. They were secured below by a cable being placed over the fo'c'sle hatch.

The schooner was then ransacked, the mail examined and 20,000 dollars taken. Before leaving in the boat, the pirates unshipped the tiller and threw it overboard. As soon as the wretches had quitted the vessel, the mate came down from aloft, released the crew and brought the *Neva* back to Hongkong.

The surprising thing about all these Hongkong piracies was the way in which merchants and shippers trusted specie in small ill-armed vessels, in which the only white men were the officers.

The *Neva* had an adventurous career. When her opium carrying days were finished, she became a copra schooner under the ownership of the notorious Bully Hayes, the South Sea pirate, who bought her from a trader on Strong's Island in October, 1871.

The Fate of the "Falcon."

The end of Jardine Matheson's flagship, the *Falcon*, has always been shrouded in mystery. All sorts of rumours were current about her disappearance in China; some declared that they knew it for a fact that she had been run away with by mutineers or scuttled by pirates; others swore that she had been sighted dismasted and waterlogged in the pyramid seas of a typhoon; others again said she had been sold and changed her name. I even have the photograph of a captain who is supposed to have commanded her in the late 'sixties, but *Falcon* is a common name for ships and every master was fond of calling his command a clipper. At any rate she seems to have disappeared about the middle of the 'fifties.

I have in my possession a scarce little book of sea yarns, written by a country captain and published in the 'sixties. One of these yarns may quite possibly be the true story of the *Falcon's* end, though the ship is disguised under the name of *Shadow*, but the

"WILD DAYRELL"

[*See page* 340

H.M.S. "RALEIGH"

National Maritime Museum, Greenwich

[*See page* 342

following description only fits the *Falcon* out of the whole opium fleet:

> The *Shadow* was a smart little full-rigged ship of 400 tons burden—in fact, one of the smartest in the service. She carried a strong European crew with a sufficient complement of Chinese sailors to man one boat besides other Celestials as servants.
>
> The rakish little *Shadow* was also fully equipped with an armament of twelve 18-pounders (six on either broadside) and a long 24 was a pivot gun amidships. Many a time the heavy tie-mungs or Chinese war junks found that we were quite able to fight our way, even when a dozen of them tried to effect our capture.
>
> About the end of November our vessel left Hongkong half-loaded with a valuable cargo of opium, and orders were to dispose of it at several small towns along the coast between the former town and Swatow. We had been very successful at the first place to which we had been directed and had landed more than a hundred chests of opium, for which our captain had received hard cash, with a profit more than trebling the original outlay.
>
> Then, getting under way with a strong fair wind, we sailed along the coast in search of the next port. The breeze continually increased and towards 9 p.m. we were dashing along at about 3 miles from the land when the lookout on the fo'c'sle-head shouted: "Breakers ahead! Hard a-port!"
>
> The next moment before a rope could be touched or a spoke of the wheel shifted, our doomed vessel crashed with terrific force on a sunken rock, the high ripple of a rising sea on which had warned the lookout. Being built for speed, to attain which it was necessary to sarcifice strength, the *Shadow* was stove bodily at once. We had been dashing along before the gale at fully 11 knots an hour, when we went upon some unknown rock off Breaker Point—a projecting headland some 60 miles South of Swatow.

There are rocks and shoals extending out for two miles round Breaker Point and sailing directions warn one to keep well out from the shore at night or in thick weather. The narrator was the third mate of the ship; he goes on:

> Most of the crew were drowned in their hammocks, for even as the mast came crashing over the side, the ship, having, I believe, run up the side of a sloping rock, heeled right over and with her hold already full of water slipped off and sank.
>
> I had been enjoying a cheroot under the lee of the weather bulwarks amidships. When the ship struck I was hurled right across the deck, striking with great violence against the carriage of the long-tom. When I recovered myself, she was sinking and, amid falling spars, shouting men, dashing waves and the terrible grind-grind, crash-crash of the poor old vessel's hull upon the rocks, I seized one of the lifebuoys hanging to the poop rail and sprang overboard. I jumped to leeward, knowing well that if I took the other side, I should either be drifted under the hull or get into the chow-chow water rushing and eddying around the rocks.

The Mate of an Opium Clipper becomes a Taiping General.

The third mate of the ill-fated clipper then describes how he is saved and dragged ashore through the surf by his Madras bearer, Ali. The only other member of the crew to reach the land alive was Dick Savage, the second officer. The three survivors found themselves in the midst of a Taiping army which was about to fight a battle with the Imperialists for the possession of Swatow.

All three sailors took an active part on the side of the Taipings in the battle, which was a very desperate affair, but ended in a victory for the Taipings, who were most grateful to the mates of the wrecked ship for the efficient way in which they had handled the Chinese artillery, which had been put in their charge. After the battle the third mate, who pays a glowing tribute to the way in which he was treated by the Taipings, took his leave of the rebels and boarded a British ship lying at anchor off Double Island. Dick Savage, however, elected to stay on with the Taipings and became one of their most trusted generals. "Six years later," wrote Lindley, "I found Dick Savage was well known as a favourite general of the celebrated Chung-Wong-Le, the commander-in-chief of the Taiping armies."

In the published life of General Fred Townsend Ward I find this sentence: "In September, 1861, a brilliant English officer, named Savage, successfully defended Tsing-Poo with 2000 Taipings against General Ward and his levies."

A history of China has this to say about the ex-mate: "The attack on Sunkiang by Ward's force was repulsed by Taipings directed by an Englishman, named Savage. Chung Wang drove Ward from attacking Tsing-Poo and captured the positions of the Imperial commander, Li Aidong, but failed in an attempt to recover Sunkiang, in which his English colleague, Savage, was so seriously wounded that he died some weeks later at Nankin."

Dent's Schooners.

By the beginning of the 'fifties the brig rig in China was fast being supplanted by that of the topsail schooner, which had always been the favourite rig of the fruiter and other craft built for speed on the coasts of Great Britain.

During the 'fifties a great many very beautiful, fine-lined, heavily rigged topsail schooners came out from England and took their places in the opium coasting trade.

Amongst these were the *Nina*, *Eamont*, *Undine*, *Violet*, *Vindex*, *Wild Dayrell*, *Waterwitch*, *Chin-Chin*, *Salamander* and *Spray*.

The greater number of the above were specially built by J. & R. White of Cowes, the great gun-brig, and yacht builders, for Dent & Co.

These Cowes-built opium clippers cost more per ton than the finest yacht, being built of the very best materials with a cabinet-maker's finish to even the bunk boards in the fo'c'sle; all their woodwork was carefully seasoned and selected teak or mahogany and their metal work chased copper or brass.

As regards their sail plans a skysail yard was often crossed on the foremast in light weather and a full suit of stunsails, a ringtail, water sails and other flying kites were always carried.

The mainboom of the *Eamont*, which was launched in 1854 and registered about 200 tons, was 110 ft. long, so that her mainsail took some handling when it came on to blow.

They were all fitted with racks of muskets and boarding pikes, stands of small arms, specially built magazines and broadside guns of brass, four 18-pounders aside, in addition to which a long brass 18-pounder pivot gun stood on the fo'c'sle-head. Amidships there was the usual long-tom also on a pivot—Dent & Co. favoured the Armstrong 68-pounder.

With so much weight on deck and aloft these fine-lined schooners required close on 200 tons of iron kentledge stowed in their limbers as stationary ballast.

A Dent or Jardine Matheson schooner of under 200 tons always carried a captain and three mates; and the rates of pay were about double those paid in first-class merchantmen of six times their tonnage, whilst European A.B.'s received as much as 45 dollars a month. There were usually 18 to 20 men before the mast besides the usual sea-cunnies or quartermasters, the boatswain and 2 mates, gunner and mate, carpenter, cooks, compradore, 2 schroffs and officers' Chinese servants. Luckily the cargo—either opium or treasure—never took up much room in the hold. With so many hands these opium coasters of the 'fifties vied with the smartest gun-brigs and corvettes in their spick and span appearance and quickness of sail drill. When lying at anchor in Hongkong Harbour or the Shanghai River they fairly shone as the rays of the sun sparkled on their brass guns and glinted off the bright metal of their rails and deck fittings. It was the day of shining black topsides, burnished copper, gold streaks and much gingerbread scroll work and carving at bow and stern. Belaying pins were mostly of copper; ropes were all pointed or else brass-capped, and Flemish coiled on the snow-white decks. What wonder if these little schooners were the pride of their officers and the delight of their owners.

Here is a description, taken from the *Illustrated London News*, of Dent's *Wild Dayrell*, which was launched in 1855:

> The new schooner *Wild Dayrell* has been lately constructed by Messrs. John & Robert White of the Medina Docks, Cowes, for the old established firm of Messrs. Dent & Co. of Hongkong.
>
> The yacht-like appearance of this schooner attracted the notice of several members of the Royal Yacht Squadron at Cowes. Her form for beauty, speed and seagoing qualities is most admirable: and she is so constructed as to give her the greatest possible strength to contend with the tempestuous weather of the China Seas. She has a heavy and most complete armament for protection against the swarms of pirates that now infest the coast of China. She is commanded by Captain Walter Macfarlane, who expects his *Wild Dayrell* to prove herself the fastest model afloat.

The *Vindex* was not a Cowes schooner, but came from the drawing board of Alexander Hall, being the only vessel he designed specially for the Dents. She was a slightly larger schooner than the *Wild Dayrell*.

Three of these coasting opium schooners belonged to their masters. The *Nina*, built by White in 1852, was a smaller schooner than the others. Captain George Stanford commanded and owned her for many years.

Then there was the *Waterwitch*, of 236 tons, which was built at Newcastle in 1855 for Captain Reynell, who had commanded Dent's famous barque of that name for so many years and whose last command had been the *Sea Witch*.

The third was the *Salamander*, of 115 tons. She was built in 1856 by Hall for the Earl of Selkirk. In 1859 she was consigned to Dent & Co. and Captain Barcham brought her out to Hongkong from

Aberdeen with a general cargo in 110 days (April 13 to August 1). Dents put her up for sale by public auction on November 7, and she was bought by a Mr. Alosch, the price being 11,000 dollars. In the early 'sixties a very old China hand, Captain Alfred Roper, late of *Corsair*, *Zephyr* and *Vindex*, bought her, and commanding her himself, ran her on charter to Jardine, Matheson & Co. at 1000 dollars a month and a commission on sales of opium at non-treaty ports.

Old Hands amongst the Coasters.

There are few men still alive who can remember any of the old hands of opium clipper days, such old sea dogs as Charlie Bolton who commanded in turn the *Anonyma*, *Gazelle*, *Mazeppa* and *Mor* and ended up as Jardine, Matheson's first marine superintendent. Then there was Johnny Saunders, who began coasting as second mate of the *Mazeppa*, and was afterwards mate of the *Gazelle* and master of the *Neva* and finally of the *Chin-Chin*. He became Lloyd's Surveyor at Foochow. Before taking out the *Wild Dayrell*, Wallie Macfarlane commanded *Mazeppa* and *Island Queen*. Duncan Forbes, still alive a few years ago, had *Omega* and *Kelpie*. Then there was Oliver, who was master of the *Red Rover* for six years, after first commanding the *Harlequin* and *Audax*, and who ended up with the *Eamont*; and Barcham who, after having the *Denia*, brought the *Vindex* out from Glasgow in 1856 and the *Salamander* from Aberdeen in 1859. All these were household names on the coast at that time.

The last of the real old timers, Brodie Clarke, died in the autumn of 1931. Though not bred to the sea but to the counting house, he served aboard the *Salamander* as Roper's third mate in 1864-5. He had the cheery spirit of the true coaster, spreading happiness and gaiety, energy and courage around him down to the day of his death. And he was a sportsman of the true Scottish type. In his 80th year at the St. Andrew's Day ball at Shanghai he joined the young folk at a foursome reel to the skirl of the bagpipes and kept it up with the best for fully twenty minutes.

For some years before his death it was his custom to be out at cockcrow at the Race Club watching the ponies training for the

Shanghai autumn season. Such early risers were known as the "Coffee and Roll Brigade;" and old Brodie took such a pride in being the first on the scene that anyone arriving ahead of him would hide until the old man had shown up, so that his record of always being the early bird should not be broken.

A very different character was Captain D. A. de Sainte Croix, a Jerseyman and one of Jardine Matheson's favourite skippers. Here is a description of him, which I found in an old *Chamber of Commerce Journal.*

> To look at this very precise old gentleman who habitually used to wear long stockings with most immoral garters made of ribbon with flapperesque bows of the most fascinating type and high heeled Parisian shoes, it was difficult to imagine him reefing topsails in a gale or grappling with Chinese pirates, yet his body was gashed and cut about in a fashion which left one no reason to doubt but that in his youth he must have enjoyed a series of particularly exciting, not to say lurid, experiences.

For the most part, in spite of their many ups and downs, their blood-curdling encounters with Chinese and Malay pirates and their soul-battering experiences in typhoons, the old China hands were a jovial crowd, who loved the life, loved their ships and took a pride in being in the service of Jardine, Matheson & Co. or Dent & Co.

The coasters indeed were a happy family who knew each other's intimate concerns and rejoiced in a chaff and a gup, a sport and a service, that was all their own.

The Little Commodore in the Second Chinese War.

The outbreak of the second China war in 1857 brought Harry Keppel out to the East again—as a commodore in one of the finest 50-gun frigates in Service, the ***Raleigh***. ***Raleigh*** is not a lucky name in Chinese waters; the first was dismasted, the second foundered.

As Keppel was approaching Macao on April 14, 1857, at the end of his passage out, the ***Raleigh*** ripped her bottom up on an uncharted reef. Keppel sailed on in the hope of being able to beach her in shallow water before the sea became too much for the pumps. The anchorage was in sight and in the roadstead lay the French Admiral.

As the ***Raleigh*** slowly approached in a water-logged condition, Keppel gave the order for the usual salute to be fired. Though the gun deck was already under water, the *Raleigh*'s crew with perfect discipline fired their salute with the China Sea sluicing around their feet, and scarcely had the last round been fired before the *Raleigh* quietly subsided beneath the wave in full sight of a large fleet of ships and whilst the French Admiral was returning her salute.

Keppel was heart-broken, but the last salute of the *Raleigh* will always be remembered as one of those actions of which the British Navy has cause to be proud.

The little commodore, as he was lovingly called by everyone, recovered his spirits directly there was any fighting to do, and in the battle of Fatshan Creek as he stood on the paddle box of the gunboat *Hongkong*, directing operations with his blue trousers tucked into the tops of his Crimean boots and a white pith helmet on his head, he was evidently thoroughly enjoying himself, and later when his galley was cut in half by a round shot and sank under him, killing several of his boat's crew, his cheery voice and devil-may-care laugh heartened the whole British force.

There is not space in this book to deal with the second China war as well as the first—but it pursued much the same course with important results as regards trade, five additional ports, Niuchwang, Tangchau, Taiwan, Chaochau (port of Swatow) and Cninug being opened to foreign trade as well as the river Yang-tze-kiang.

The Opium Clipper "Wynaud" in the 1858 Tea Race.

The last of the clippers as distinguished from the coasters was the beautiful little *Wynaud*, a full-rigged ship of 521 tons, built on the Thames in 1854 and classed 13 years A1. Dent & Co. were her owners and Captain David Reid of Peterhead her first master.

Like all craft built for the Dents she was most beautifully fitted and luxuriously appointed besides being well armed. Her battery consisted of six 9-pounder carronades, which were in charge of a trained gunner, and gun drill was regularly carried on aboard her.

I have no record of her opium passages, but she was undoubtedly a very fast ship, though requiring careful handling, owing to being so lofty.

In the autumn of 1858, there was a large amount of tea awaiting shipment as soon as the Canton River should be opened to trade on the ratification of the peace treaty.

The *Wynaud* was amongst the ships lying at Hongkong waiting to load up at Whampoa at the first opportunity.

Jardine Matheson's representative was the famous *Cairngorm*, commanded at this date by the sedate John Ryrie, who had at last been persuaded to leave his old *Marian*. Gibb, Livingstone & Co. had Willis' *Lammermuir*, commanded by Andrew Shewan. She was a full-built ship and not a clipper, but like many vessels with apple cheeks and a fine run, very fast in light winds. Then there was the Jersey-built crack *Chieftain*, the American *Morning Star*, and as whipper-in, the Sunderland frigate-built ship *Warrior Queen*.

Things were a bit difficult at Hongkong that autumn. The Viceroy of Canton was up to all the old tricks of the first China war. After first trying to poison the British community by sending poisoned flour into Hongkong, he next cut off all supplies from the mainland, and on this form of blockade failing he thereupon ordered all Chinese servants to leave the island.

In this dilemma the ships in the harbour came to the aid of the houses and hongs ashore, and many a great lady in Hongkong was dependent on a sea cook for her meals.

At last a day came when it was known that peace was about to be ratified. The ladies of Hongkong at once decided to celebrate the occasion by a grand ball. The *Lammermuir* with her lofty 'tween decks, her fine cabin accommodation and her long poop was offered by Captain Shewan as a ballroom, and Captain Jock Stewart of the *Pique* frigate produced the band, whose German valses and English gallops were not approved by the Highland captain of the *Wynaud*, who was a fiddler himself with a strong affection for reels and strathspeys.

"Look-a-here, Shewan," he is said to have exclaimed; "there's nae music in yon lot a'va. To Hades wi' their toot-a-toot-toot. Tell 'em to play up 'Auld Lang Syne.' "

Davie Reid was a character; no doubt he had his way before the ball—which was a great success—ended in the small hours of the morning, when, under the influence of much excellent champagne, many a dignified Scottish skipper was tempted to join the dancers in the hot 'tween decks.

Peace was ratified on October 24 and immediately there was a rush to load.

Cairngorm, *Wynaud* and *Chieftain* got away from Whampoa on November 6, and the bigger *Lammermuir* two days later.

This was the first tea race with an agreed bonus for the first ship in, a gratuity of £200 being offered to the master and mates, to be divided *pro rata*, of the first ship to dock.

With a favourable monsoon of good strength the bigger ships had a slight advantage, carrying sail for all they were worth so that Ryrie carried away two stunsail booms and Shewan broke his main topgallantyard before they were up with Pulo Sapata. The smaller ships were somewhat overpowered, yet *Wynaud* entered Banka Strait close on the heels of the *Cairngorm*. A very famous ship-master served his time on the little *Wynaud*. This was Captain Tom Bowling, whose grandfather, a gunner of one of Nelson's ships at Copenhagen and Trafalgar, is supposed to have been the original of Dibdin's hero.

Captain Tom Bowling, who is still well remembered by shipping people in New Zealand as the master of the *Invercargill*, had vivid memories of those 1858 tea races and especially of the *Wynaud's* run through the Banka Strait.

He related this experience in the *Canterbury Times*. Let me quote some of his graphic words:

> After working down through the China Sea, with the forest-hung mountains of Borneo close on the port hand, the clipper would pass through Banka or Gaspar Straits into the Java Sea.
>
> All these waters, reef-dotted and shoal-infested, and the coasts of the great islands, that hemmed in the shallow seas, wooded from the water's edge to their cloudy summits swarmed with pirates of the Malay and China breeds. Borneo, Sumatra, Java, Banka, Billiton, Lambok and a hundred smaller islands harboured their ruffians of the seas: and when the wind came ahead in restricted waters and the ship had to anchor to save herself from being swept back or shorewards by the strong currents, a close and anxious watch was kept for the silently stealing proas.
>
> Sometimes the anchor was let go for the night so close to the islands of Banka and Sumatra that the monkeys could be heard chattering in the trees and the tropic birds singing and screaming, while the roar of the tiger was heard as "Stripes" came down to drink at some creek mouth.

On such occasions an armed anchor watch was set, one man with a loaded rifle on the poop and another similarly armed on the forecastle-head, with orders to fire the instant any boat was seen approaching. The 6-pounders were kept loaded and the poker ready heated in the galley fire. The shot used was canister and grape, the most effective projectiles for crowded proas.

In the China Sea the weather was often shockingly bad, rain in tropical sheets, thunder and lightning something terrible. We'd be wet through all day and whenever the wind came fair it was out with the stunsails: no possible chance was lost, for it was always a race.

We boys had to be roused out in our watch below to set topgallant and royal stunsails, and we'd be perched aloft reeving and unreeving gear and setting and taking in sail half a dozen times a day.

The *Wynaud* and *Cairngorm* were unlucky in Banka Strait to find light airs and calms. They felt their way through the mud flats during the night with the lead going steadily. Bowling further records:

Old Captain Reid would be lying down in his long chair on the poop. "Now then, youngster," he would say, "what watter ha'e ye gotten?" When there was a longer interval than usual between the apprenctice's reports, there came "Dom it; are ye asleep?"

The old man thought a lot of his boys, and made them do all the sounding and much other seamen's work;

"Ah!" he would say, "Ye'll nae gang awa' frae me an' say I didna mak' sailors o' ye."

We are only concernd with the *Wynaud* in this race. Other incidents, such as when *Lammermuir* sailed round *Cairngorm*, I have related in *The China Clippers*.

Lammermuir and *Cairngorm* were off Anjer on November 20, with *Wynaud* only twenty-four hours behind.

The late Captain Shewan of *Norman Court*, the son of the master of *Lammermuir*, gives the result of the race as a win for *Lammermuir* in actual time by 6 hours, Whampoa to Downs 92 days; *Cairngorm* gained the bonus for first ship in by docking 40 hours ahead of *Lammermuir*.

Wynaud was the third arrival, the *Chieftain* fourth, *Morning Star* fifth and *Warrior Queen* last.

All made good passages, *Warrior Queen* arriving only 104 days out, whilst both *Wynaud* and *Chieftain* were under 100.

Captain Shewan, junior, in referring to this race, compares

Wynaud's experience in Banka Strait to that of an unfortunate clipper in the "Straits of Bally Bang-jang, where the sailors could not get the yards swung on account of the overhanging trees, and the monkey's tails getting jammed in the brace blocks!"

Casualties in the September Typhoon of 1858.

A number of well-known opium clippers besides many other vessels came to grief in the September typhoon of 1858, which was at its worst off Swatow. Amongst those vanquished by this blow were the *Anonyma*, *Pantaloon*, *Gazelle*, and *Mazeppa*.

The *Anonyma* dragged ashore and was turned bottom up in the surf. She became a total wreck, but only one of her crew was drowned and her treasure was afterwards recovered.

The *Pantaloon* went on the rocks off Otao village. Captain Mooney and his crew were also successful in getting ashore, but when they came back to her at low water after the storm had blown over they found that she had been completely gutted and stripped by the Chinese.

The *Gazelle* (Captain Fox) arrived from Amoy and anchored off Double Island about 5 p.m. on September 20 at the beginning of the blow. It was then thick and hazy, a heavy swell was running in, and the wind was blowing in stronger and stronger gusts from the N.E. with the barometer falling rapidly. At midnight heavy rain was falling and the gale still increasing. Between 1 and 2 a.m. the typhoon was at its worst with the barometer, according to some readings, below 28. With waves running into the anchorage, which were judged to be as high as 40 ft., the anchored fleet had a terrible time of it. The glass did not start to rise until 3.30 a.m., when the wind suddenly veered into the South and East. At daybreak not a vessel was to be seen afloat except the schooners *Hazard* and *Eamont*. The latter had 150 fathoms of chain out and a second anchor backed on it at 60 fathoms. They were obliged, however, to cut away her masts; but she had smart officers. Captain Oliver hung his spars astern, refitted her in four days and then, with shortened lower masts and treble-reefed lowers, ran down to Amoy, where the schooner was given a complete overhaul and refit.

The *Gazelle* went down at her anchors, so that only her topmasts were showing above water. Only her captain and three Lascars were saved, picked out of the water the following morning.

The *Mazeppa*, the fourth victim amongst the opium coasters, had put back to Swatow in August leaking badly and with her bows opened up, six men having to be kept continually at the pumps. She went on to Hongkong where she was patched up and surveyed by John Rickett, surveyor to the Canton Marine Insurance, who, after caulking her, passed her as seaworthy for dry and perishable goods. It was rumoured, however, that Captain G. Heaton, who had surveyed her at the same time, had reported her to be in very bad condition.

Captain Bolton, who had succeeded Aleck Ryrie, also considered that she was pretty well worn out and used up as far back as April, 1857, but it had then been decided to give her another year's service as she was such a fast, useful little ship. After the caulking she was sent North and ran slap into the typhoon when abreast of Swatow, sinking off Double Island. The rumour was that she gybed her mainboom all standing in a squall and capsized, but many believed that she had opened up under the stress of wind and sea and filled.

After the typhoon had passed on, H.M.S. *Fury* busied herself in trying to salve the foundered ships and their valuable cargoes, as these were all in shallow water. She first of all anchored over the wreck of the *Mazeppa* and sent divers down, but it was found impossible to do anything there so she steamed into Swatow harbour and commenced operations on the *Gazelle*. The latter was found embedded deep in mud and sand, and after breaking both her bower cables, the *Fury* gave up all idea of raising the schooner; but there were 80,000 dollars worth of specie aboard, which she succeeded in recovering.

The Fate of Other Opium Clippers.

By this date many of the early clippers had disappeared from the lists. I believe that the last passage made by the famous *Waterwitch* was from Calcutta to Hongkong under Captain Mann, May 11 to June 11, 1853—31 days. The following March we find her moored as a receiving ship in the Min River with Captain Hely in charge.

Red Rover was lost in the 'sixties and *Lady Hayes* broken up in 1868. *Cowasjee Family* was sold to the Imaum of Muscat in 1861. *Hellas* went missing in 1855, *Black Joke* was lost in 1847 and *Syed Khan* was taken off the register in the same year. *Columbine* was wrecked in 1844. *Clown* was sold to the Chinese Government in 1853 and lost two years later. *Emma* foundered at sea in 1850 and *Arratoon Apcar* became an Indian Railway Company's hulk in 1860. *Time* was lost under Cama's flag. *Sydney* succumbed to a Bay of Bengal cyclone in 1868 and *Royalist* went to Tahiti to become an island trader. *Zephyr* was sold by the Dents to foreigners in October, 1859, and the *Spray* was sold to the U.S.A. in 1869; *Chin Chin* also ended her days under a foreign flag.

The *Antelope* was lost in August, 1852, on her way up from Woosung to Shanghai—her wreck was afterwards sold by auction for the benefit of the underwriters. The speedy little *Nymph* left Hongkong for Shanghai on October 2, 1854, and was never heard of again. The *Rustomjee Cowasjee* left Calcutta on June 23, 1850, with a cargo worth 800,000 dollars, passed Singapore on July 26, and went missing.

On October 9 a Chinese sugar junk reported a large ship which she saw in the hands of 15 pirate junks, whose crew and passengers had been landed at Tae-ho. The Portuguese sent out three armed lorchas, manned by sailors from the Portuguese men-of-war, but the ship, which had been plundered off St. Johns, turned out to be the country ship *Good Success*, Captain Henry Fraser's old ship, and not the *Rustomjee Cowasjee*.

Since his rescue of the junkmen and the sea-cunny of the *Rose* in the 1841 Hongkong typhoon, Captain Fraser had had the misfortune to lose the *Bombay Castle*, belonging to Sir Jamsetjee Jejeebhoy, which was burnt on her way down the Hooghly in May, 1846, probably by spontaneous combustion as she was loaded with cotton, though Captain Fraser feared it was the work of some of his crew.

The *Sir Edward Ryan* was bought by Augustine Heard & Co. in 1853 and was turned into a receiving ship.

The *Rob Roy* was lost in October, 1853, on her way from Calcutta to China.

Gradually as the steamers began to break into the clippers' trade from Calcutta and Bombay, the clippers themselves went off seeking.

Will o' the Wisp and *Corsair* went into the Honolulu trade; *Frolic* left for San Francisco in 1850; *Lanrick*, we find in 1863, bound for Sourabaya from Newcastle having been sold to the Prince of Nagots; and many even of the small brigs and schooners took cargoes home like the *Enigma*, though they mostly came out again.

The Looting of the "Three Brothers."

I have been unable to verify the following yarn which came from the lips of an old China captain many years ago and I am unable to give the date except that it was about the middle 'fifties.

The steamer *Three Brothers*, bound from Hongkong to Shanghai with both specie and opium in her hold, ran hard and fast ashore on Cape Good Hope near Swatow one very dark night, when the coast was not lighted as it is now. At daybreak several pirate junks made their appearance, and the boldest of them dropped her anchor about 200 cable lengths from the wreck and opened fire upon her.

The steamer was heeling over so far that it was impossible to train a gun upon the pirate, but after a bit her crew managed to lash a 9-pounder to the main bitts. This cannon was roughly laid in the direction of the junk and fired, but the very first shot, or at any rate the second, dismounted the gun and smashed the bitts.

It was at this exciting moment that Dent's schooner *Undine* appeared upon the scene, and, anchoring about half a mile off, sent in two armed boats to take the steamer's crew off.

Meanwhile the steamer's boats had also been lowered. One of these was actually alongside being loaded up with officers' gear, when a junk swooped down upon her, hooked her with long boat-hooks, and dragged her away, killing the men in her in spite of musketry fire from the *Three Brothers*. When the *Undine's* boats arrived the captain of the steamer ordered her to be abandoned.

When all the boats were loaded, strict orders were given to keep close together on the pull to the schooner. But the latter's captain's gig, in charge of the serang, with 30,000 dollars in specie aboard, being faster than any of the other boats, slipped off by herself only to be caught by two of the pirates and carried off.

Where wrecks or strandings occurred the pirates and even the local fishermen were always tempted to unusual deeds of daring, led on by the hopes of loot.

When Jardine Matheson's steamer *Europe* was wrecked at the mouth of the Min River in 1881, her crew abandoned her, leaving her under the protection of a Chinese gunboat. But during that night the steamer was completely gutted, though lying under the guns of the warship, and when her crew boarded her on the lee side in the morning, she was apparently intact and untouched, so cleverly had the robbers gone to work.

The Opening up of Japan, 1858.

In the year 1858 after some months of negotiation, a commercial treaty was at last concluded with Japan, which had been closed to foreign vessels for 200 years. In the treaty the Japanese were given 12 months to open three ports to foreign trade—those of Nagasaki, Kanagwa and Hakodate.

Both Jardine, Matheson & Co. and Dent & Co. took a keen interest in the future of Japan and did everything possible to forward the negotiations.

Dent's schooner *Eamont* was used as a sort of despatch vessel carrying emissaries and negotiators backwards and forwards between Shanghai and Nagasaki. There was a strong conservative party in Japan who were against the opening of the country to foreigners. The first time that the *Eamont* anchored at Nagasaki, this party sent about fifty row boats to tow the schooner out of the harbour again. They made fast their lines to bobstay, martingales and bowsprit shrouds, and tugged away with all their might for an hour or two, quite oblivious of the fact that her anchor was down and had a firm hold on the bottom. In the early days of the negotiations unwary foreigners were caught like wild beasts in pits carefully hidden by a light layer of bamboo poles, etc. Others were set upon and slashed about and even killed by fanatical Samurai with their terrible swords.

Yet the sights that the lucky officers of the *Eamont* saw in that absolutely unspoilt and uncontaminated land amply repaid them for falling into pits full of horrible mud and garbage or being attacked by ferocious swordsmen.

One of the first ships to take a cargo away from Japan was the *Troas* of 700 tons (Captain Holmes), chartered by Jardine, Matheson & Co., which arrived at Nagasaki on February 9, 1859, with 200 tons of sugar and took away 300 tons of seaweed, which was used as a food at Hongkong.

William Keswick, of Jardine, Matheson & Co., then a young man of 25 years, accompanied Captain Holmes and was actually left behind as Jardine Matheson's agent in Japan.

Joseph Jardine was then the Tai-pan or head partner in China, whilst James Whittall had succeeded Alexander Grant Dallas as head in Shanghai. It was Whittall who chartered the *Troas* and sent young Keswick to Nagasaki.

The *Eamont*, which played such an important part in the opening up of Japan, was eventually lost on the East coast of that beautiful country. It must be remembered that in those early days there were no reliable charts of the coast, and log, lead and lookout were of more use than chart and compass.

It is possible that the *Eamont* was wrecked in the same typhoon which did for the beautiful gun-sloop *Camilla*. The latter left Hakodate on September 1, 1860, for Kanagwa, the port of Jeddo, and is supposed to have foundered in the storm which swept the coast on September 9. Not the smallest trace of her was ever found.

There is no space in this book to describe the opening up of Japan to the world, in which the little opium clippers played such a prominent part. Those were the days when there was still a large slice of the world which was utterly free from the contaminating effects of Europe's boasted civilisation; and the lucky officers of the opium schooners, who adventured to Nagasaki or Hakodate, always used to speak of Japan as a sort of Garden of Eden before the fall.

The China Station in the 'Fifties.

Ever since the opium war the British squadron in Chinese waters, with its headquarters at Hongkong, was a command which

"MAZEPPA" CAREENING ALONGSIDE HULK, APRIL, 1847

From a Drawing by A. G. Dallas

[*See page* 348

S.S. "LY-EE-MOON"

National Maritime Museum, Greenwich

[*See page* 370

grew yearly in importance. The station extended from Singapore to the Bering Sea. Its fast growing trade had to be protected from the pirates both Malay, Dyak and Chinese, who seemed to increase in the same ratio as the merchant shipping. Its little known coasts had to be surveyed. Its open ports had to be guarded and its shallow inland waters patrolled. For these duties a variety of ships were required from stately battleships and haughty frigates to saucy gun-brigs and shallow draught long funnelled gunboats.

In 1850 there were two stationary ships at Hongkong, the *Minden*, store-ship, and the *Alligator*, hospital ship; in 1857 the *Princess Charlotte*, which once mounted 104 guns and was Lord Exmouth's flagship at the bombardment of Algiers, came out to take their place.

She took six months sailing out under a jury rig of frigate's spars and a crew of 600 men. Her guns, except for a saluting battery, had been left behind and her middle deck was fitted up with cabins.

At Simon's Town she came in for a hard blow, and with both bowers out to the clinch it became necessary to prepare her sheet cable. This was a huge hemp rope, 101 fathoms long, 26 inches in the round and with an Elliot's eye on the end for shackling on the anchor. It was quite a job bringing this monster rope up from the after orlop deck, where it was stowed, and ranging it on deck ready for use.

The majestic *Queen Charlotte* caused quite a stir amongst the Chinese water population as with slow, stately grace she sailed into Hongkong Harbour. "Hi-yah! Hi-yah!" came the cries from junk, lorcha and tanka-boat. "Lookee see! one big three piecey bamboo, flour dlecks!"

By this date, owing to the second Chinese war, there were as many as 63 British men-of-war in the East, headed by the *Calcutta* (84 guns), Sir Michael Seymour's flagship.

Amongst the gun-brigs were the *Acorn* (Commander Hood), considered one of the smartest ships at sail drill in the Navy; the *Bitterne*, commanded by Vansittart, a great chastiser of pirates, and the *Camilla*, perhaps the finest brig ever designed by Sir William Symonds.

These little vessels, which ever since the first Georges had been the "maids of all work" in the British Navy, were fast being replaced by rakish-looking screw gunboats, clipper-bowed and barque-rigged, with only a slender funnel and skeleton bridge to show that they possessed engines. For river work there was also a number of tiny two-gun screw steamers, the forerunners of the torpedo-boat.

Yet even as late as 1857 there were still some smart frigates in commission out East, such as the famous *Pique*, commanded by Sir F. W. E. Nicholson, Bart., and the *Surprise* (40 guns, Commodore the Hon. C. G. J. B. Elliot), and a couple of 26's, the *Actaeon* and *Amethyst*.

Though steam was slowly superseding sail, as a means of propulsion at sea, during the 'fifties the form of the ship, whether man-of-war or merchant, had not yet undergone the change in design which engines and iron plates helped to bring about; and even paddle and screw steamers, with their conventional black sides, yellow superstructures, raking funnels and masts, and web-like rigging, were still very handsome to the eye; for the designer still considered that beauty in a ship was as necessary a quality as speed or seaworthiness; thus Hongkong Harbour in the 'fifties was a fair vision of tall ships and graceful steamers.

CHAPTER IX.

THE LAST DAYS OF THE TRADE.

There is a way, a wide way,
  Where the calling sea-gulls cry,
And when the night is darkest,
  The great, grey ships go by.
The men they carry are strong and bold,
The things they see can never be told,
The things they hear they can never unfold,
  On the tide-way, the wide way,
  Where the great grey ships go by.

—VIOLET GILLIESPIE.

Early Trade up the Yang-tze-kiang.

ON March 9, 1861, the Yang-tze-kiang was declared open to all British ships as far as Hankow, a distance up the "Son of the Sea" from the lightship at its mouth of just under 600 miles.

Great stretches of the river as well as Nankin itself were then in possession of the Taipings, and the enterprising traders who first adventured up the great river found a variety of enemies to overcome besides the ever present dangers of the navigation amidst shoals and rapid currents, shifting sand bars and overfalls. From the first, piracy was a continual plague, the river being infested with robbers of every description, from large outside pirate junks from the coast to small lorchas manned by fishermen. But the early traders also had to contend against imperialist war junks, which were often the worst pilongs of the lot, and the conduct of the Taipings was another very uncertain factor in a river voyage.

Dent & Co. were the first to attempt to trade opium with the Taipings; they stationed the receiving ship *Nimrod* at Wahu (50 miles above Nankin), for six months, but did not have the success they expected.

As soon as the river was opened to Europeans, large profits were made by many daring seamen not only in opium but in smuggling salt, which at Eching, the great salt mart for the interior, a large village on the North bank 18 miles above Chinkiang, sold at the same price as common rice—about three taels (£1 sterling) per picul (130 pounds weight), but further up sold at double that price.

The first ships used on the great river by European traders were either small schooners, shallow draught paddle-wheel steamers or lorchas. These lorchas had European hulls and Chinese mat sails. They were generally two-masted, with often a couple of small square topsails on the main. They sailed well and were handy for tracking, but they were rather weakly manned to contend against all the piratical gentry they had to fight their way through.

The first ship of any size to adventure up the Yang-tze was the famous tea clipper *Challenger* which, in 1863, when commanded by Captain Macey, loaded the first tea cargo at Hankow.

Gunboats were sent up the river to look after and protect British traders, but they could not be everywhere at once, and during the first few years after the opening of the river to trade scarcely a vessel made the voyage to Hankow and back without being attacked.

The most difficult navigation was at the dreaded Langshan Crossing, where the channel took a sharp turn towards the Langshan Hills. Here many a vessel was lost. The steamer *Kate*, for instance, on her first voyage up the Yang-tze ran ashore, was capsized by the fierce stream, slid off the bank into deep water, and sank with her valuable cargo of specie, many of her passengers and crew being drowned.

At Chinkiang, the first of the river treaty ports, the current ran so swiftly that small river steamers could not steam round the South End of Silver Island against the stream.

At Nankin, the Taiping capital, H.M.S. *Centaur* was stationed, and British vessels had to obtain permits from her before proceeding further.

When the river was opened those gigantic 1000 feet piles of rock, the Pillars, which the Chinese called the "Gates of the Upper River," were also in the hands of the Taipings, who had fortified

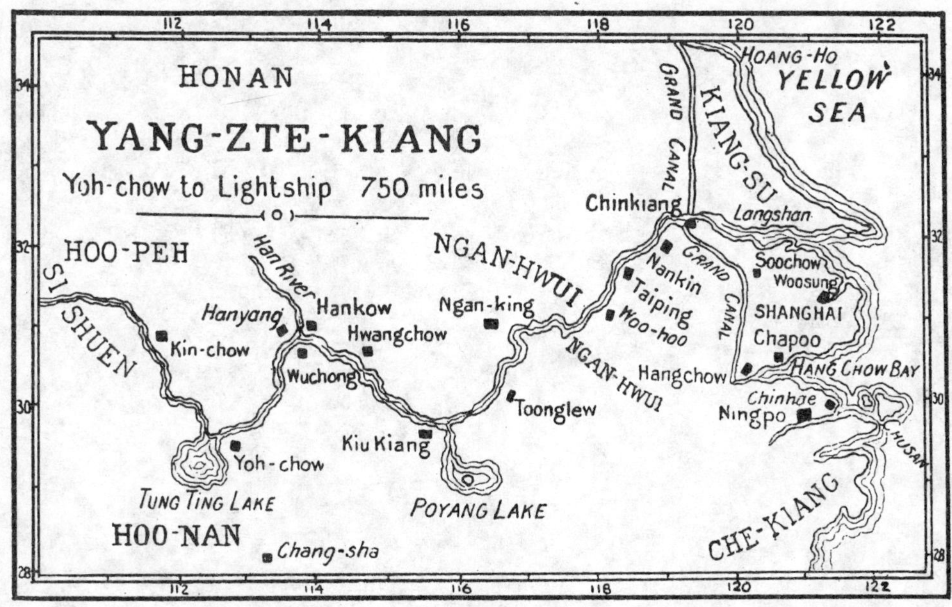

YANG-ZTE-KIANG

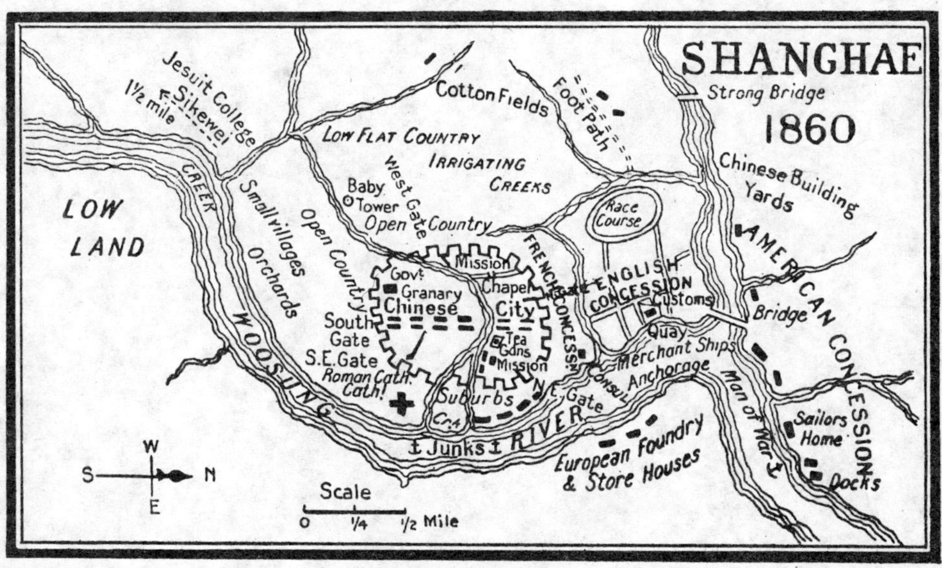

SHANGHAE, 1860

[To face page 356

their summits and erected batteries at the water level. The Pillars are about 40 miles above Nankin, and mark the limit of the flood tide.

Off the city of Tunglin, 380 miles from the river mouth, lorchas, schooners and even steamers were often compelled to bring up in a sheltered nook owing to the violence of the storms, which lashed the river into breaking seas and sent the stream roaring down in a fury. Here the low hilly country, which was uncultivated, simply swarmed with pheasants, and sportsmen from the weather-bound vessels were able to make good bags. In the early days some of the adventurers up the Yang-tze were Californian and Australian diggers, who found many good prospects on the hills about Tunglin and even washed gold dust and nuggets out of the river itself at a place they called Hen Point, 20 miles below Ngan-kiang.

The chief landmark before reaching the treaty port of Kew-kiang was that famous rock, the Little Orphan, whose 500 ft. summit was crowned by a Buddhist temple, which could only be reached by steps cut in the face of the rock by the priests. Here the Chinese demons who inhabited the temple were supposed to be particularly hostile to foreign devils. The clear transparent waters of the Poyang Lake, which were such a contrast to the thick muddy stream of the Yang-tze, bounded by magnificent cliffs, dense under-woods sprinkled with giant forest trees, were a welcome sight to the schooner captain, for here he was able to fill his water casks.

It was some time before Kew-kiang settled down to trade with the foreigner. At first, in spite of the presence of a British gun-boat, the British concession and consulate were continually being attacked by undisciplined imperial troops, and the mandarins pretended that they were unable to control their soldiery.

Between Kew-kiang and Hankow, the scenery is grandly wild and mountainous, cliffs rising to more than 1000 ft. straight up from the water's edge. At one place, called Ke-tow—the Cockshead—a great overhanging mountain echoed with the rushing sound of birds' wings, as myriads of shags rose from its honeycombed face at the beat of a steam-boat's paddles, the air literally became black with birds, and the shrill, discordant cries of the Bramley kites and the screams of gulls were so deafening as to notify the

Chinese for miles around that foreign devils were passing the Cockshead.

Further on again the voyager passed through the gloomy chasm of Pwan-pieu-shan—the Split Hill—with its towering, perpendicular sides, into a cultivated land of paddy-fields, tropical foliage, reed huts, and low hills covered with wild tea, until the great mart of Hankow came into view.

Hankow was a dangerous place for the foreigner in the early days of the concession, and a favourite trick of Chinese robbers was to set fire to a European's house in the dead of night and then to loot it under the pretence of putting out the flames.

It must not be supposed that the traveller up the Yang-tze could sit on his quarterdeck or paddle box and enjoy the view all the time.

A Smuggling Schooner's Adventures.

Let me transcribe the experience of a little English trading schooner, a salt and opium smuggler with a British captain, Linley, a Greek mate, a Malay boatswain and a Chinese crew, which was bound to Shanghai from Hankow soon after the river was opened. Captain Linley wrote:

> At Chin-kiang I heard terrible rumours of pirates about the Lang-shan Crossing and entrance of the river. In spite of much exaggeration the danger was really too great to be despised and I made arrangements to sail down to Shanghai in company with two European vessels bound there, one a fore-and-aft French schooner, the other an American lorcha.

His first encounter was during the first night after leaving Chin-kiang. The moon was shining brightly. About half a mile away a schooner with an English ensign union down was distinguished approaching.

The smuggler was leading his two consorts, and as he passed he caught the hail:

"Come on board, I will anchor."

The distressed stranger's anchor almost at once plunged overboard. The skipper of the smuggler told his mate to work up close to the other and also anchor, whilst he jumped into his boat and rowed off to the other vessel. As he ran alongside he noticed two armed Europeans aft, and a number of fiery excited Chinamen forward; upon which he loosened his revolver in its holster. As he stepped up the gangway ladder a Chinaman suddenly made a rush at him.

The wide-awake captain caught his assailant round the shoulders and flung him clean over his head into the gurgling tide of the Yang-tze. The man gave one cry and then disappeared forever. The captain then sprang over the rail with drawn pistol just as the rest of the Chinamen came for him.

A bullet sang among them. The schooner's crew drew back; at the same moment her captain thrust a cutlass into the smuggler's hand and gasped out the word, "Mutiny!"

Then, brandishing bamboo spears and long knives, and yelling like demons let loose, the Celestials came jumping and gesticulating to the attack of the three white men, who with their revolvers poised hesitated to shoot. The leader of the mutineers started the battle by letting drive point blank with a couple of heavy horse-pistols, which made the most horrible din and smoke. The aim was bad, and the man was at once shot down by his own captain. The melee then began in earnest, cutlass and revolver against spear and horse-pistol.

Let me quote the smuggler:

> My next perception was that I was engaged with half-a-dozen men pushing fiercely at me with their spears. For some seconds I defended myself desperately with the cutlass, successfully warding all their thrusts, actually forgetful of the revolver I held in my left hand.
>
> I was soon reminded of its use by another man coming towards me, pointing a huge pistol, like the first two which had so nearly finished me. This entirely recalled my presence of mind, and bringing my revolver into play I had the satisfaction of seeing him fall in the smoke. At the same instant, however, the slight distraction had nearly proved successful to my spear assailants; one transfixed me, as I thought, though afterwards it appeared I was barely scratched, and the transfixing sensation was caused by the spear tightly pinning my clothes; while before I could parry it another made a thrust full at my breast.
>
> With no time to sweep my cutlass round, I dropped it and seized the spear haft within an inch of my body, at the same time using my revolver and shooting the man. Before I could level at another enemy, the man whose spear was fast in my clothes abandoned it and closed with me. Over and over we rolled on the deck. I was unable to use my pistol and he to use his knife. My left wrist was firmly grasped by his right

hand, while my right hand was fully engaged restraining his left, armed with a large dagger.

While struggling on the deck I saw several Chinamen approaching with uplifted spear to slaughter me in my helpless condition, but each time I had seen the schooner's mate jump over me, exclaiming as he thrust with his sword: "La! La!" and each time I had seen an enemy fall.

At last I received a severe blow on the head and, half stunned, felt my antagonist releasing his left hand. Just at this moment I was sensible of someone dragging himself along the deck close to me, and ere I could distinguish who or what it was, my revolver was taken from my hand, the Chinaman who had hitherto been holding it abandoned his grip and knocked my right hand from his left. Instead of feeling his knife pierce me, a pistol was discharged so close that the flash singed my hair and the Chinaman fell motionless across me. From the effect of the blow I had received and the shock of the near report, I lay for a moment unable to move. I was then aroused by the mate of the schooner dragging the Chinaman off me and assisting me to rise, exclaiming:

"Eh, monsieur capitaine, hope I, be gar, vous have no die. Zese sacre—all dead, all run down le fond de calle—de hole, by gar!"

When I recovered my feet, I saw the deck was deserted, except by ourselves and seven or eight Chinamen lying dead or wounded and the captain of the schooner, who was sitting on the deck with my revolver in his hand, for he it was who had so opportunely rescued me from my antagonist.

The ball from one of the horse-pistols had struck the captain's breast-bone and glancing off passed through his left arm. Of the Chinese four were dead and four severely wounded. The Frenchman turned out to be not the mate but the part owner of the schooner, which was bound to Chin-kiang with a cargo of opium. When close to Langshan Crossing, the lowder (Chinese captain) who was at the helm suddenly altered the course to the North where there was a well-known pirate haunt.

The two white men seized the lowder, the Frenchman putting his revolver to his head, whilst the captain held off the rest of the crew with levelled rifle. At this the crew retreated forward, snatching up boarding pikes, and they held off until boarded by the stranger. But for the dexterous swordsmanship of the French owner, the three men must have been overpowered, but nine killed and wounded were due to his cut and thrust, for five of those who had fled below were wounded. The Frenchman had been a *maitre d'armes* in a French regiment. Let me give his gallant end in the words of Captain Linley, the smuggler:

Some little time afterwards he was killed by pirates, almost upon the scene of our encounter, when, after bravely defending himself alone on the deck of his vessel against a host of assailants and killing sixteen with his own hand, the pirates, unable to overcome his splendid swordsmanship, retired to their own vessel and killed him by throwing stink-pots upon him.

Hardly was the fighting over before the lorcha and French schooner anchored close alongside and sent armed parties aboard to find out what all the firing had been about. The Chinamen were all made fast after they had bound up their own wounds; and soon afterwards a passing steamer took the *maitre d'armes* schooner in tow for Chin-kiang.

The other three vessels then continued their voyage down stream. Towards dusk the Langshan Hills came in sight and Captain Linley judged it prudent to anchor for the night, it being too dangerous to attempt the difficult navigation of the crossing in the dark. About midnight the smuggler and his Greek mate were roused out by the lookout man rushing aft with the cry;

"Jeu-dow-li! Jeu-dow-li!"

"Pirates coming! Pirates coming!"

The moon had gone down and the night was fairly dark, but less than a quarter of a mile up stream two heavy junks were observed, apparently at anchor some considerable distance apart.

But the captain and mate soon recognised what had alarmed the lookout. There was a stout coir rope between the two junks and they were fast dropping down upon the schooner on the swift ebb. This was a favourite trick of the pirates. As the tide swept them noiselessly down upon their unsuspecting prey, they carefully tended the rope, hauling in or giving out aboard each junk as necessary so that when it finally caught on the cable or bows of their victim, they were quickly swept alongside by the tide, one to port and one to starboard, and in a moment after a shower of stink-pots, hordes of long tails would pour down upon the deck of the unfortunate vessel. Several fast schooners and lorchas had been caught in the Yang-tze in this way when they could easily have escaped by their superior sailing.

On the above occasion Captain Linley's consorts had anchored over a mile below him; also they mounted cannon, whilst his schooner only carried small arms.

He immediately got his anchor as quietly as possible and began to drop down stream, making no use of his sails or yulos (heavy sweeps) so as to avoid giving his action away to the pirates, who did not discover that he was drifting also until he was within a quarter of a mile or so of his consorts.

Then the junks gave up the whole hope of surprise, set their sails in chase and opened fire, the loudness and rapidity of their reports warning the experienced Linley that they were the formidable West Coast Ti-mungs mounting ten guns or more of calibres from 12 to as large as 32-pounders.

The lorcha and French schooner carried a pair of long-nines apiece. Captain Linley, as soon as he had closed them, left the lowder in charge of his schooner, and with six of his best men and Philip, his Greek mate, pulled aboard his two consorts, boarding one himself with three men and sending the mate and three men aboard the other. Linley took charge of the fight, his plan being to try to separate the Ti-mungs, and fight them in turn. For this purpose he hailed his own schooner to keep away, and one Ti-mung going after her, he was by this means able to keep the two in line abreast, so that only one could bring her broadside to bear on the lorcha and French schooner, who could make good play with their swivel guns.

The pirates' firing though rapid and heavy was very ineffective, as they could only aim with any accuracy when directly abeam, and this the faster consorts took care to avoid, sailing completely round their antagonists and bearing down to close Linley's defenceless schooner, which had tacked and with the other junk in chase had fetched a compass so as not to get cut off.

The action finished by the lorcha and French schooner luffing up across the bows of the two junks at 50 yards and letting fly a salvo. Shrieks out of the dark night told of its effect—and the Ti-mungs then hauled off and crowded sail to escape.

It was now the turn of the smugglers, and blazing away with their long-nines, they followed the junks in amongst the Langshan shoals, with the result that the vessel, aboard of which Captain

Linley had been directing operations, being in the lead, ran hard ashore on a bank. He was able to warn his consorts in time, and a line taken off to them soon hove him off into deep water where all three anchored for the rest of the night.

Their casualties were one man killed, one wounded by a splinter and another by a grape shot, and the captain of the lorcha's pet monkey missing. The victors celebrated their victory by splicing the main brace, and topping off the grog with a well-earned breakfast.

The following day the three consorts were held up by fog which kept blowing up in thick wreaths, blotting out every landmark and even the vessels from each other. It was late in the day before they dared to heave up their anchors and proceed by the North Channel of Langshan Crossing, where they had good soundings to steer by.

In the midst of the passage, the sky cleared for a few minutes and a large fleet of trading junks passed, bound up from Shanghai. These reported that they had been attacked by pilongs in long, low rowing boats about a mile or so and two of their number had been captured. This warning caused the three consorts to prepare once more for battle. Linley and his mate again went aboard the lorcha and French schooner, their vessel under the lowder, leading the way with a consort on each quarter.

Unfortunately the fog again closed down, so that Linley's schooner was lost sight of, but a tremendous uproar aboard the hidden vessel and cries of "Jeu-dow" (pirates) and then the bang of a cannon, the scream of grape and canister and the splashing of oars, caused the captain to jump off the pivot gun upon which he was sitting, depress the muzzle to its lowest limit and fire it by touching it off with the lighted cigar in his hand. He had laid it on a dark patch in the mist; the next moment a fast-boat, full of dead and dying Chinamen, crashed alongside, turned over and sank.

Nothing more could be seen, though the noise of oars sounded on every side; then, where the fog thinned, the stern of a boat was sighted for a moment and received a dose from the French schooner's foremost pivot gun. That was the last round fired. When a few minutes later, the fog cleared away, there was a squadron of small imperialist gun-boats, pulling inshore as fast as they could. These found it more profitable battening on the trade up the Yang-tze than joining battle with the dreaded Taipings.

I have given these Yang-tze-kiang combats in some detail, for they show so very clearly how hazardous was the navigation of that river in the early 'sixties.

Further instances could be given in which the "Jeu-dows" were not so unsuccessful. Until the river steamers cut them out, the small schooners and lorchas, which dared the turbid waters of the "Son of the Sea," made a great deal of money smuggling salt and opium, though they literally had to fight their way through pirates, Taipings and Imperialists.

Trading with the Wild Formosans.

Owing to the treatment of the shipwrecked crews from the *Ann* and *Nerbudda*, the island of Formosa had a very bad reputation amongst the coasters and no attempts had been made to open up a trade with a people who were considered to be the wildest of savages.

In the year 1860, however, rumours reached Hongkong that one or two adventurous captains had managed to open up a very profitable trade with a port named Taku at the South-west end of the island.

The opium firms were always on the lookout for new markets, and like pearl lagoons these were always kept as secret as possible by their fortunate discoverers, yet, before long, the news always leaked out and found its way to the native godowns in Hongkong. In the case of Taku, the Dents were amongst the first to hear of its possibilities, and immediately sent off their schooner *Eamont* to investigate, with a full cargo of the drug on board.

It was the typhoon season when the *Eamont* left Hongkong and she ran into an ominous calm before she was through the Ly-ee-moon Passage. Her impatient skipper, Gulliver, at once ordered her 40 ft. sweeps to be run out of the gun-ports. These, each one manned by six hands, sent the sweet-lined schooner along at from 3 to 4 knots an hour and she was soon through the pass; but when she was within a day's sail of Amoy the threatened typhoon fell upon her. Though the *Eamont* was shortened down as quickly as possible, the gaff topsail, which had a 28-ft. yard on its head, was too much for a bosun's mate and eight hands and, filling like a balloon, tore itself out of their grasp and blew away into space like a great white bird. By dark the schooner, under reefed fore-staysail and fore-trysail, was flying before the storm. All through the night she scudded round and round in circles in the midst of a dense mist of spray and driving rain. The land was somewhere close aboard and the centre of the commotion was growing ever nearer.

By 10 the following morning the barometer was down to 27.30, the four lee broadside guns had chafed through their breechings and gone overboard, the quarter boat to windward had been smashed to staves against its davits, and that to leeward gone altogether, whilst the schooner, as each squall struck her, lay ever farther over on her side. By this time the carpenter and his mates were standing by the masts with their sharpest axes, whilst reliable hands were stationed by the weather shrouds and backstays ready to cut the lanyards.

The squalls were coming in one long dismal howl, a deep booming note told of the stormfiend's fury, whilst a high-pitched shrieking was drawn from the tortured rigging. At six bells in the forenoon a terrific gust laid the *Eamont* flat on her broadside with her cross-trees in the water. The captain lifted his trumpet to give the order to cut, but before he could get out a word the schooner brought her spars upright in the midst of a sudden breathless calm—she was in the centre of the typhoon.

For half an hour she lay tossing in a confused maelstrom of heaving waters, then the storm struck her again on the starboard beam and hove her down until again it was "Stand by to cut." A new fore-staysail and jib, which had been hurriedly bent during the calm interval, blew away with a report like thunder, then the gallant little *Eamont* righted and scudded away before the gale under her close-reefed fore-trysail. The worst was now over, the wind began to ease and the glass to rise, and soon after noon the schooner was able to lay her course.

The following morning found her at Amoy, safely moored

within a cable's length of Dent's receiving ship, with boarding nettings triced up and armed sentries at the gangway.

It took a week to refit after the typhoon. The next thing was to find Taku, of which the latitude and longitude were only approximately known. Having arrived on the supposed position, the schooner was sailed slowly along the Formosan coast, with every eye on the lookout for an opening. At last a small passage was made out, leading in between the hummocks, but between it and the *Eamont* a long line of heavy surf betrayed a coral reef blocking the way. The monsoon was blowing strongly through the day but at sundown when it eased up, a raft, holding a couple of fishermen, paddling out from the shore, showed where a passage through the reef existed. The fishermen were caught and interrogated, and from them the rough depth of the channel was ascertained to be somewhat less than the actual draught of the *Eamont*. Captain Gulliver, however determined to trust the propelling power of her sails and the height of the surf to carry her over, relying upon the strength of her build to withstand the thumping of her keel on the hard rocky bottom. Such risks were all in the day's work when looking for new markets.

The "Eamont" bumps over the Reef.

Let me quote Captain Lindsay Anderson, a late P. & O. commander, who was then third mate of the schooner and with the second mate and two sea-cunnies was at the wheel during the passage of the reef:

> The *Eamont* having fore-reached a little to the Northward, while standing offshore, was then put about so as to run in with a good impetus on the starboard tack, the wind being well on the quarter. As soon as she was round and the yards trimmed, the balloon square sail was set and the main-boom sheet eased off as far as necessary.
>
> Away flew the *Eamont* before the breeze, like a greyhound just slipped from his leash. The captain took his station with the two natives and a Chinese schroff on the weather side of the quarterdeck, and from there conned the *Eamont* to what might be her doom or the success of his daring enterprise.
>
> Flying through the water as if she were a thing of life being hunted to death, the *Eamont* soon came to the edge of the surf, which was falling wave over wave with the noise of a cataract. One length of herself within this mass of seething, hissing foam, and bump she came, striking heavily on the ground, and making her spars tremble and

shake like willow wands, while she herself paused in her mad career. Another mass of seething water came along, filling the decks fore and aft, but lifting her up to hurl her further on her way. While running on this second roller she attempted to broach-to and lay her broadside open to the sea, but luckily for us her momentary stoppage and the force of water thrown into the mainsail when this second roller came along, carried away the main-sheet, the boom swung right off, losing its power, the head-yards and jibs made her pay off, and thus saved us from what might have been a capsize right in the middle of the reef.

Hands jumped aft at the captain's call, with spare tackle to secure the boom, but before they had found their way aft amidst the blinding spray the *Eamont* had struck again, and paused again as if to shake herself and make ready for another bound. A second of breathless suspense, another roller was upon us, hitting her with sledge-hammer force as she lay fast on the reef, knocking in part of the taffrail and nearly doubling me and Nealance in two over the wheel; while the quartermasters, from whom we had taken charge of the wheel when we came to the edge of the reef, were washed along and hanging on to the midship gun.

Rising on the crest of this third roller, the *Eamont* again rushed on like a mad deer before the hounds. When on the highest point of the breaking roller, she shook herself free of the water on her deck, and as she subsided in the hollow left behind this crested wave a lusty cheer was shouted out by all hands, for this time no bump was felt on mother earth to stop us on our onward way. We were through the surf, the water was a dark blue and comparatively smooth.

Traders, Wreckers and Pirates encountered.

Their difficulties now seemed to be over, a snug harbour was found inside, in which lay a jury-rigged receiving-ship flying the Stars and Stripes, an island brig from Sydney, N.S.W., a Dutch schooner and a number of junks. These ships had come over the reef in ballast on a calm day. The schooner and brig were taking in a cargo of cheap Formosan sugar, but it was the well-armed, snugly moored receiving-ship which roused the curiosity of the *Eamont's* crew.

The business of getting in touch with the local merchants was undertaken by the schooner's compradore and schroffs; by wisely distributing cumshaw they soon discovered that this new market was likely to prove decidedly profitable.

Champagne flowed when the local big-wigs came aboard to inspect the cases of Malwa, Patna and Benares, and bargaining was soon in full swing. Meanwhile the *Eamont's* officers were not idle. Every day they were out in the harbour sounding and surveying, and they actually managed to take a line of soundings through the passage over the reef with the aid of a boat's crew of New Caledonians from the Sydney brig.

Shortly before the *Eamont* was ready to sail with a hold full of specie, another typhoon came to test her afresh. It came roaring down on the anchorage after a close black night, throughout which long rolls of clattering rumbling thunder heralded zigzags and spirals of upward shooting lightning along the horizon. Every ship in the harbour of Taku had time to prepare with springs on their cables, spars and topmasts on deck and everything trebly lashed. A junk which looked much like a pilong drifted across the bow of the *Eamont*, swung round, and became tightly wedged between the schooner's lee bow and the shore. Captain Gulliver in the midst of the hurly-burly of the storm deemed it wise to take possession of the junk and disarm her crew.

Of the European shipping only the Amsterdam schooner came to grief. She went adrift and stranded along the shore inside the reef, where she speedily fell a prey to wreckers, the Dutch captain and three of his crew being murdered. Crews from the other three ships took prompt action; under the lead of the three captains, the village of the wreckers was burnt to the ground.

The Formosans responded by sending four heavily armed junks against the three ships. But these were captured one by one, as they sailed in round the high hummock which marked the entrance to the harbour. This squashed all further resistance, the Formosans came to terms, and a trade agreement between the Tootai and the captains was celebrated in the usual way, by a grand spread on the white deck of the little schooner, when much wine was drunk and many toasts proposed with great enthusiasm.

King Tom in Trouble.

The success of the *Eamont* encouraged other opium firms and schooner captains to exploit Formosa, but not all of these were as successful as Captain Gulliver. One of the most daring of the owner-captains in the very last days of the trade was an Irishman, Captain O'Donovan, known on the coast as "King Tom." He owned a big clipper schooner of 255 tons, called the *Spray*, which,

THOMAS DENT

Lent by L. A. Dent, Esq.

ALFRED DENT

Lent by L. A. Dent, Esq.

[*See page* 374

curiously enough, had been commanded by Rooney, the master of the American receiving-ship at Taku, some eight or ten years before.

King Tom attempted to follow Rooney's example in a still wilder spot than Taku named Tam Sui, fell into the hands of the Formosans and only escaped with his life, having been beaten black and blue with split bamboos. He came sailing into Hongkong, vowing vengeance with a vocabulary which was the envy of every sailorman on the coast. But he was so knocked about that he had to be slung aboard the nearest British gunboat in a hammock, in order that he might spin his yarn to her captain. And he did not stop talking until the Admiral permitted the gunboat H.M.S. *Snake,* Captain Moresby to go in search of his enemies.

King Tom himself acted as pilot: and in due course the Taotai of Tam Sui had good cause for regretting that he had ever dared to lay a bamboo across the broad back of Captain O'Donovan of the opium schooner *Spray.*

Opium Racing Steamers.

By the end of the 'fifties the opium clippers on the Bombay and Calcutta runs were fast being replaced by racing steamers, such vessels as Jardine Matheson's *Riever,* of 778 tons and 400 h.p. *Clan Alpine,* of 942 tons and 400 h.p., *Glengyle,* of 1266 tons and 400 h.p., and *Glenartney,* of 1088 tons and 300 h.p.

The Dent's were represented by the *Ly-ee-moon,* which came out in 1860, and for some time held the record as the fastest opium steamer afloat. She was built by the Thames Shipbuilding Company from designs by Mr. James Ash. She had a tonnage of 1001 tons gross and 753 net, was 270 ft. long between perpendiculars, 292 ft. overall, 27 ft. 3 ins. in breadth and 16.5 ft. deep. Her oscillating engines of 350 h.p. from designs by William C. Taylor drove her at a speed of 17 knots. She was a very handsome steamer as may be seen from her portrait, and we are told that she was decorated internally in the most magnificent style.

Other steamers which deserve a mention were the little Napier-built *Lancefield,* of only 173 tons and 60 h.p., and the Denny-built *Thales,* of 775 tons and 200 h.p.

At first the steamers were fully rigged, such as the *Thunder* and *Lightning*, belonging to the Armenian firm of Apcar, which though proudly boasting two smoke stacks a piece were heavily masted and sparred.

The *Thunder* came to grief at the mouth of the Hooghly in the 1867 cyclone, but nothing was known of her fate until July, 1869, when her wreck was discovered in the Sunderbunds and the treasure with which she was freighted recovered.

The *Lightning* survived her sister ship for many years, though a second *Lightning*, of 2124 tons net, was built by the firm.

The *Armenian*, of 870 tons and 60 h.p. was built at Hartelpool in 1857 for the Apcars, but proved a better sailer than steamer. She was followed in 1861 by a new *Arratoon Apcar*, of 1480 tons gross. The little *Confucius* of 430 tons was sent out to Russell & Co. in 1853, but the Americans did not consider her a worthy representative and three years later they sold her to the Chinese Government to go pirate hunting with H.M.S. *Hornet*.

Another well-known steamer was the *John Bright* belonging to the Parsees in Bombay.

Amongst the best known of the racing steamer captains were Charles Bolton of the *Riever*, Sandy Hutchinson of the *Clan Alpine*, (both Jardine Matheson 17 knotters,) Burney Lloyds, of the *Thales*, and Hill of the *Ly-ee-moon*.

These men had mostly come from the clippers and ran their steamers as hard as they had carried on in the sailing ships. For some years the rivalry between the different firms and their steamers was just as keen as it had been with the clippers.

Jardine, Matheson & Co. had a private signal code and signal station above West Point, at Hongkong. From this station they used to communicate with their steamers at a great distance, give them instructions as to the state of the market and regulate their arrival in Hongkong Harbour accordingly. This signal station was instituted after a second mate had been sent ashore at the back of the island with very important information, which he allowed to leak out over a glass of port and thus lost his firm a great deal of money.

It was during the 'fifties and early 'sixties that the rivalry of the two leading firms in China—Jardine, Matheson & Co. and Dent

& Co.—became so intense that it was even extended to the dinner table and the racecourse. Sir Robert Jardine, who afterwards became famous on the turf in the Old Country, started his racing career on the racecourse in Happy Valley. But I believe it was John Dent who paid £10,000 for a racehorse in order to win the Hongkong Cup.

The Panic Year of 1865.

The great days of the Hongkong merchant princes came practically to an end in 1865, the panic year, when tea freights fell below £3 per ton, an immense fleet of ships lay idle in Hongkong Harbour and many an old standing house, both in England and China came to grief, amongst the victims being the famous firm of Dent & Co., though their rivals, Jardine, Matheson & Co., survived.

Some years ago an officer of one of Jardine Matheson's steamers told me how they saved their balances in the various Eastern banks, but he did not wish the name of the steamer to be divulged, so I fear I must leave it blank.

Here is his yarn in his own words:—

Our vessel was one of the fleetest craft in Eastern Seas, specially built for the opium trade; but there was no opium on board, nothing in fact but a full supply of the finest steam coal.

We were anchored abreast of Armenian Ghaut in the Calcutta River. Our orders were to proceed to Penang and make every possible effort to get there before the English mail from Point de Galle. If she beat us and was in first, we were not to enter George Town but make for Singapore; if beaten there, we were to go for Hongkong.

Our captain came off in a shore dinghy; the mate was at the accommodation ladder to meet him. No sooner was his foot on deck than he asked if steam was up.

"Yes, sir!"

"Stand by in the engine-room!"

"All ready, sir!"

"Slip the cable, go ahead full speed!"

We had no pilot—half an hour's delay would have obtained one; we had to pay him anyway. However we were a light draught and we all knew the river. Away she steamed down Garden Reach safely over the James and Mary quicksand, past Diamond Harbour and Kedgeree, past Saugor Roads, past the pilot brig with the signal flying "No pilot on board"—onward down the Bay of Bengal to the thunder of our paddles and the hiss of our steam pipe; on, on, for hundreds of miles until one would have thought every bearing was at melting point. At last there came a cry of "Land Ho!"

"Where away?" asked our skipper.

"Starboard beam, sir!"

"That's not land. Take a glass aloft and see if it is the smoke from the mail boat's funnel."

"It is smoke, sir!" came down from aloft.

The captain walked to the engine-room hatch. "Tell the chief engineer I want him," he called down.

Up came the chief, the perspiration pouring from him. An engine room of that date in the Bay of Bengal was a veritable inferno.

"How are the engines, Mac—doing their best, eh?" asked the captain.

"Well, sir, any fool can break them down."

"Exactly ; do you see the smoke yonder on our beam?"

"Yes, sir."

"That man's contract speed is 10 knots: he is a mile nearer his anchorage than we are, we have 47 miles to run; beat him by an hour and you get 500 rupees and every mother's son on the articles a month's extra pay; only—consider the engines are meant to take us in."

"All that man can do, I will do, sir," said Mac.

Mac did it, We ran close inshore.

"Stop her!"—"Turn astern!"—"Stop her! Stand clear of the chain! Let go the anchor!"

The doctor and the harbour master came alongside. We were given "pratique." Ashore went the captain with a bag full of what looked like bank notes, and in fifty minutes he was back with some of the papers and a boat load of specie, mostly English gold, though there were many cases of Mexican, Spanish and American dollars.

As he stepped aboard, he sang out: "Heave up the anchor: bear a hand, boys, you shall have your money as soon as we are clear of the port."

How that mud-hook rose!

"Anchors aweigh, sir!" cried the mate.

"Hand to the wheel. Go ahead with the engines!" was the captain's next order. There was no engine-room telegraph in those days. Every order was given by word of mouth.

Off we steamed along the Straits of Malacca for Singapore.

"Watch below, lay aft. As soon as you are paid relieve the watch on deck and send them aft," came the order from the bridge. There is nothing like the prompt redemption of a promise.

We had a long start of the mail and in any case could have offered her a tow rope.

On arrival at Singapore, a similar performance was gone through: the specie boat came alongside, there was more money than the treasure room would hold.

Before the mail came in we were out again on our passage of 1630 miles back to Calcutta.

There we heard all about it. The bank our owners banked with had stopped payment on receipt of a telegram from the head office, London. We had been sent to the branches to draw out deposits and cash as many notes as possible, before advices reached them. There were no cables then to the Straits Settlements. This we just managed to do, and so made a huge profit instead of a loss, as the notes were bought for a mere song when the news was known. I doubt if there ever was a bigger money stake on a race.

The Demise of Dent & Co.

The failure of the famous firm of Dent & Co. to survive the black year of 1865 has generally been ascribed to the rashness of John Dent; the firm had not been well managed for some years and it had been rather too adventurous and go-ahead even with its large resources.

The collapse did not come until 1867, when the firm declared itself bankrupt on July 9. A few months previous to this date their fleet had been sold for 550,000 taels (roughly £183,000). Writing to his father in England young Alfred Dent declared: "It was a bitter moment when we had to haul down the old house-flag. I am glad, however, that they are to remain under the English flag and the captains and crews to be kept on as before. Dent & Co.'s skippers were the only ones who knew the Yang-tze and their steamers were never ashore."

John Dent sailed for home to face his London partners, Thomas Dent (senior partner of Dent, Palmer & Co., London, the father of Alfred and the original founder of the China house) and Wilkinson Dent, Thomas's brother.

Meanwhile Alfred Dent, who had scarcely been three years in the East, worked like a Trojan to "save the face" of the family; and to such good purpose did he use his energy and brains that by 1868 the new firm of Alfred Dent & Co. was doing business at Shanghai in the old hong.

The "Princess Royal" sails for Home.

It is now time to take our leave of the Flowery Land. I fear we cannot do it in the lordly style of the old three-decker *Princess Royal*, the last of Britain's wooden walls in commission on the China station.

She left for home in March, 1867. Though full-rigged, she bore the blight, according to all good sailors, of an engine; and with this chunking and smoking, to the extreme chagrin of her commander who would have sailed out of the harbour had there been wind, she slowly steamed through the shipping.

She had a blue-jacket standing on each truck waving a boat flag, and the bladder of her homeward bound pennant bobbed along in her wake at least a ship's length astern. As she passed each anchored ship, her best ensign was slowly dipped. Every single ship in the roads cheered her, and her crew, manning the rigging in clean whites, returned cheer for cheer.

Forward her fiddlers scraped away like men possessed, whilst aft her band, their brass sparkling and the red tunics of the Marines flashing in the sun, played the grand old homeward bound chanty:—

The wind blows hard from East North-east,
Our ship she does 10 knots at least.
The anchor's aweigh and the sails unfurled,
We're bound to plough the watery world,
For now we're homeward bound;
Hurrah! We're homeward bound.

APPENDIX

APPENDIX A.

"Magicienne's" Passages.

During the first part of her commission she was roving about the Indian Ocean, but in the summer of 1832 she was ordered to China, by easy stages, the dates of her passages being:—

1832	Aug.	23	6 p.m.	Left Malacca.	
	,,	24	12 p.m.	Anchored. Pulo Pisang bearing N.E.½ E.	
	,,	25	6 a.m.	Left Pulo Pisang.	
	,,	25	10 p.m.	Anchored Singapore.	
	,,	29	6 a.m.	Left Singapore.	
	Sept.	7	7 p.m.	Anchored Batavia.	
	,,	9	6 a.m.	Left Batavia.	
	Oct.	2	12 p.m.	Anchored Trincomalee.	
	Dec.	8	5 p.m.	Left Malacca	4 days.
	,,	12	2 p.m.	Anchored Penang	
	,,	13	2 p.m.	Left Penang	7 days.
	,,	20	7 p.m.	Anchored Madras	
1833	Sept.	14	11 a.m.	Left Singapore	11 days.
	,,	25	4 p.m.	Anchored Manila	
	Oct.	31	4 a.m.	Left Manila	5 days.
	Nov.	5	9 p.m.	Anchored Lintin	

Dec. 17 5·30 a.m. Left Lintin. Wind N.N.E., moderate and fine. Returned a salute of 7 guns to the merchant ships at Lintin.

8 a.m. Macao W. by N. 7 miles.

9·30 a.m. Spoke Dutch ship *Atlas* from Batavia.

Noon. Lat. 21° 48′ N., Long. 113° 26′ E. Course S. 28 W.

P.M. Fresh breezes and fine. Trimmed sails.

4 p.m. Mustered at quarters. In first reefs and topgallant studding sails. Carried away the starboard tack of main topsail.

6 p.m. Fresh breezes. Logging 9 knots. Carried away larboard mizen topmast quarter backstay. Knotted ditto.

9·30 p.m. In 2nd reefs, mizen topsail, royals and topmast studding sails. Logging 9·6 knots.

Wednesday, December 18.

A.M. Fresh breezes N.N.E. and fine.

7 a.m. Set lee foretopmast studding sail. In main topgallant sail and lowered main topsail to repair.

9 a.m. Mustered at quarters. Set main topsail and topgallant sail. Carpenters caulking upper deck.

11·30 a.m. Down jib.

Noon. Fresh breezes East. Trimmed sails. Lat. 18° 30′ N., 111° 36′ E. Distance 250 miles. Logging 10·2 knots. Exercised boys with muskets.

4·30 p.m. Mustered at quarters.

5 p.m. In fore topmast studding sail and fore topgallant sail. Reefed courses and close reefed mizen topsail. In 3rd reefs of fore and main topsails.

10 p.m. Squally, in topgallant sails. Wind E.N.E.

10·30 p.m. Set topgallant sails. Logging 10 knots.

Thursday, December 19.

A.M. Moderate S. by W. wind. Course S. ½ W.

6 a.m. Trimmed sail. Out reef of courses and reef of topsails, set driver and flying jib.

8 a.m. Crossed royal yards and set the sails. Wind E.S.E.

11 a.m. Set fore topmast and topgallant studding sails.

Noon. Light E.N.E. breeze and fine. Logging 5·2 knots. Lat. 14° 58′ N., Long. 110° 57′ E.

P.M. Set lower and main topmast studding sail.

3·30 p.m. In ditto.

5 p.m. Mustered at quarters. Exercised boats' crews with muskets. In 1st reefs.

9 p.m. Trimmed sail. Moderate North wind and cloudy. Carried away strop of lower studding sail halyards. In ditto and fore topmast studding sail.

Friday, December 20.

A.M. Moderate North wind and fine. Course S.E. by S.

2 a.m. Latitude by Polaris 12° 22′ N.

5 a.m. Made sail.

7 a.m. Lowered main topsail to repair.

7·30 a.m. Set ditto.

9 a.m. Made all sail. Down jib.

10 a.m. In spanker. Logging 7·6 knots.

Noon. Lat. 11° 52′ N., Long. 111° 55′ E. Wind moderate N.E. Pulo Sapata S. 55 W., 141 miles.

Friday, December 20 (*cont.*)

1·30 p.m. Set starboard fore topmast studding sail and topgallant studding sails. Shifted over lower studding sails and in larboard ditto.

8 p.m. In lower studding sails and shifted fore topmast studding sail. Carried away the yard.

Midnight. Moderate and fine N.N.E. Logging 8·4 knots.

Saturday, December 21.

A.M. Moderate N.E. and cloudy. Course S.S.W.

3 a.m. Squally. In royals and studding sails.

4 a.m. Moderating. Set royals.

6 a.m. Out reefs. Set studding sails.

7·30 a.m. Punished John Green (marine) with 24 lashes for neglect of duty; Thomas Rogers (seaman) with 24 lashes for repeated drunkenness; H. Lonnidge (seaman) with 36 lashes for drunkenness and insolence to Messrs. Bedford and Clarke.

8 a.m. Logging 11·4 knots.

Noon. Lat. 8° 15′ N., Long. 110° 38′ E. Moderate and fine.

5 p.m. Exercised pikemen with muskets.

7·40 p.m. Latitude by lunar 7° 8′ 19″ N.

Sunday, December 22.

A.M. Wind N.E. moderate and fine. Course S.W. by S.

6·30 a.m. Set main topmast studding sail. Logging 8·6 knots.

8 a.m. Mustered at quarters.

10 a.m. Performed divine service, read articles of war. Mustered by open list. 13 men sick (boils).

Noon. Lat. 5° 15′ N., Long. 108° 31′ E. Moderate and fine.

3 p.m. Trimmed. Set starboard studding sails.

5 p.m. Mustered at quarters.

8 p.m. Light breezes and fine.

Monday, December 23.

A.M. Moderate N.E. wind and fine. Course S.W. ½ S.

5·40 a.m. Observed land.

6 a.m. Set starboard lower studding sail.

8 a.m. Light breezes. Great Anambai E. ½ S.

11 a.m. Pulo Aor bearing S.E. by E.

Noon. Lat. 3° 1′ N., Long. 106° 59′ E. Pulo Aor S. 54 W., 44 miles.

P.M. Calm and cloudy. Rain at times. In all studding sails and royals and braced up on larboard tack.

2 a.m. Squally.

Monday, December 23 (*cont.*)

4 p.m. Light airs and fine Pulo Timor West. Made sail. Exercised general quarters. Cleaned trucks and axletrees.

8 p.m. Light variable breezes. Pulo Aor W.½ N., 10 or 12 miles.

9 p.m. Lat. by moon 2° 27′ N.

11 p.m. Up mainsail.

Midnight. Calm and fine.

Tuesday, December 24.

4 a.m. Light airs and fine. Course South.

7 a.m. Set starboard studding sails; in spanker.

9 a.m. Set mainsail and spanker.

Noon. Lat. 1° 44′ N., Long. 106° 26′ E. Singapore N. 89 W. 57 miles.

P.M. Light airs. Trimmed and set jib.

4 p.m. Pedro Blanca W. by N., 5 or 6 miles.

5 p.m. Mustered at quarters. Exercised pikemen.

6·30 p.m. In studding sails.

9·30 p.m. Burnt a blue light. Observed Singapore light.

10 p.m. Running for the anchorage.

11 p.m. Shortened sail and came to in 13 fathoms, veered to 30 fathoms.

1834	Jany.	1	6 a.m.	Left Singapore.
	,,	2	1·30 p.m.	Anchored Malacca.
	,,	5	6 a.m.	Left ,,
	,,	10	2·30 p.m.	Anchored Penang.
	,,	20	12·30 a.m.	Left ,,
	,,	30	5·15 p.m.	Anchored Madras.
	Feb.	10	6 a.m.	Left Madras.
	,,	16		Arrived Trincomalee.
	,,	22		Left ,,
	Mar.	23	11 a.m.	Anchored Bombay.

During the summer of 1834 the *Magicienne* went to Zanzibar from Bombay. It was a disastrous trip, for her crew were struck down by malaria, and when she returned to Bombay in August she had lost her master, carpenter and two mates. In October she was sent round to Madras, preparatory to sailing for home.

She left Madras homeward bound on December 15, 1834, and had 14 days without wind before she took the trades; this she made up for by sailing 2017 miles in 8 days and averaging 252 miles a day, arriving at Mauritius on January 10, 1835. Here she remained only a few hours, before proceeding direct to St. Helena, where she hove to on February 2 for 7 hours, having been only 22 days between Mauritius and St. Helena and averaged 200 miles a day. Off the Cape she experienced very heavy weather, but came through it in admirable fashion like the splendid sea boat she was, without straining or carrying away a ropeyarn though she kept her topgallant masts fidded.

Fayal was sighted on March 1, and nine days later, on March 10 she anchored in Plymouth Sound, her dispatches from India and China being landed on the 85th day from Madras.

This is one of the fastest passages ever made from India by a man-of-war, and considering that she had been becalmed for a whole fortnight in the Bay of Bengal was considered a truly marvellous performance.

It is interesting to compare this passage with those of other men-of-war and merchantmen.

As far back as 1804 the *Medusa* (32-gun frigate Captain Sir John Gore), took out the new Governor-General the Marquis Cornwallis, to India; and made the return passage in 84 days at sea, averaging 160 miles a day and covering 13,831 miles in 82 days. This was considered the fastest passage ever made. It was this frigate which bore Nelson's flag at the attack on the Boulogne flotilla in August, 1801.

About seven years after the *Medusa's* performance the 36-gun frigate *Caroline*, (Captain Christopher Cole), made the run home in 94 days, during seven of which she was becalmed.

Coming to the time of the opium clippers, in 1838 the *Rattlesnake* (26 guns), left Madras on August 24, Trincomalee on September 3, Cape of Good Hope on October 6, Ascension on October 28, after spending two days there and reached Plymouth on November 27, 95 days from Madras.

In 1843 all these passages were rivalled, if not beaten, by that of the *Endymion* (44 guns, Captain the Hon. F. W. Grey); this frigate was only 76 days from Bombay, including a three days' stay at St. Helena.

In the following year the well-known 18-gun corvette *Dido*, commanded by Harry Keppel, whilst on her passage home broke the record from the Cape to Spithead, which distance she covered in 40 days without once reefing topsails.

Her master, Mr. R. C. Allen, in writing about the passage declared: "She passed scores of merchant ships, everyone of them with double-reefed topsails, and with iibs and mainsails stowed, while the saucy *Dido* careered along with whole topsails, topgallant sails, jib and mainsail, reminding them no doubt of the *Flying Dutchman.*"

Turning to the opium clipper passages, *Sylph's* run from Calcutta to Singapore in 9 days 20 hours in 1833 held the record for some years.

As regards *Magicienne's* run of 7 days from Lintin to Singapore during the favourable monsoon, this was equalled by the *Red Rover* in November, 1835, by the *Cowasjee Family* in March, 1836, and by the *Rob Roy* in December, 1837, whilst several vessels including *Waterwitch*, *Lady Grant* and *Antonio Pereira* had all done it in 8 days, but I can find no instance of this week's run being beaten.

APPENDIX B.

Register of the Opium Fleet.

Date entrd. Trade	Name	Rig	Tons	Length ft.	Breadth ft.	Depth ft.	Where and when built	Chief Owner
1823	*Jamesina*	brig	382	100	30·6	12·9	Ex-R.N. sloop, Bridport, 1811	Magniac
1828	*Louisa*	,,	162	—	—	—	Calcutta 1828	Capt. W. Clifton.
1830	*Falcon (I)*	,,	175	84	22	11·5	Cowes 1815	H.E.I. Co.
1830	*Red Rover*	barque	254	97·7	24	11·10	Howrah 1829	Capt. W. Clifton
1830	*Lady Hayes*	,,	314	99·10	26·10	18	Kidderpore 1829	James Matheson
1831	*Waterwitch (I)* ..	,,	363	104·11	27·10	17·6	Kidderpore 1831	Dent
1831	*Sylph*	,,	304	100·5	26	12·5	Howrah 1831	R. Cowasjee
1832	*Lady of the Lake* ..	ship	243	83	25·10	15·3	Chittagong 1820	T. Bridges
1833	*Fairy*	brig	161	77	22·6	11·8	Liverpool 1833	Jardine Matheson
1834	*Syed Khan*	schooner	191	91·7	22·9	9·5	Slaver captured 1831	Capt. J. McKinnon
1835	*Sir Herbert Compton*	barque	346	104	27·3	15·5	Bombay 1835	Aga Sherazee
1836	*Cowasjee Family* ..	,,	431	106·10	30·3	13·6	Howrah 1835	R. Cowasjee
1836	*Lady Grant*	brig	239	90·6	24·4	—	Mazagon 1835	Mottichund
1836	*Ardaseer*	barque	422	117	29·6	—	Bombay 1836	C. Cowasjee
1836	*Ann*	brig	252	101·10	24	10	Slaver captured 1834	Capt. H. Pybus
1836	*Antonio Pereira* ..	,,	140	94	21·4	10·8	Blackwall Yard 1836	Capt. Wm. O. Young
1836	*Rose*	schooner	150	—	—	—	Boston	Russell
1836	*Harriet*	,,	100	—	—	—	Macao	Jardine Matheson
1837	*Sir Edward Ryan* ..	barque	320	102·6	23·2	17·2	Moulmein 1837	Capt. H. Pybus
1837	*Pearl*	brigantine	118	68·10	19·9	10·6	Bombay 1837	C. Cowasjee
1837	*Rob Roy*	barque	352	101	28	13·1	Howrah 1837	De Souza
1837	*Ariel (I)*	,,	368	106	27·10	16	Kidderpore 1837	Dent
1837	*Omega*	schooner	178	—	—	—	Cowes 1837	Dent
1837	*Psyche*	schooner	100	80·6	19·6	10·4	Slaver captured 1834	Dent
1838	*Black Joke* ..	brig	113	85·8	20·7	10	Slaver captured 1836	Capt. J. Miller
1838	*Nymph (I)*	barque	157	89	23·9	11·11	Howrah 1838	J. D. Gow
1838	*Poppy*	brigantine	250	97	24	14·1	Kidderpore 1838	Dent
1838	*Hellas*	schooner	209	91·4	23	14·10	Waterford 1832	A. Grant
1838	*William*	brig	205	78	21·4	16·1	Bombay	J. W. Shearman
1839	*Time*	,,	139	85·9	19·9	10·9	Poplar 1832	Capt. Joseph Pybus
1839	*Mary Gordon* ..	brig	250	—	—	—	Mazagon 1839	Furdonjee Limjee
1839	*Clown*	schooner	143	77·5	18·25	13·16	Moulmein 1839	Donald C. MacKey
1839	*Columbine*	,,	146	79·16	18·16	13·16	,, ,,	,,
1839	*Harlequin*	,,	145	79	18·16	13·16	,, ,,	,,
1840	*Mor*	ship	280	121·5	28·5	14	London 1839	Jardine Matheson

Register of the Opium Fleet.—Continued.

Date entrd. Trade	Name	Rig	Tons	Length ft.	Breadth ft.	Depth ft.	Where and when built	Chief Owner
1840	*Audax*	brig	151	88·4	20·6	13	Cowes 1840	Jardine Matheson
1840	*Spy*	,,	120	—	—	—		,,
1840	*Dido*	,,	230	104·4	23·3	16·6	Calcutta 1840	Donald C. Mackey
1840	*Falcon (II)*	ship	351	113·7	27·5	18·33	Fishbourne 1826	H. Rustomjee
1840	*Gazelle*	schooner	121	103·1	14·7	8·7	Aberdeen 1840	——
1840	*Tartar*	barque	567	125·4	26·5	19·6	Blackwall Yard 1840	Green & Wigram
1841	*Anglona*	,,	90	—	—	—	New York 1840	Russell
1841	*Ariel (II)*	,,	98	—	—	—	Medford 1841	Jardine Matheson
1841	*Black Swan*	brigantine	113	69·3	20	10·6	Wexford 1838	John B. Elden
1841	*Pantaloon*	brig	202	94·2	20·1	13·2	Moulmein 1841	Donald C. Mackey
1841	*Sea Queen* ..	barque	389	113·6	27·10	18·3	Howrah 1841	Fergusson Bros.
1841	*Corsair*	brig	150	—	—	—	——	R. Cowasjee
1841	*Linnet*	schooner	90	—	—	—	Chittagong 1841	R. Cowasjee
1841	*Caroline*	,,	85	66	16·3	9·8	Bombay	C. Fearon
1841	*Bengal Packet* ..	barque	231	—	—	—	——	Lindsay & Co.
1841	*Island Queen*	schooner	194	93	22	13·9	Cowes 1840	Dent
1841	*Lyra*	,,	165	—	—	—	——	J. A. Durran
1841	*Prince Albert* ..	ship	303	—	—	—	Blackwall Yard	Shepherd
1842	*Mazeppa*	schooner	175	92·5	20·5	9·5	New York	Jardine Matheson
1842	*Zephyr*	,,	150	—	—	—	Boston	Dent
1842	*Sidney*	,,	184	84·6	20·8	13·7	Limehouse 1841	Jardine Matheson
1842	*Spec*	,,	105	85·6	22·6	—	New York	Pybus Bros.
1842	*Young Queen* ..	,,	85	—	—	—	——	Jardine Matheson
1842	*Royal Exchange* ..	,,	130	—	—	—	——	Rustomjee & Co.
1842	*Vixen*	,,	106	71·7	17·9	8·7	Bally 1840	Jardine Matheson
1842	*Zoe*	,,	117	—	—	—	——	McVicar & Co.
1842	*Kelpie*	brigantine	109	80	20	9·4	Ex-slaver, captured 1836	A. Grant
1842	*Anonyma*	brig	257	114·7	26	13·3	Gosport	Jardine Matheson
1842	*Prima Donna* ..	ship	222	88·6	20·9	15	Blackwall Yard 1839	Dent
1842	*Will of the Wisp* ..	schooner	101	76	18	10·5	Liverpool 1841	S. J. Hallam
1842	*Gem*	brig	226	—	—	—	——	Gilman & Co.
1842	*Mavis*	brig	113	—	—	—	——	——
1843	*Celestial*	schooner	50	57·10	16·4	7	Hongkong 1843	C. Jamsetjee
1843	*Antelope*	brig	370	—	—	—	Boston 1843	Russell
1843	*Lanrick*	,,	283	108·4	26·9	15·1	Liverpool 1843	Jardine Matheson
1843	*Royalist*	schooner	141	72·8	22	6·8	Fishbourne 1834	Boustead
1843	*Emma*	,,	64	62	17	8	Mazagon 1843	Cama Bros.
1843	*Pelorus*	brig	380	—	—	—	Ex-R.N. sloop	J. Pybus
1843	*Marsdeu*	barque	247	—	—	—	Country built	D. Burjorjee

Register of the Opium Fleet.—Continued.

Date entrd. Trade	Name	Rig	Tons	Length ft.	Breadth ft.	Depth ft.	Where and when built	Chief Owner
1843	*Don Juan* ..	schooner	175	—	—	—	New York	Russell
1844	*Coquette*	barque	450	—	—	—	Boston	,,
1844	*Arratoon Apcar* ..	brig	275	94·6	21·9	15·2	Howrah 1844	Apcar & Co.
1845	*Torrington*	schooner	144	104·6	20·2	11·2	Aberdeen 1845	Jardine Matheson
1845	*Nymph (II)*	,,	106	92·6	21	11	Ex-slaver captured 1831	Thomas Horsburgh
1845	*Enigma*	,,	84	75	17·5	9·3	Calcutta 1845	——
1845	*Frolic*	brig	212	—	—	—	American built	Russell
1845	*Corcyra*	,,	184	—	—	—	——	Gilman & Co.
1846	*Astarte*	brig	328	—	—	—	Cowes 1846	Capt. T. Crossley
1846	*Anna Eliza*	,,	201	96·2	24·9	12·7	Southampton 1827	A.B. & P.B. Fuckeeragee
1846	*Denia*	schooner	133	84·2	20·1	12·5	Cowes 1840	Dent
1848	*Sea Witch*	barque	401	—	—	—	London 1848	Taylor & Co.
1851	*Minna*	schooner	300	—	—	—	Portsmouth, N.H. 1851	Russell
1852	*Brenda*	,,	300	—	—	—	Portsmouth, N.H. 1852	Russell
1852	*Nina*	,,	115	72·3	17·7	10	Cowes 1851	Dent
1853	*Eamont*	,,	120	87	20	12	Cowes 1852	Dent
1854	*Wynaud*	ship	521	150	29	17·9	London 1854	Dent
1855	*Wild Dayrell* ..	schooner	158	103·3	23·7	13·3	Cowes 1854	Dent
1855	*Vindex*	,,	176	107	23·8	13·2	Aberdeen 1855	Dent
1855	*Waterwitch (II)* ..	,,	236	114·6	24·1	13·6	Newcastle 1855	Captain H. Reynell
1856	*Salamander*	,,	115	109	21·7	11	Aberdeen 1856	Capt. A. Roper
1858	*Spray*	3-m. schnr.	255	117·4	26·4	10·8	——	J. Farr
1858	*Neva*	schooner	90	91	21·5	10·1	St. Petersburg 1853	John Darby Gibb
1859	*Undine*	,,	143	134	19	8·5	Hongkong 1849	D. Lapraik
1860	*Chin Chin*	3-m. schnr.	263	119·8	26·5	10	——	Capt. J. C. Saunders

Besides these vessels, there were a number of fine lined craft, which after making a voyage or two either left the trade or came to grief. Of such was the brig *Brigand*, with which Captain Jim Paddon started his sandalwood station in the Loyalty group in 1843. Then there was the notorious schooner *Black Dog*, with which Captain Bobby Towns initiated the Fiji and Queensland "black-birding" traffic. Even Bully Hayes' beautiful *Leonora* began life on the China coast, though it is doubtful if she ever carried the drug.

INDEX

INDEX

PRINTED IN GREAT BRITAIN BY BROWN, SON AND FERGUSON, LTD., GLASGOW

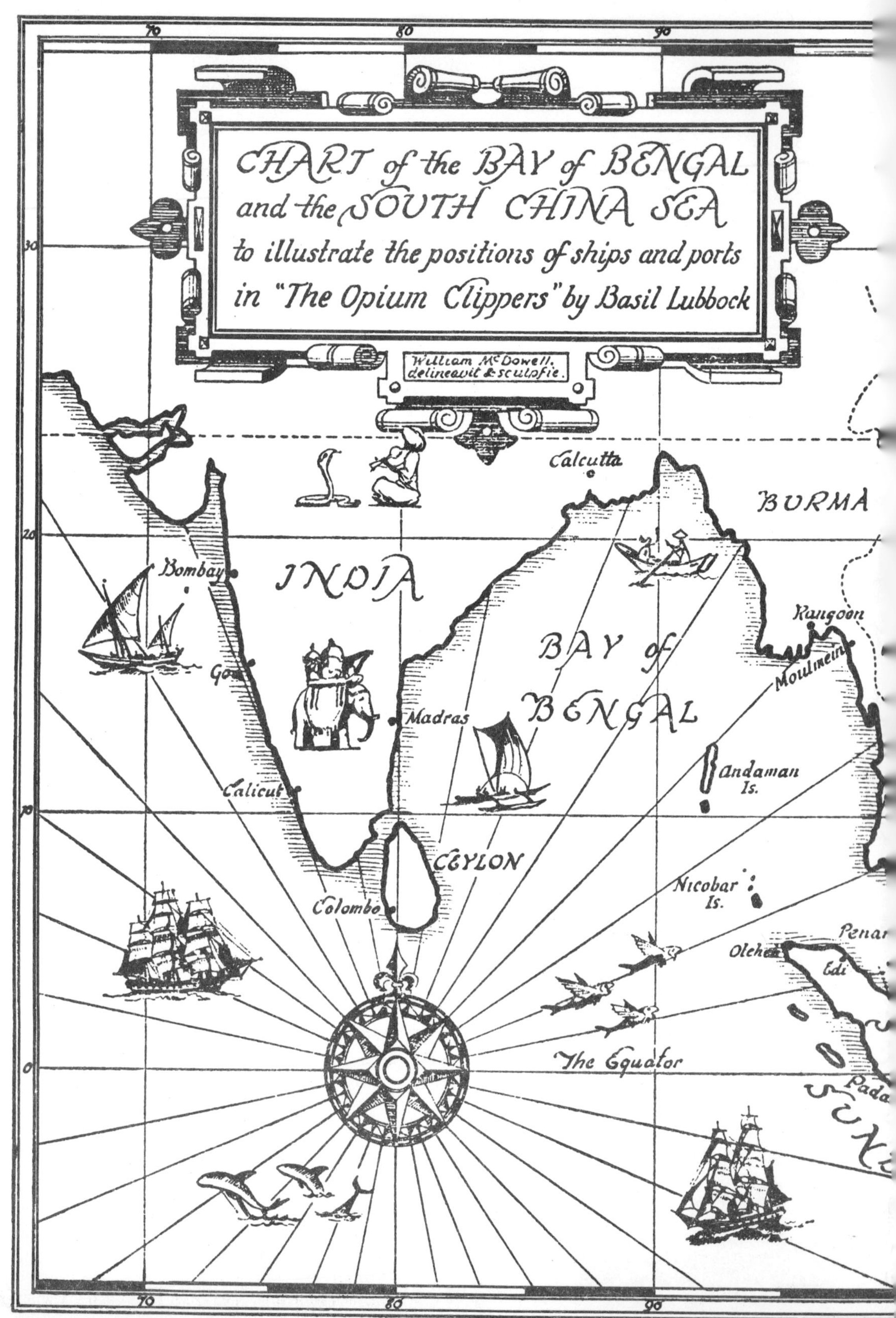
CHART of the BAY of BENGAL
and the SOUTH CHINA SEA
to illustrate the positions of ships and ports
in "The Opium Clippers" by Basil Lubbock
William McDowell,
delineavit & sculpsit.
70
80
90
30
20
10
0
Calcutta
BURMA
Bombay
INDIA
Rangoon
BAY of
BENGAL
Moulmein
Madras
Andaman
Is.
Calicut
CEYLON
Nicobar
Is.
Colombo
Olehen
Edi
The Equator